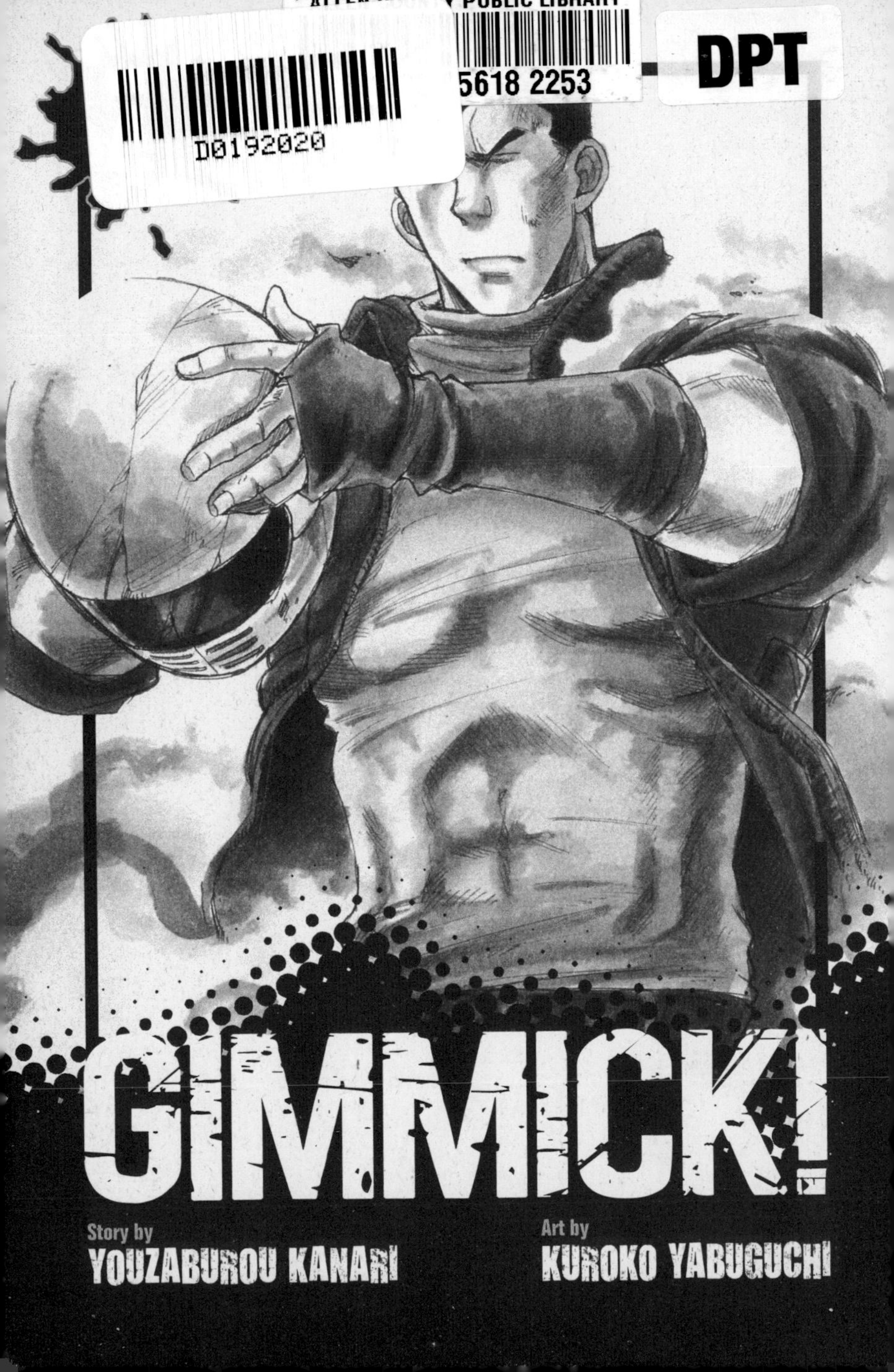

GIMMICK!

Story by
YOUZABUROU KANARI

Art by
KUROKO YABUGUCHI

GIMMICK!

CONTENTS

VOL 4

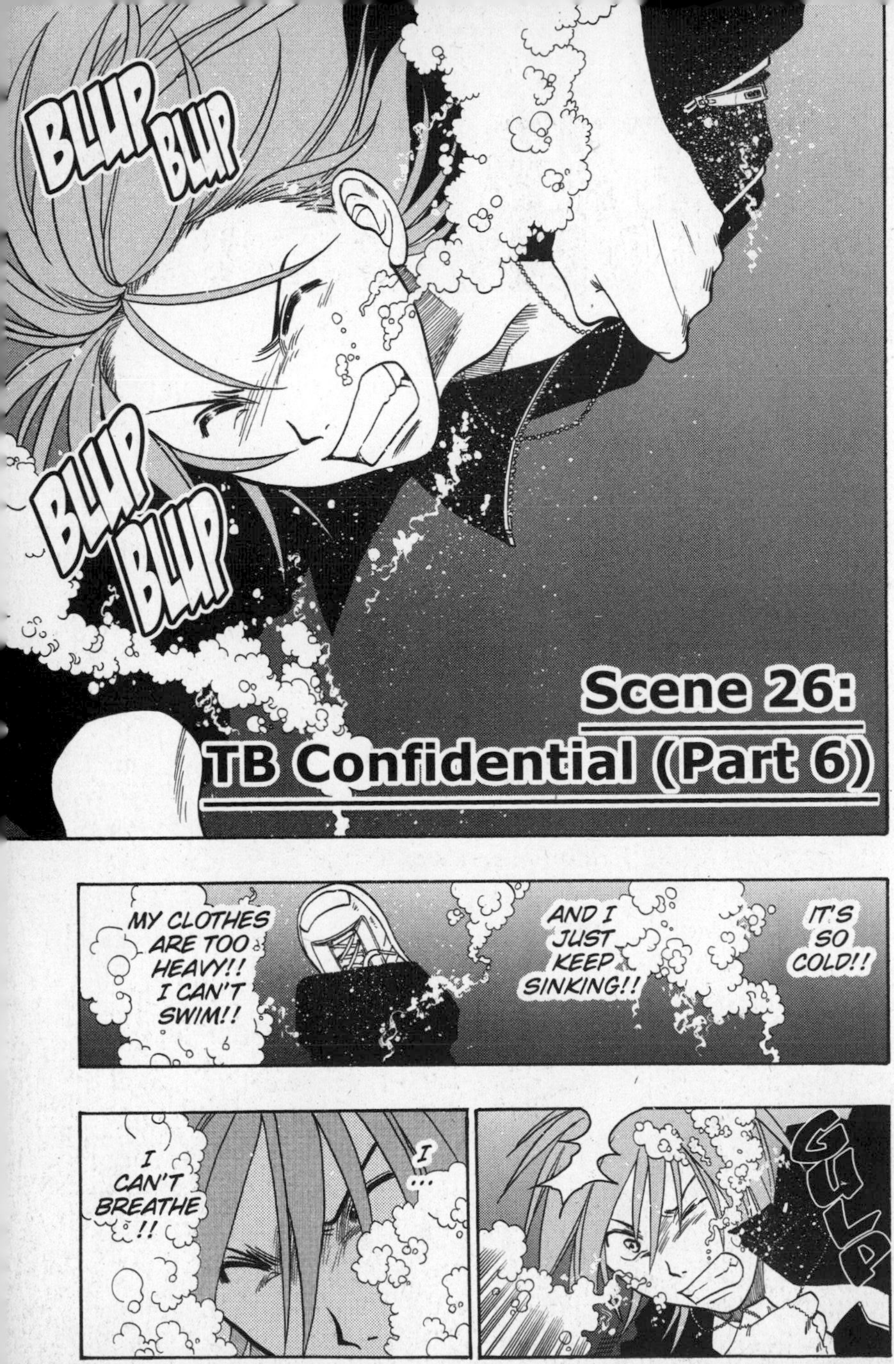
BLUP BLUP
BLUP BLUP
Scene 26:
TB Confidential (Part 6)
IT'S SO COLD!!
AND I JUST KEEP SINKING!!
MY CLOTHES ARE TOO HEAVY!! I CAN'T SWIM!!
GULP
I ...
I CAN'T BREATHE!!

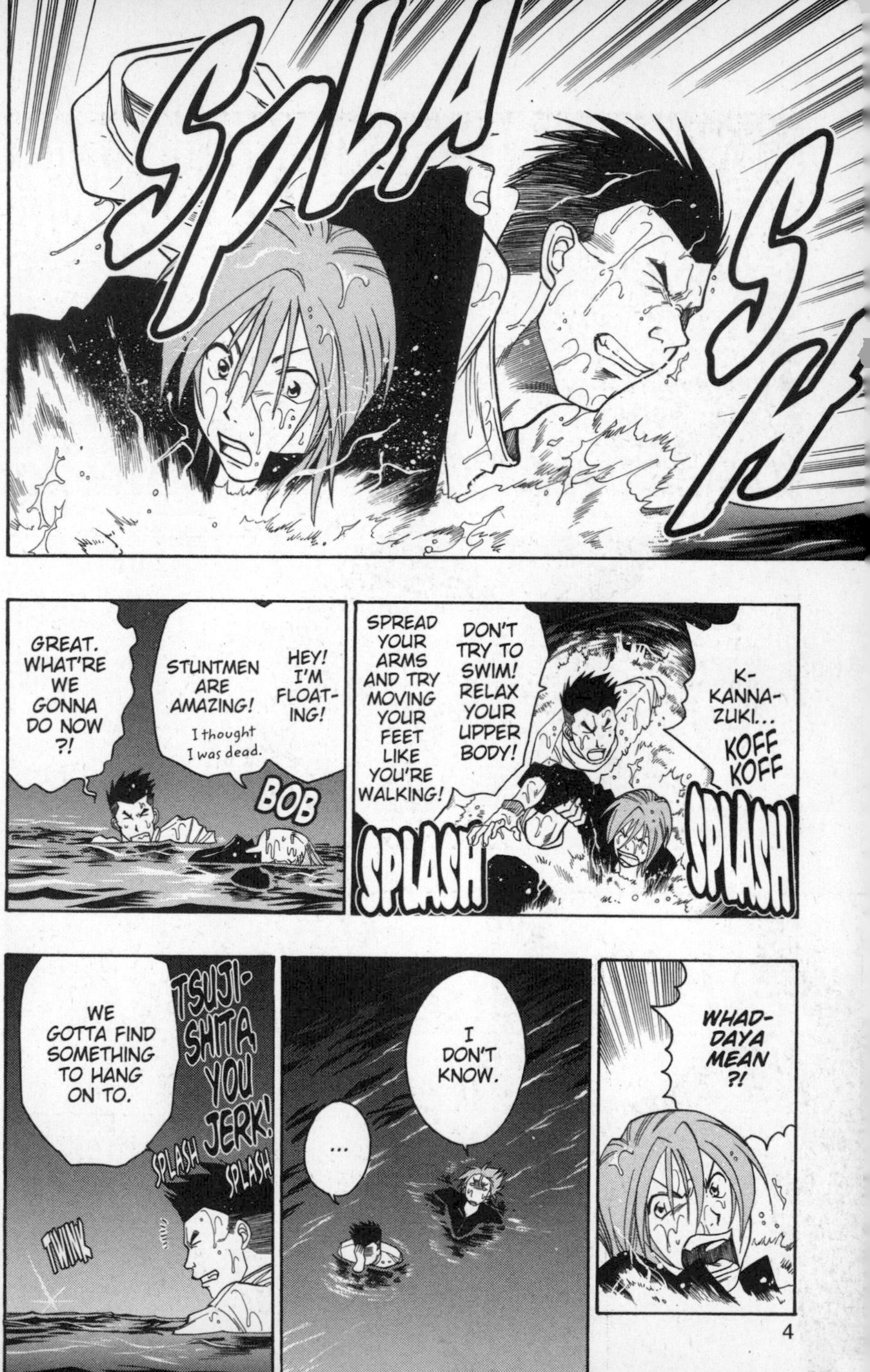
SPLA
K-KANNA-ZUKI... KOFF KOFF
DON'T TRY TO SWIM! RELAX YOUR UPPER BODY!
SPREAD YOUR ARMS AND TRY MOVING YOUR FEET LIKE YOU'RE WALKING!
SPLASH
SPLASH
HEY! I'M FLOAT-ING!
STUNTMEN ARE AMAZING!
I thought I was dead.
BOB
GREAT. WHAT'RE WE GONNA DO NOW ?!
WHAD-DAYA MEAN ?!
I DON'T KNOW.
...
TSUJI-SHITA YOU JERK!
WE GOTTA FIND SOMETHING TO HANG ON TO.
SPLASH
SPLASH
TWINK

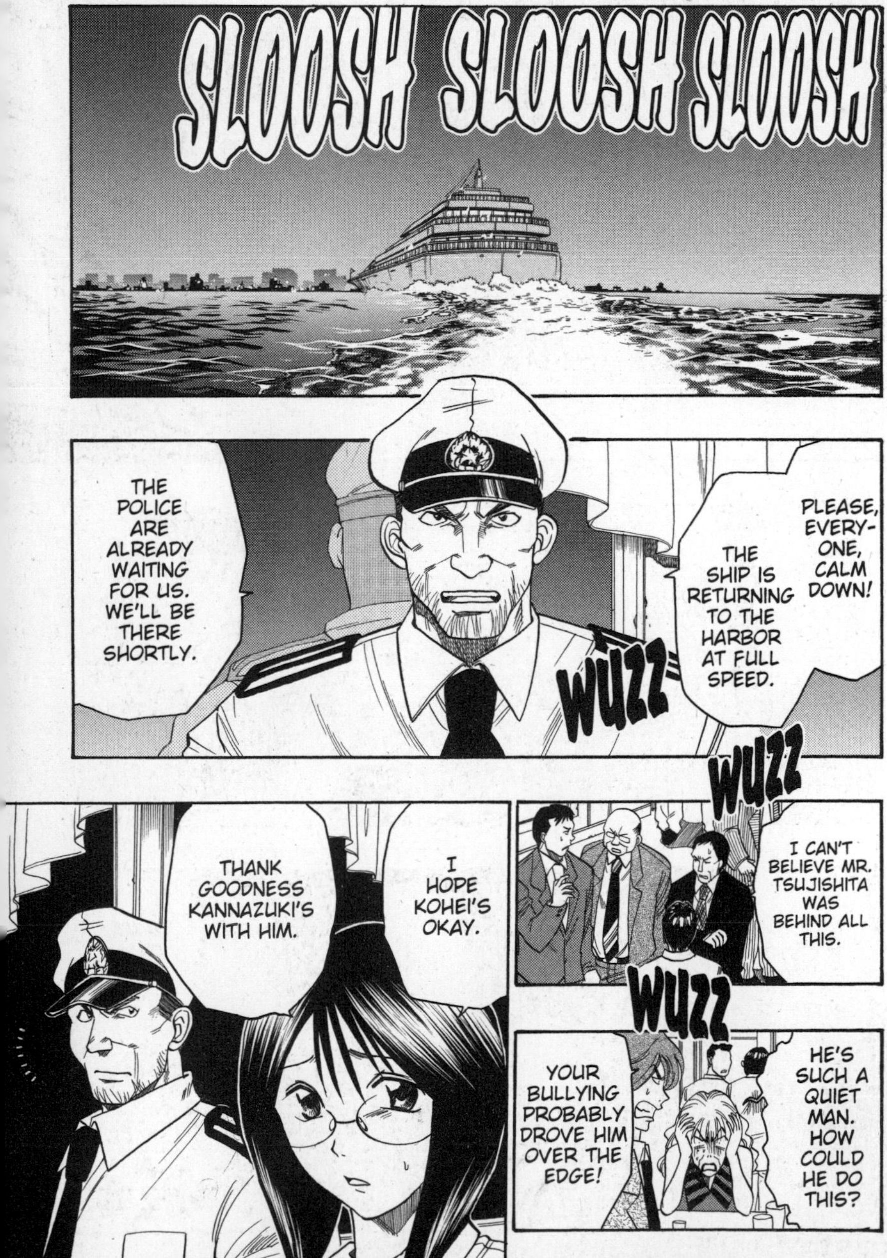
SLOOSH SLOOSH SLOOSH
PLEASE, EVERYONE, CALM DOWN!
THE SHIP IS RETURNING TO THE HARBOR AT FULL SPEED.
WUZZ
THE POLICE ARE ALREADY WAITING FOR US. WE'LL BE THERE SHORTLY.
WUZZ
I CAN'T BELIEVE MR. TSUJISHITA WAS BEHIND ALL THIS.
WUZZ
HE'S SUCH A QUIET MAN. HOW COULD HE DO THIS?
YOUR BULLYING PROBABLY DROVE HIM OVER THE EDGE!
I HOPE KOHEI'S OKAY.
THANK GOODNESS KANNAZUKI'S WITH HIM.

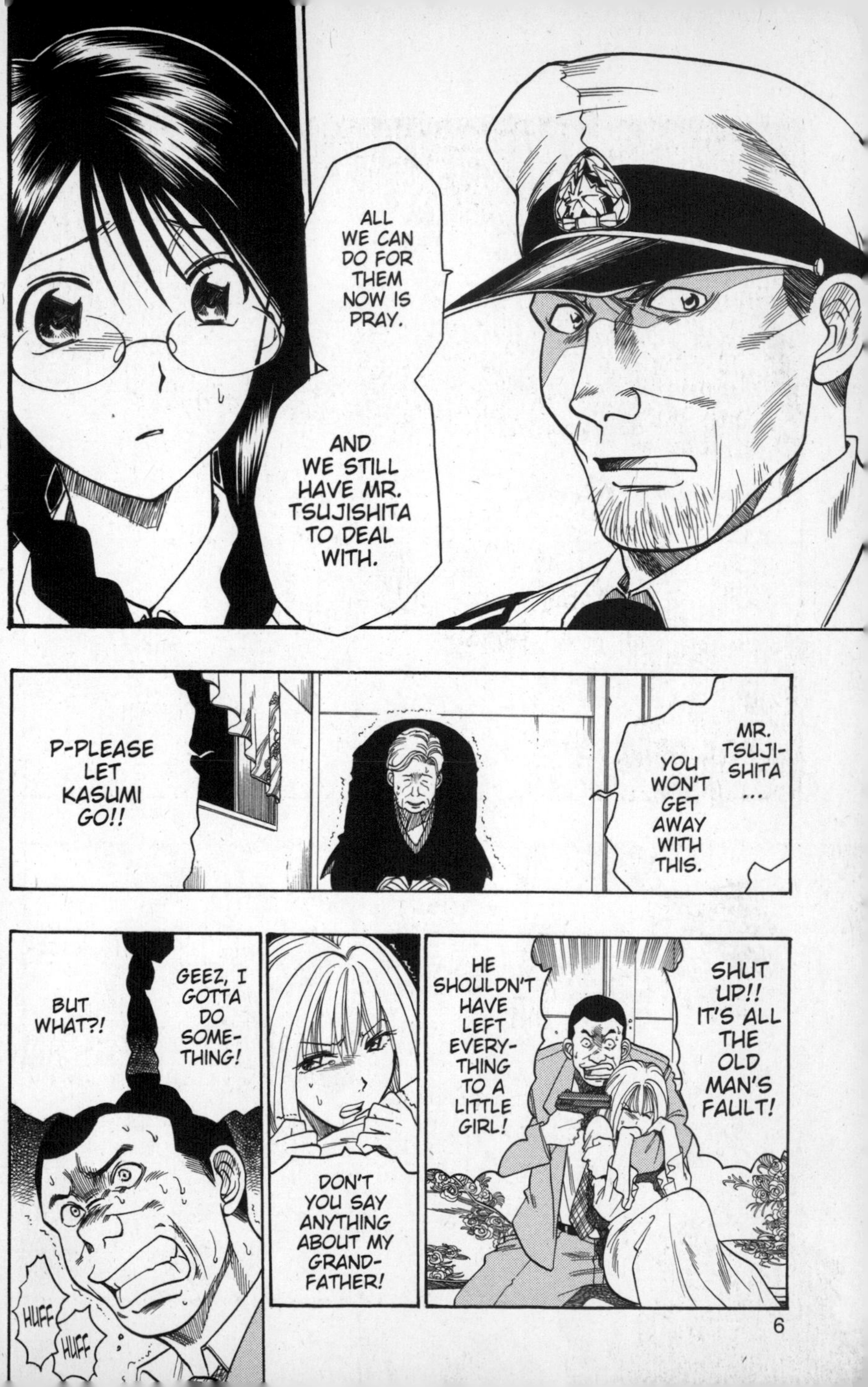
ALL WE CAN DO FOR THEM NOW IS PRAY.
AND WE STILL HAVE MR. TSUJISHITA TO DEAL WITH.
MR. TSUJISHITA...
YOU WON'T GET AWAY WITH THIS.
P-PLEASE LET KASUMI GO!!
SHUT UP!! IT'S ALL THE OLD MAN'S FAULT!
HE SHOULDN'T HAVE LEFT EVERYTHING TO A LITTLE GIRL!
DON'T YOU SAY ANYTHING ABOUT MY GRANDFATHER!
GEEZ, I GOTTA DO SOMETHING!
BUT WHAT?!
HUFF
HUFF

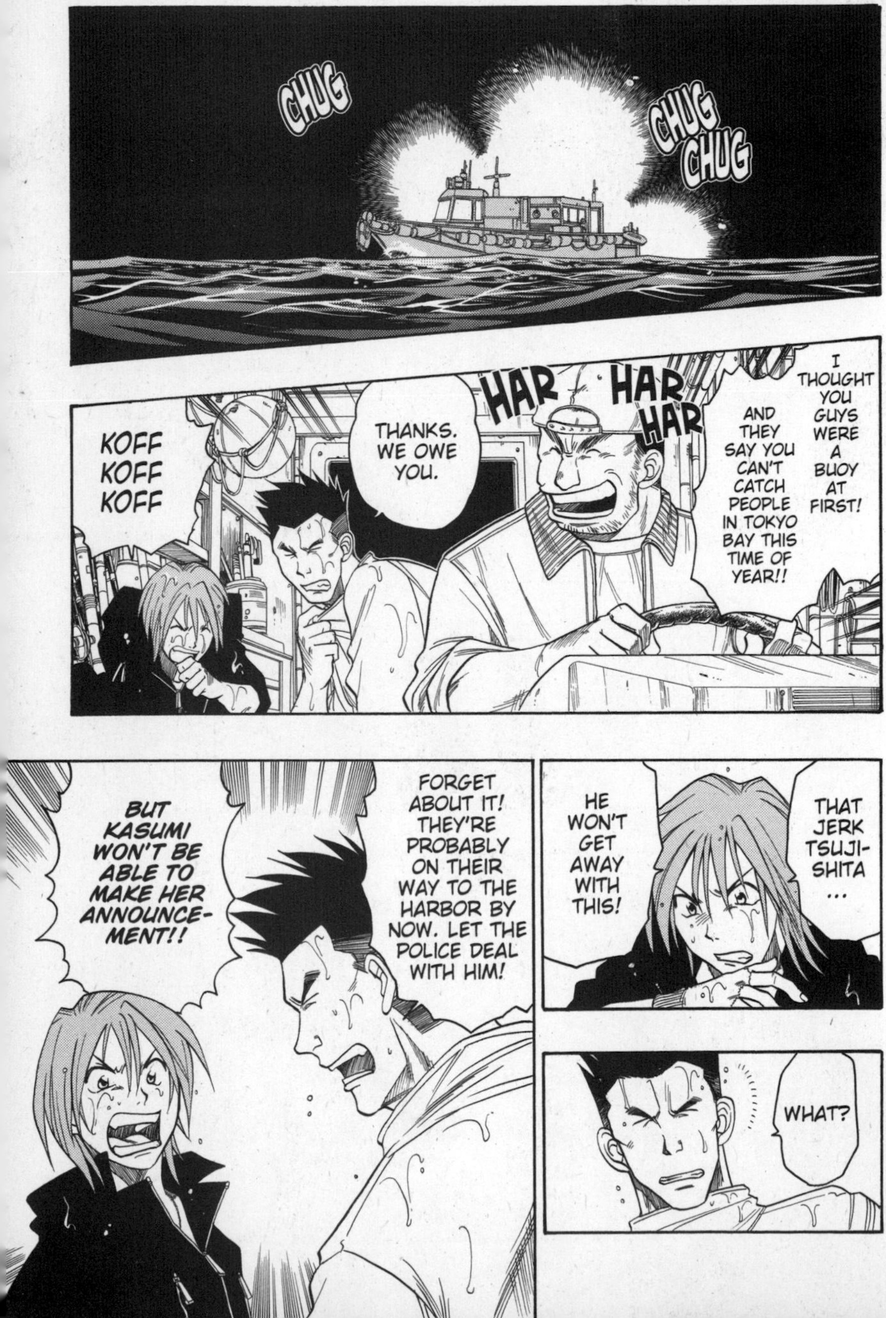
CHUG CHUG
CHUG
I THOUGHT YOU GUYS WERE A BUOY AT FIRST!
AND THEY SAY YOU CAN'T CATCH PEOPLE IN TOKYO BAY THIS TIME OF YEAR!!
HAR HAR HAR
THANKS. WE OWE YOU.
KOFF KOFF KOFF
THAT JERK TSUJI-SHITA...
HE WON'T GET AWAY WITH THIS!
WHAT?
FORGET ABOUT IT! THEY'RE PROBABLY ON THEIR WAY TO THE HARBOR BY NOW. LET THE POLICE DEAL WITH HIM!
BUT KASUMI WON'T BE ABLE TO MAKE HER ANNOUNCE-MENT!!

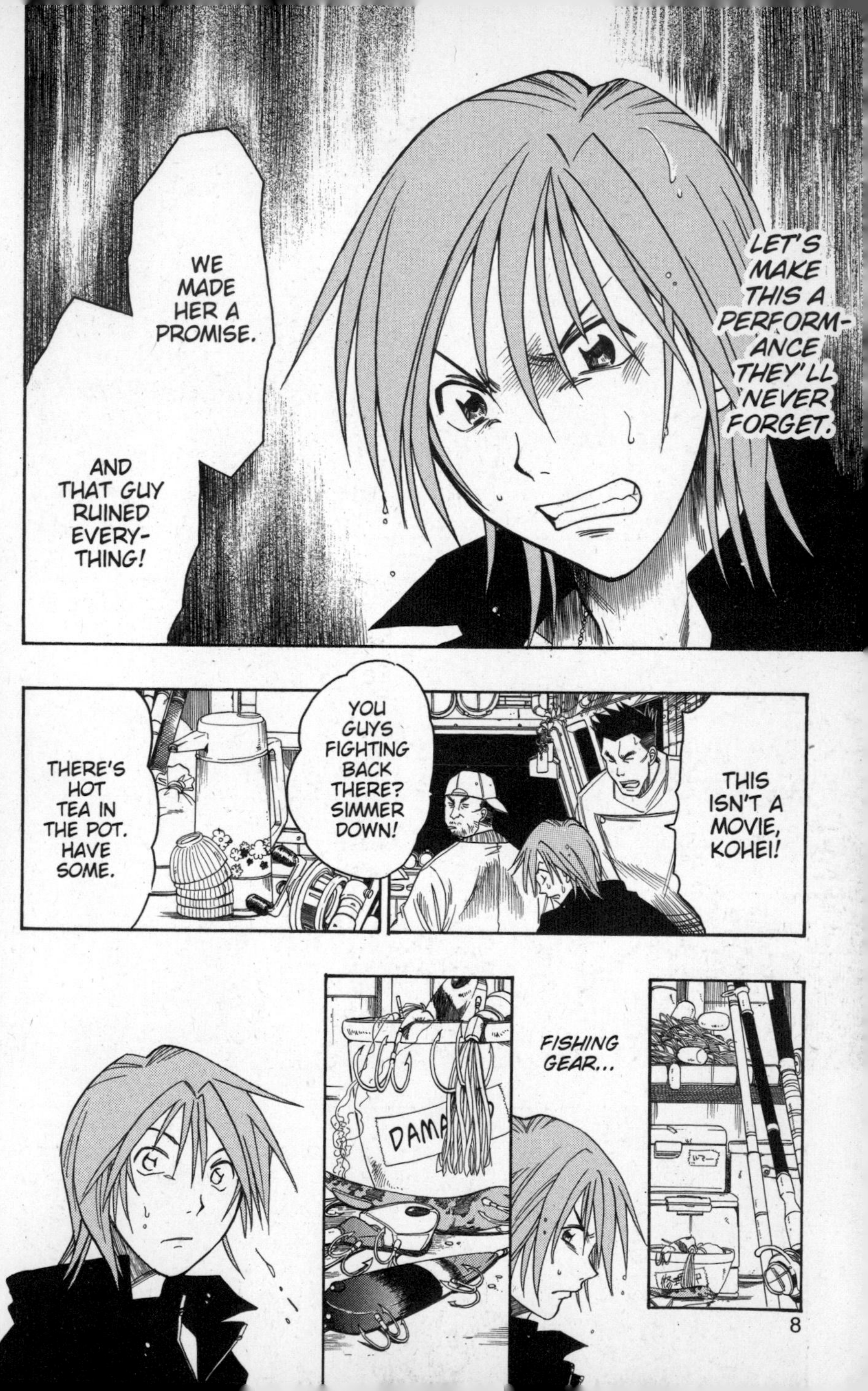
LET'S MAKE THIS A PERFORMANCE THEY'LL NEVER FORGET.
WE MADE HER A PROMISE.
AND THAT GUY RUINED EVERYTHING!
THIS ISN'T A MOVIE, KOHEI!
YOU GUYS FIGHTING BACK THERE? SIMMER DOWN!
THERE'S HOT TEA IN THE POT. HAVE SOME.
FISHING GEAR...
DAMA

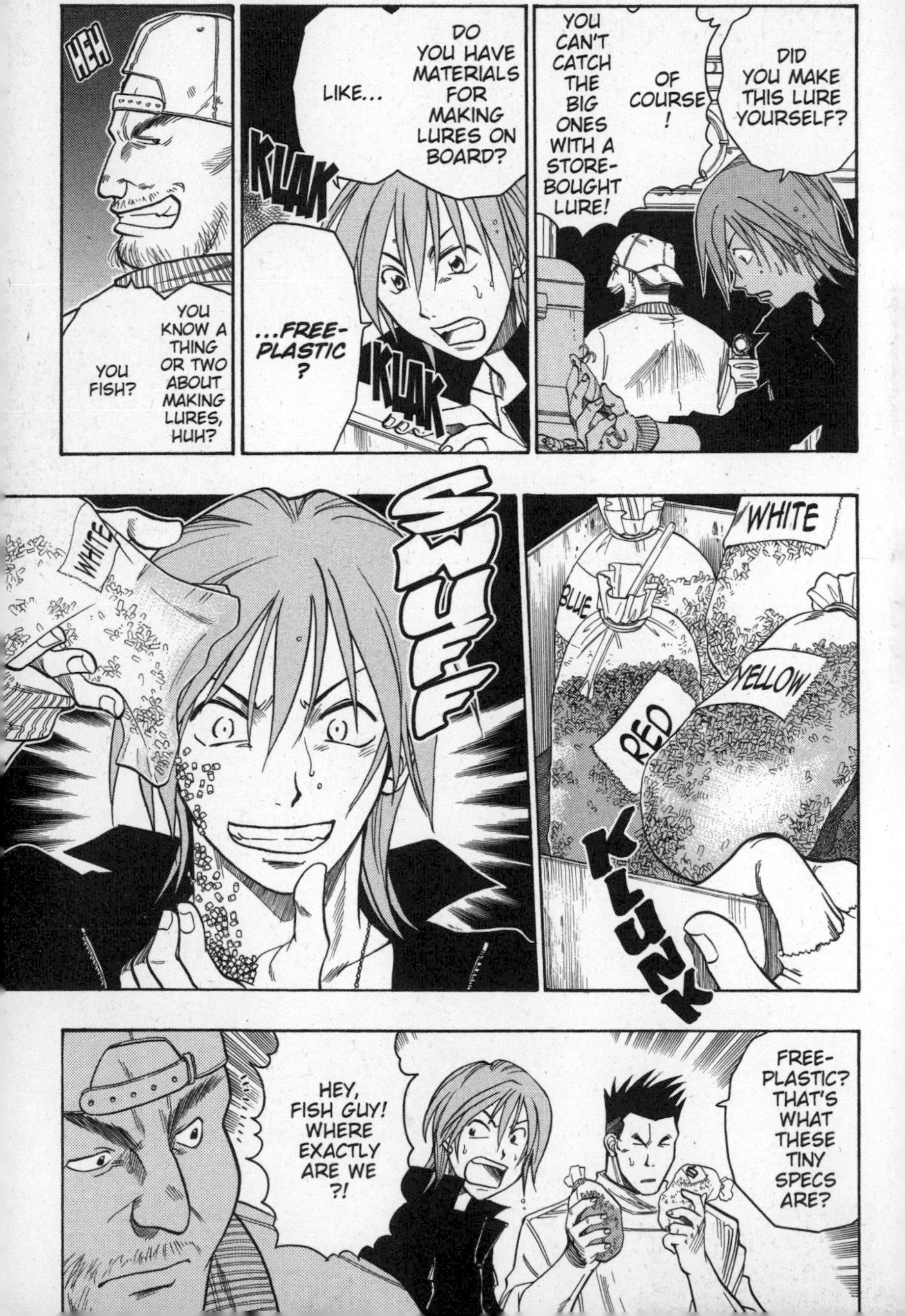
DID YOU MAKE THIS LURE YOURSELF?
OF COURSE!
YOU CAN'T CATCH THE BIG ONES WITH A STORE-BOUGHT LURE!
DO YOU HAVE MATERIALS FOR MAKING LURES ON BOARD?
LIKE...
KLAK
KLAK
...FREE-PLASTIC?
HEH
YOU KNOW A THING OR TWO ABOUT MAKING LURES, HUH?
YOU FISH?
WHITE
BLUE
YELLOW
RED
KLUNK
WHITE
FREE-PLASTIC? THAT'S WHAT THESE TINY SPECS ARE?
HEY, FISH GUY! WHERE EXACTLY ARE WE?!

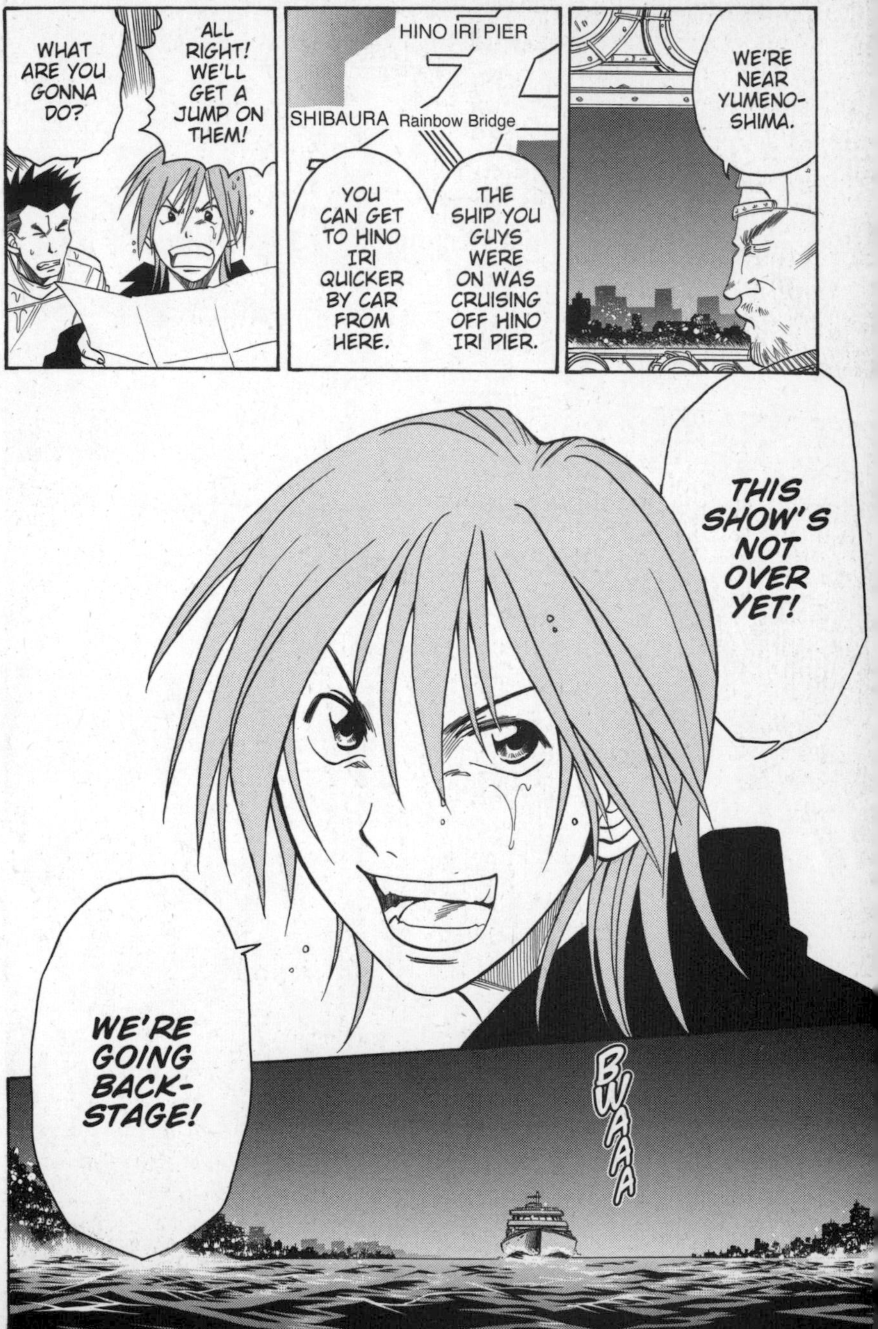
WE'RE NEAR YUMENO-SHIMA.
HINO IRI PIER
SHIBAURA
Rainbow Bridge
THE SHIP YOU GUYS WERE ON WAS CRUISING OFF HINO IRI PIER.
YOU CAN GET TO HINO IRI QUICKER BY CAR FROM HERE.
ALL RIGHT! WE'LL GET A JUMP ON THEM!
WHAT ARE YOU GONNA DO?
THIS SHOW'S NOT OVER YET!
WE'RE GOING BACK-STAGE!
BWAAAA

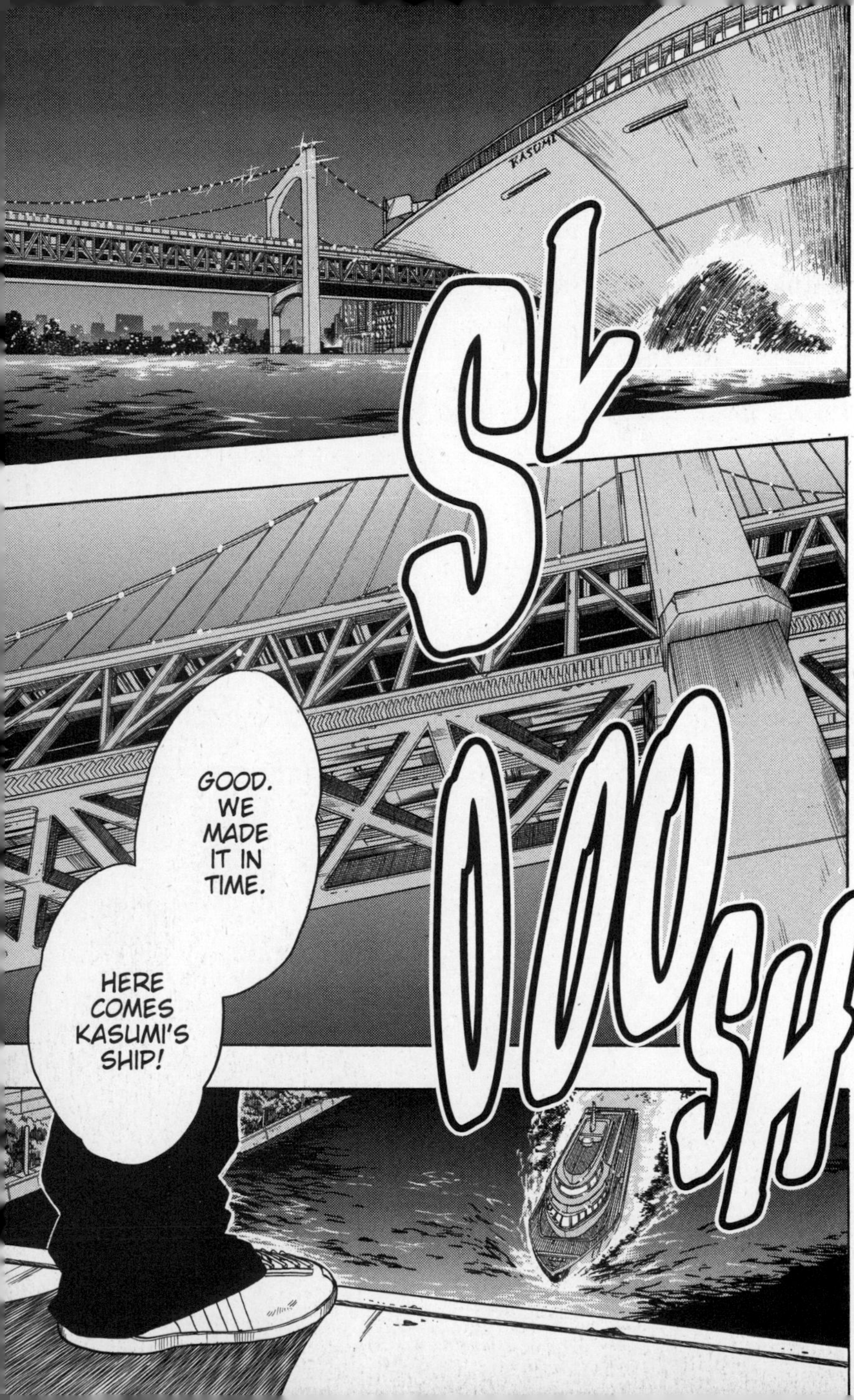
SLOOOSH
GOOD. WE MADE IT IN TIME.
HERE COMES KASUMI'S SHIP!
KASUMI

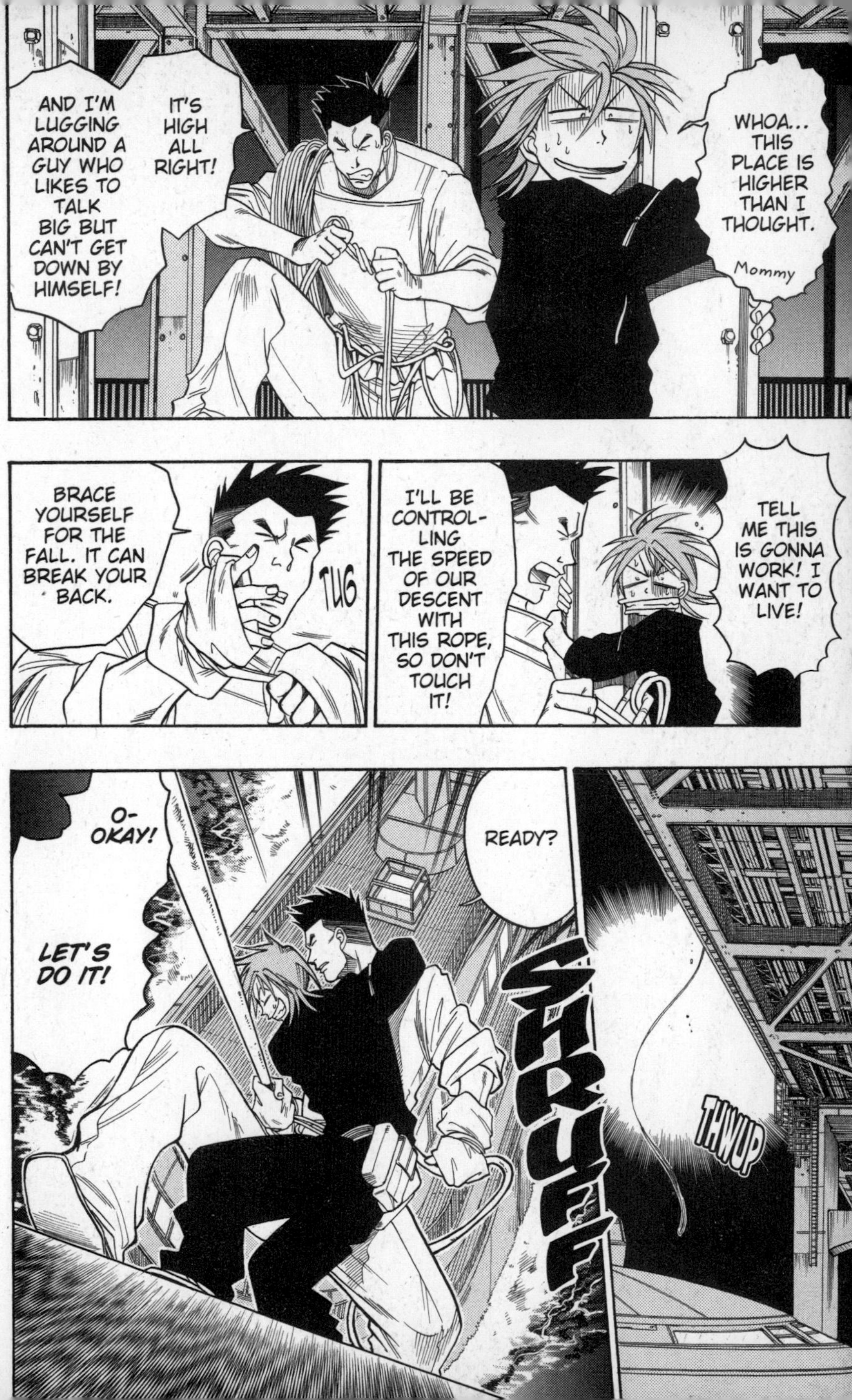
WHOA... THIS PLACE IS HIGHER THAN I THOUGHT.
Mommy
IT'S HIGH ALL RIGHT!
AND I'M LUGGING AROUND A GUY WHO LIKES TO TALK BIG BUT CAN'T GET DOWN BY HIMSELF!
TELL ME THIS IS GONNA WORK! I WANT TO LIVE!
I'LL BE CONTROL-LING THE SPEED OF OUR DESCENT WITH THIS ROPE, SO DON'T TOUCH IT!
BRACE YOURSELF FOR THE FALL. IT CAN BREAK YOUR BACK.
TUG
READY?
O-OKAY!
LET'S DO IT!
SHRUFF
THWUP

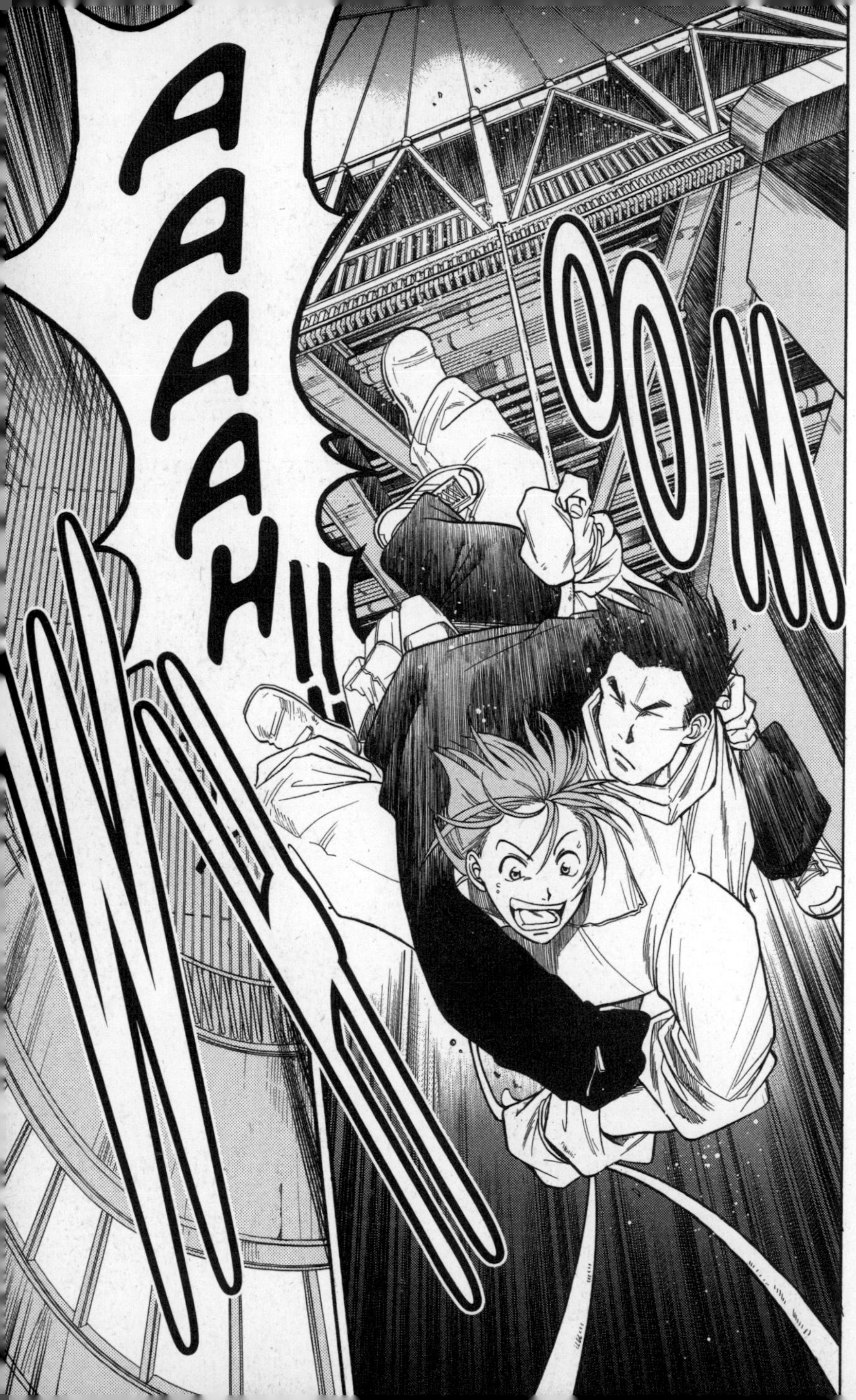
OOM
AAAAH!!

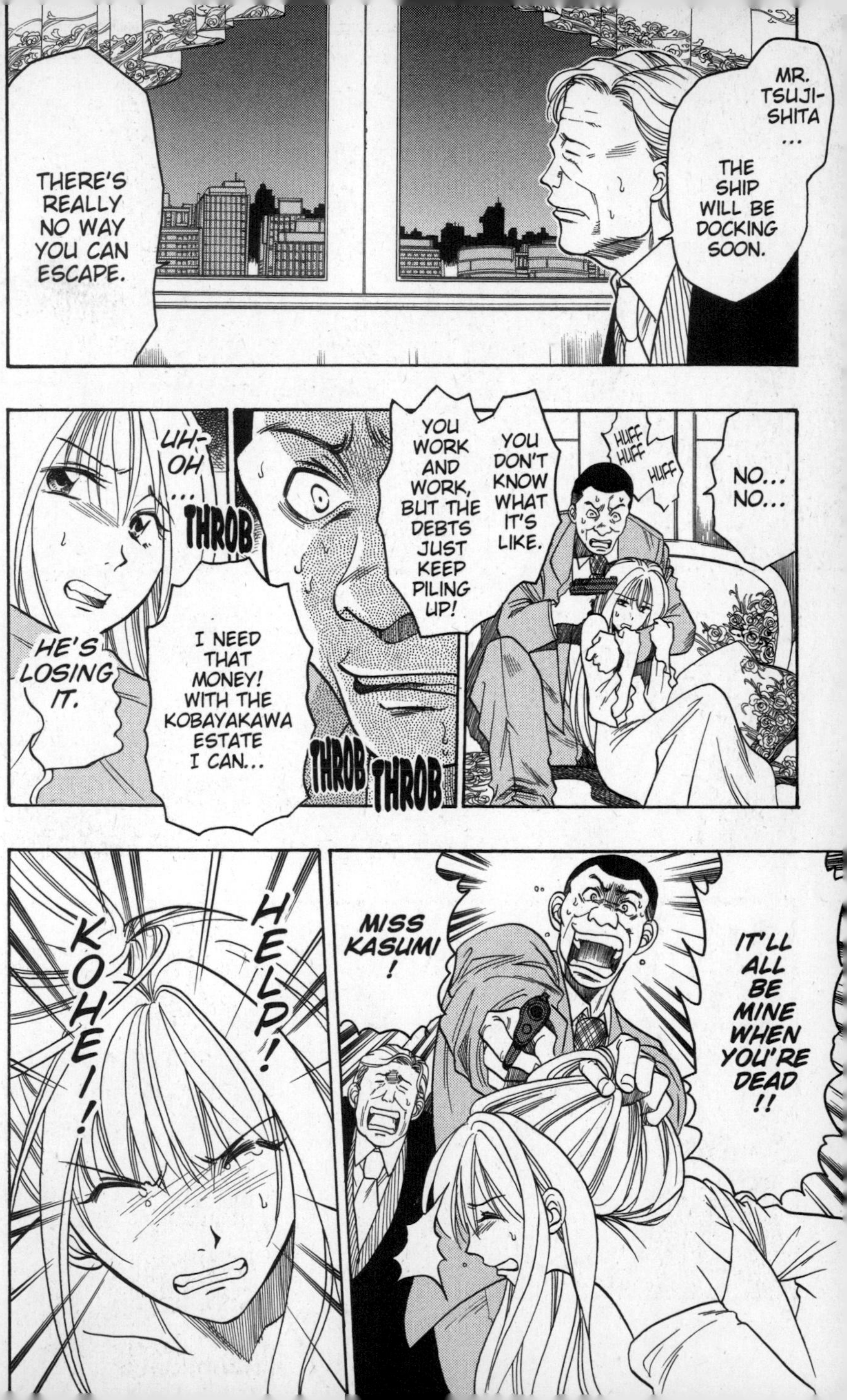
MR. TSUJISHITA...
THE SHIP WILL BE DOCKING SOON.
THERE'S REALLY NO WAY YOU CAN ESCAPE.
NO... NO...
HUFF HUFF
HUFF
YOU DON'T KNOW WHAT IT'S LIKE.
YOU WORK AND WORK, BUT THE DEBTS JUST KEEP PILING UP!
THROB THROB
I NEED THAT MONEY! WITH THE KOBAYAKAWA ESTATE I CAN...
UH-OH...
THROB
HE'S LOSING IT.
IT'LL ALL BE MINE WHEN YOU'RE DEAD!!
MISS KASUMI!
HELP!
KOHEI!!

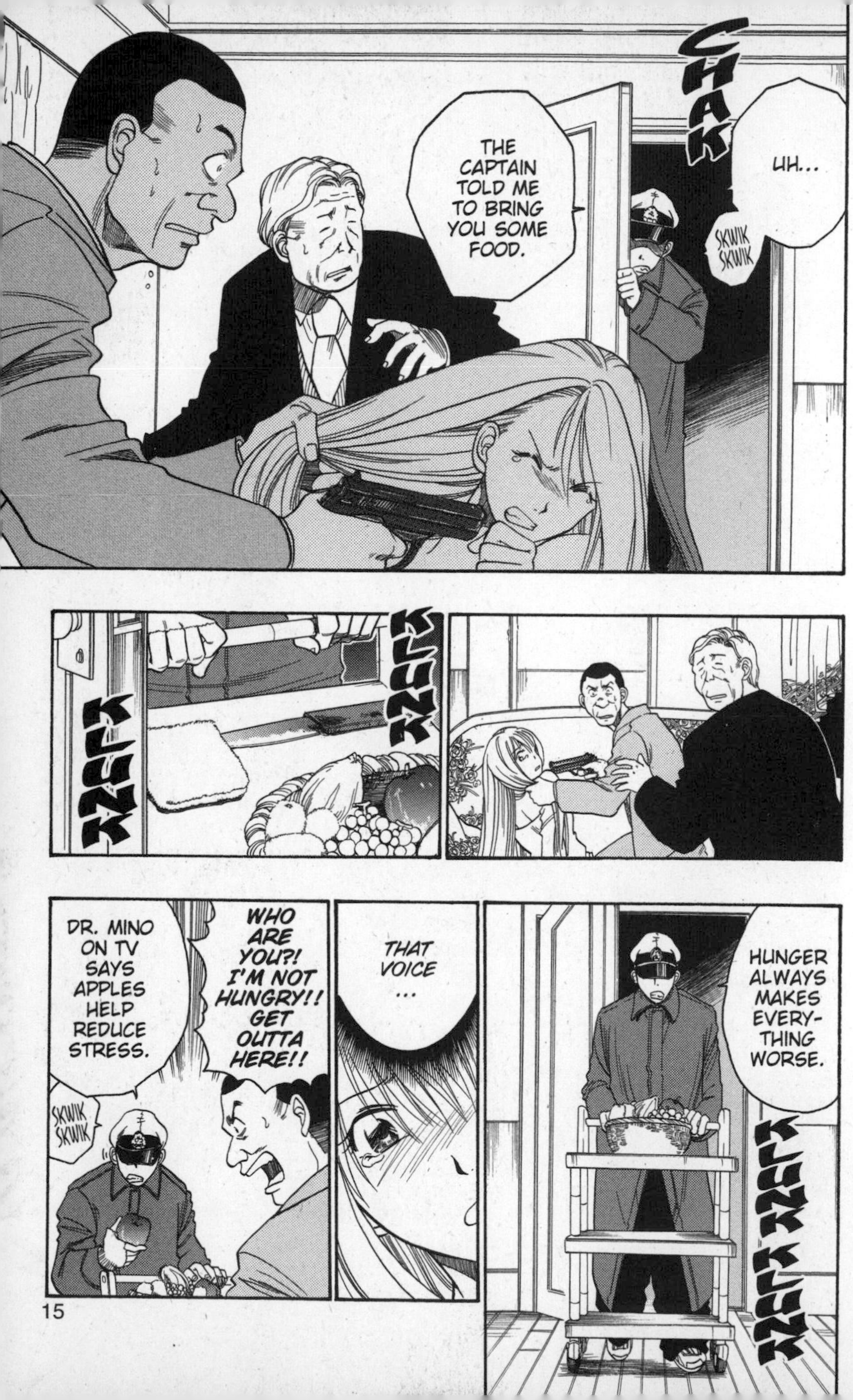
CHAK
UH...
SKWIK SKWIK
THE CAPTAIN TOLD ME TO BRING YOU SOME FOOD.
KLUNK KLUNK
HUNGER ALWAYS MAKES EVERY-THING WORSE.
KLUNK KLUNK
THAT VOICE ...
WHO ARE YOU?! I'M NOT HUNGRY!! GET OUTTA HERE!!
DR. MINO ON TV SAYS APPLES HELP REDUCE STRESS.
SKWIK SKWIK

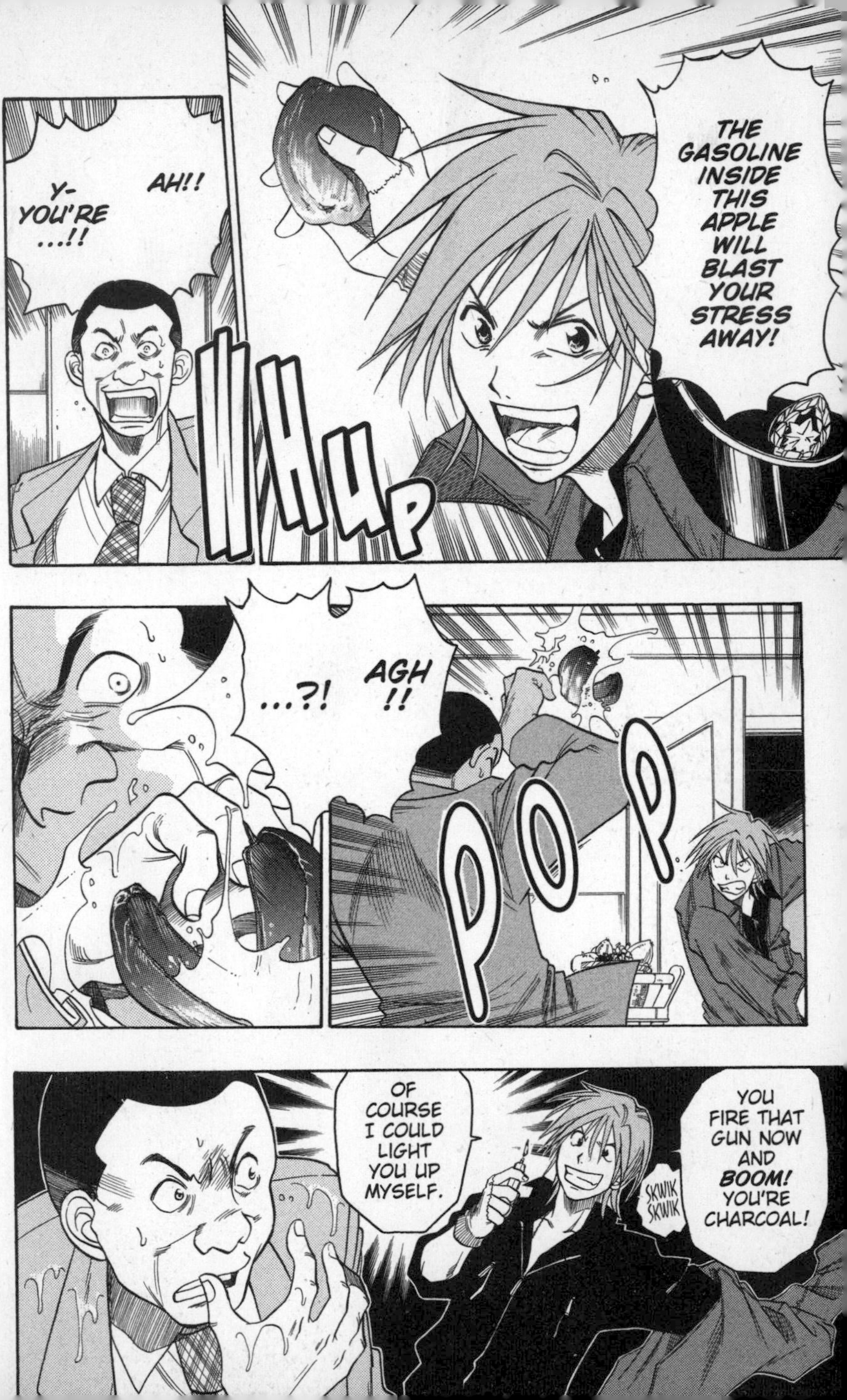

THE GASOLINE INSIDE THIS APPLE WILL BLAST YOUR STRESS AWAY!
HUP
AH!!
Y-YOU'RE ...!!
AGH !!
POP
...?!
YOU FIRE THAT GUN NOW AND BOOM! YOU'RE CHARCOAL!
SKWIK SKWIK
OF COURSE I COULD LIGHT YOU UP MYSELF.

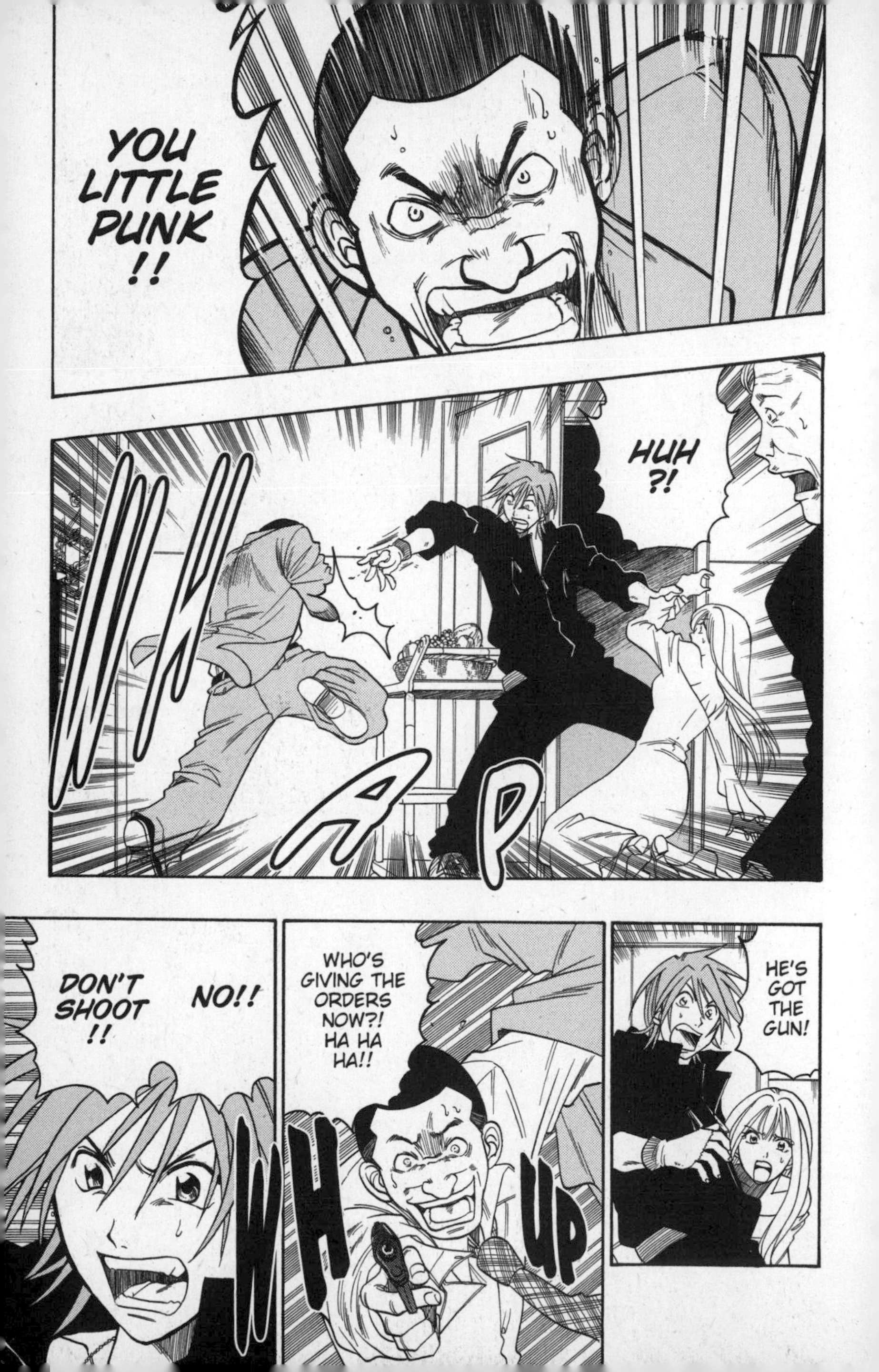
YOU LITTLE PUNK!!
HUH?!
WHAP
HE'S GOT THE GUN!
WHO'S GIVING THE ORDERS NOW?! HA HA HA!!
WHUP
NO!!
DON'T SHOOT!!

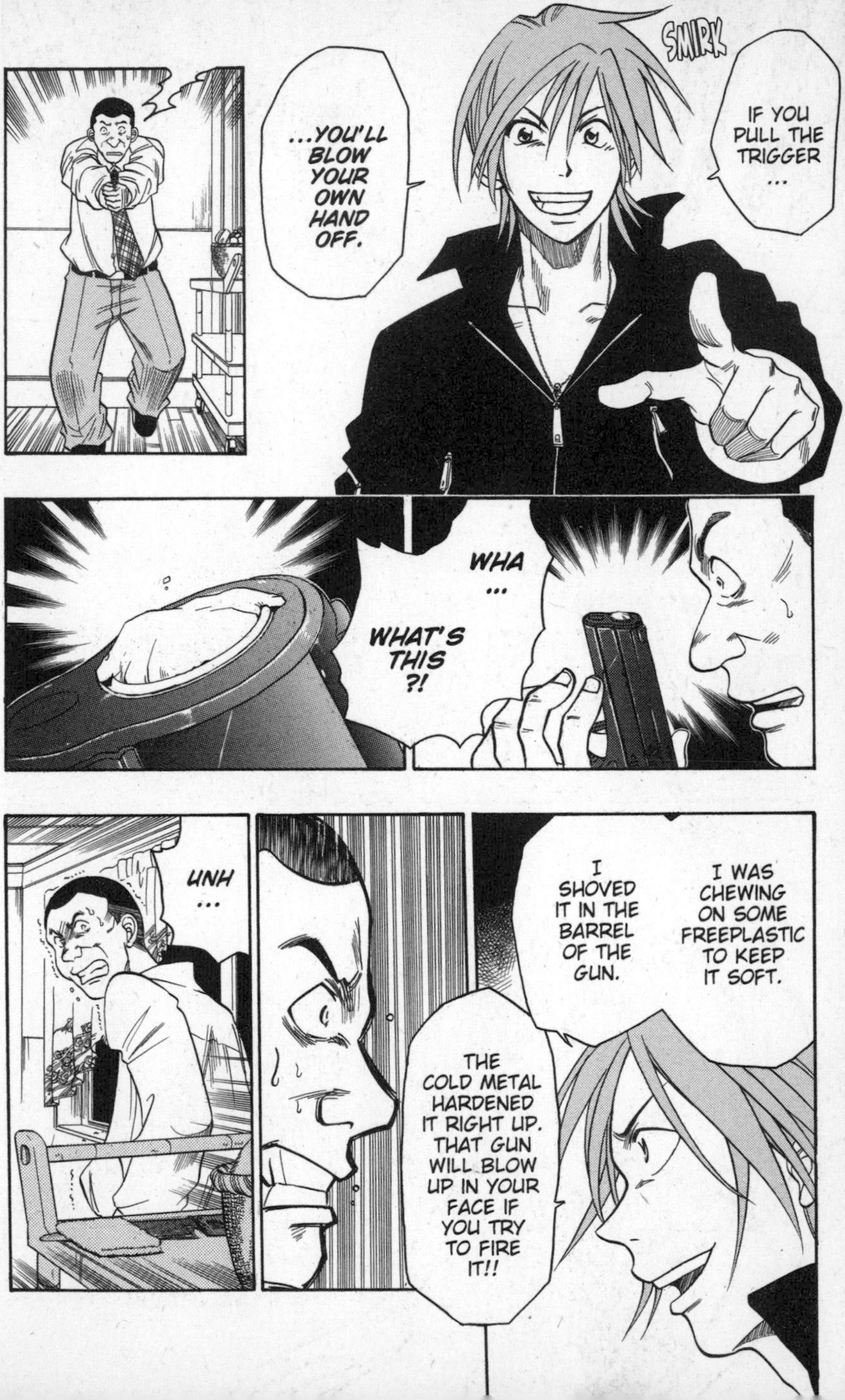
SMIRK
IF YOU PULL THE TRIGGER ...
...YOU'LL BLOW YOUR OWN HAND OFF.
WHA ...
WHAT'S THIS ?!
I WAS CHEWING ON SOME FREEPLASTIC TO KEEP IT SOFT.
I SHOVED IT IN THE BARREL OF THE GUN.
THE COLD METAL HARDENED IT RIGHT UP. THAT GUN WILL BLOW UP IN YOUR FACE IF YOU TRY TO FIRE IT!!
UNH ...

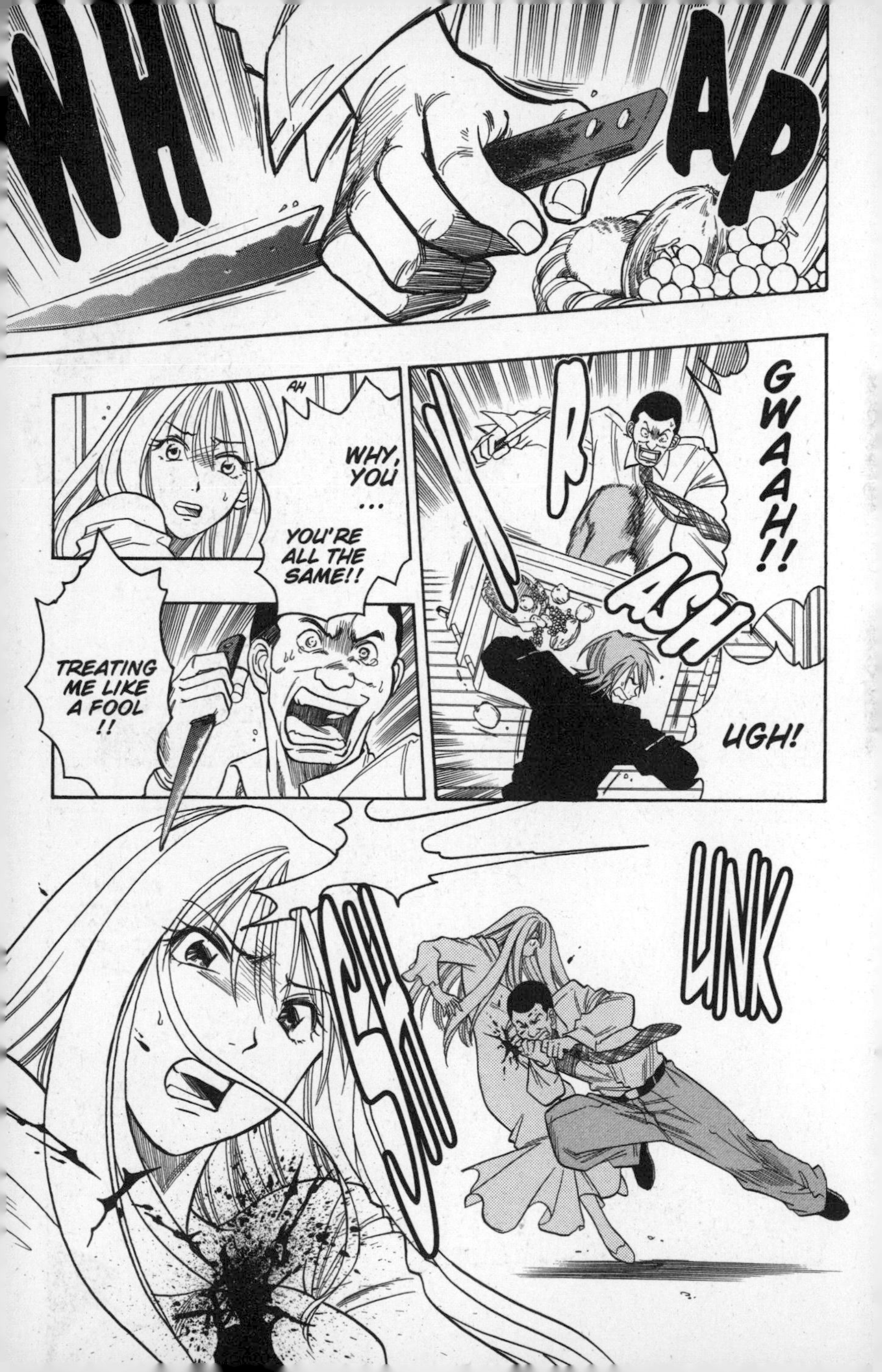
WH
AP
GWAAAH!!
R
ASH
UGH!
AH
WHY, YOU ...
YOU'RE ALL THE SAME!!
TREATING ME LIKE A FOOL !!
UNK

You think I could be a special effects artist too?

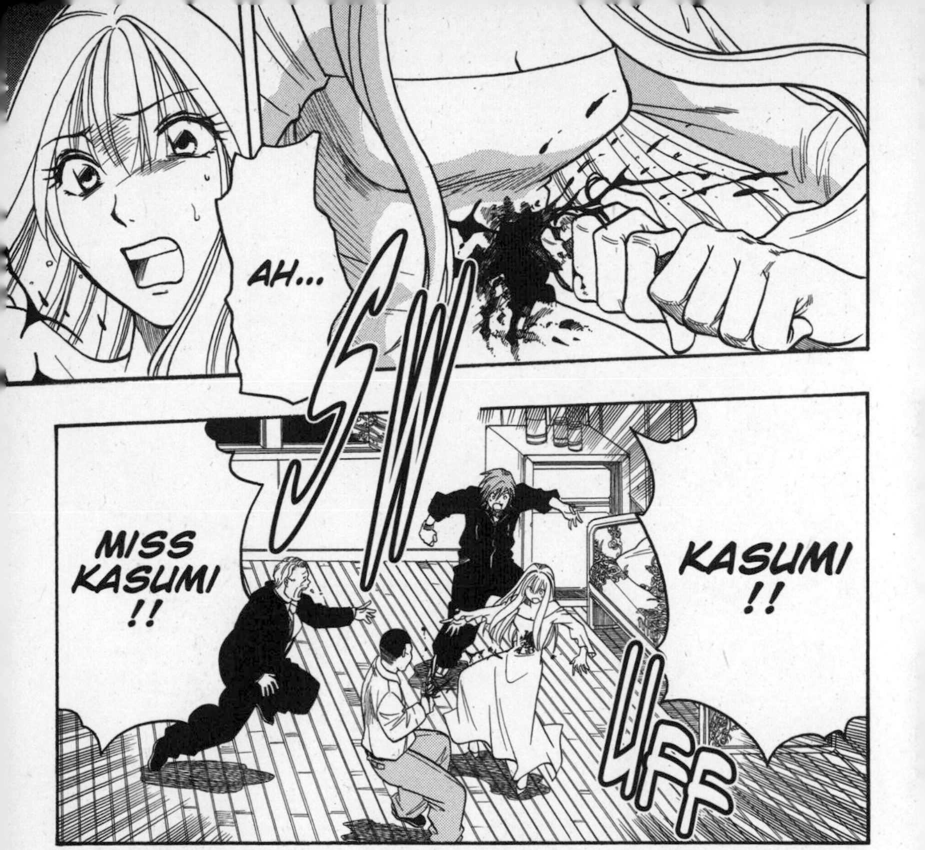
AH...
KASUMI !!
MISS KASUMI !!

Scene 27: TB Confidential (Part 7)

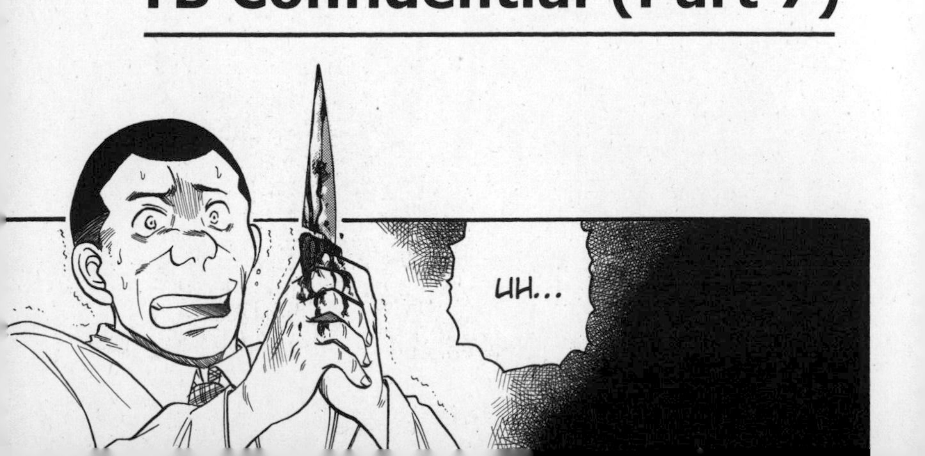
UH...

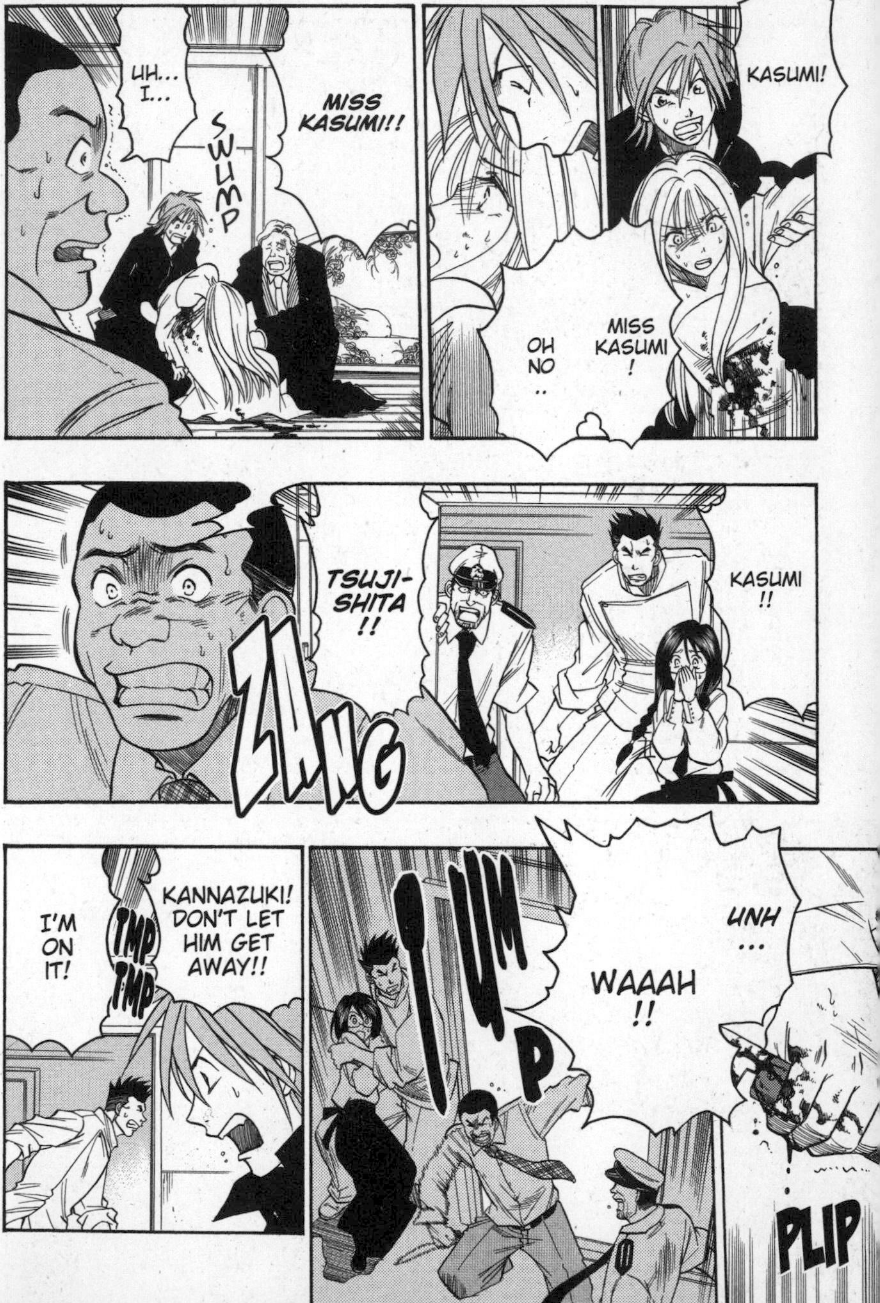
KASUMI!
MISS KASUMI!
OH NO ..
MISS KASUMI!!
UH... I...
SWUMP
KASUMI !!
TSUJI-SHITA !!
ZANG
UNH ...
WAAAH !!
THUMP
PLIP
KANNAZUKI! DON'T LET HIM GET AWAY!!
TMP TMP
I'M ON IT!

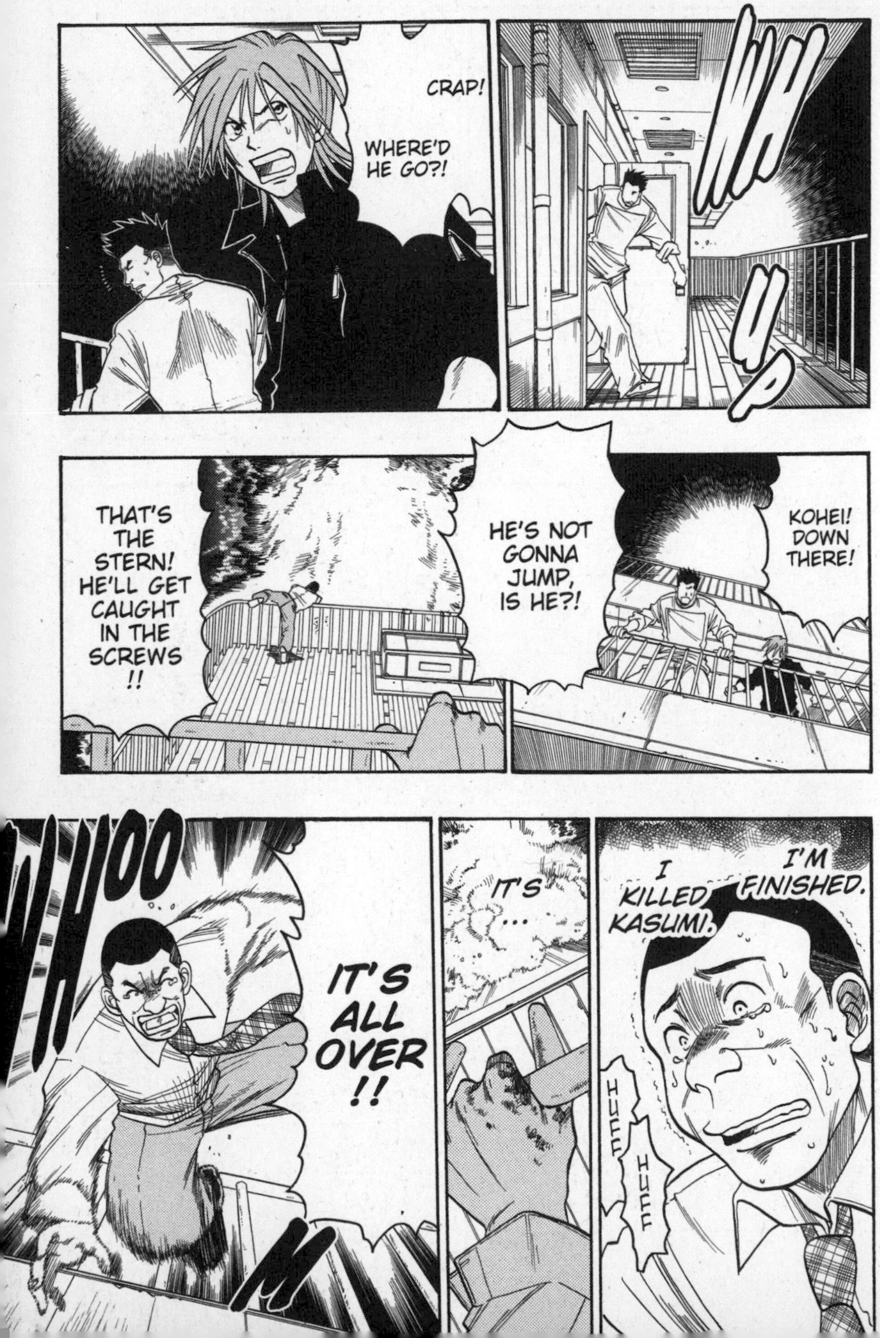
WHUP
CRAP!
WHERE'D HE GO?!
KOHEI! DOWN THERE!
HE'S NOT GONNA JUMP, IS HE?!
THAT'S THE STERN! HE'LL GET CAUGHT IN THE SCREWS!!
I'M FINISHED.
I KILLED KASUMI.
HUFF HUFF
IT'S...
IT'S ALL OVER!!
WHOOM

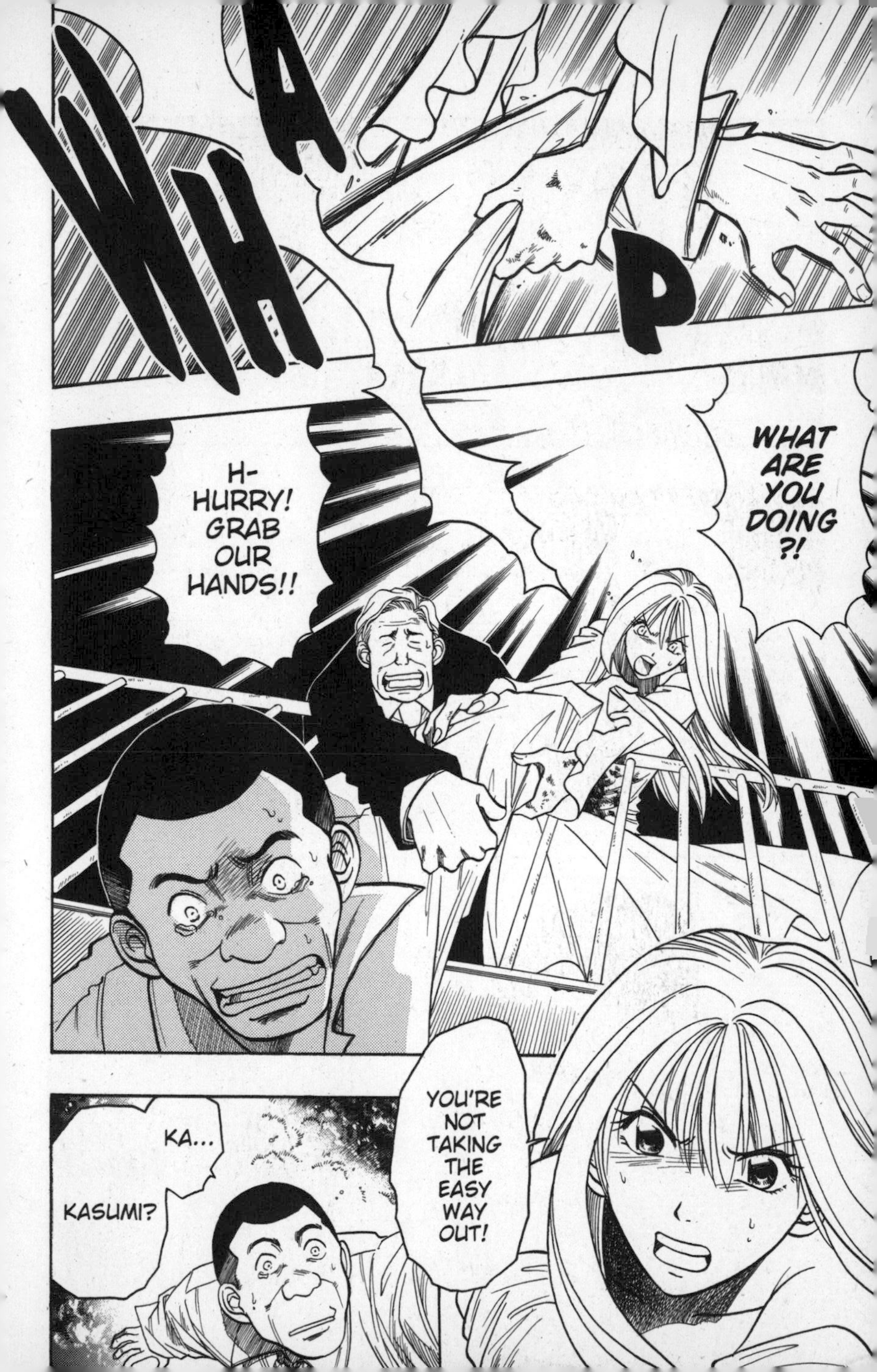
WHAP
WHAT ARE YOU DOING?!
H-HURRY! GRAB OUR HANDS!!
YOU'RE NOT TAKING THE EASY WAY OUT!
KA...
KASUMI?

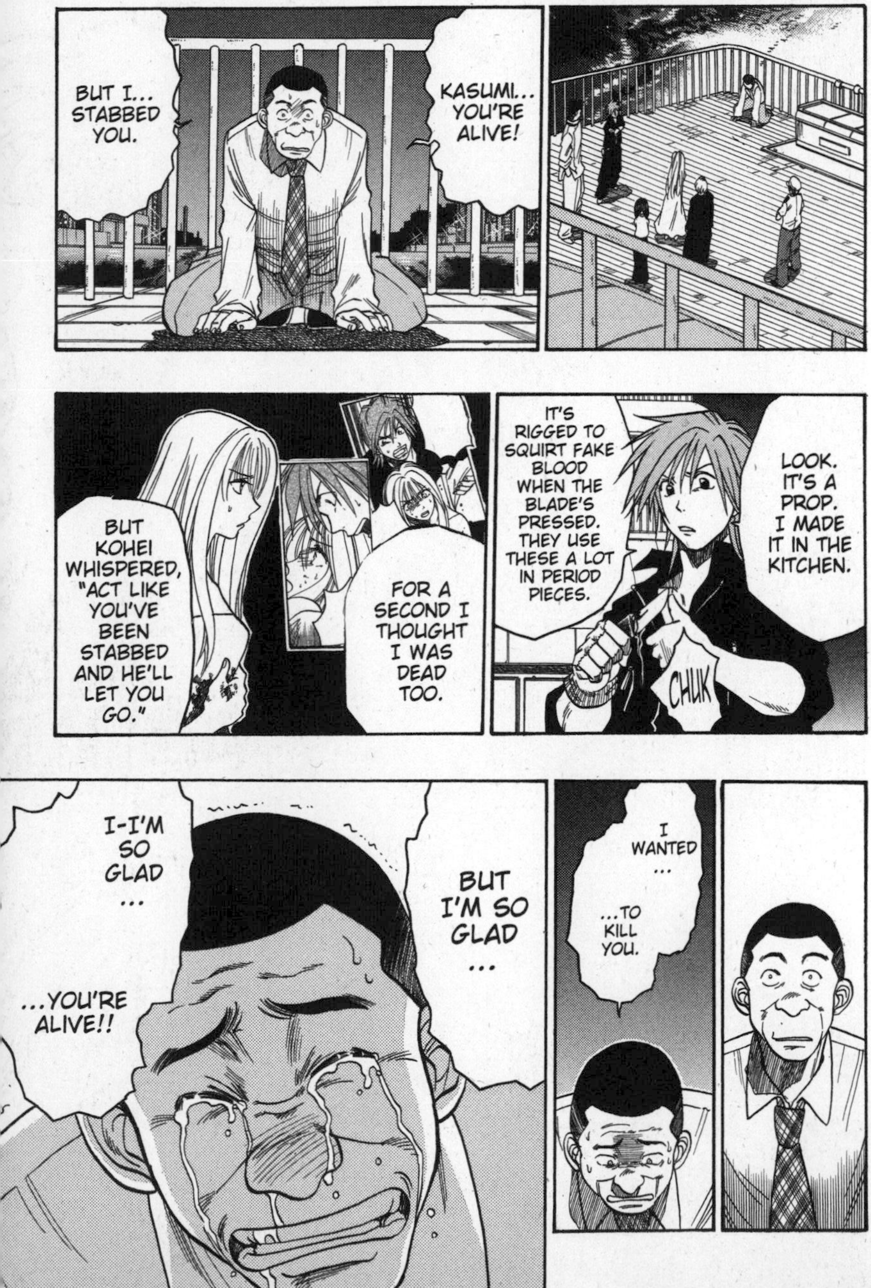
KASUMI... YOU'RE ALIVE!
BUT I... STABBED YOU.
LOOK. IT'S A PROP. I MADE IT IN THE KITCHEN.
IT'S RIGGED TO SQUIRT FAKE BLOOD WHEN THE BLADE'S PRESSED. THEY USE THESE A LOT IN PERIOD PIECES.
CHUK
FOR A SECOND I THOUGHT I WAS DEAD TOO.
BUT KOHEI WHISPERED, "ACT LIKE YOU'VE BEEN STABBED AND HE'LL LET YOU GO."
I WANTED ...
...TO KILL YOU.
BUT I'M SO GLAD ...
I-I'M SO GLAD ...
...YOU'RE ALIVE!!

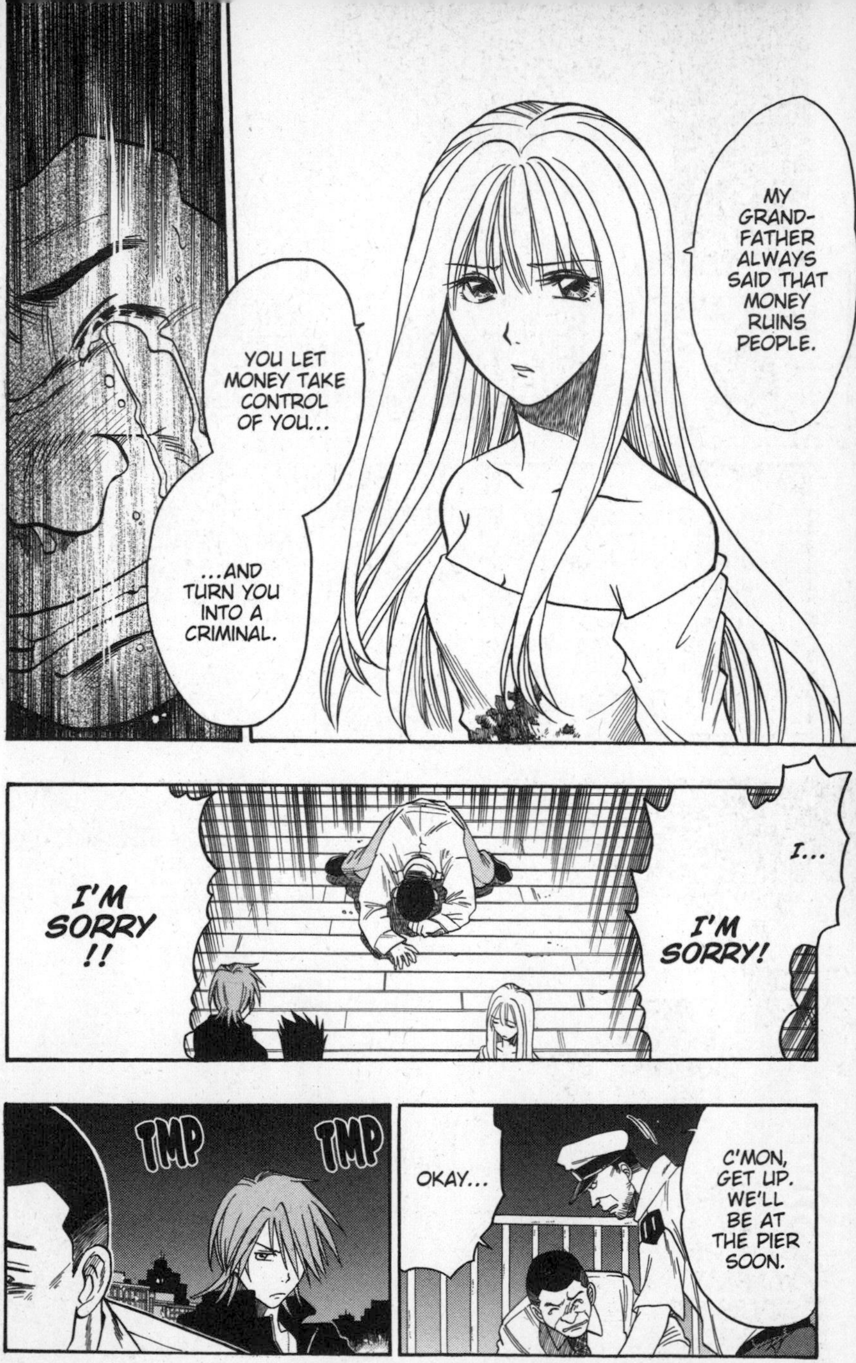
MY GRANDFATHER ALWAYS SAID THAT MONEY RUINS PEOPLE.
YOU LET MONEY TAKE CONTROL OF YOU...
...AND TURN YOU INTO A CRIMINAL.
I...
I'M SORRY!
I'M SORRY!!
C'MON, GET UP. WE'LL BE AT THE PIER SOON.
OKAY...
TMP
TMP

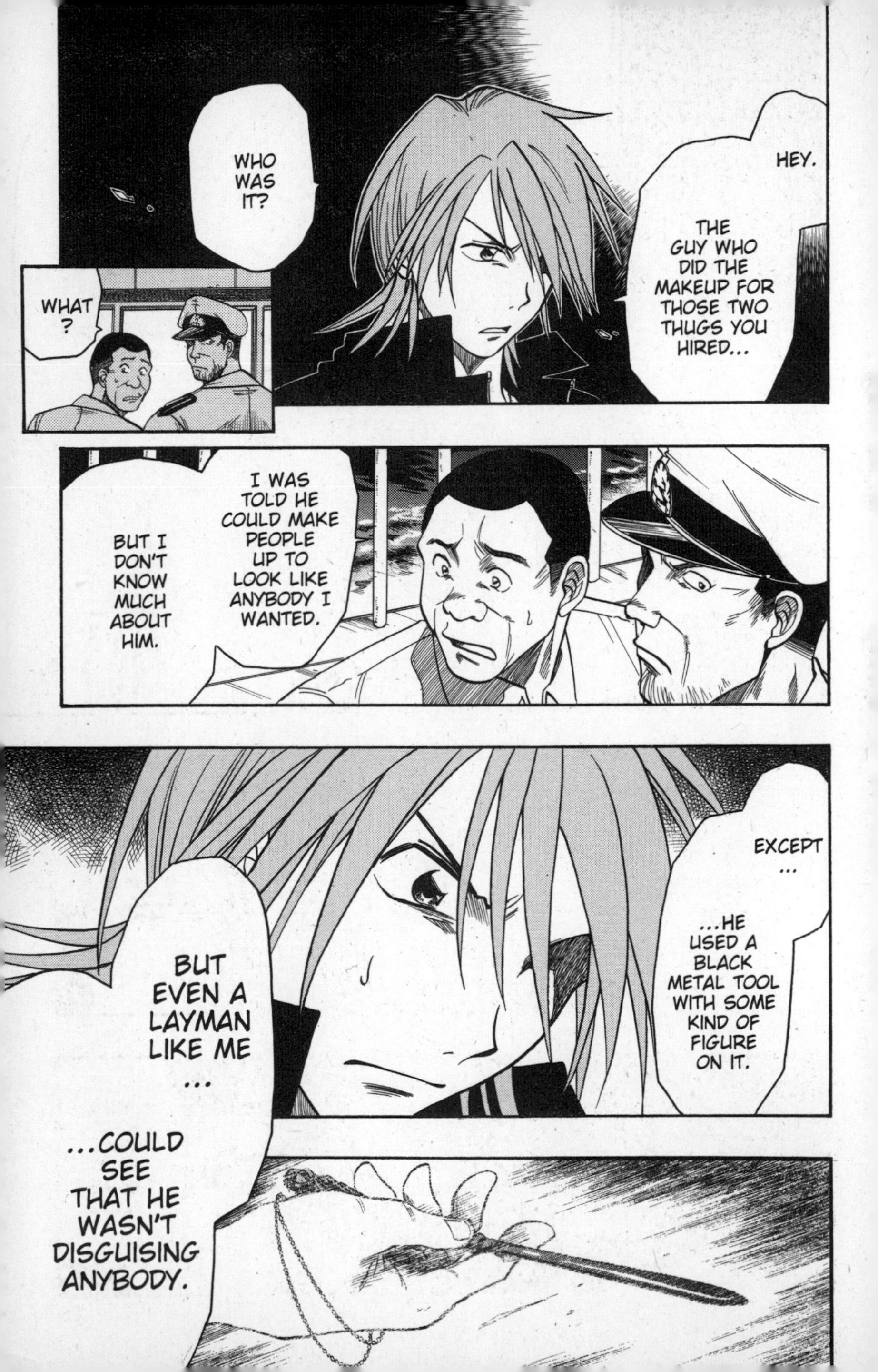
HEY.
THE GUY WHO DID THE MAKEUP FOR THOSE TWO THUGS YOU HIRED...
WHO WAS IT?
WHAT?
I WAS TOLD HE COULD MAKE PEOPLE UP TO LOOK LIKE ANYBODY I WANTED.
BUT I DON'T KNOW MUCH ABOUT HIM.
EXCEPT...
...HE USED A BLACK METAL TOOL WITH SOME KIND OF FIGURE ON IT.
BUT EVEN A LAYMAN LIKE ME...
...COULD SEE THAT HE WASN'T DISGUISING ANYBODY.

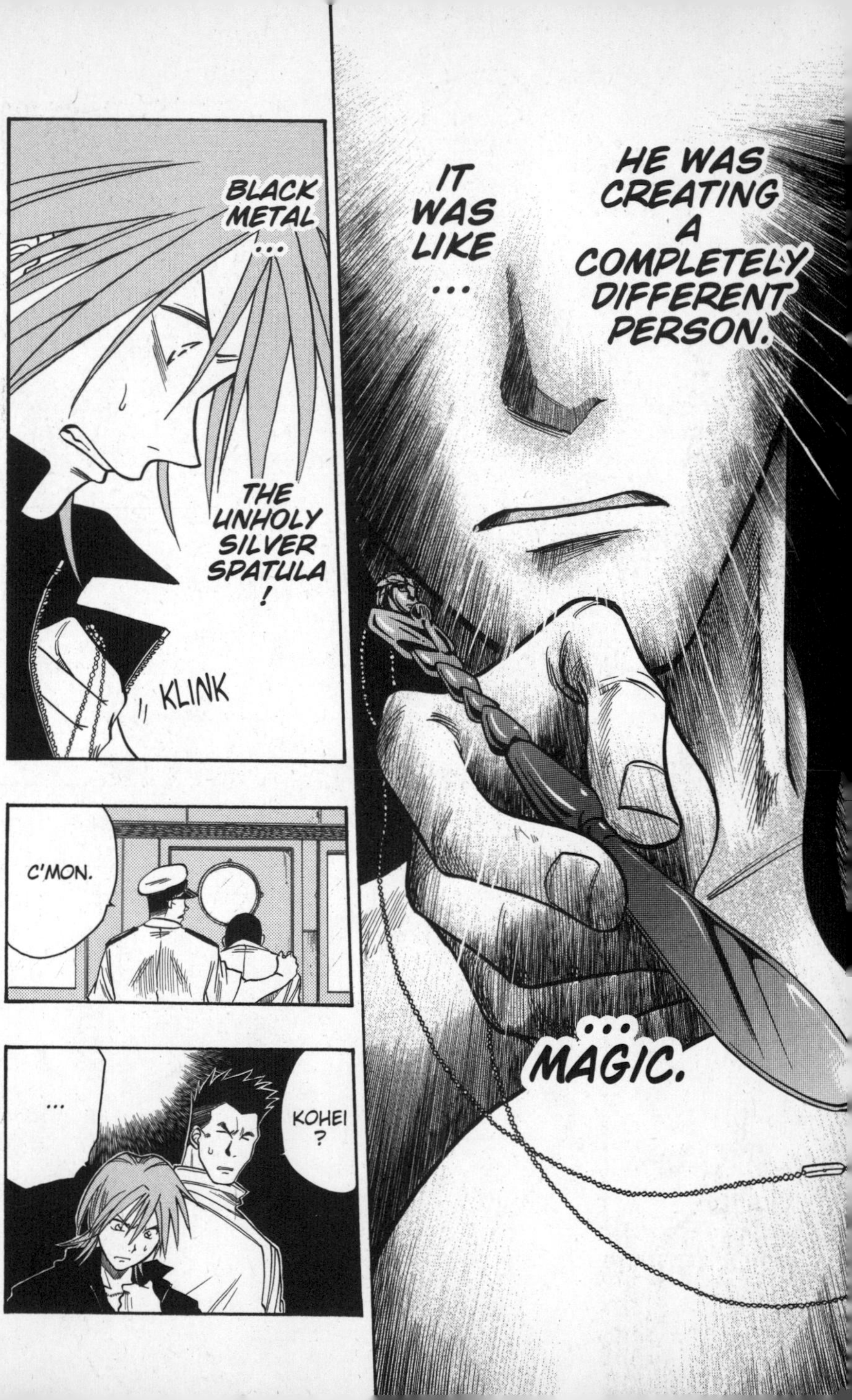
HE WAS CREATING A COMPLETELY DIFFERENT PERSON.
IT WAS LIKE ...
... MAGIC.
BLACK METAL ...
THE UNHOLY SILVER SPATULA!
KLINK
C'MON.
KOHEI?
...

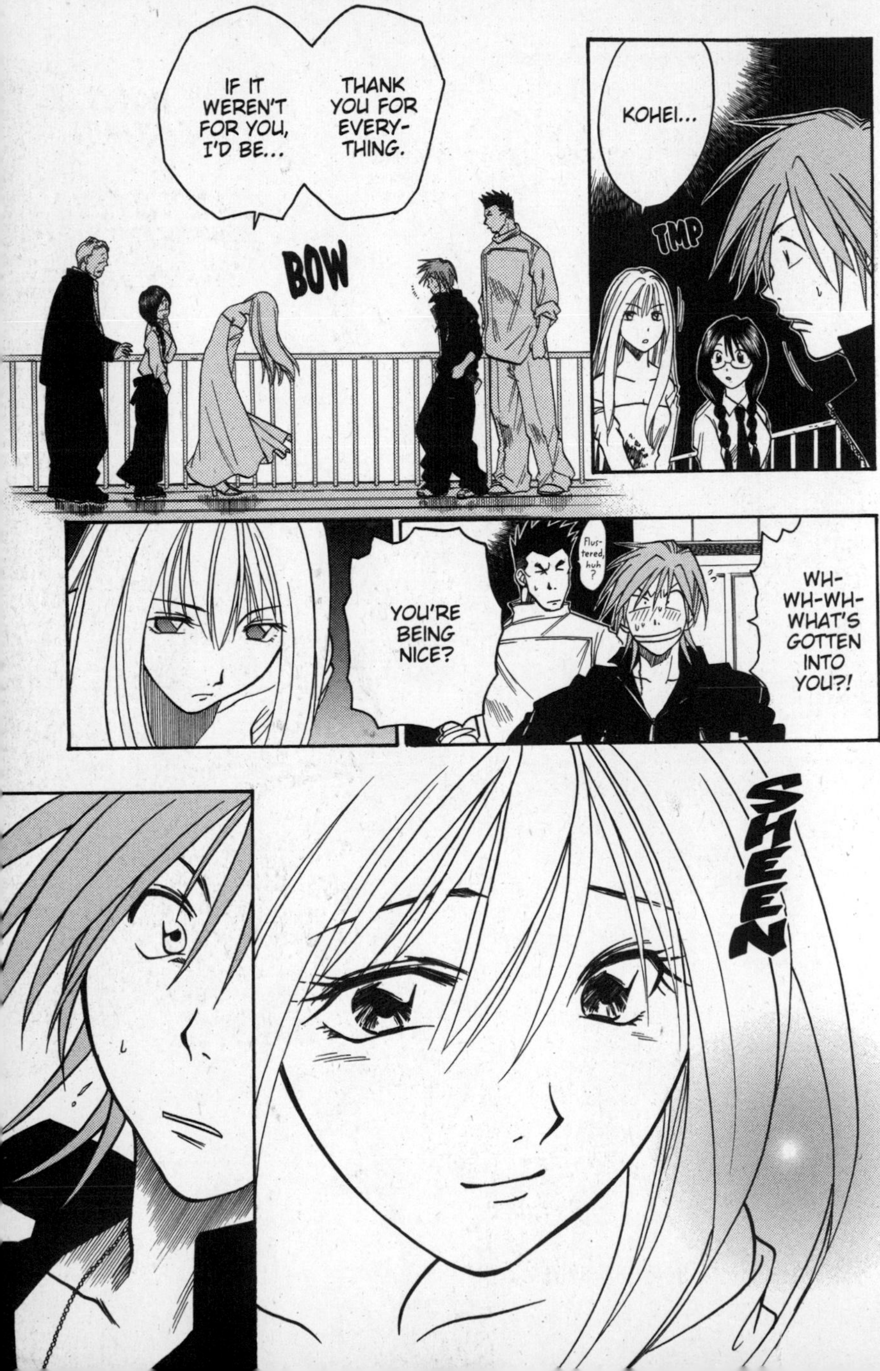
KOHEI...
TMP
THANK YOU FOR EVERY-THING.
IF IT WEREN'T FOR YOU, I'D BE...
BOW
WH-WH-WH-WHAT'S GOTTEN INTO YOU?!
Flus-tered, huh?
YOU'RE BEING NICE?
SHEEN

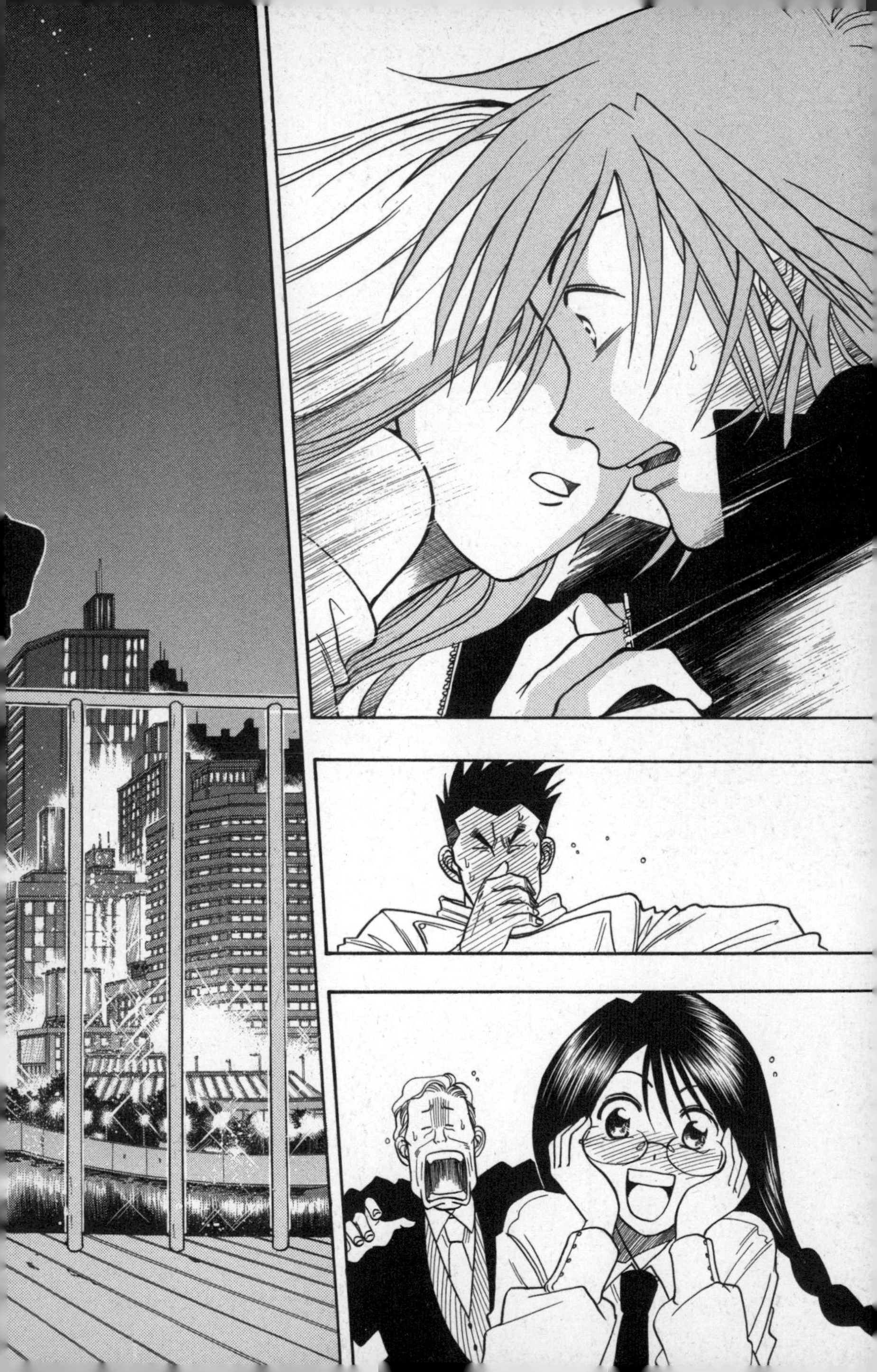

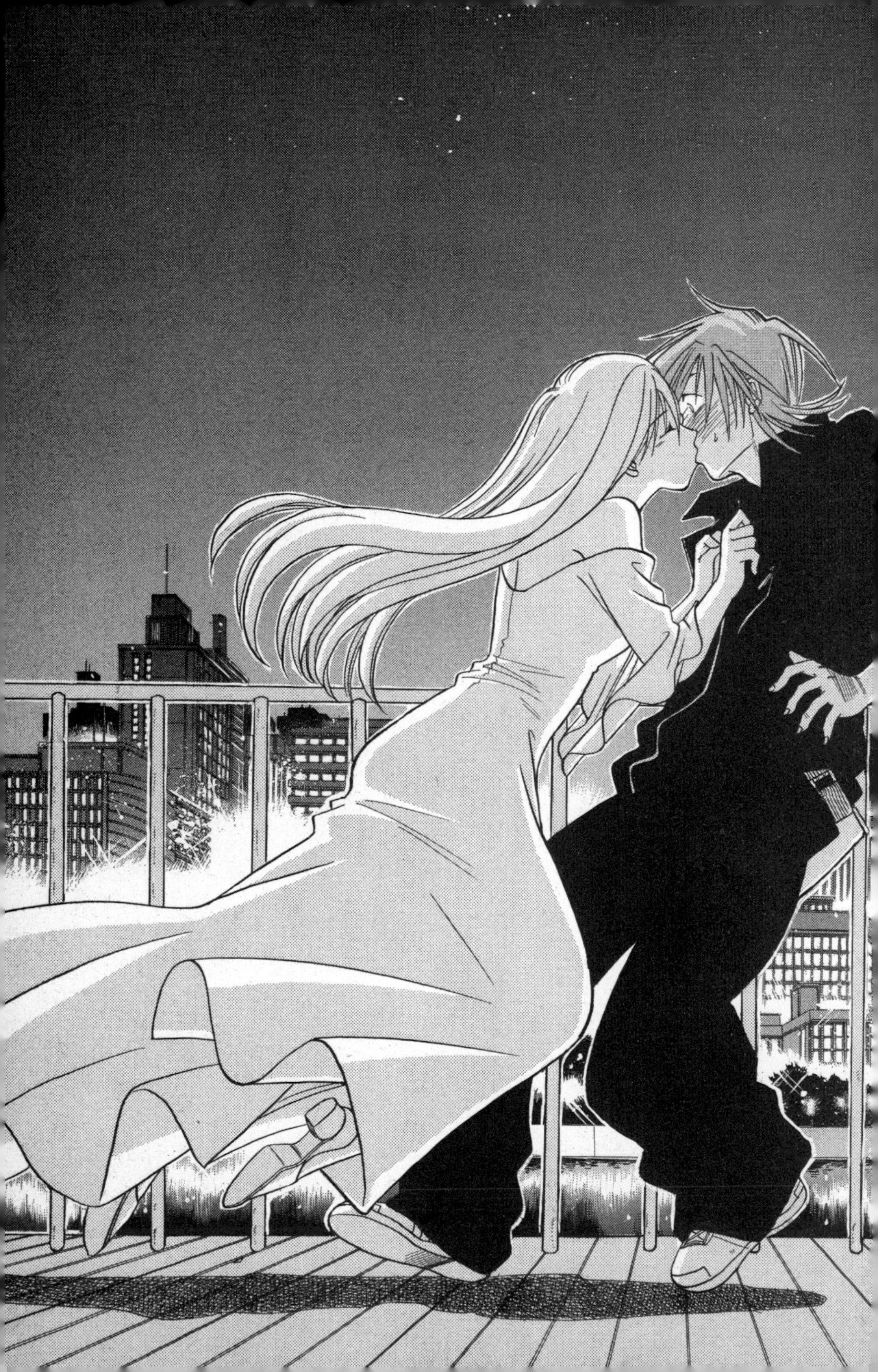

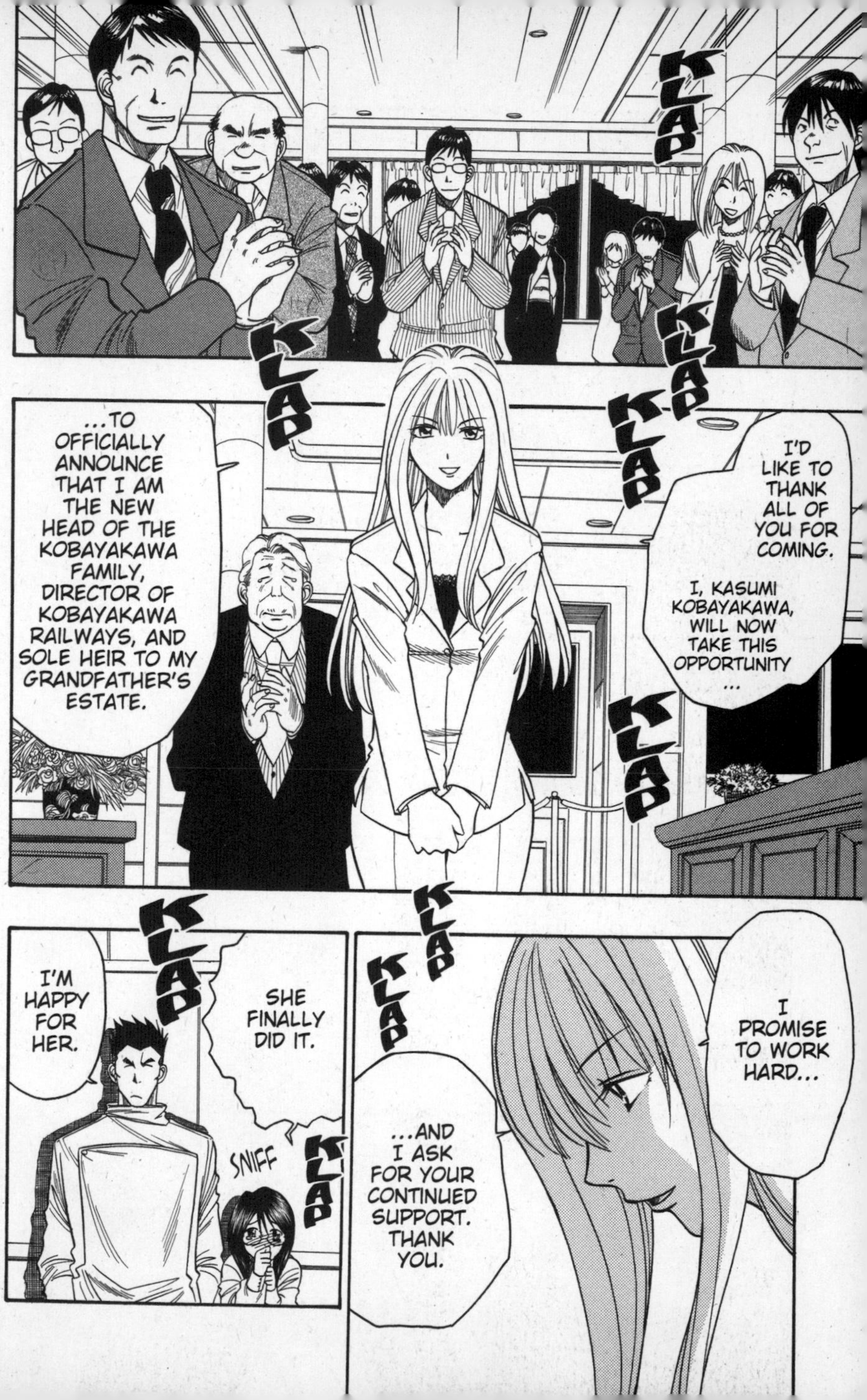
KLAP
KLAP
KLAP
KLAP
I'D LIKE TO THANK ALL OF YOU FOR COMING.
I, KASUMI KOBAYAKAWA, WILL NOW TAKE THIS OPPORTUNITY...
...TO OFFICIALLY ANNOUNCE THAT I AM THE NEW HEAD OF THE KOBAYAKAWA FAMILY, DIRECTOR OF KOBAYAKAWA RAILWAYS, AND SOLE HEIR TO MY GRANDFATHER'S ESTATE.
KLAP
KLAP
KLAP
I PROMISE TO WORK HARD...
...AND I ASK FOR YOUR CONTINUED SUPPORT. THANK YOU.
KLAP
SHE FINALLY DID IT.
I'M HAPPY FOR HER.
KLAP
SNIFF

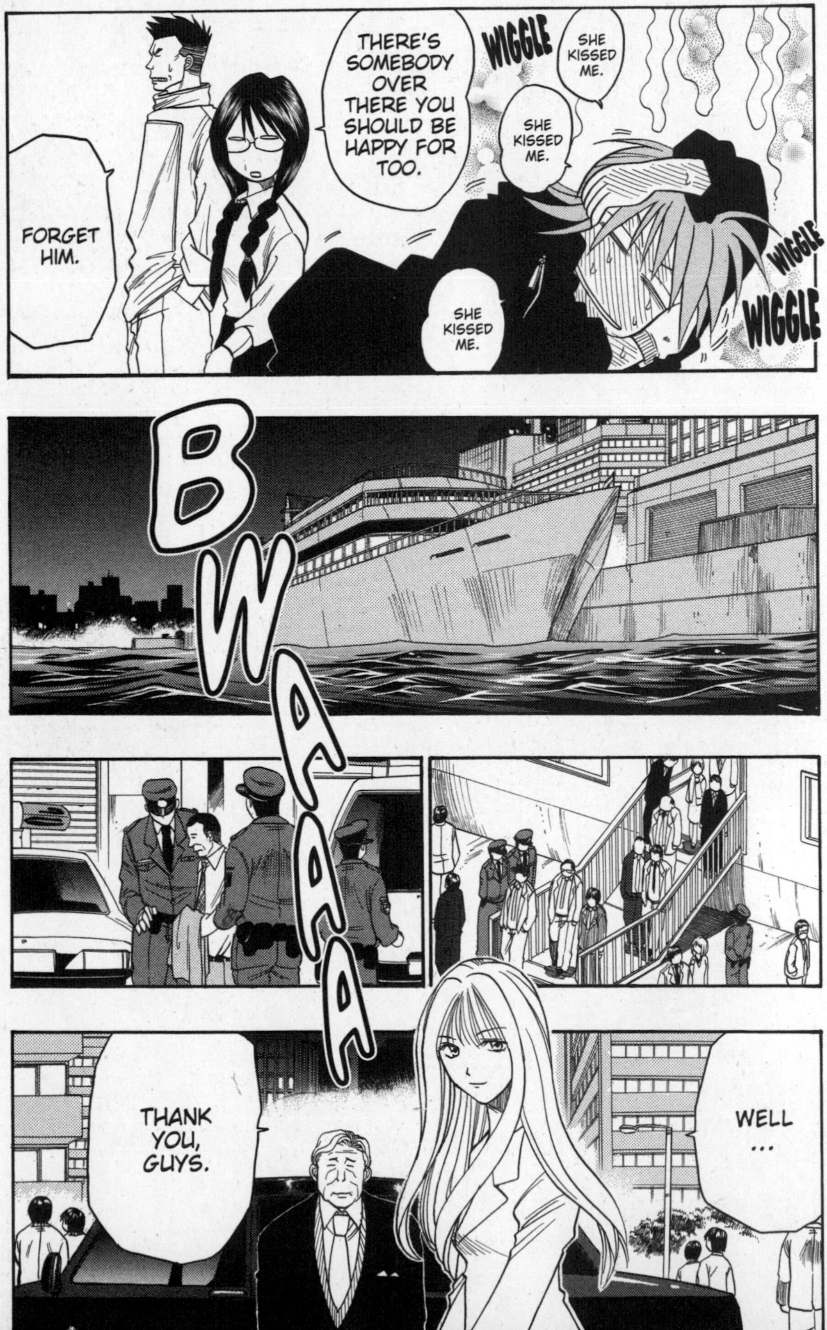
SHE KISSED ME.
SHE KISSED ME.
WIGGLE
WIGGLE
WIGGLE
THERE'S SOMEBODY OVER THERE YOU SHOULD BE HAPPY FOR TOO.
SHE KISSED ME.
FORGET HIM.
BWAAAAA
WELL ...
THANK YOU, GUYS.

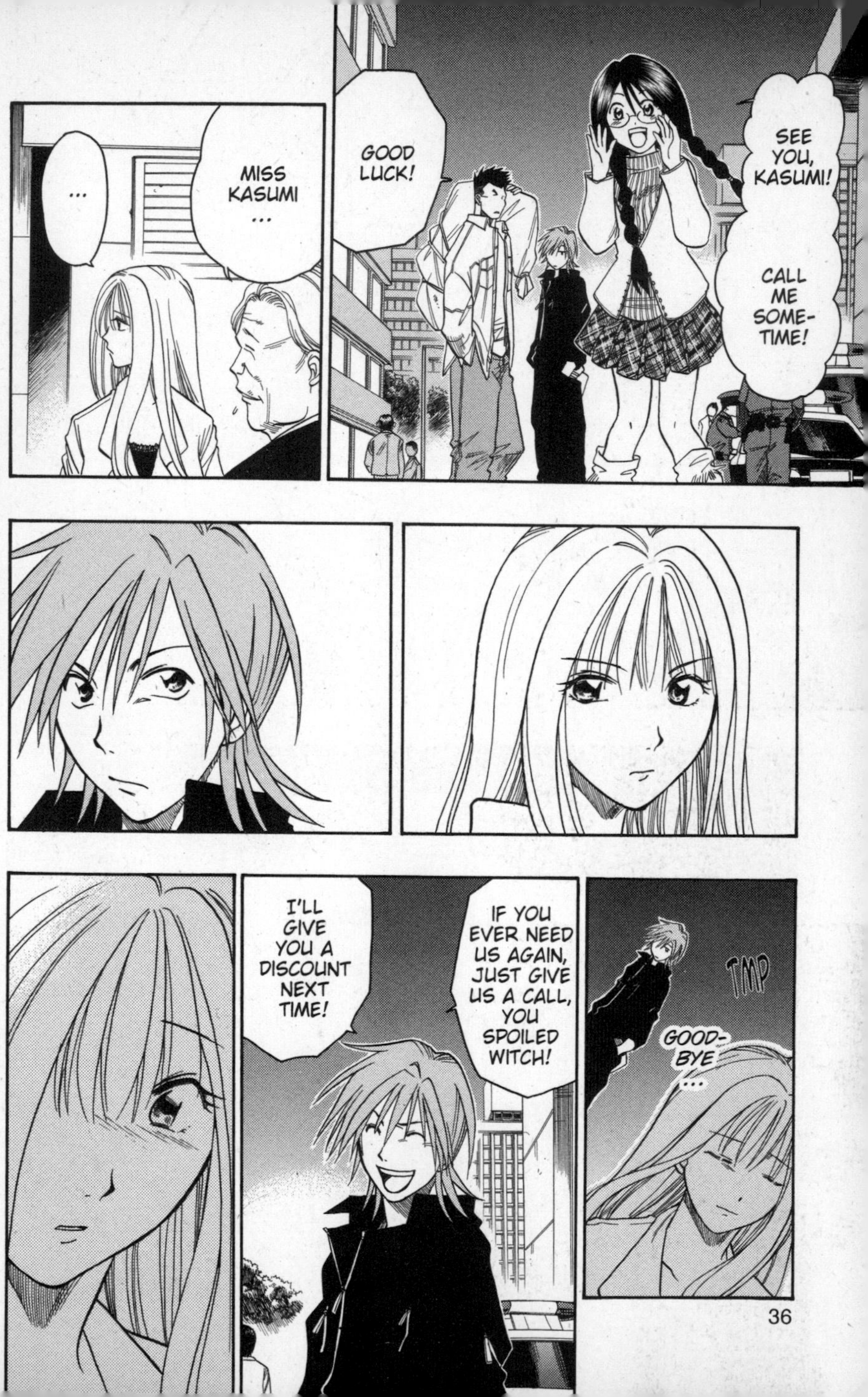
SEE YOU, KASUMI!
CALL ME SOME-TIME!
GOOD LUCK!
MISS KASUMI ...
...
TMP
GOOD-BYE ...
IF YOU EVER NEED US AGAIN, JUST GIVE US A CALL, YOU SPOILED WITCH!
I'LL GIVE YOU A DISCOUNT NEXT TIME!

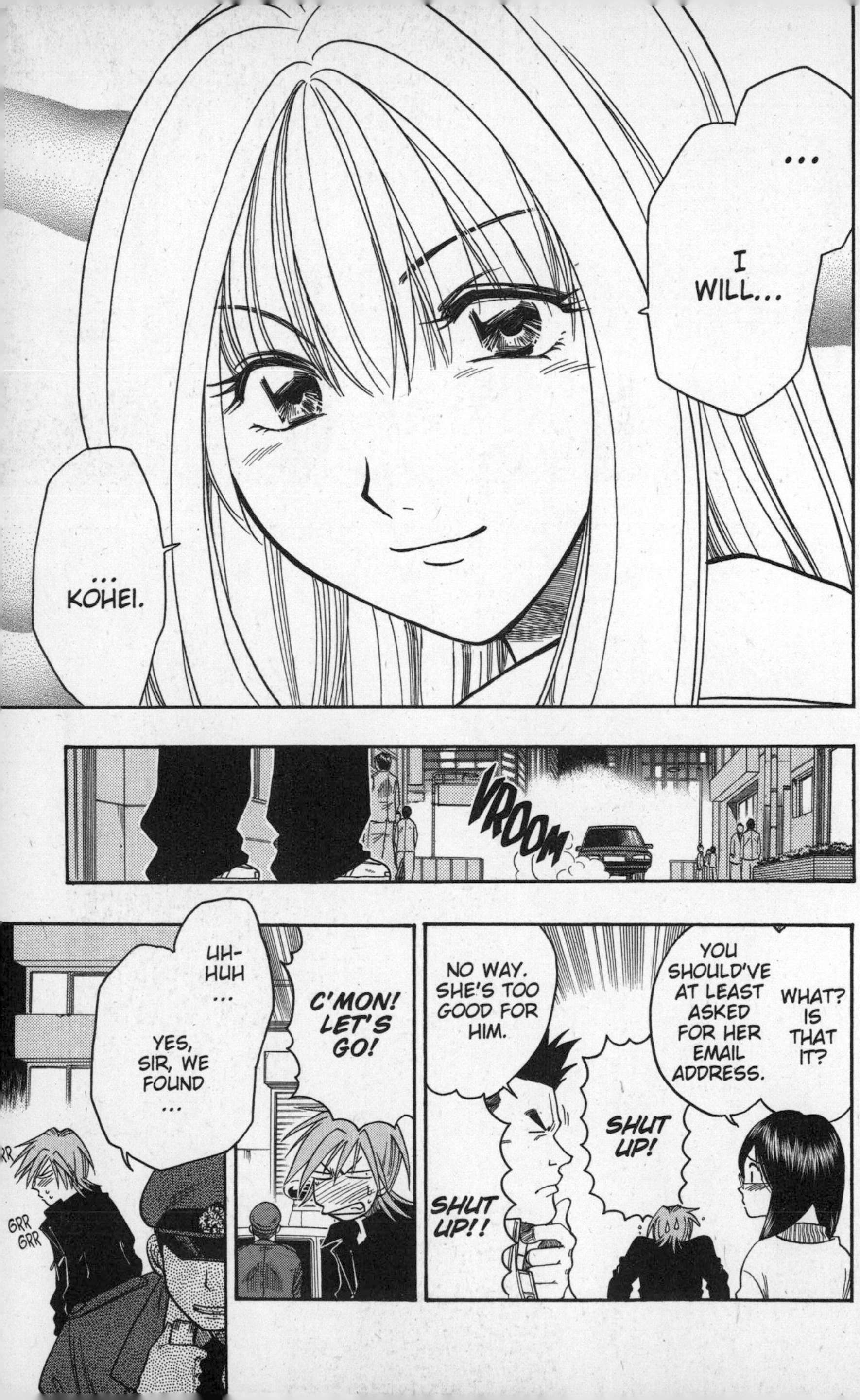
... I WILL...
... KŌHEI.
VROOM
WHAT? IS THAT IT?
YOU SHOULD'VE AT LEAST ASKED FOR HER EMAIL ADDRESS.
NO WAY. SHE'S TOO GOOD FOR HIM.
SHUT UP!
SHUT UP!!
C'MON! LET'S GO!
UH-HUH... YES, SIR, WE FOUND...
GRR GRR

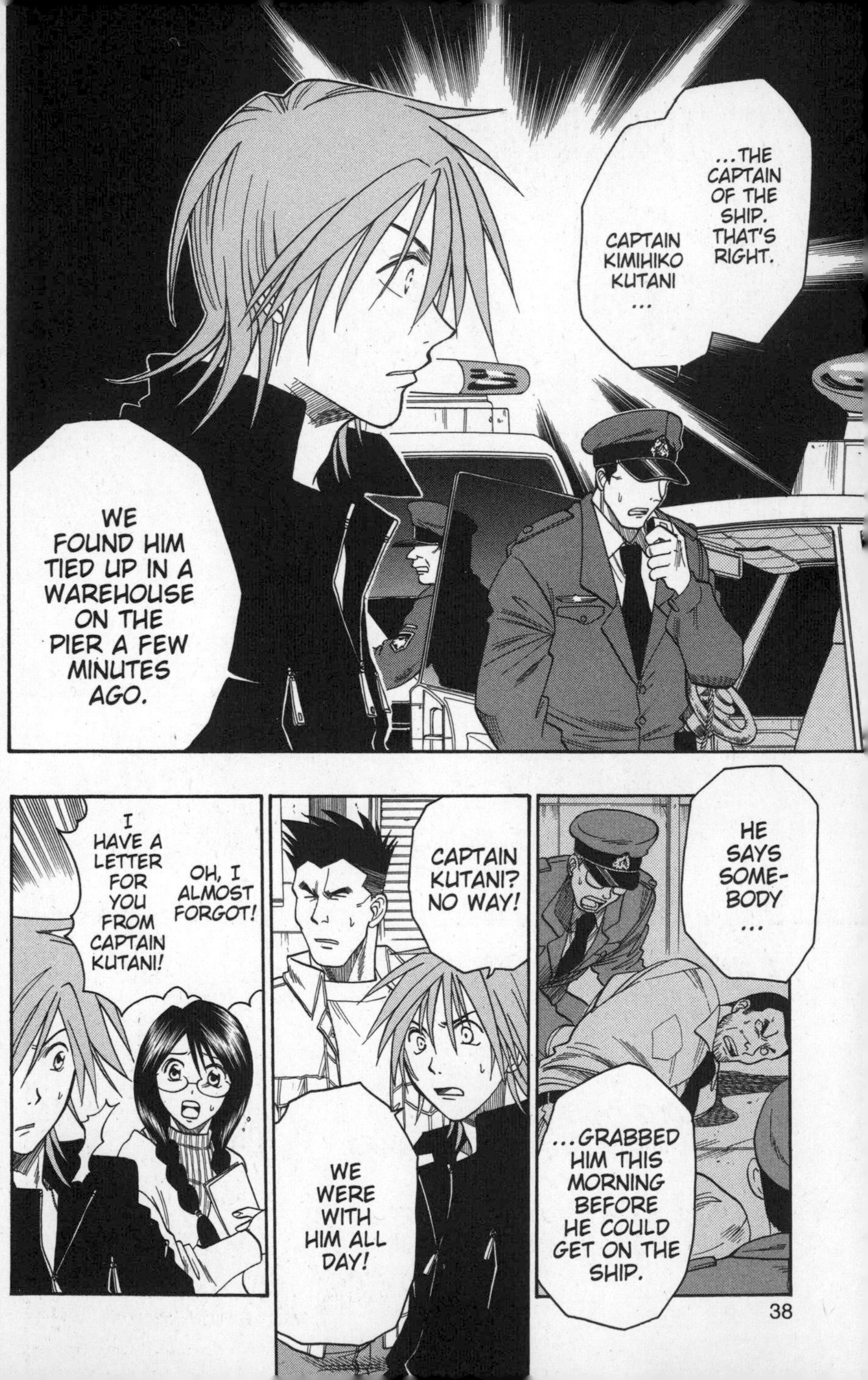
...THE CAPTAIN OF THE SHIP. THAT'S RIGHT.
CAPTAIN KIMIHIKO KUTANI ...
WE FOUND HIM TIED UP IN A WAREHOUSE ON THE PIER A FEW MINUTES AGO.
HE SAYS SOMEBODY ...
...GRABBED HIM THIS MORNING BEFORE HE COULD GET ON THE SHIP.
CAPTAIN KUTANI? NO WAY!
WE WERE WITH HIM ALL DAY!
OH, I ALMOST FORGOT!
I HAVE A LETTER FOR YOU FROM CAPTAIN KUTANI!

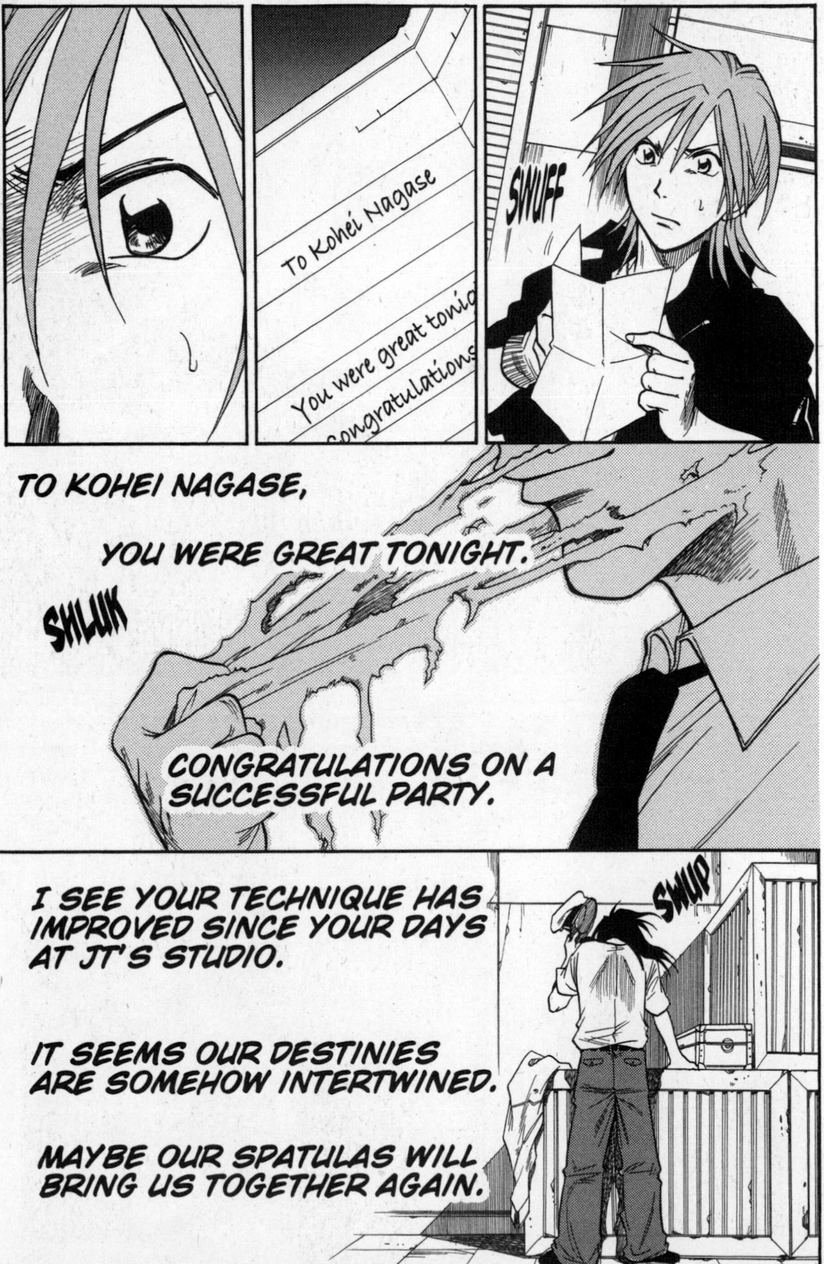
SWUFF
To Kohei Nagase
You were great tonig
Congratulations
TO KOHEI NAGASE,
YOU WERE GREAT TONIGHT.
SHLUK
CONGRATULATIONS ON A SUCCESSFUL PARTY.
SWUP
I SEE YOUR TECHNIQUE HAS IMPROVED SINCE YOUR DAYS AT JT'S STUDIO.
IT SEEMS OUR DESTINIES ARE SOMEHOW INTERTWINED.
MAYBE OUR SPATULAS WILL BRING US TOGETHER AGAIN.

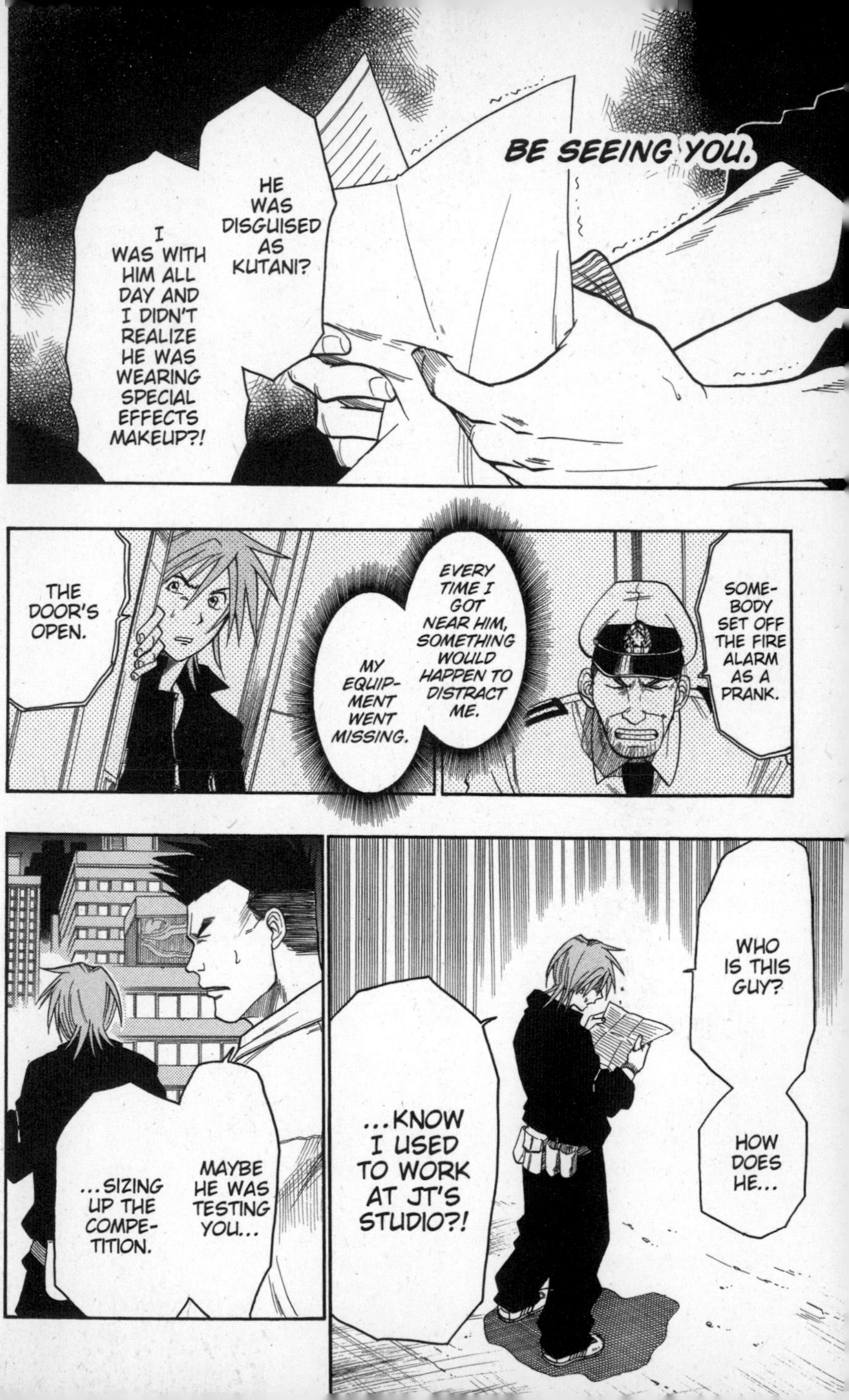
BE SEEING YOU.
HE WAS DISGUISED AS KUTANI?
I WAS WITH HIM ALL DAY AND I DIDN'T REALIZE HE WAS WEARING SPECIAL EFFECTS MAKEUP?!
SOME-BODY SET OFF THE FIRE ALARM AS A PRANK.
EVERY TIME I GOT NEAR HIM, SOMETHING WOULD HAPPEN TO DISTRACT ME.
MY EQUIP-MENT WENT MISSING.
THE DOOR'S OPEN.
WHO IS THIS GUY?
HOW DOES HE...
...KNOW I USED TO WORK AT JT'S STUDIO?!
MAYBE HE WAS TESTING YOU...
...SIZING UP THE COMPE-TITION.

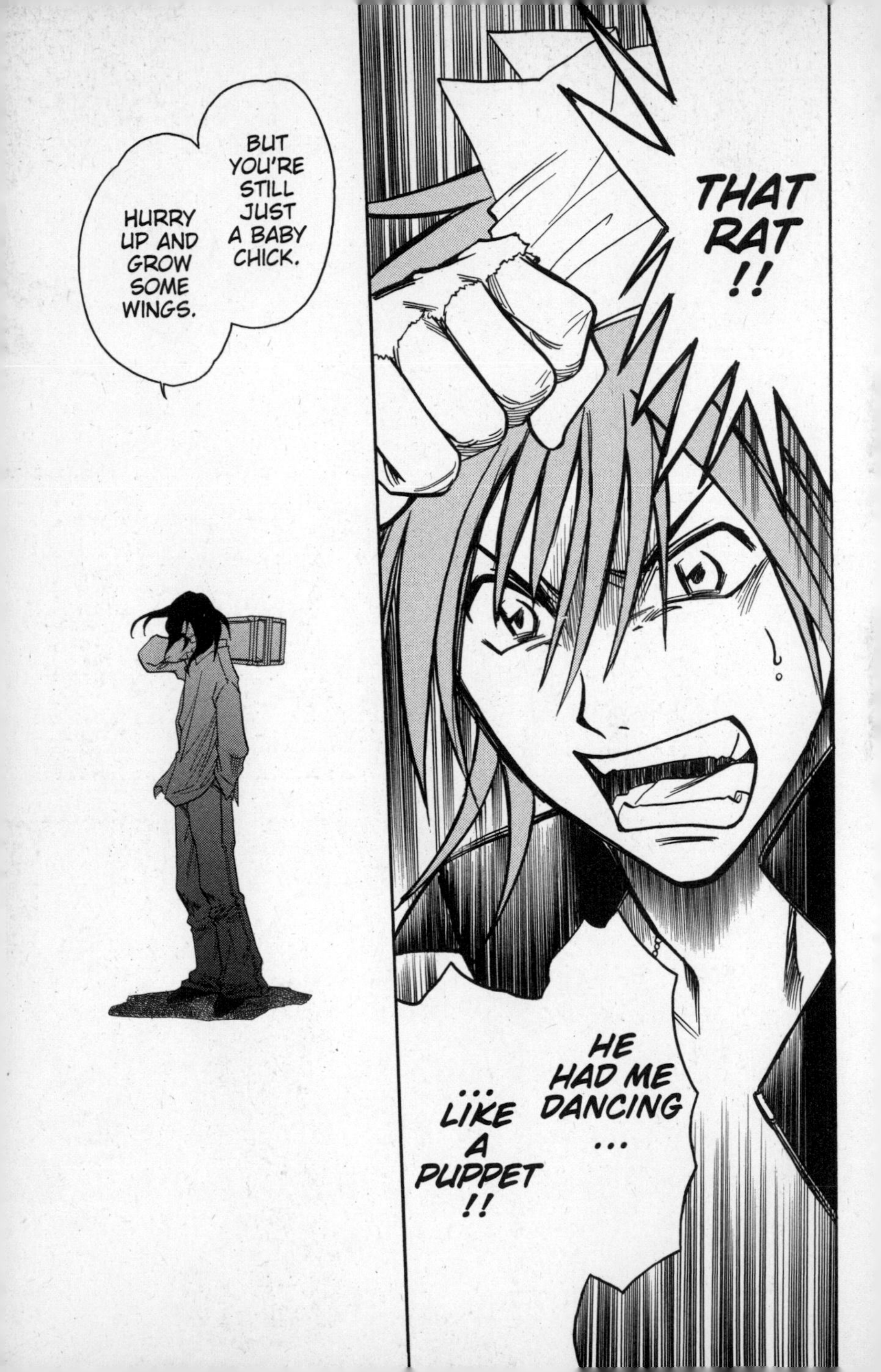
THAT RAT!!
HE HAD ME DANCING...
...LIKE A PUPPET!!
BUT YOU'RE STILL JUST A BABY CHICK.
HURRY UP AND GROW SOME WINGS.

Scene 28: MONE-Y TRAIN

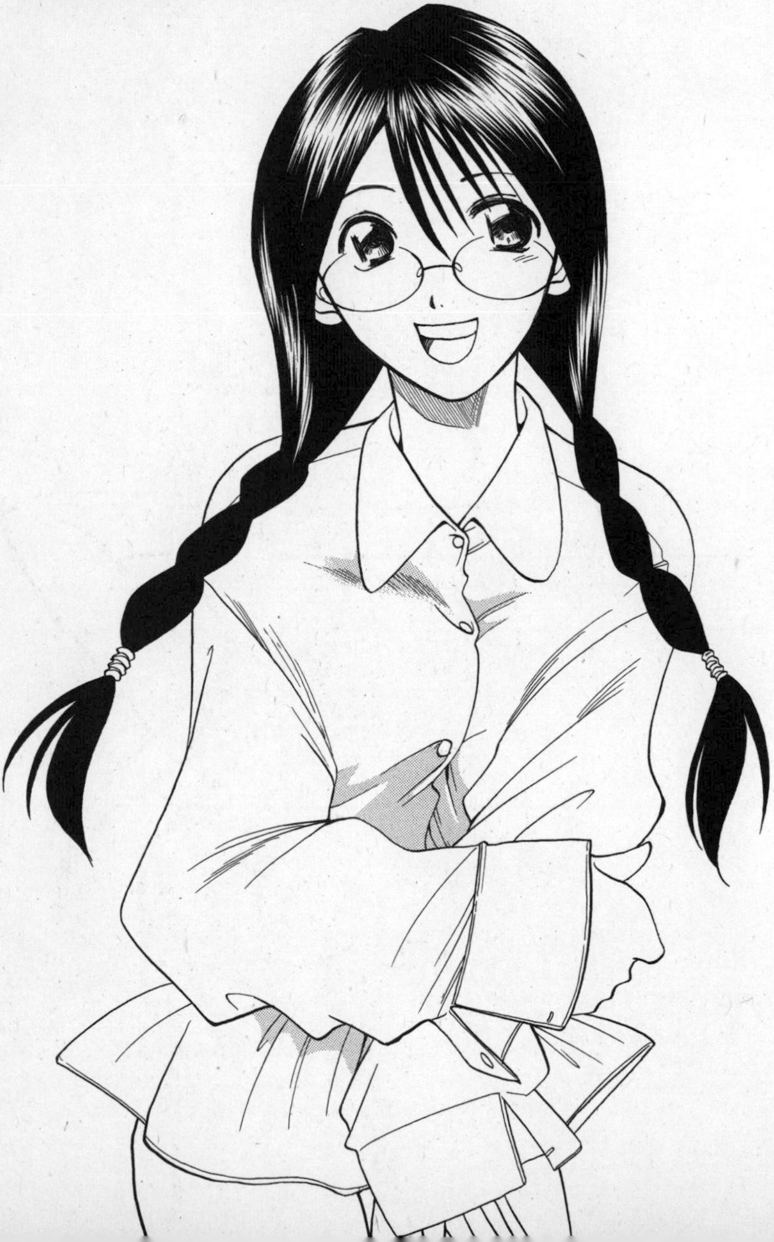

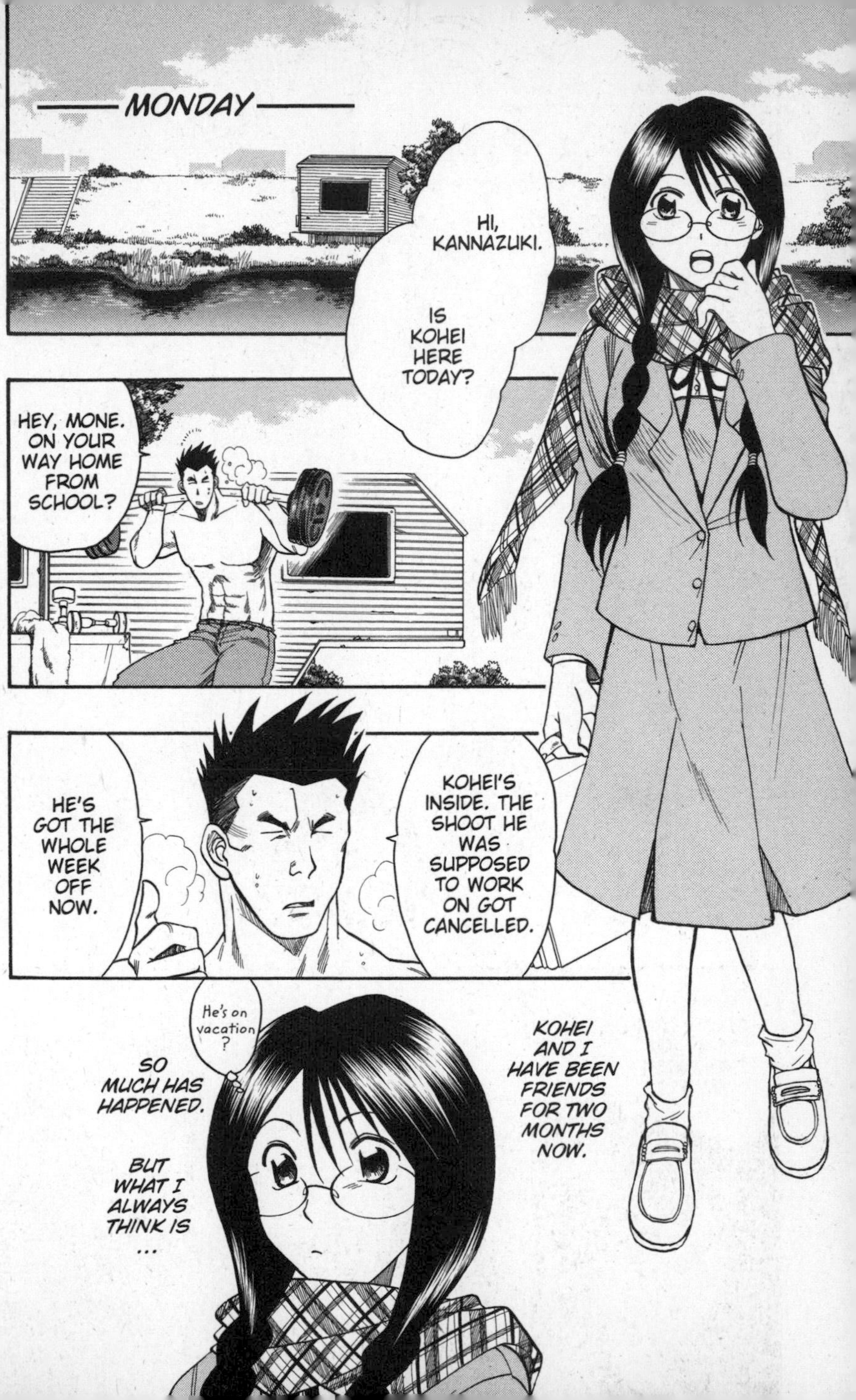
MONDAY
HI, KANNAZUKI.
IS KOHEI HERE TODAY?
HEY, MONE. ON YOUR WAY HOME FROM SCHOOL?
KOHEI'S INSIDE. THE SHOOT HE WAS SUPPOSED TO WORK ON GOT CANCELLED.
HE'S GOT THE WHOLE WEEK OFF NOW.
He's on vacation?
KOHEI AND I HAVE BEEN FRIENDS FOR TWO MONTHS NOW.
SO MUCH HAS HAPPENED.
BUT WHAT I ALWAYS THINK IS ...

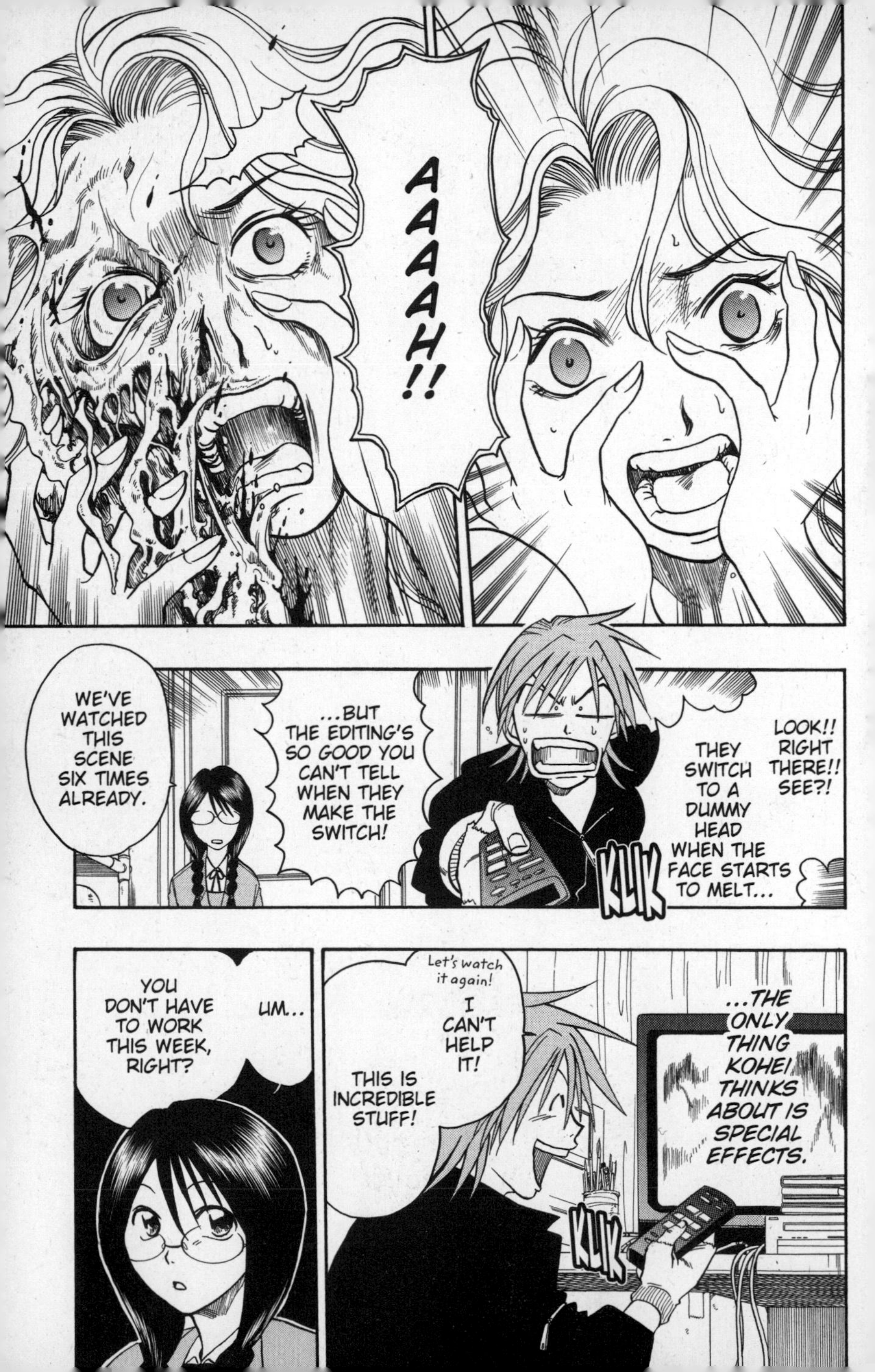
AAAAAH!!
LOOK!! RIGHT THERE!! SEE?!
THEY SWITCH TO A DUMMY HEAD WHEN THE FACE STARTS TO MELT...
KLIK
...BUT THE EDITING'S SO GOOD YOU CAN'T TELL WHEN THEY MAKE THE SWITCH!
WE'VE WATCHED THIS SCENE SIX TIMES ALREADY.
...THE ONLY THING KOHEI THINKS ABOUT IS SPECIAL EFFECTS.
Let's watch it again!
I CAN'T HELP IT!
THIS IS INCREDIBLE STUFF!
KLIK
UM...
YOU DON'T HAVE TO WORK THIS WEEK, RIGHT?

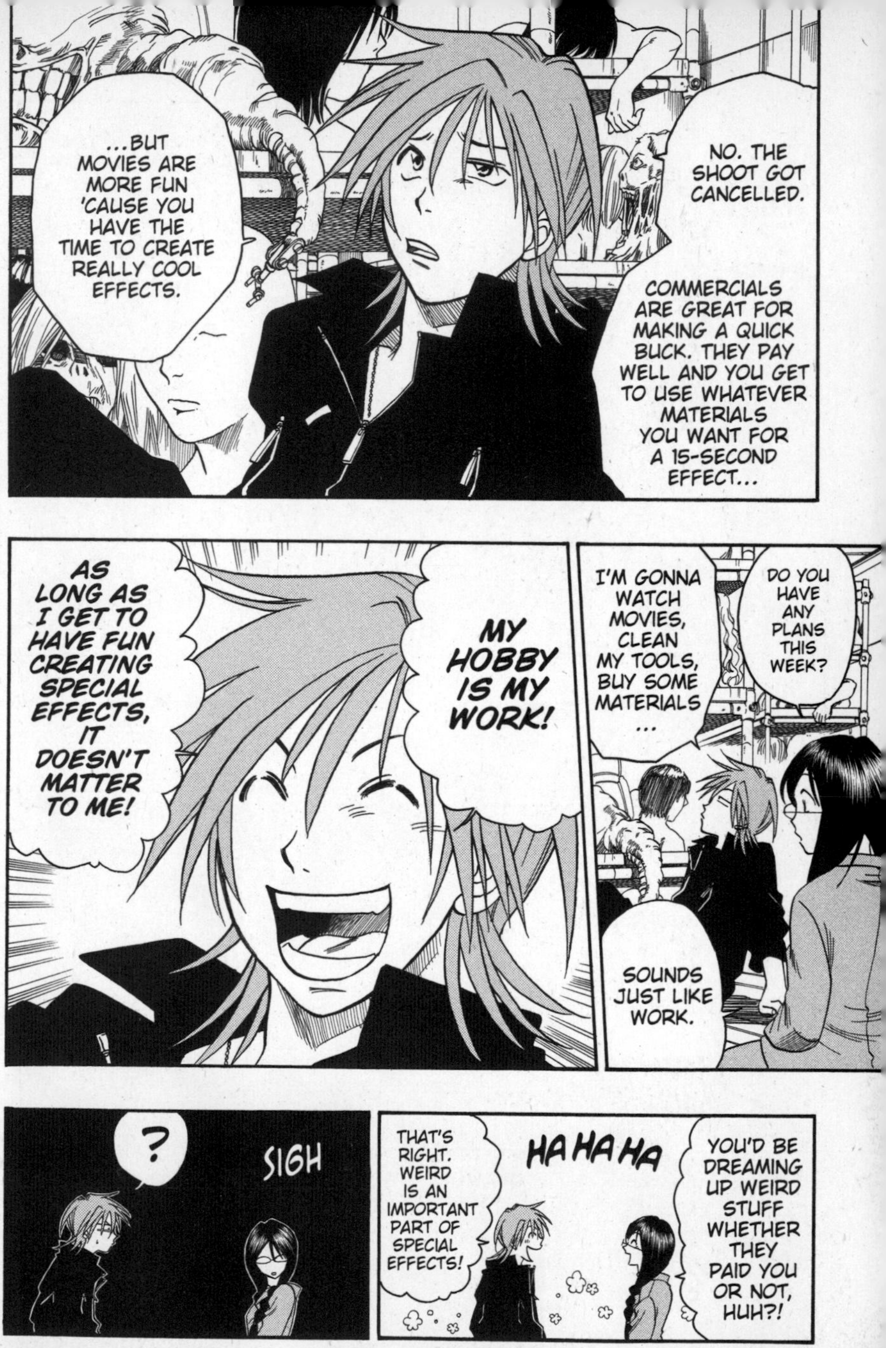
NO. THE SHOOT GOT CANCELLED.
COMMERCIALS ARE GREAT FOR MAKING A QUICK BUCK. THEY PAY WELL AND YOU GET TO USE WHATEVER MATERIALS YOU WANT FOR A 15-SECOND EFFECT...
...BUT MOVIES ARE MORE FUN 'CAUSE YOU HAVE THE TIME TO CREATE REALLY COOL EFFECTS.
DO YOU HAVE ANY PLANS THIS WEEK?
I'M GONNA WATCH MOVIES, CLEAN MY TOOLS, BUY SOME MATERIALS...
SOUNDS JUST LIKE WORK.
MY HOBBY IS MY WORK!
AS LONG AS I GET TO HAVE FUN CREATING SPECIAL EFFECTS, IT DOESN'T MATTER TO ME!
YOU'D BE DREAMING UP WEIRD STUFF WHETHER THEY PAID YOU OR NOT, HUH?!
HA HA HA
THAT'S RIGHT. WEIRD IS AN IMPORTANT PART OF SPECIAL EFFECTS!
SIGH
?

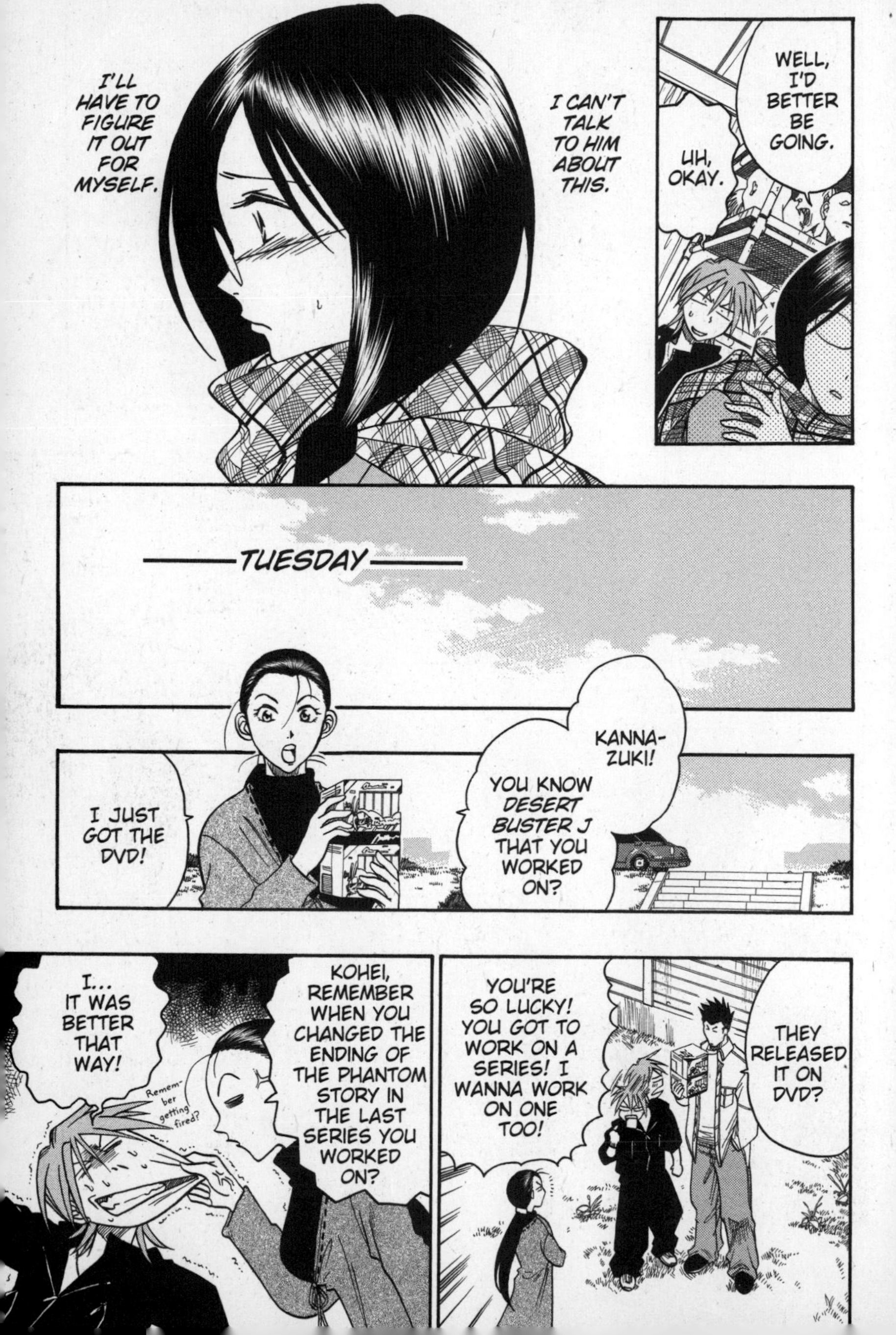
WELL, I'D BETTER BE GOING.
UH, OKAY.
I CAN'T TALK TO HIM ABOUT THIS.
I'LL HAVE TO FIGURE IT OUT FOR MYSELF.
—TUESDAY—
KANNA-ZUKI!
YOU KNOW DESERT BUSTER J THAT YOU WORKED ON?
I JUST GOT THE DVD!
THEY RELEASED IT ON DVD?
YOU'RE SO LUCKY! YOU GOT TO WORK ON A SERIES! I WANNA WORK ON ONE TOO!
KOHEI, REMEMBER WHEN YOU CHANGED THE ENDING OF THE PHANTOM STORY IN THE LAST SERIES YOU WORKED ON?
Remember getting fired?
I... IT WAS BETTER THAT WAY!

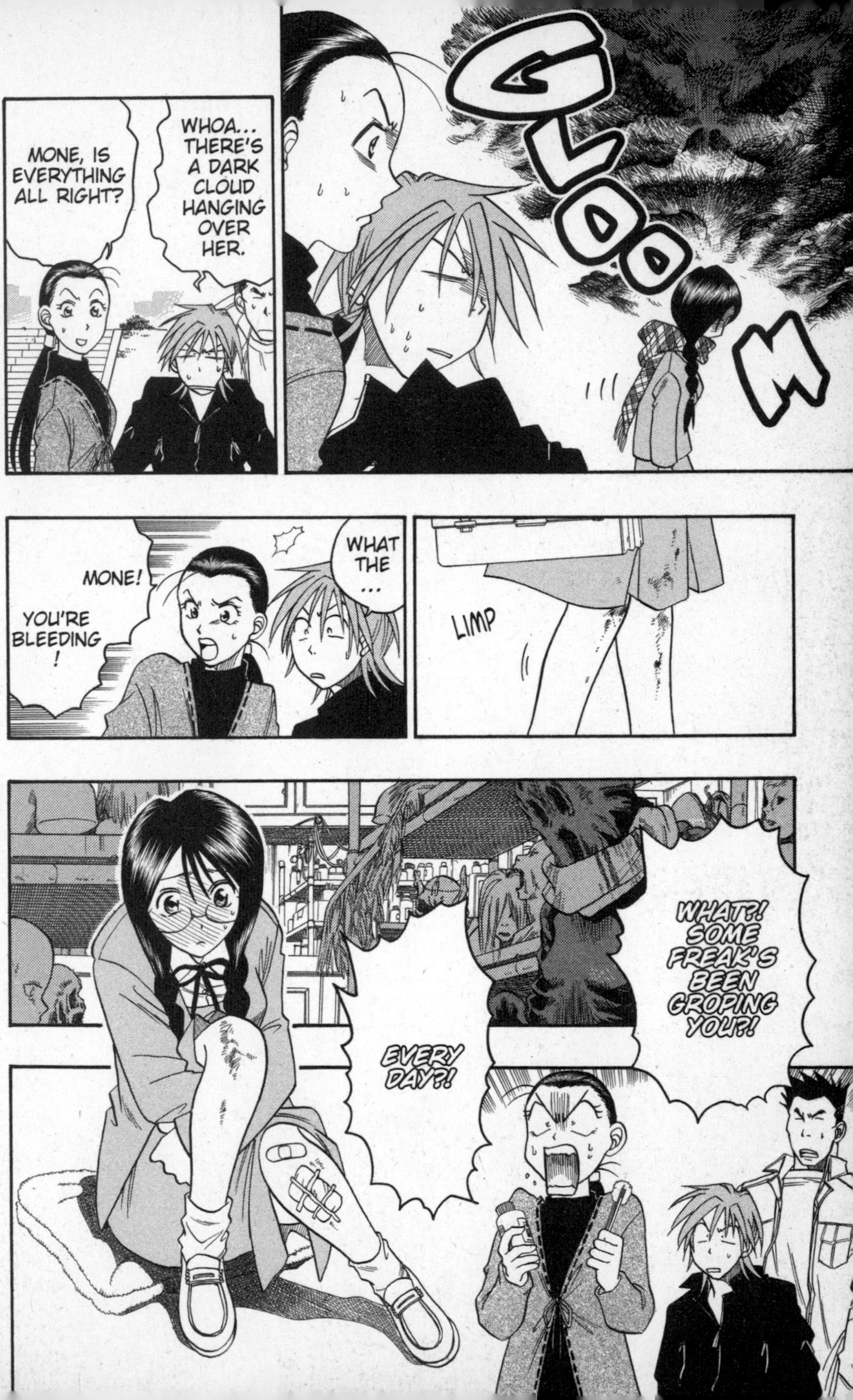
GLOOOM
WHOA... THERE'S A DARK CLOUD HANGING OVER HER.
MONE, IS EVERYTHING ALL RIGHT?
LIMP
WHAT THE ...
MONE! YOU'RE BLEEDING!
WHAT?! SOME FREAK'S BEEN GROPING YOU?!
EVERY DAY?!

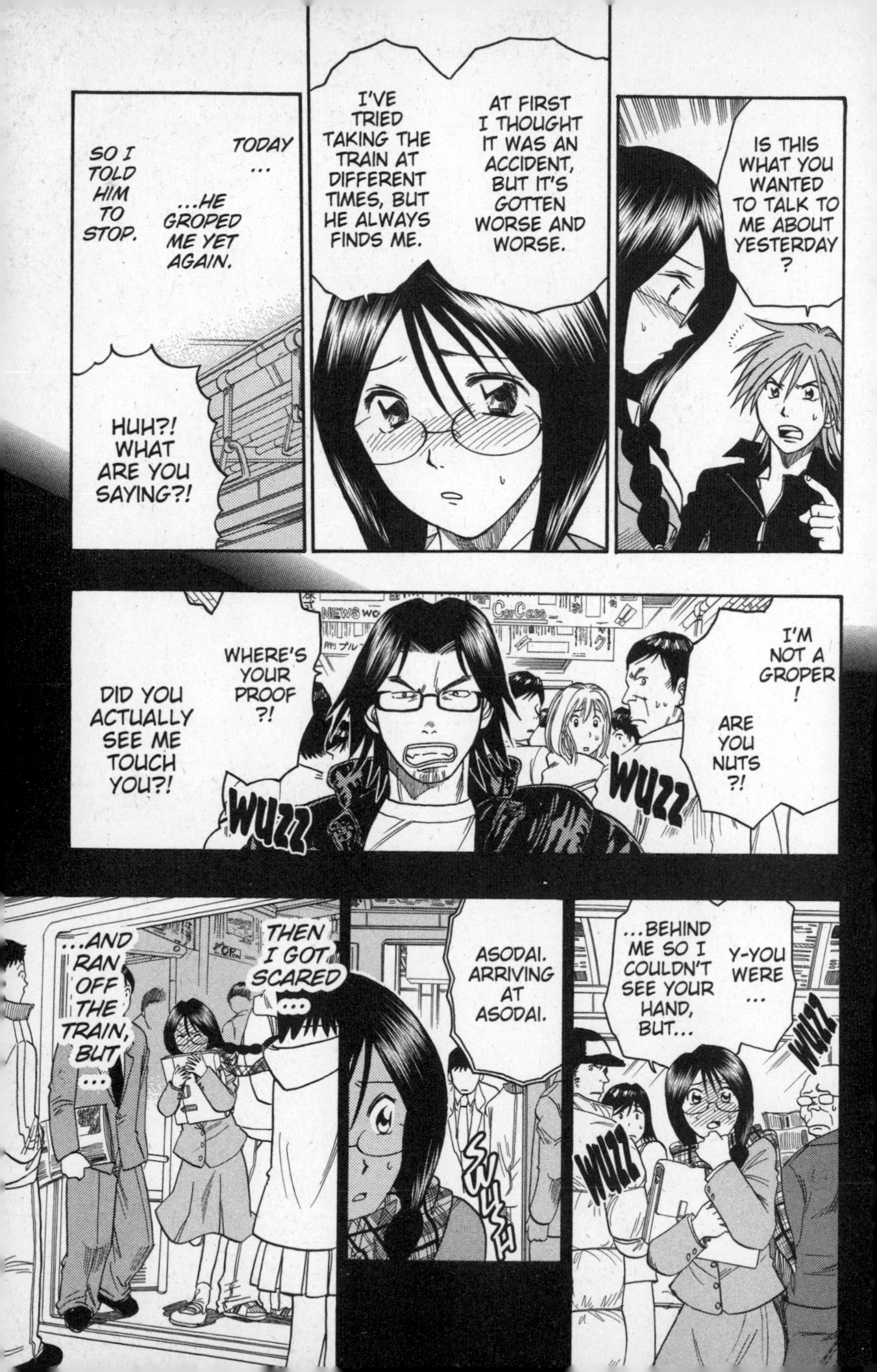
IS THIS WHAT YOU WANTED TO TALK TO ME ABOUT YESTERDAY?
AT FIRST I THOUGHT IT WAS AN ACCIDENT, BUT IT'S GOTTEN WORSE AND WORSE.
I'VE TRIED TAKING THE TRAIN AT DIFFERENT TIMES, BUT HE ALWAYS FINDS ME.
TODAY...
...HE GROPED ME YET AGAIN.
SO I TOLD HIM TO STOP.
HUH?! WHAT ARE YOU SAYING?!
I'M NOT A GROPER!
ARE YOU NUTS?!
WUZZ
WHERE'S YOUR PROOF?!
DID YOU ACTUALLY SEE ME TOUCH YOU?!
WUZZ
Y-YOU WERE...
...BEHIND ME SO I COULDN'T SEE YOUR HAND, BUT...
WUZZ
WUZZ
ASODAI. ARRIVING AT ASODAI.
THEN I GOT SCARED...
...AND RAN OFF THE TRAIN, BUT...

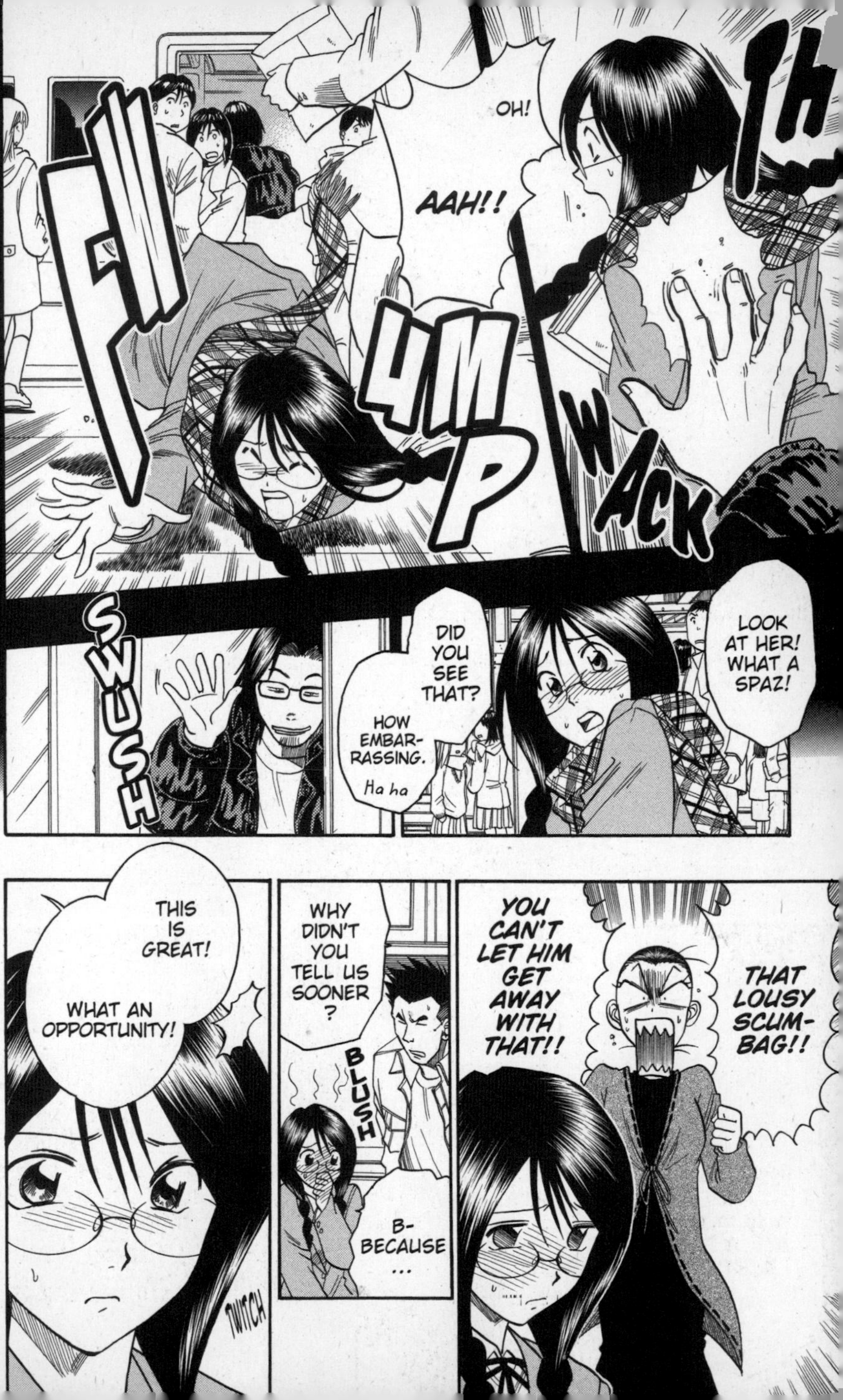
OH!
WHACK
AAH!!
LOOK AT HER! WHAT A SPAZ!
DID YOU SEE THAT?
HOW EMBARRASSING.
Ha ha
SWUSH
THAT LOUSY SCUMBAG!!
YOU CAN'T LET HIM GET AWAY WITH THAT!!
WHY DIDN'T YOU TELL US SOONER?
BLUSH
B-BECAUSE...
THIS IS GREAT!
WHAT AN OPPORTUNITY!
TWITCH

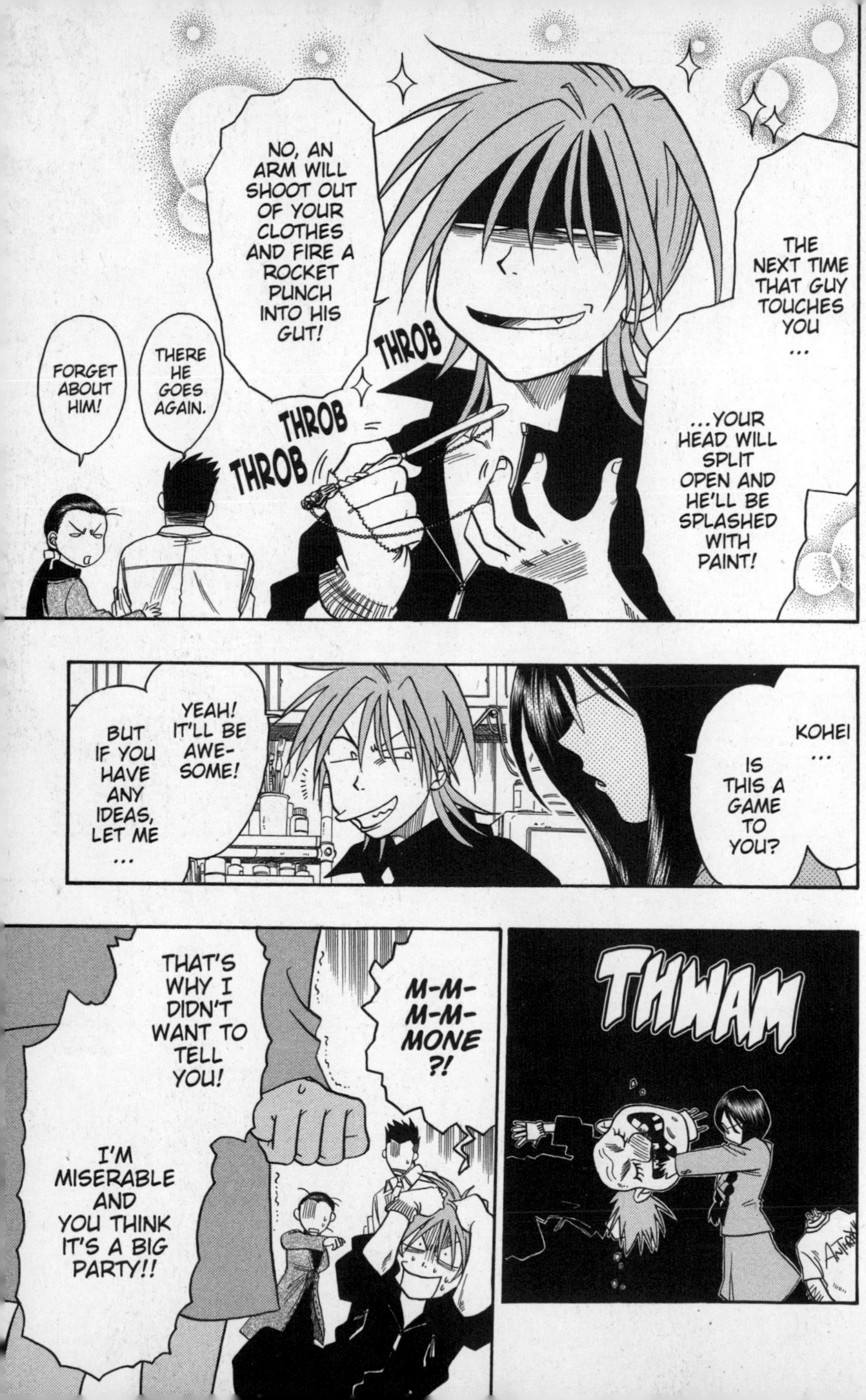
THE NEXT TIME THAT GUY TOUCHES YOU ...
...YOUR HEAD WILL SPLIT OPEN AND HE'LL BE SPLASHED WITH PAINT!
NO, AN ARM WILL SHOOT OUT OF YOUR CLOTHES AND FIRE A ROCKET PUNCH INTO HIS GUT!
THROB
THROB
THROB
THERE HE GOES AGAIN.
FORGET ABOUT HIM!
KOHEI ...
IS THIS A GAME TO YOU?
YEAH! IT'LL BE AWE-SOME!
BUT IF YOU HAVE ANY IDEAS, LET ME ...
THWAM
M-M-M-M-MONE ?!
THAT'S WHY I DIDN'T WANT TO TELL YOU!
I'M MISERABLE AND YOU THINK IT'S A BIG PARTY!!

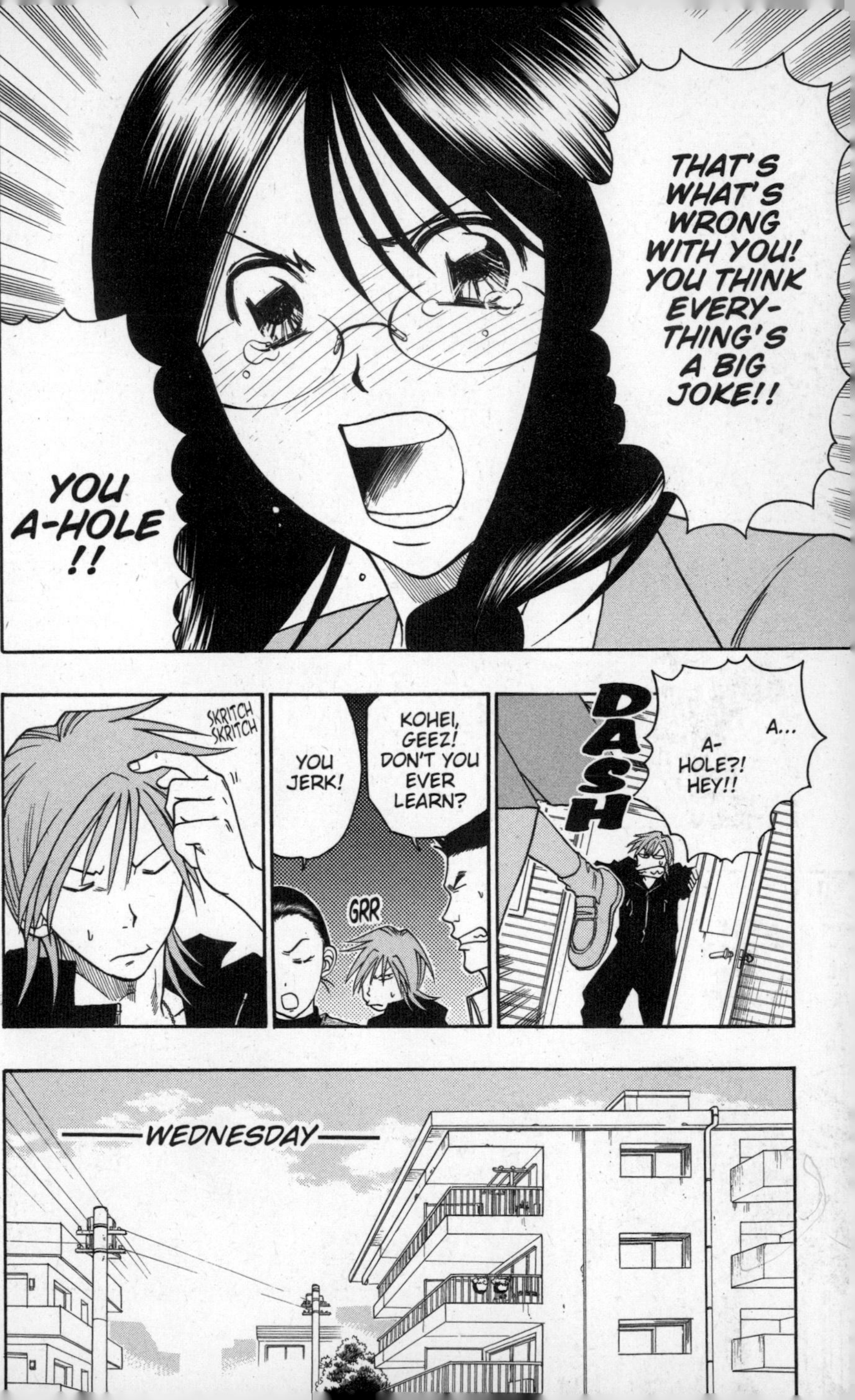
THAT'S WHAT'S WRONG WITH YOU! YOU THINK EVERY-THING'S A BIG JOKE!!
YOU A-HOLE!!
A...
A-HOLE?! HEY!!
DASH
KOHEI, GEEZ! DON'T YOU EVER LEARN?
YOU JERK!
GRR
SKRITCH SKRITCH
—WEDNESDAY—

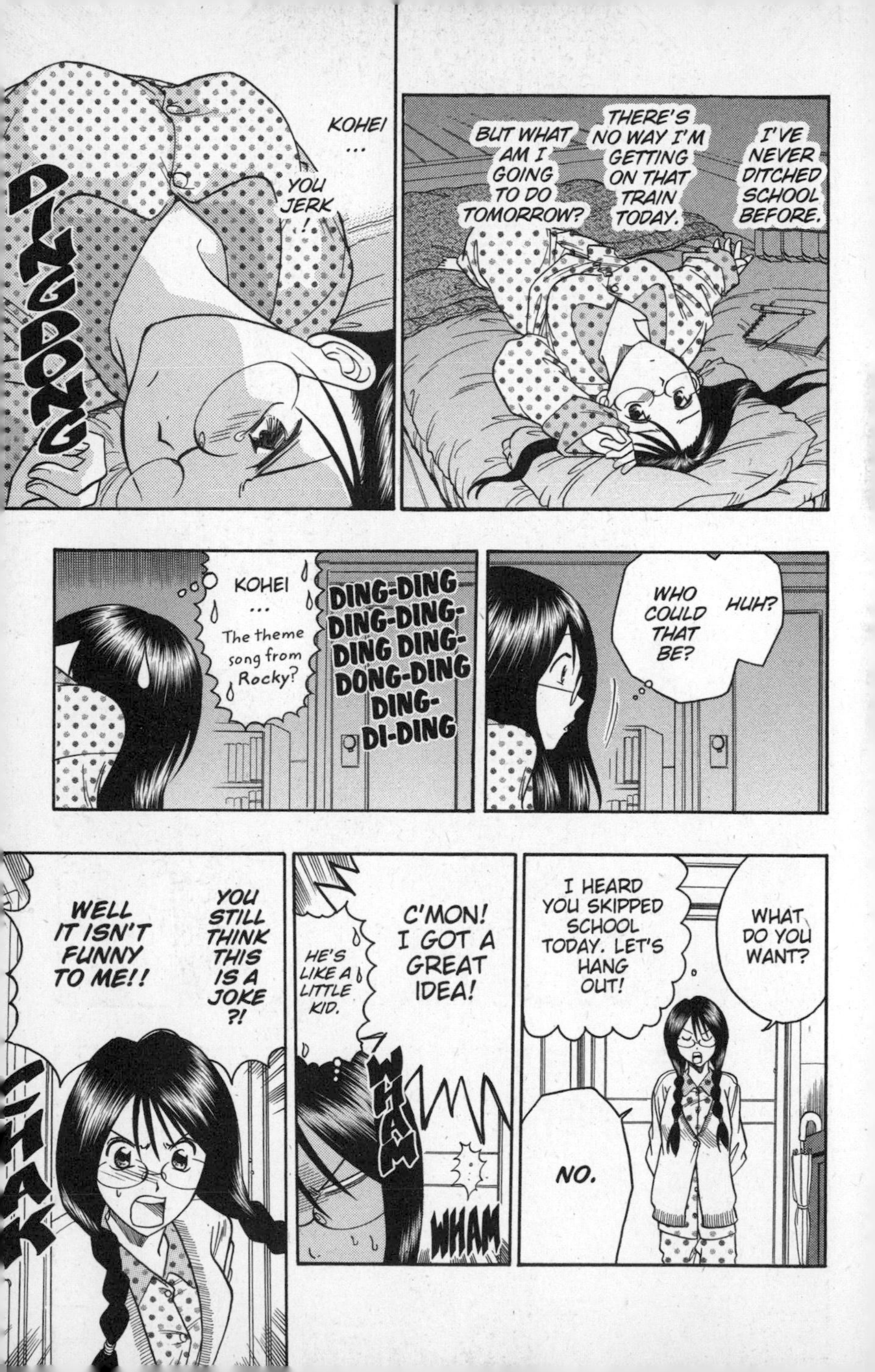
I'VE NEVER DITCHED SCHOOL BEFORE.
THERE'S NO WAY I'M GETTING ON THAT TRAIN TODAY.
BUT WHAT AM I GOING TO DO TOMORROW?
KOHEI ...
YOU JERK!
DINGDONG
HUH?
WHO COULD THAT BE?
DING-DING DING-DING-DING DING-DONG-DING DING-DI-DING
KOHEI ...
The theme song from Rocky?
WHAT DO YOU WANT?
I HEARD YOU SKIPPED SCHOOL TODAY. LET'S HANG OUT!
NO.
C'MON! I GOT A GREAT IDEA!
HE'S LIKE A LITTLE KID.
WHAM
WHAM
YOU STILL THINK THIS IS A JOKE?!
WELL IT ISN'T FUNNY TO ME!!
THAK

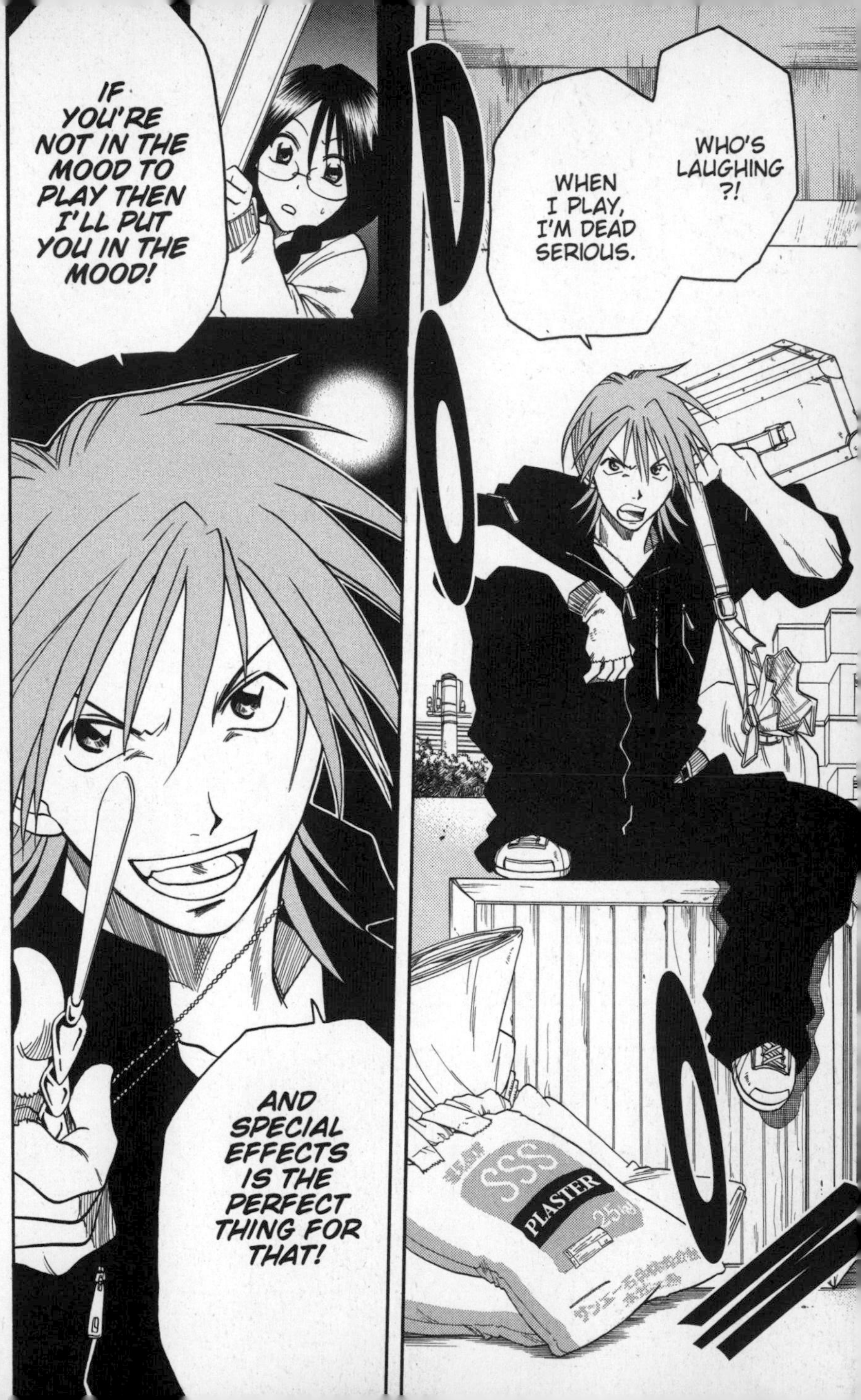
WHO'S LAUGHING ?!
WHEN I PLAY, I'M DEAD SERIOUS.
PLASTER
IF YOU'RE NOT IN THE MOOD TO PLAY THEN I'LL PUT YOU IN THE MOOD!
AND SPECIAL EFFECTS IS THE PERFECT THING FOR THAT!

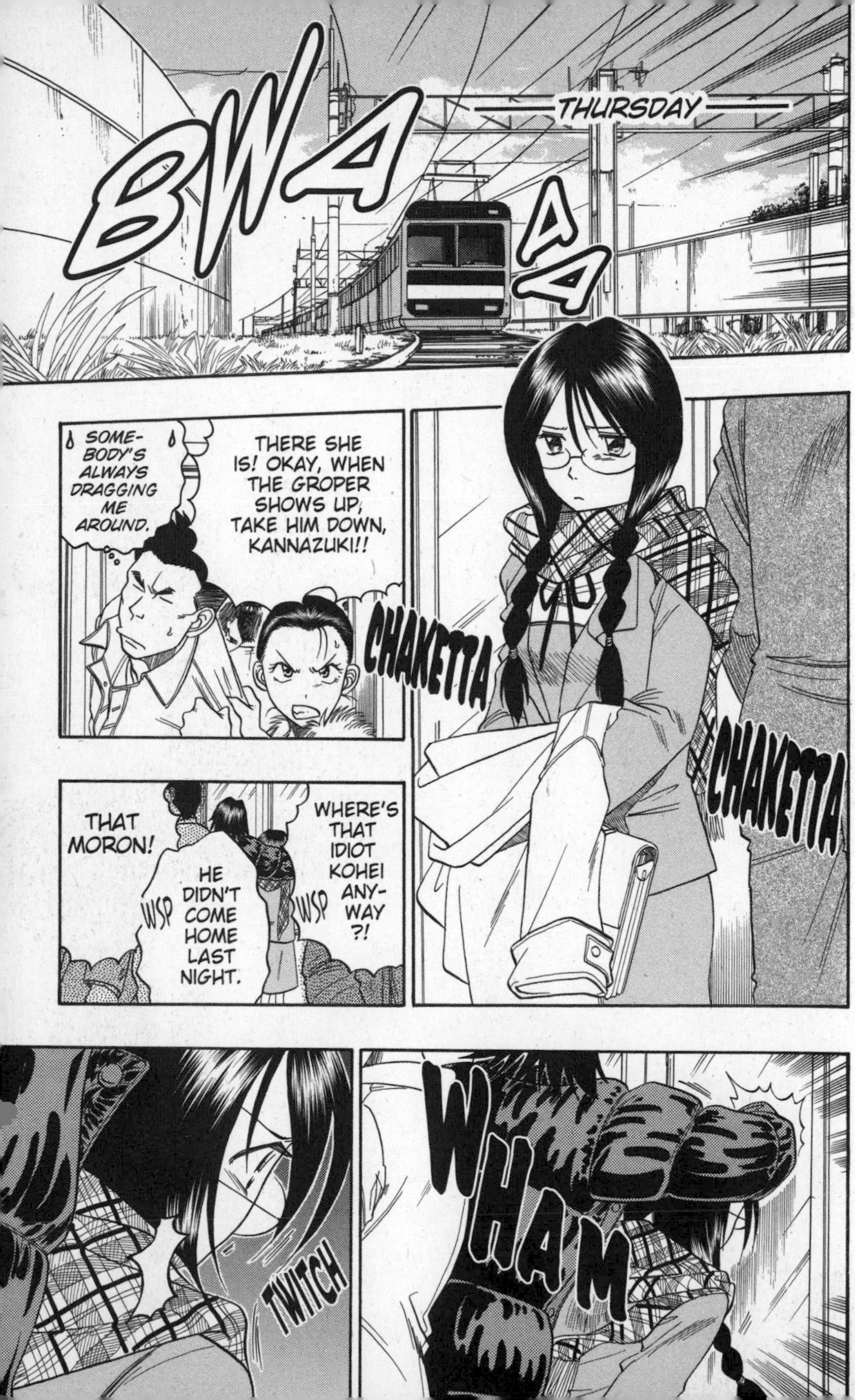
THURSDAY
BWAAA
CHAKETTA
CHAKETTA
THERE SHE IS! OKAY, WHEN THE GROPER SHOWS UP, TAKE HIM DOWN, KANNAZUKI!!
SOMEBODY'S ALWAYS DRAGGING ME AROUND.
WHERE'S THAT IDIOT KOHEI ANYWAY?!
WSP
HE DIDN'T COME HOME LAST NIGHT.
WSP
THAT MORON!
WHAM
TWITCH

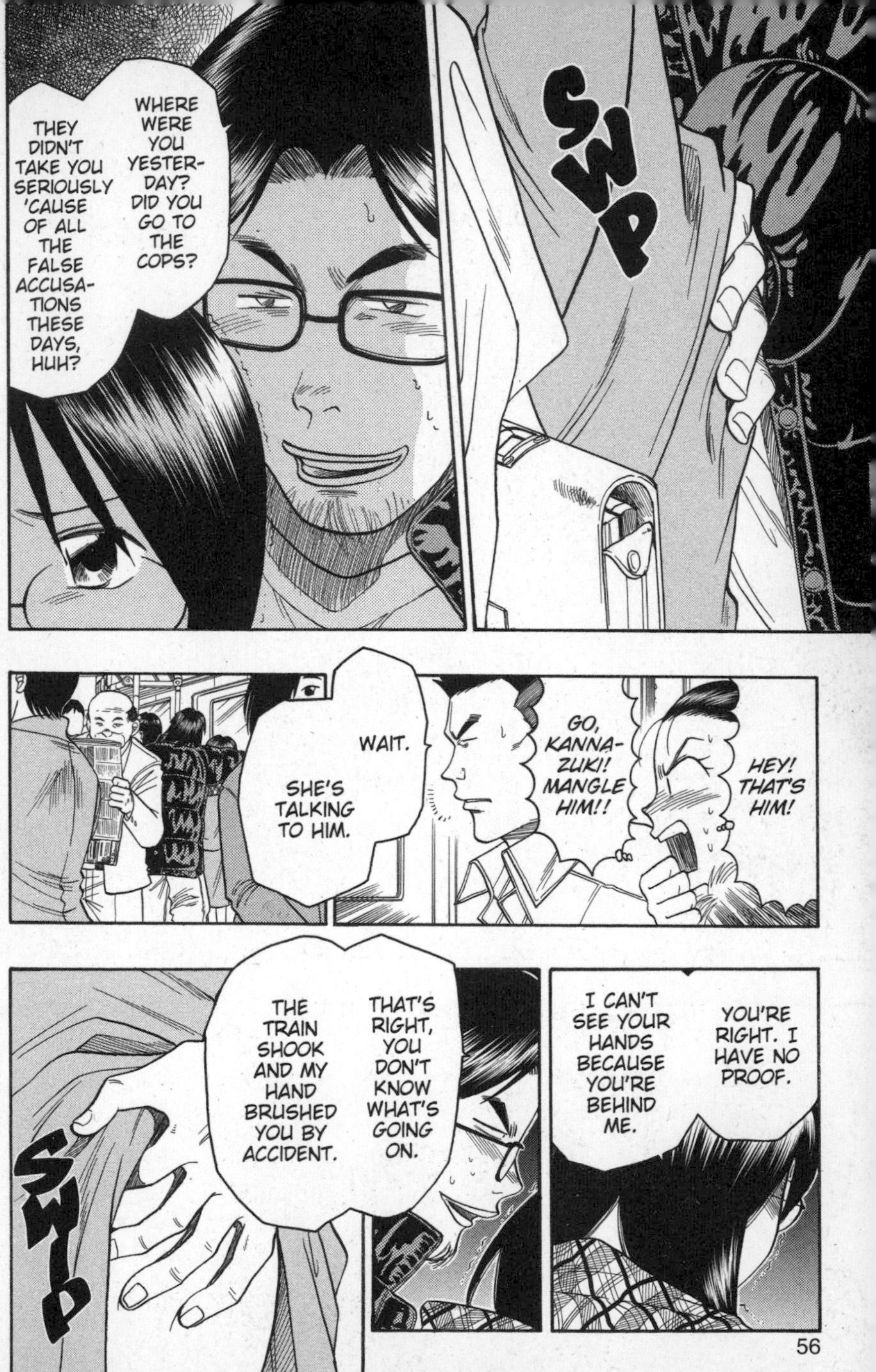
SWP
WHERE WERE YOU YESTERDAY? DID YOU GO TO THE COPS?
THEY DIDN'T TAKE YOU SERIOUSLY 'CAUSE OF ALL THE FALSE ACCUSATIONS THESE DAYS, HUH?
HEY! THAT'S HIM!
GO, KANNAZUKI! MANGLE HIM!!
WAIT.
SHE'S TALKING TO HIM.
YOU'RE RIGHT. I HAVE NO PROOF.
I CAN'T SEE YOUR HANDS BECAUSE YOU'RE BEHIND ME.
THAT'S RIGHT, YOU DON'T KNOW WHAT'S GOING ON.
THE TRAIN SHOOK AND MY HAND BRUSHED YOU BY ACCIDENT.
SWP

BUT NOT TODAY!

TODAY I CAN SEE IT!

WHAP

...WAS TRYING TO GO UNDER MY SKIRT!

THIS HAND...

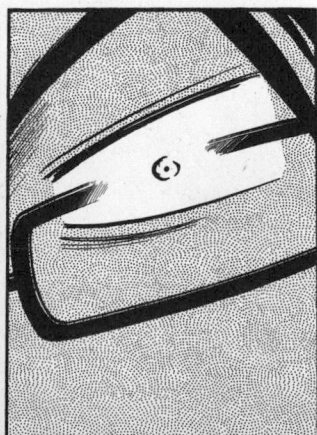

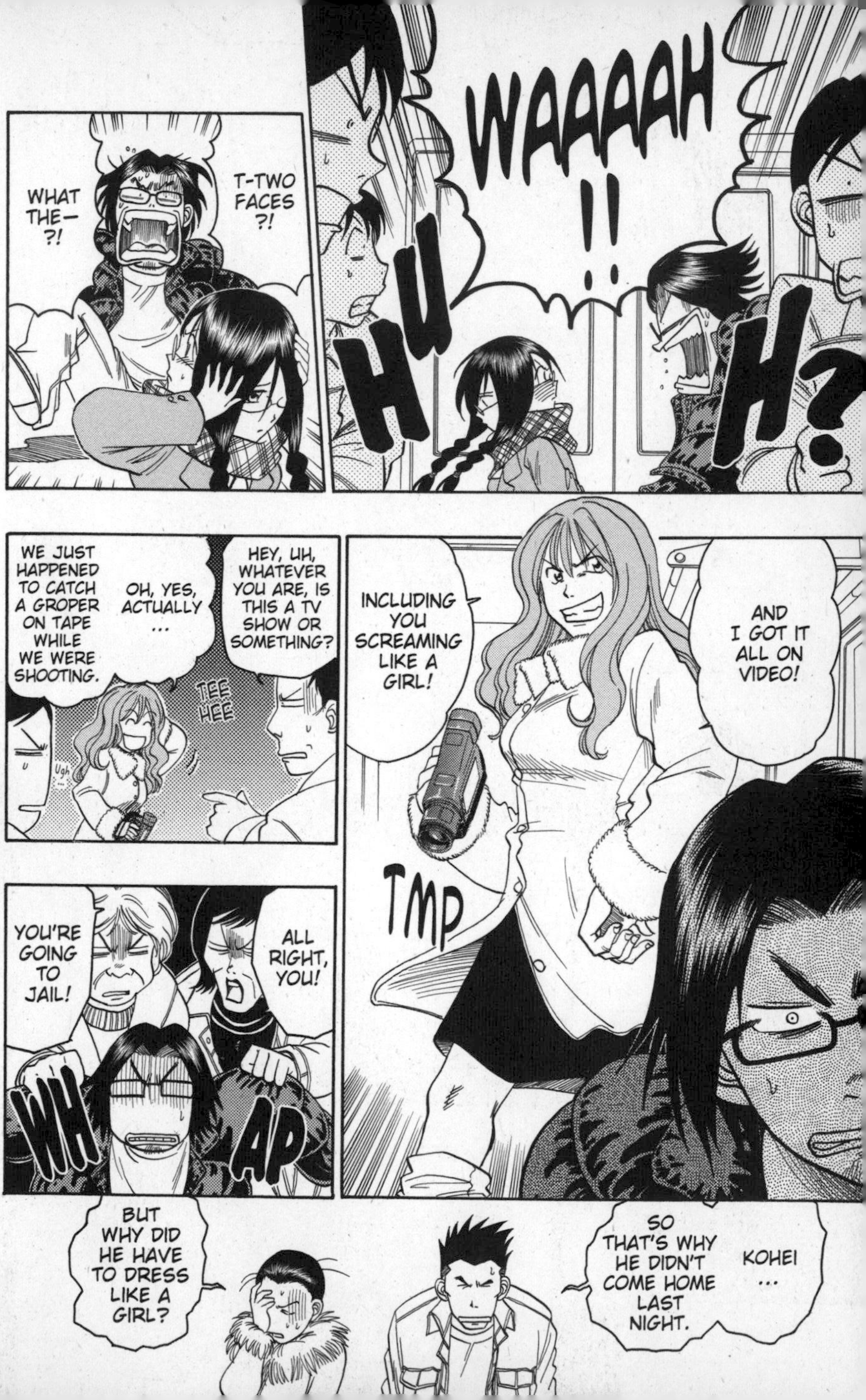
WAAAAH !!
HUH?
T-TWO FACES ?!
WHAT THE— ?!
AND I GOT IT ALL ON VIDEO!
INCLUDING YOU SCREAMING LIKE A GIRL!
TMP
HEY, UH, WHATEVER YOU ARE, IS THIS A TV SHOW OR SOMETHING?
OH, YES, ACTUALLY ...
WE JUST HAPPENED TO CATCH A GROPER ON TAPE WHILE WE WERE SHOOTING.
TEE HEE
Ugh
ALL RIGHT, YOU!
YOU'RE GOING TO JAIL!
WHAP
KOHEI ...
SO THAT'S WHY HE DIDN'T COME HOME LAST NIGHT.
BUT WHY DID HE HAVE TO DRESS LIKE A GIRL?

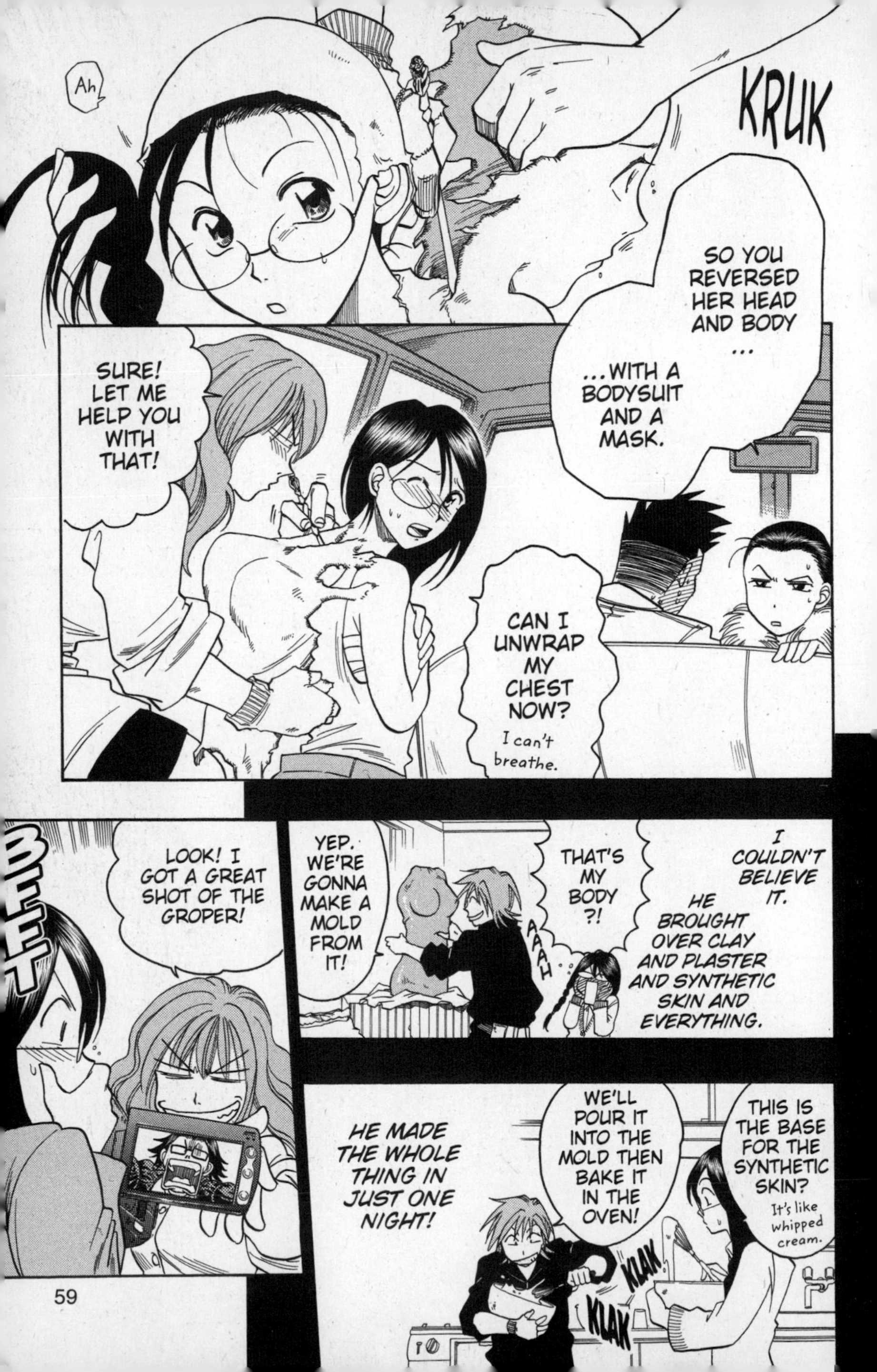
Ah
KRUK
SO YOU REVERSED HER HEAD AND BODY...
...WITH A BODYSUIT AND A MASK.
SURE! LET ME HELP YOU WITH THAT!
CAN I UNWRAP MY CHEST NOW?
I can't breathe.
I COULDN'T BELIEVE IT.
HE BROUGHT OVER CLAY AND PLASTER AND SYNTHETIC SKIN AND EVERYTHING.
THAT'S MY BODY?!
AAAH
YEP. WE'RE GONNA MAKE A MOLD FROM IT!
THIS IS THE BASE FOR THE SYNTHETIC SKIN?
It's like whipped cream.
WE'LL POUR IT INTO THE MOLD THEN BAKE IT IN THE OVEN!
HE MADE THE WHOLE THING IN JUST ONE NIGHT!
KLAK
KLAK
LOOK! I GOT A GREAT SHOT OF THE GROPER!

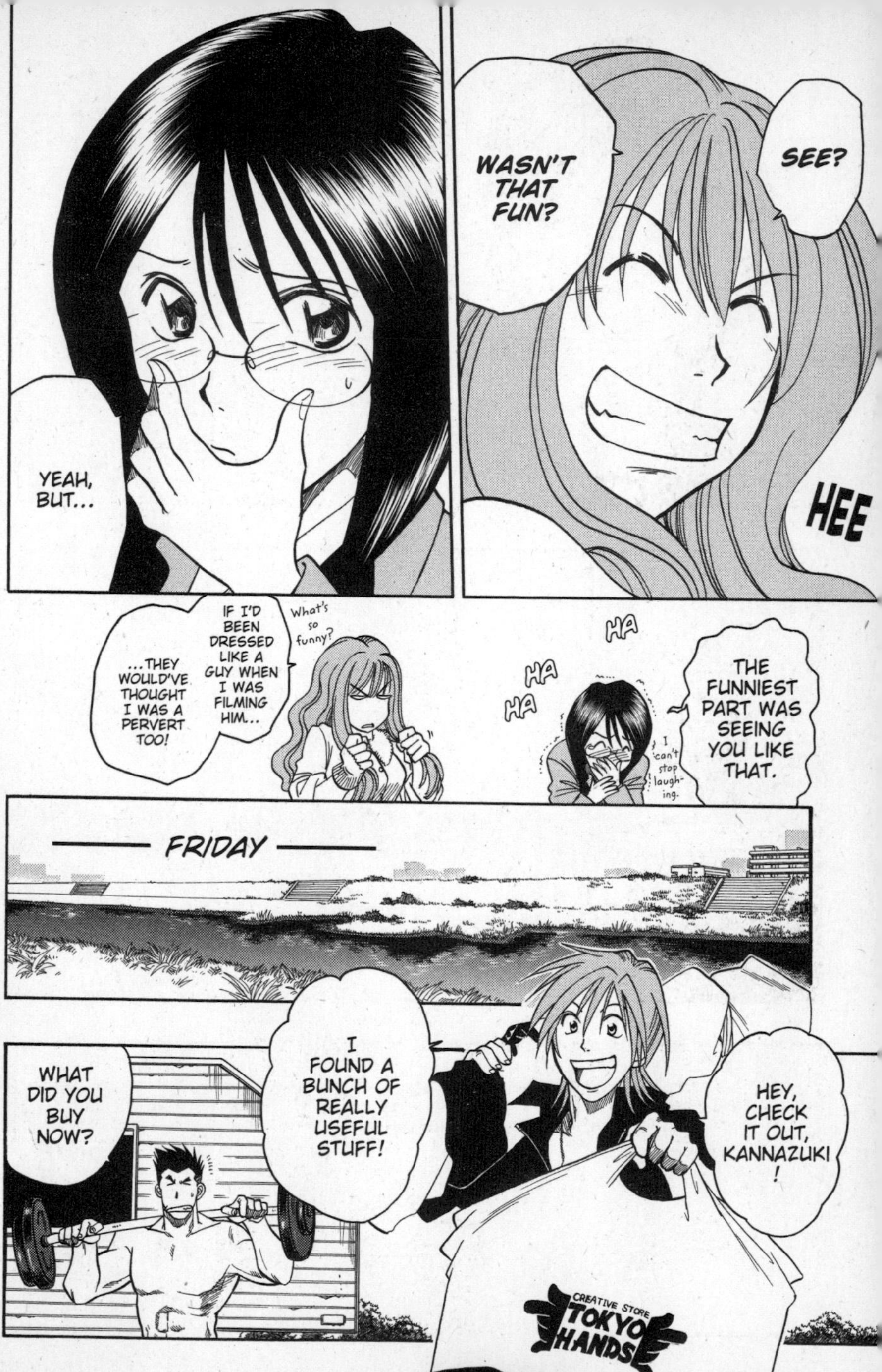
SEE?
WASN'T THAT FUN?
HEE
YEAH, BUT...
HA
HA
HA
THE FUNNIEST PART WAS SEEING YOU LIKE THAT.
I can't stop laugh-ing.
What's so funny?
IF I'D BEEN DRESSED LIKE A GUY WHEN I WAS FILMING HIM...
...THEY WOULD'VE THOUGHT I WAS A PERVERT TOO!
FRIDAY
HEY, CHECK IT OUT, KANNAZUKI!
I FOUND A BUNCH OF REALLY USEFUL STUFF!
WHAT DID YOU BUY NOW?
CREATIVE STORE
TOKYO HANDS

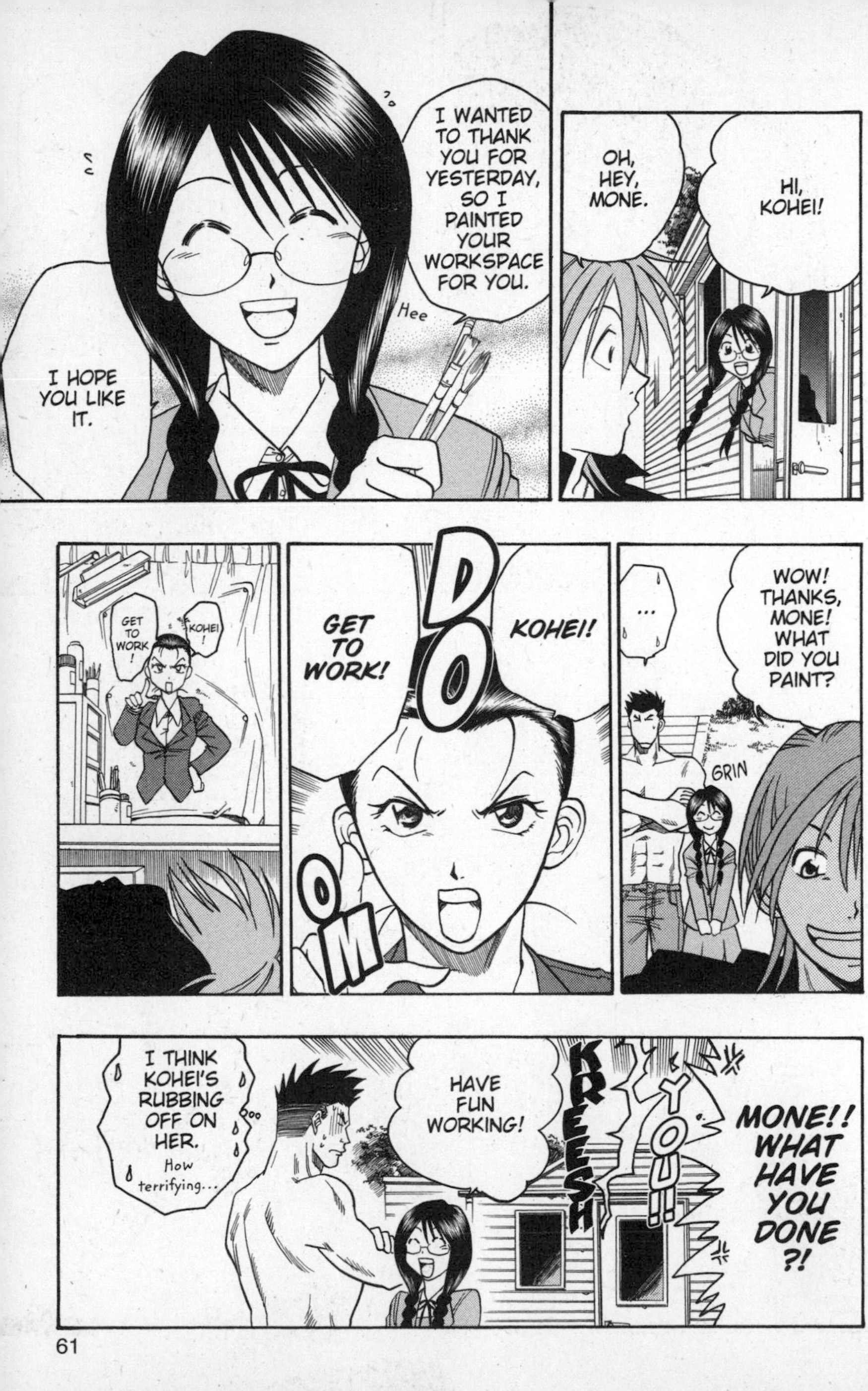
HI, KOHEI!
OH, HEY, MONE.
I WANTED TO THANK YOU FOR YESTERDAY, SO I PAINTED YOUR WORKSPACE FOR YOU.
Hee
I HOPE YOU LIKE IT.
WOW! THANKS, MONE! WHAT DID YOU PAINT?
...
GRIN
KOHEI!
DOOM
GET TO WORK!
KOHEI!
GET TO WORK!
MONE!! WHAT HAVE YOU DONE?!
YOU!!
KREESH
HAVE FUN WORKING!
I THINK KOHEI'S RUBBING OFF ON HER.
How terrifying...

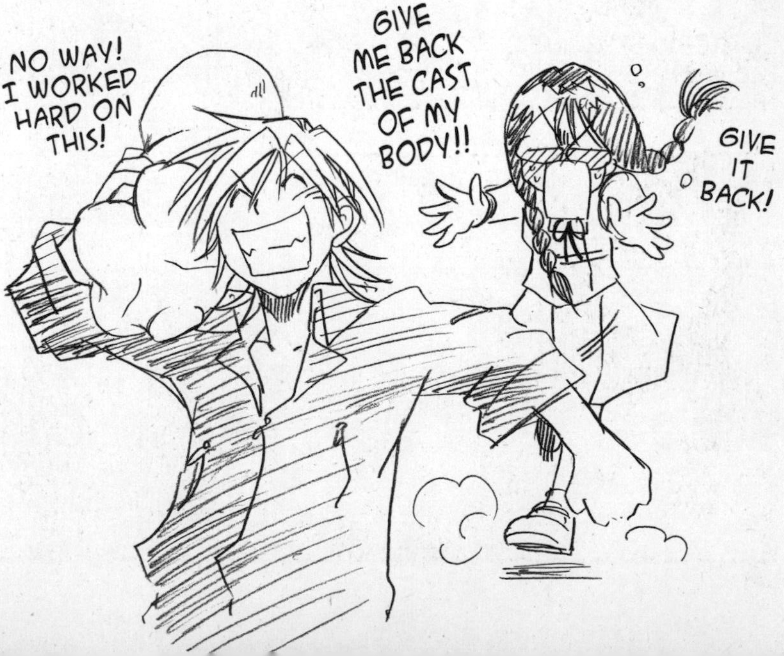
GIVE IT BACK!
GIVE ME BACK THE CAST OF MY BODY!!
NO WAY! I WORKED HARD ON THIS!

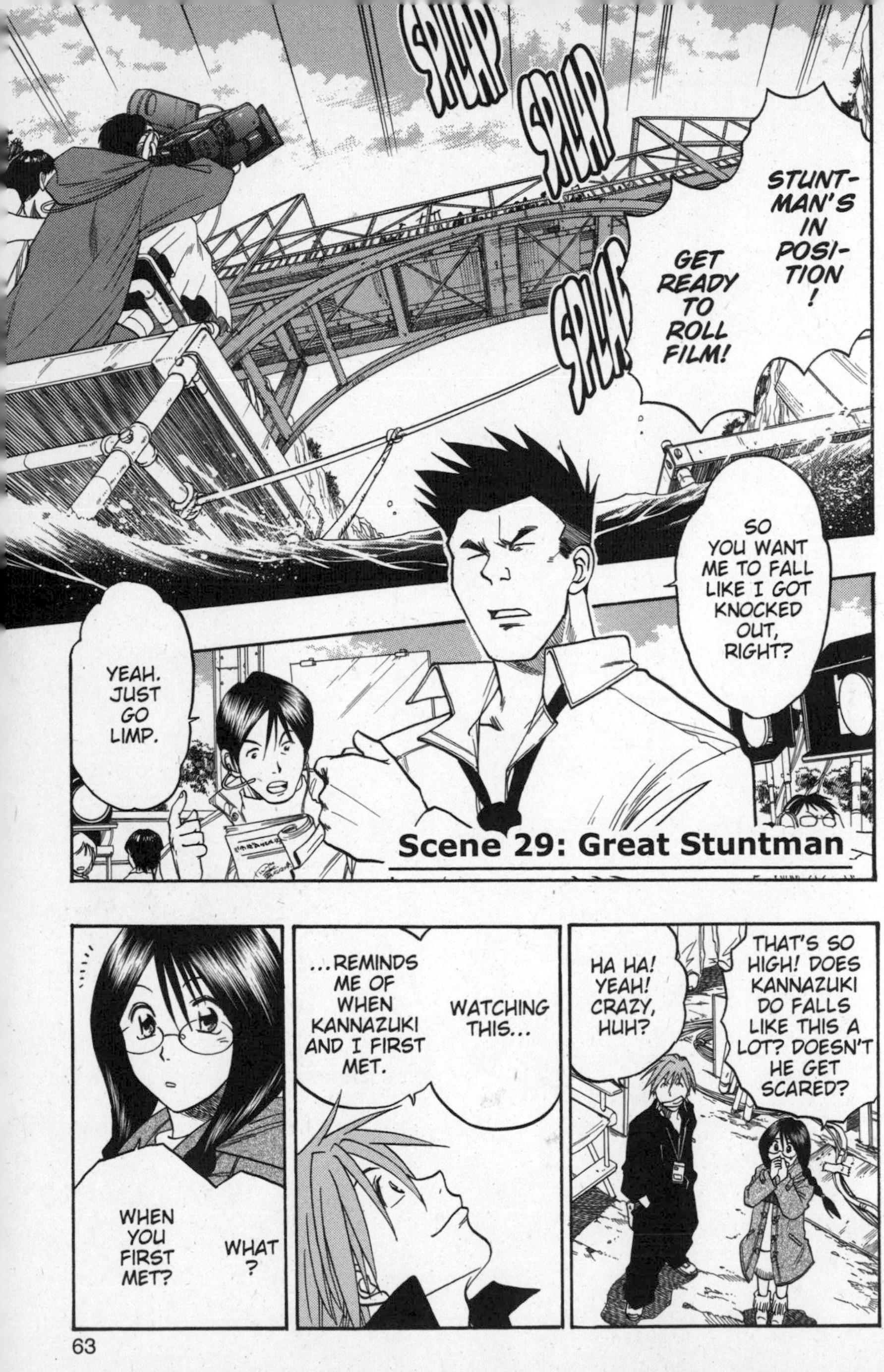
SPLAP
SPLAP
SPLAP
STUNTMAN'S IN POSITION!
GET READY TO ROLL FILM!
SO YOU WANT ME TO FALL LIKE I GOT KNOCKED OUT, RIGHT?
YEAH. JUST GO LIMP.
Scene 29: Great Stuntman
THAT'S SO HIGH! DOES KANNAZUKI DO FALLS LIKE THIS A LOT? DOESN'T HE GET SCARED?
HA HA! YEAH! CRAZY, HUH?
WATCHING THIS...
...REMINDS ME OF WHEN KANNAZUKI AND I FIRST MET.
WHAT?
WHEN YOU FIRST MET?

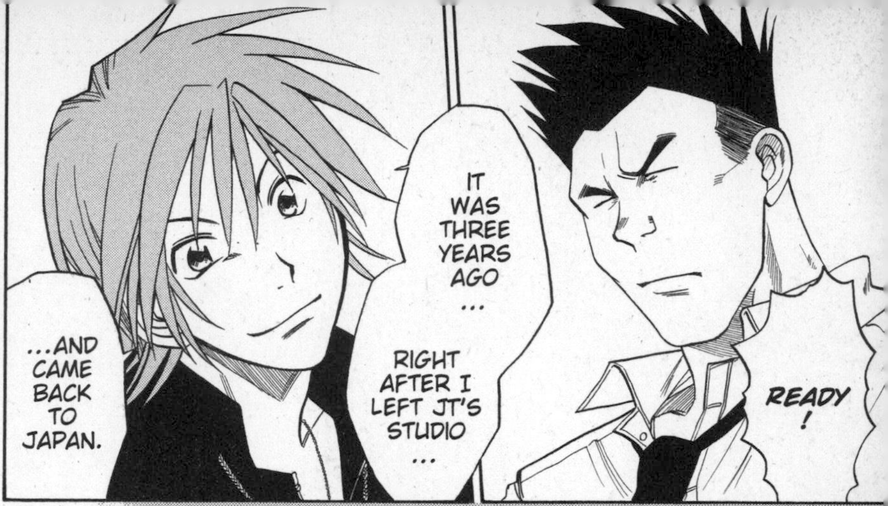
IT WAS THREE YEARS AGO ...
READY!
RIGHT AFTER I LEFT JT'S STUDIO ...
...AND CAME BACK TO JAPAN.

Scene 29: Great Stuntman

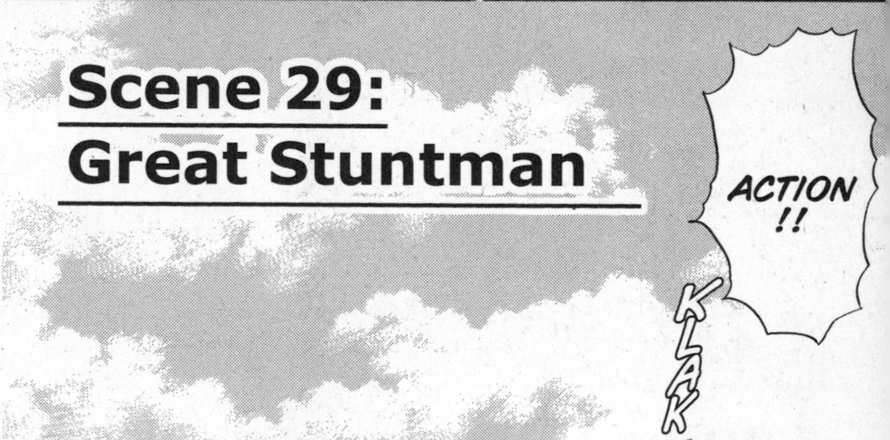
ACTION!!
KLAK

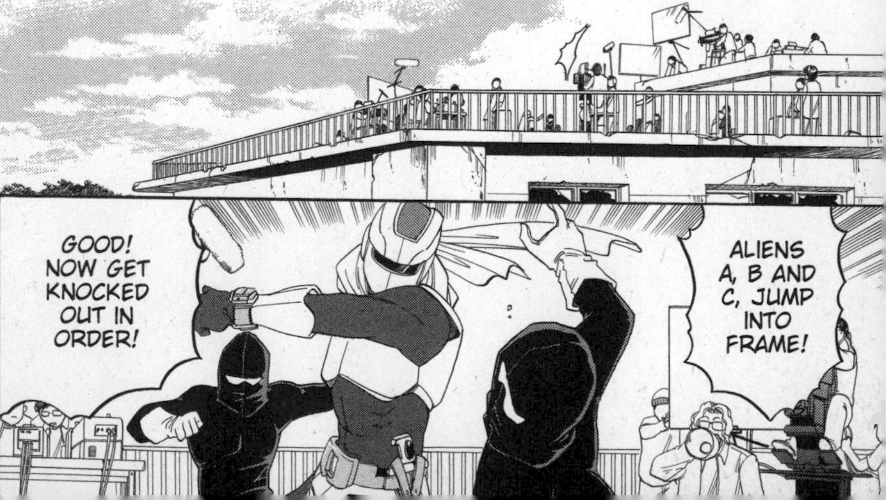
ALIENS A, B AND C, JUMP INTO FRAME!
GOOD! NOW GET KNOCKED OUT IN ORDER!

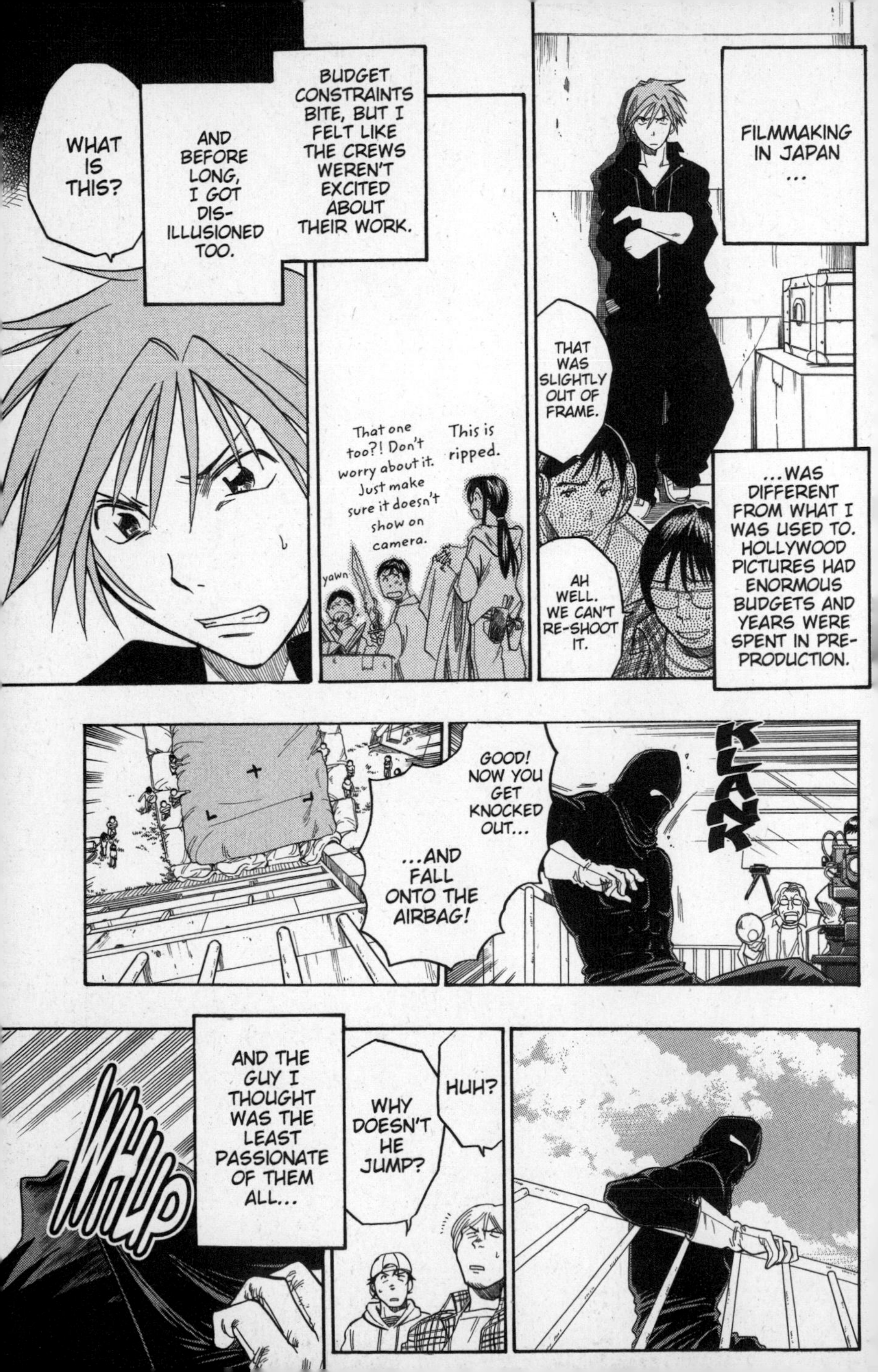
FILMMAKING IN JAPAN ...
THAT WAS SLIGHTLY OUT OF FRAME.
...WAS DIFFERENT FROM WHAT I WAS USED TO. HOLLYWOOD PICTURES HAD ENORMOUS BUDGETS AND YEARS WERE SPENT IN PRE-PRODUCTION.
AH WELL. WE CAN'T RE-SHOOT IT.
BUDGET CONSTRAINTS BITE, BUT I FELT LIKE THE CREWS WEREN'T EXCITED ABOUT THEIR WORK.
This is ripped.
That one too?! Don't worry about it. Just make sure it doesn't show on camera.
yawn
AND BEFORE LONG, I GOT DIS-ILLUSIONED TOO.
WHAT IS THIS?
KLANK
GOOD! NOW YOU GET KNOCKED OUT...
...AND FALL ONTO THE AIRBAG!
HUH?
WHY DOESN'T HE JUMP?
AND THE GUY I THOUGHT WAS THE LEAST PASSIONATE OF THEM ALL...
WHUP

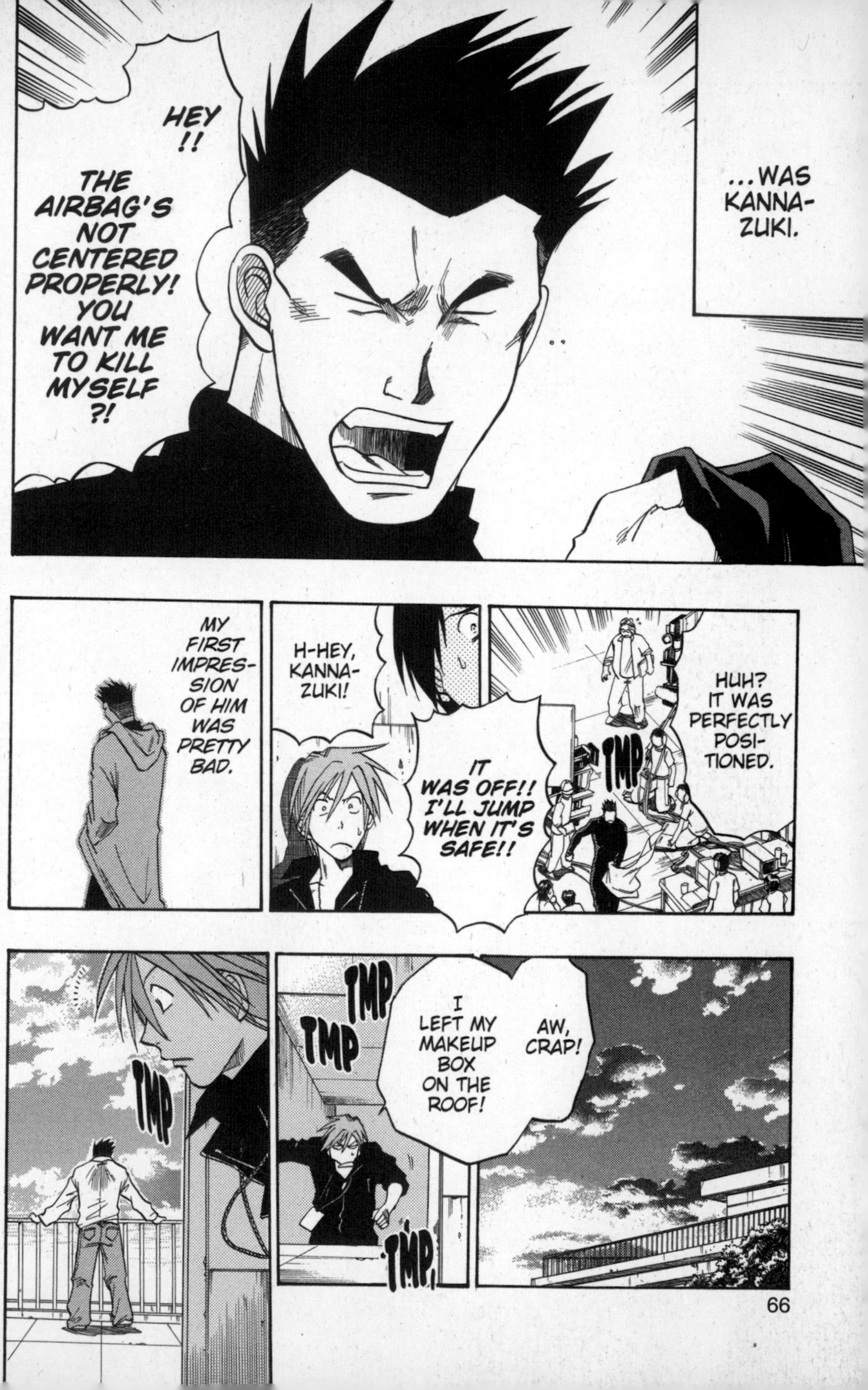
...WAS KANNA-ZUKI.
HEY !!
THE AIRBAG'S NOT CENTERED PROPERLY! YOU WANT ME TO KILL MYSELF ?!
HUH? IT WAS PERFECTLY POSI-TIONED.
TMP
IT WAS OFF!! I'LL JUMP WHEN IT'S SAFE!!
H-HEY, KANNA-ZUKI!
MY FIRST IMPRES-SION OF HIM WAS PRETTY BAD.
AW, CRAP!
I LEFT MY MAKEUP BOX ON THE ROOF!
TMP
TMP
TMP
TMP

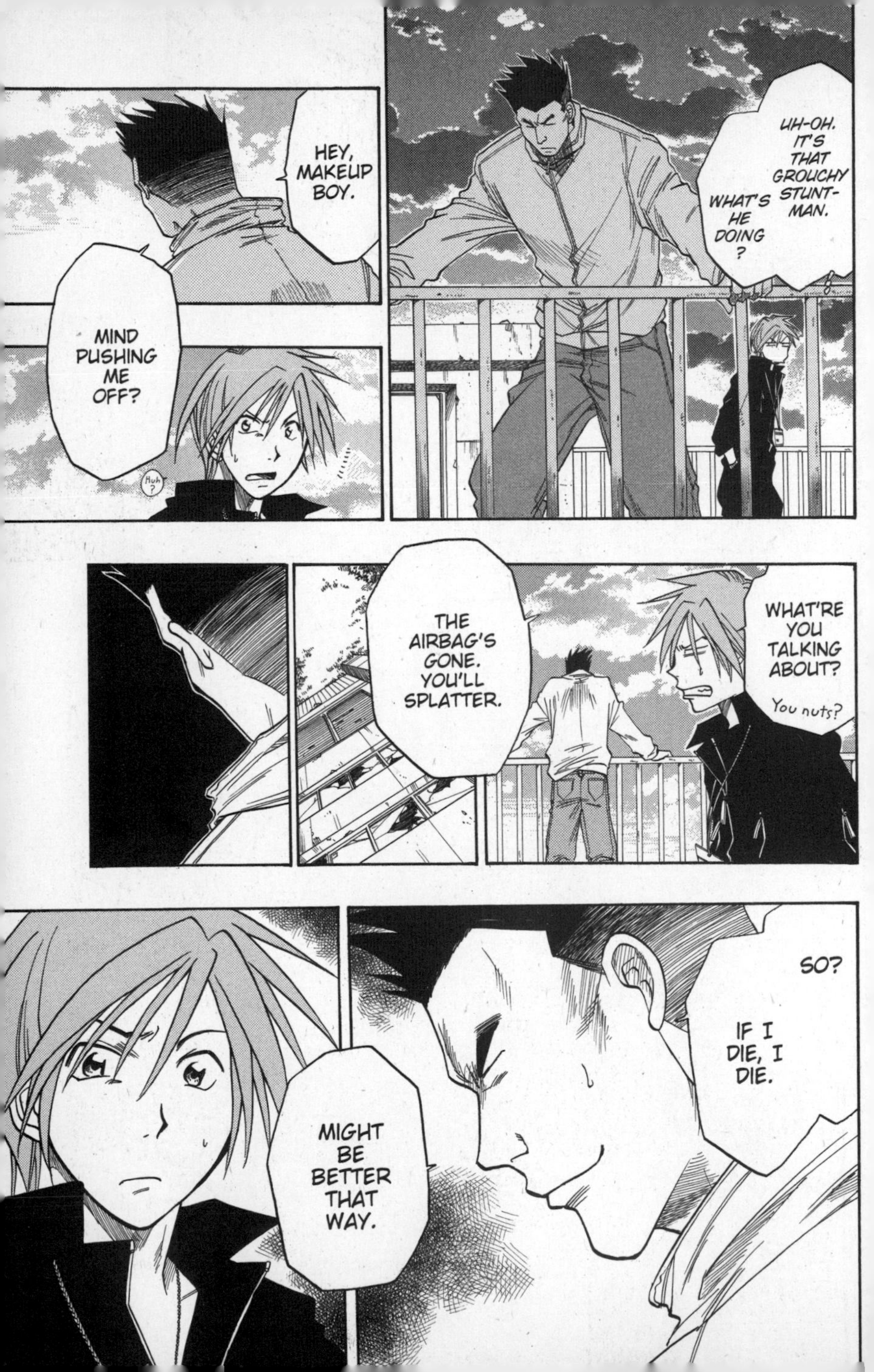
UH-OH. IT'S THAT GROUCHY STUNT-MAN.
WHAT'S HE DOING?
HEY, MAKEUP BOY.
MIND PUSHING ME OFF?
Huh?
WHAT'RE YOU TALKING ABOUT?
You nuts?
THE AIRBAG'S GONE. YOU'LL SPLATTER.
SO?
IF I DIE, I DIE.
MIGHT BE BETTER THAT WAY.

NEW WORLD RECORD!

HE'S AN EXPERT STUNTMAN. HE'S DONE LOTS OF EXTREMELY DIFFICULT STUNTS.

SHINGO KANNAZUKI?

Japanese Stuntman Shingo Kannazuki (20) Dives From Helicop...

THREE BUSES

MOTORCYCLE STUNT

THEN WHAT'S HE DOING ON THIS CRAPPY SHOW?

HA HA! HE'S BEEN DOING STUNTS ALL OVER THE WORLD SINCE HE WAS A TEENAGER.

HE'S THE SAME AGE AS ME?!

THAT GUY?

HE HASN'T BEEN THE SAME SINCE THE ACCIDENT.

WHAT A WASTE OF TALENT.

Hmm... The same age...

HE SPENT SIX MONTHS IN THE HOSPITAL. THERE WERE EVEN RUMORS THAT HE WAS DEAD, BUT THEN HE MADE AN INCREDIBLE COMEBACK.

THE CREW MESSED UP AND HE FELL WHILE DOING A WIRE STUNT.

...THEY SAY HE'S BEEN AFRAID OF HEIGHTS.

BUT EVER SINCE THAT FALL...

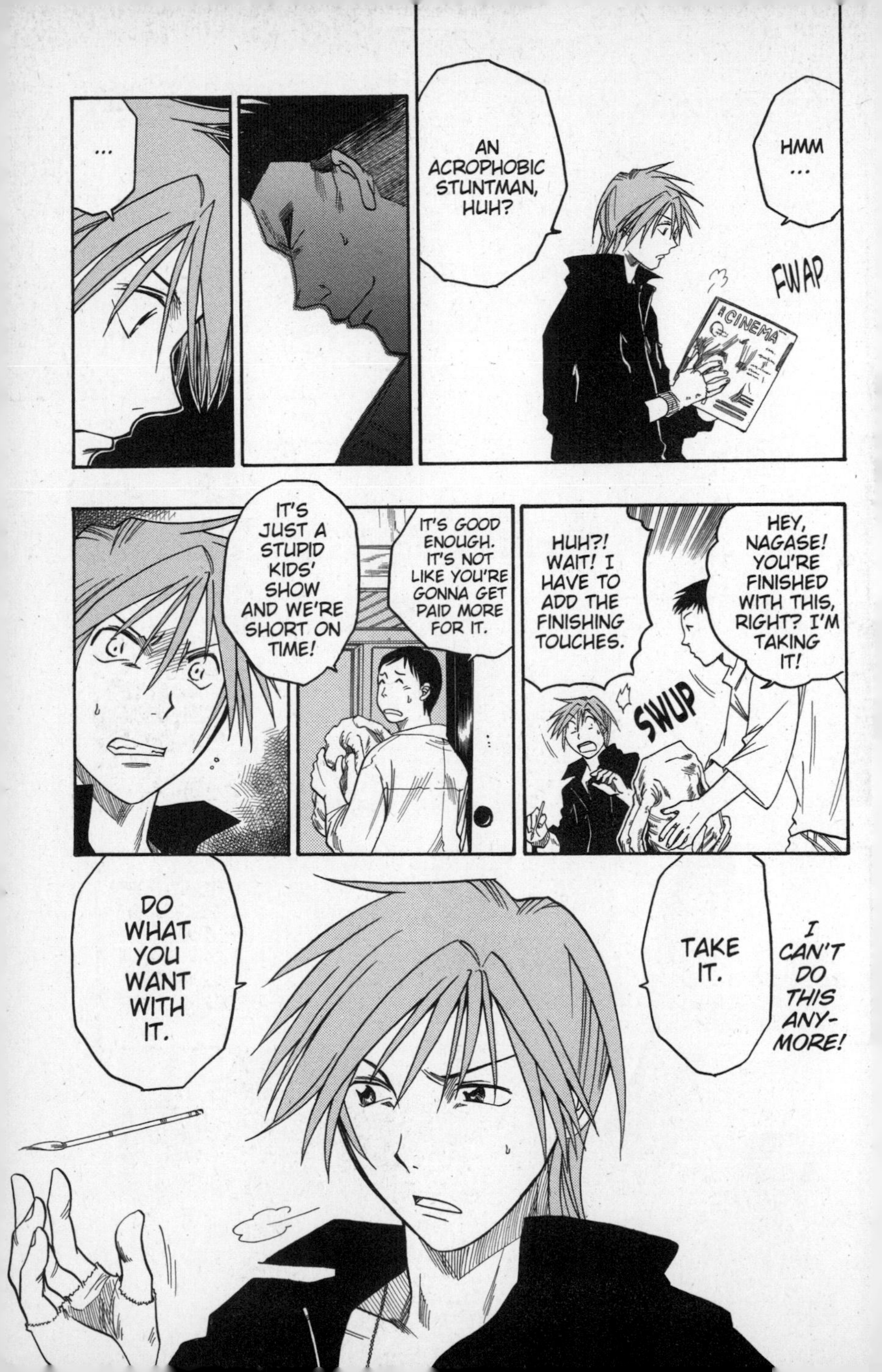
HMM ...
AN ACROPHOBIC STUNTMAN, HUH?
FWAP
CINEMA
...
HEY, NAGASE! YOU'RE FINISHED WITH THIS, RIGHT? I'M TAKING IT!
HUH?! WAIT! I HAVE TO ADD THE FINISHING TOUCHES.
SWUP
IT'S GOOD ENOUGH. IT'S NOT LIKE YOU'RE GONNA GET PAID MORE FOR IT.
IT'S JUST A STUPID KIDS' SHOW AND WE'RE SHORT ON TIME!
I CAN'T DO THIS ANYMORE!
TAKE IT.
DO WHAT YOU WANT WITH IT.

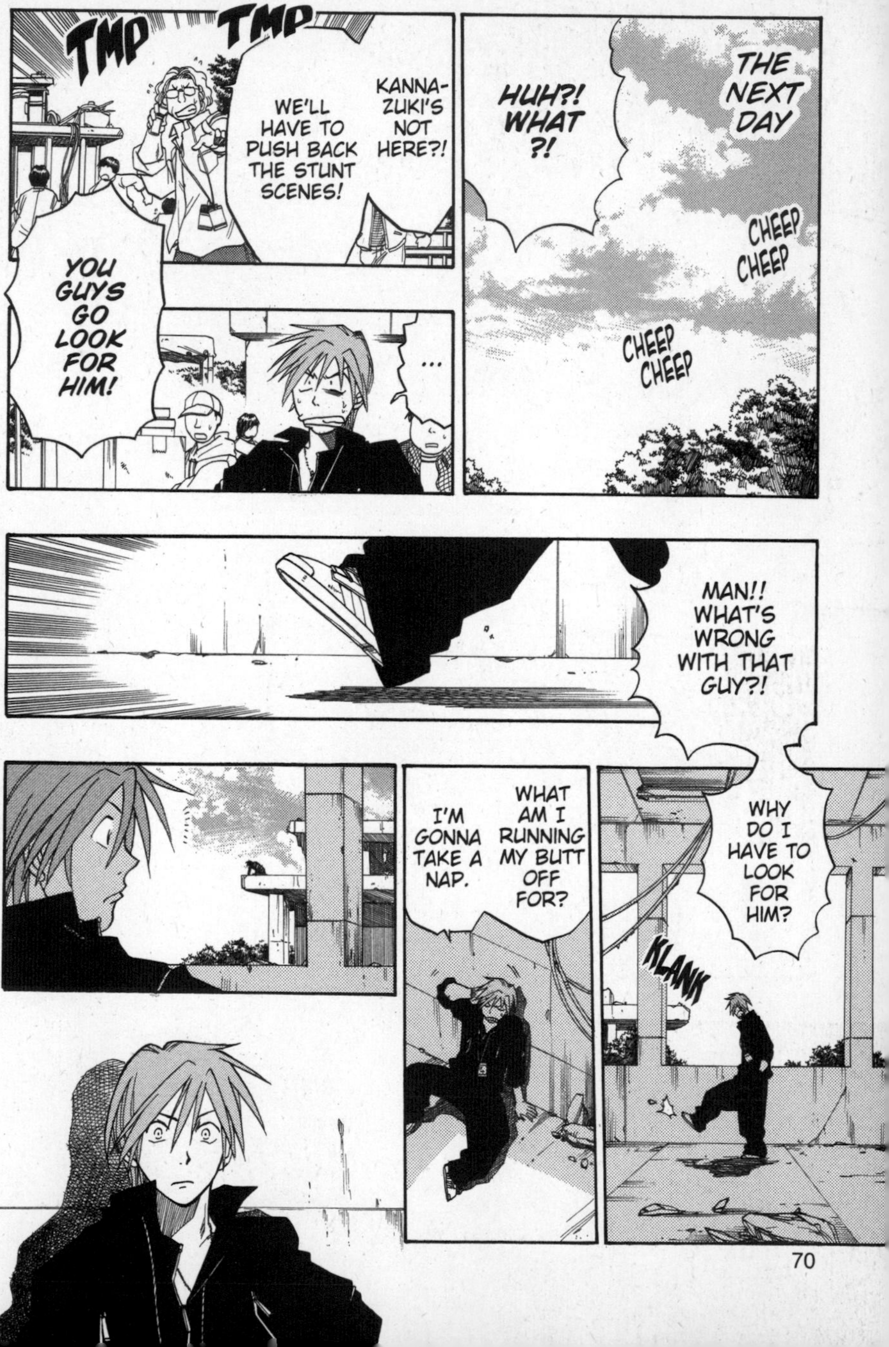
THE NEXT DAY
HUH?! WHAT?!
CHEEP CHEEP
CHEEP CHEEP
TMP TMP
KANNA-ZUKI'S NOT HERE?!
WE'LL HAVE TO PUSH BACK THE STUNT SCENES!
YOU GUYS GO LOOK FOR HIM!
...
MAN!! WHAT'S WRONG WITH THAT GUY?!
WHY DO I HAVE TO LOOK FOR HIM?
KLANK
WHAT AM I RUNNING MY BUTT OFF FOR?
I'M GONNA TAKE A NAP.

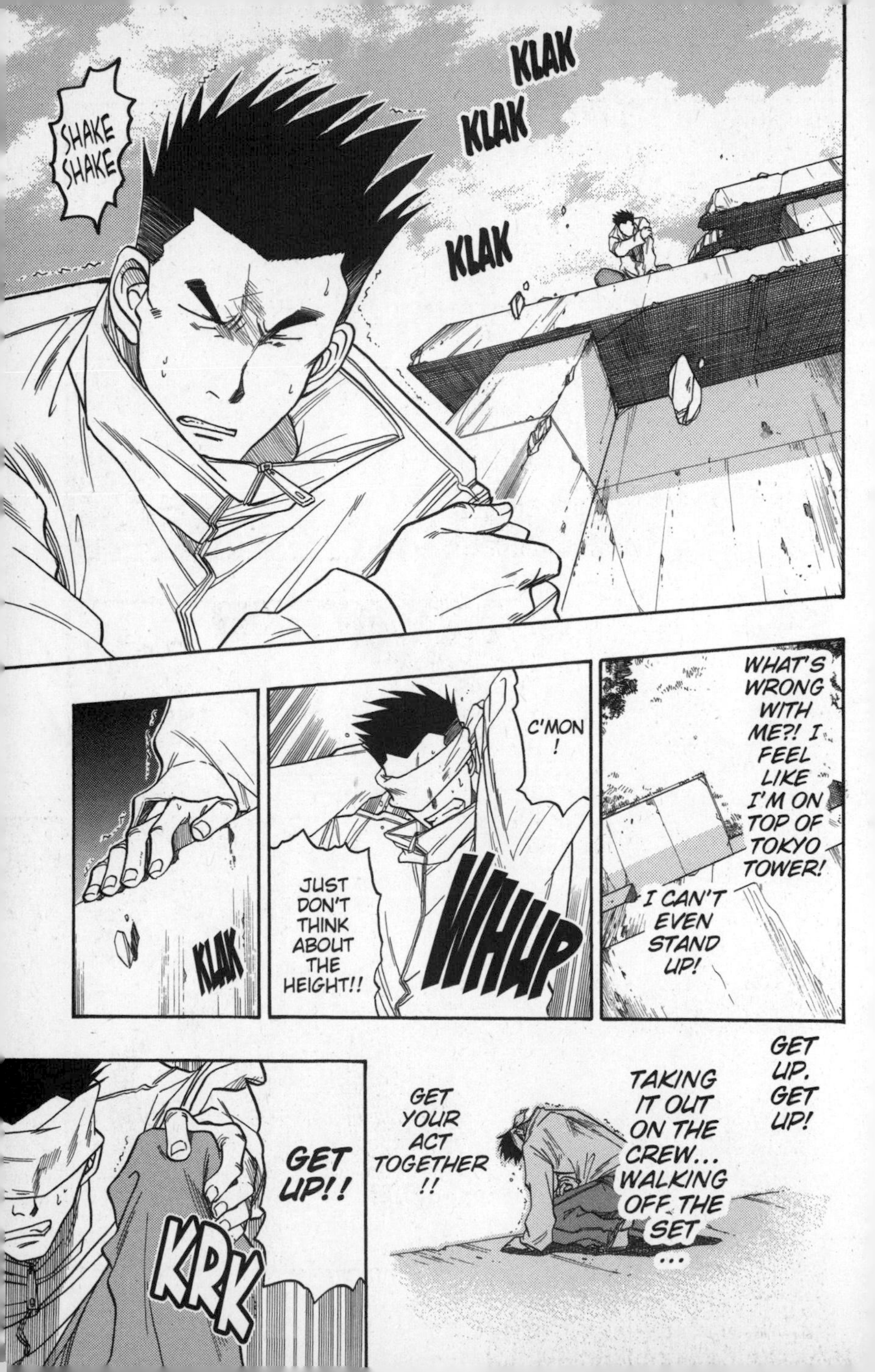
KLAK
KLAK
SHAKE SHAKE
KLAK
WHAT'S WRONG WITH ME?! I FEEL LIKE I'M ON TOP OF TOKYO TOWER!
I CAN'T EVEN STAND UP!
C'MON!
WHUP
JUST DON'T THINK ABOUT THE HEIGHT!!
KLAK
GET UP. GET UP!
TAKING IT OUT ON THE CREW... WALKING OFF THE SET...
GET YOUR ACT TOGETHER!!
GET UP!!
KRK

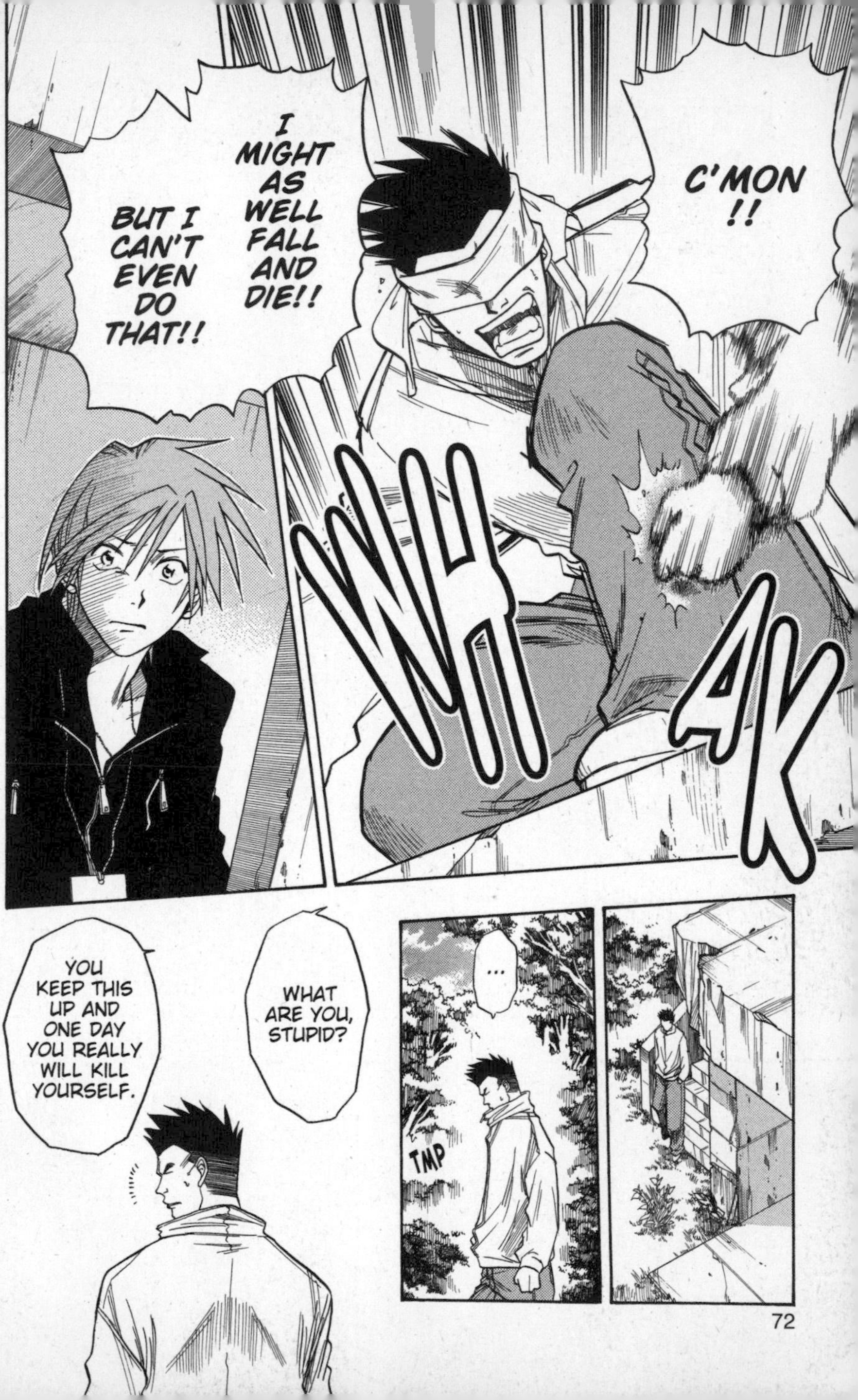
C'MON!!
I MIGHT AS WELL FALL AND DIE!!
BUT I CAN'T EVEN DO THAT!!
WHAK
...
TMP
WHAT ARE YOU, STUPID?
YOU KEEP THIS UP AND ONE DAY YOU REALLY WILL KILL YOURSELF.

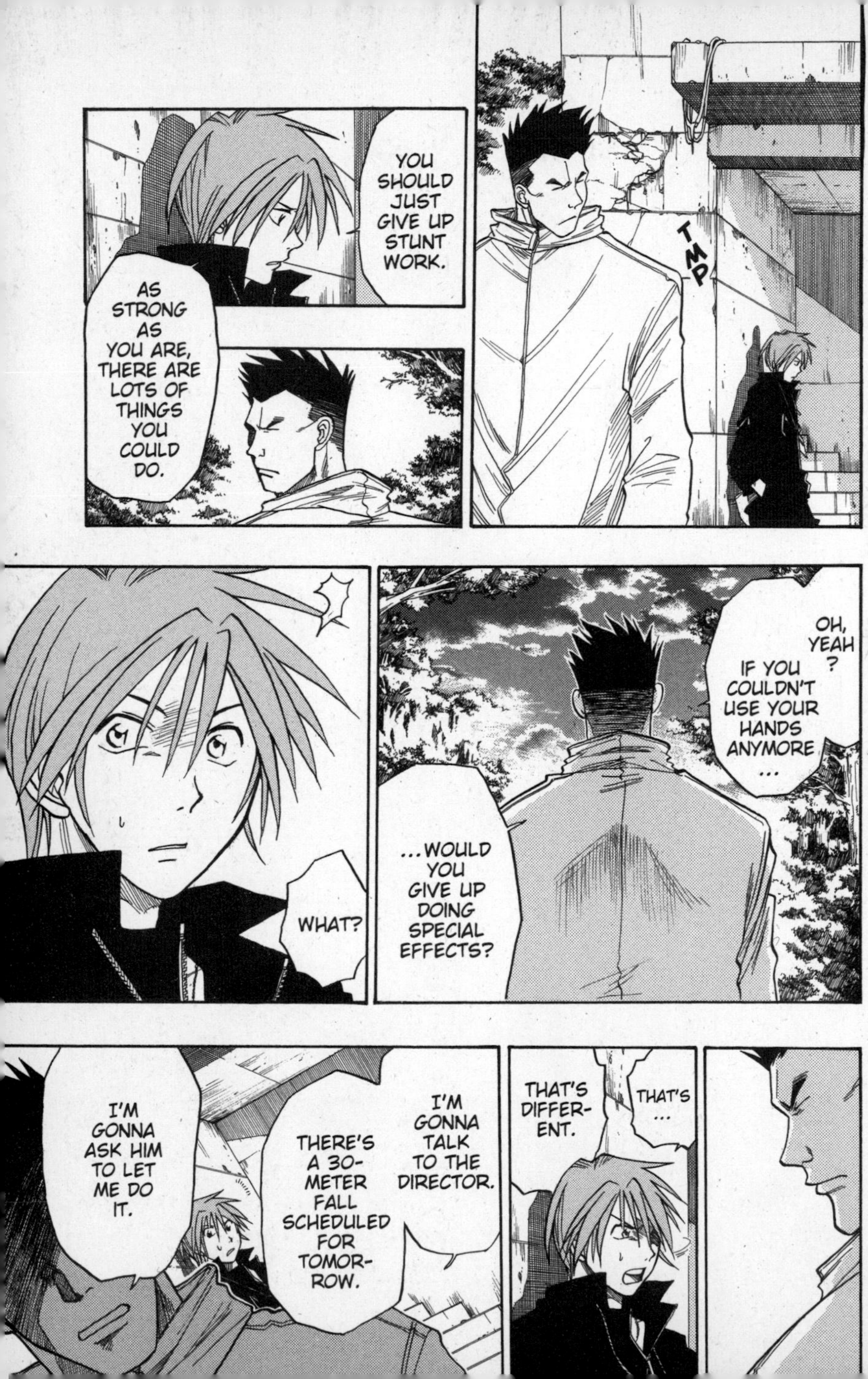
TMP
YOU SHOULD JUST GIVE UP STUNT WORK.
AS STRONG AS YOU ARE, THERE ARE LOTS OF THINGS YOU COULD DO.
OH, YEAH? IF YOU COULDN'T USE YOUR HANDS ANYMORE...
...WOULD YOU GIVE UP DOING SPECIAL EFFECTS?
WHAT?
THAT'S...
THAT'S DIFFER-ENT.
I'M GONNA TALK TO THE DIRECTOR.
THERE'S A 30-METER FALL SCHEDULED FOR TOMOR-ROW.
I'M GONNA ASK HIM TO LET ME DO IT.

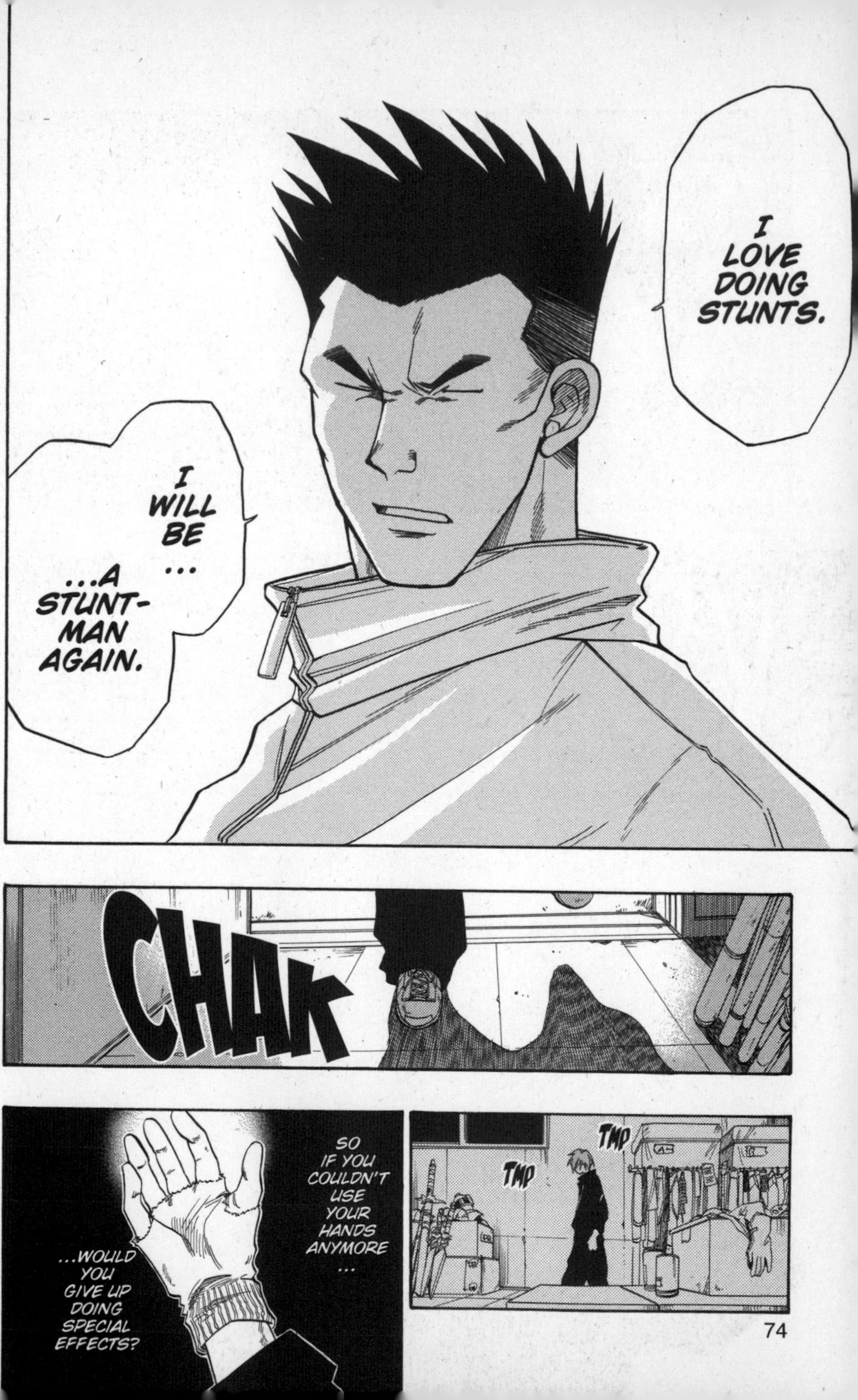
I LOVE DOING STUNTS.
I WILL BE ...
...A STUNT-MAN AGAIN.
CHAK
TMP
TMP
SO IF YOU COULDN'T USE YOUR HANDS ANYMORE ...
...WOULD YOU GIVE UP DOING SPECIAL EFFECTS?

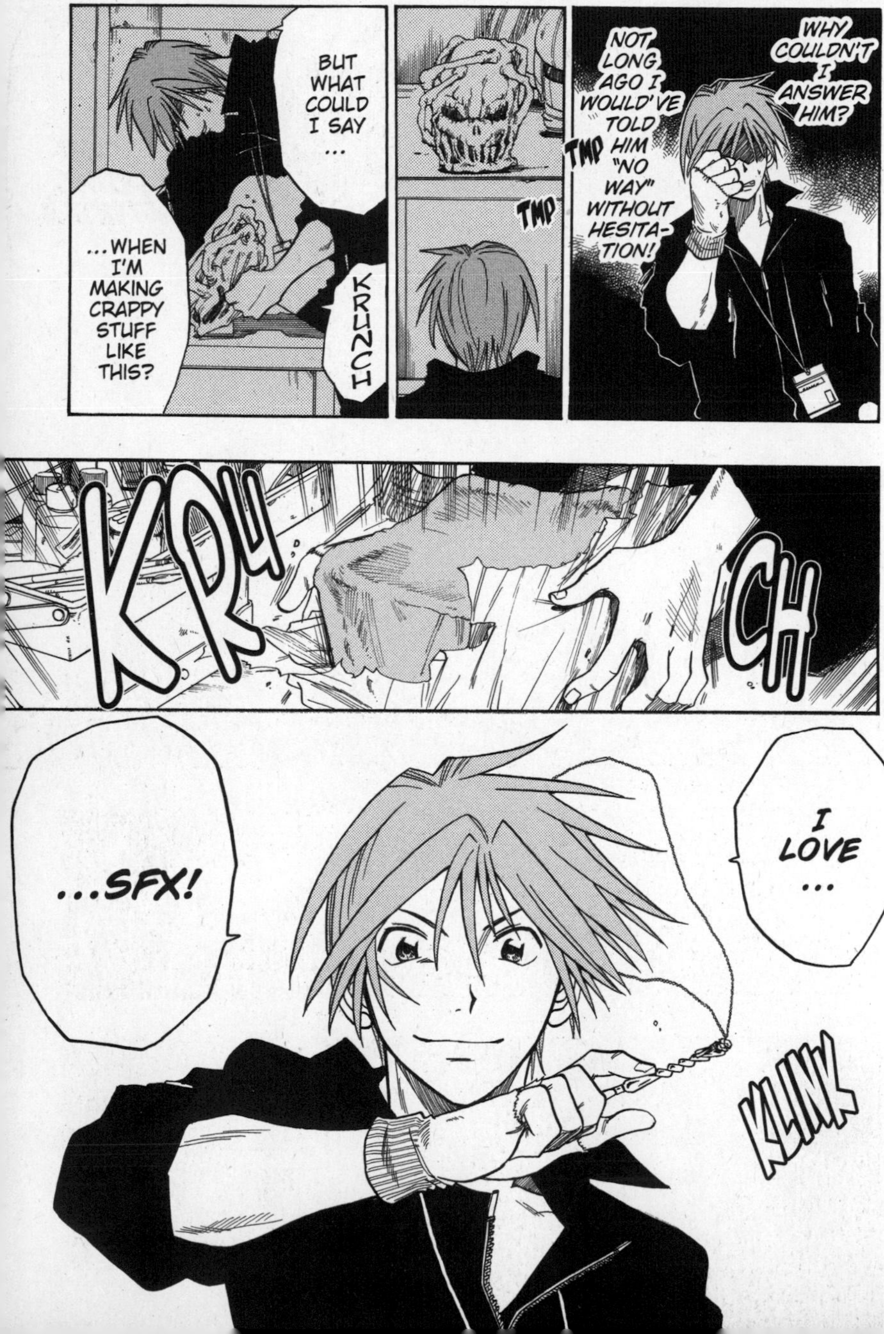
WHY COULDN'T I ANSWER HIM?
NOT LONG AGO I WOULD'VE TOLD HIM "NO WAY" WITHOUT HESITATION!
TMP
TMP
BUT WHAT COULD I SAY ...
KRUNCH
...WHEN I'M MAKING CRAPPY STUFF LIKE THIS?
KRUNCH
I LOVE ...
KLINK
...SFX!

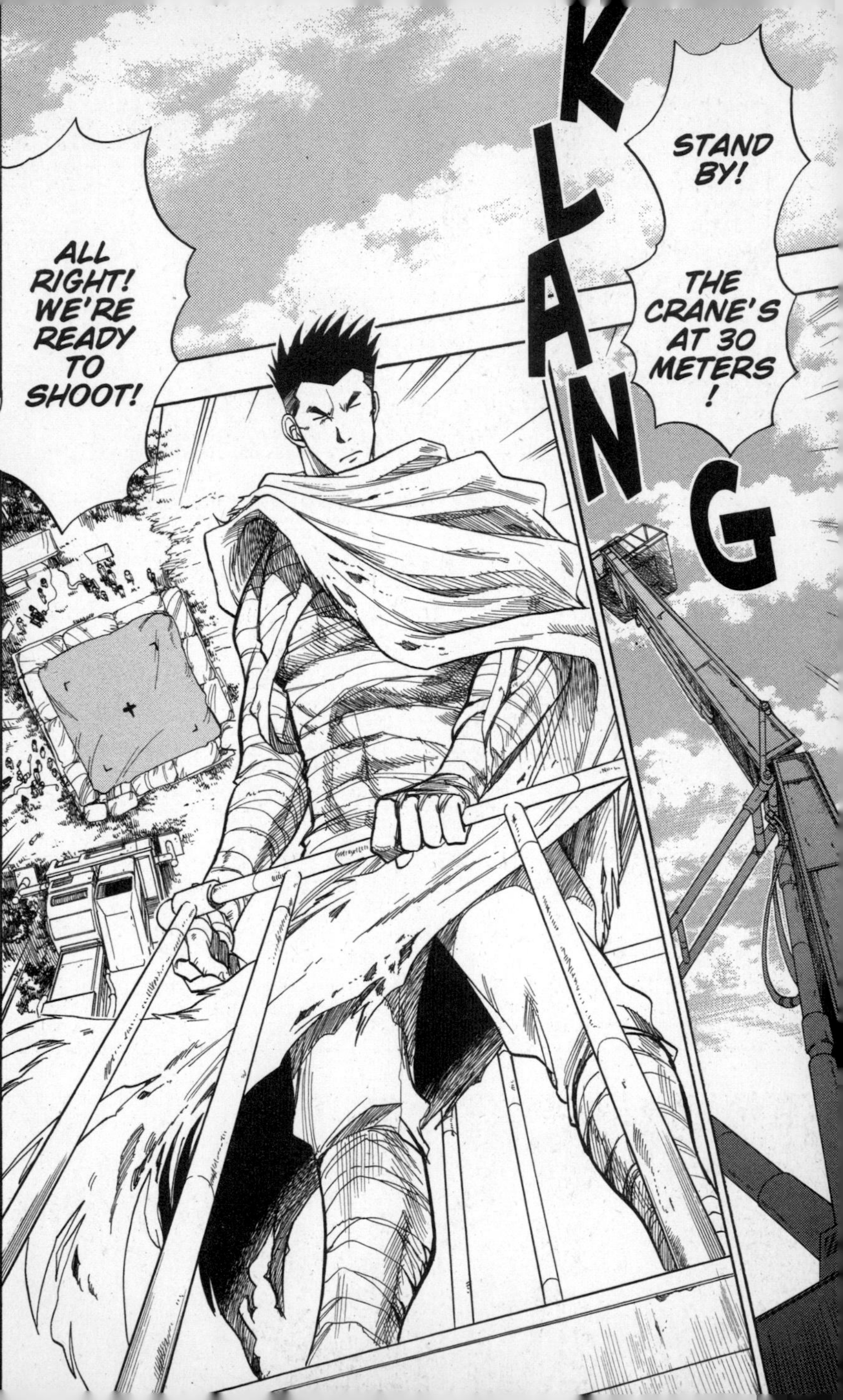
STAND BY!
THE CRANE'S AT 30 METERS!
KLANG
ALL RIGHT! WE'RE READY TO SHOOT!

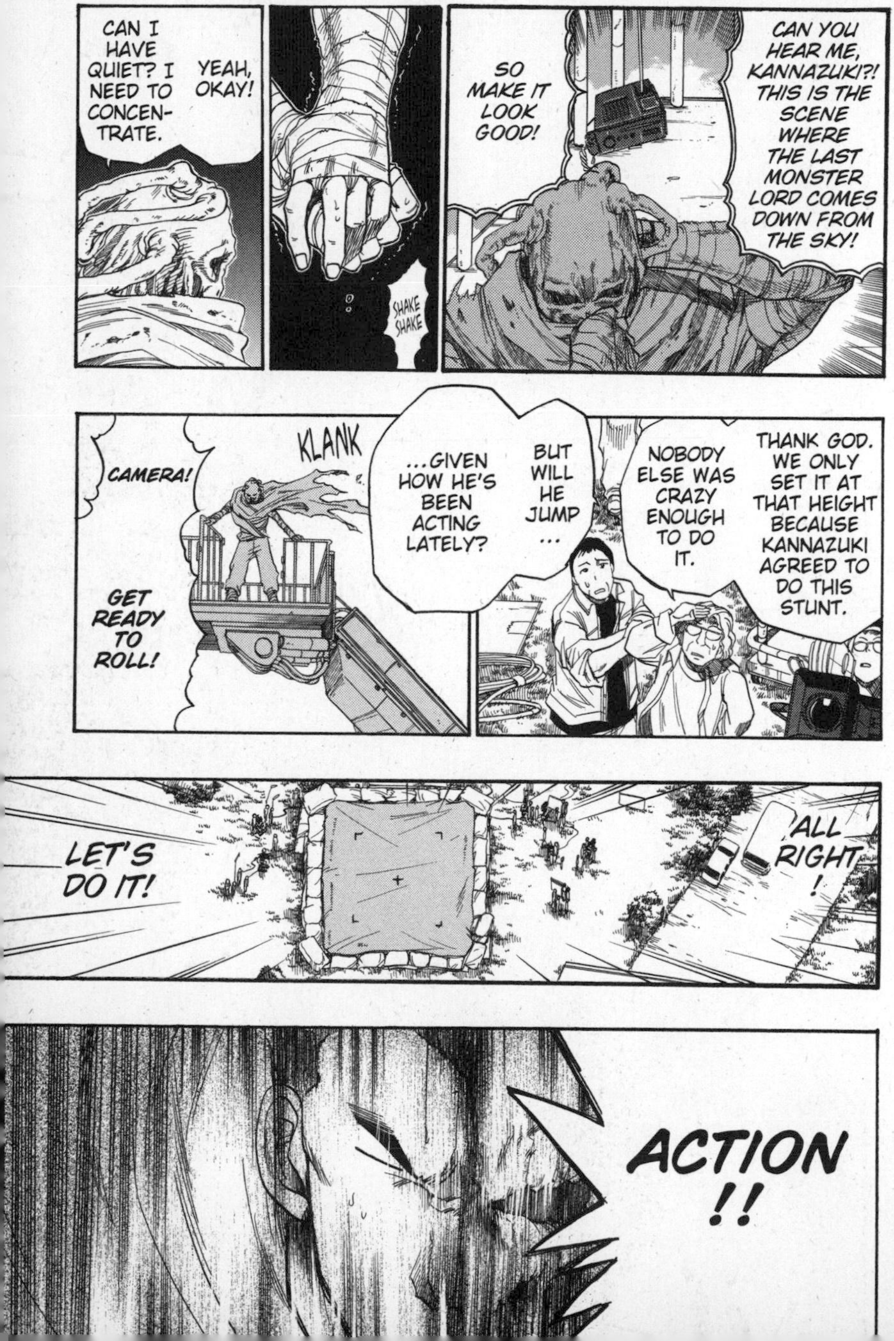
CAN YOU HEAR ME, KANNAZUKI?! THIS IS THE SCENE WHERE THE LAST MONSTER LORD COMES DOWN FROM THE SKY!
SO MAKE IT LOOK GOOD!
SHAKE SHAKE
CAN I HAVE QUIET? I NEED TO CONCENTRATE.
YEAH, OKAY!
THANK GOD. WE ONLY SET IT AT THAT HEIGHT BECAUSE KANNAZUKI AGREED TO DO THIS STUNT.
NOBODY ELSE WAS CRAZY ENOUGH TO DO IT.
BUT WILL HE JUMP...
...GIVEN HOW HE'S BEEN ACTING LATELY?
KLANK
CAMERA!
GET READY TO ROLL!
ALL RIGHT!
LET'S DO IT!
ACTION!!

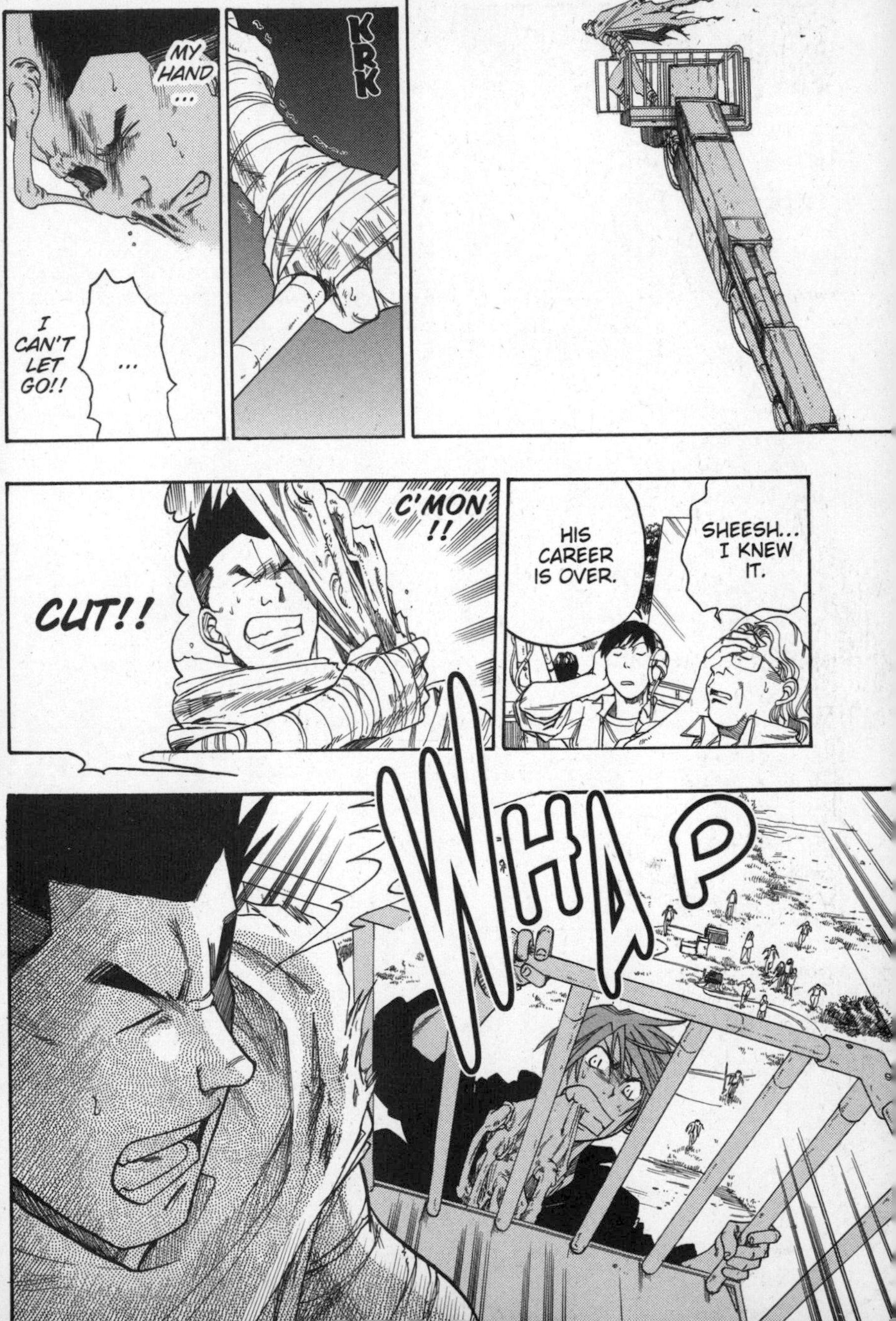
KRK
MY HAND ...
...
I CAN'T LET GO!!
SHEESH... I KNEW IT.
HIS CAREER IS OVER.
C'MON!!
CUT!!
WHAP

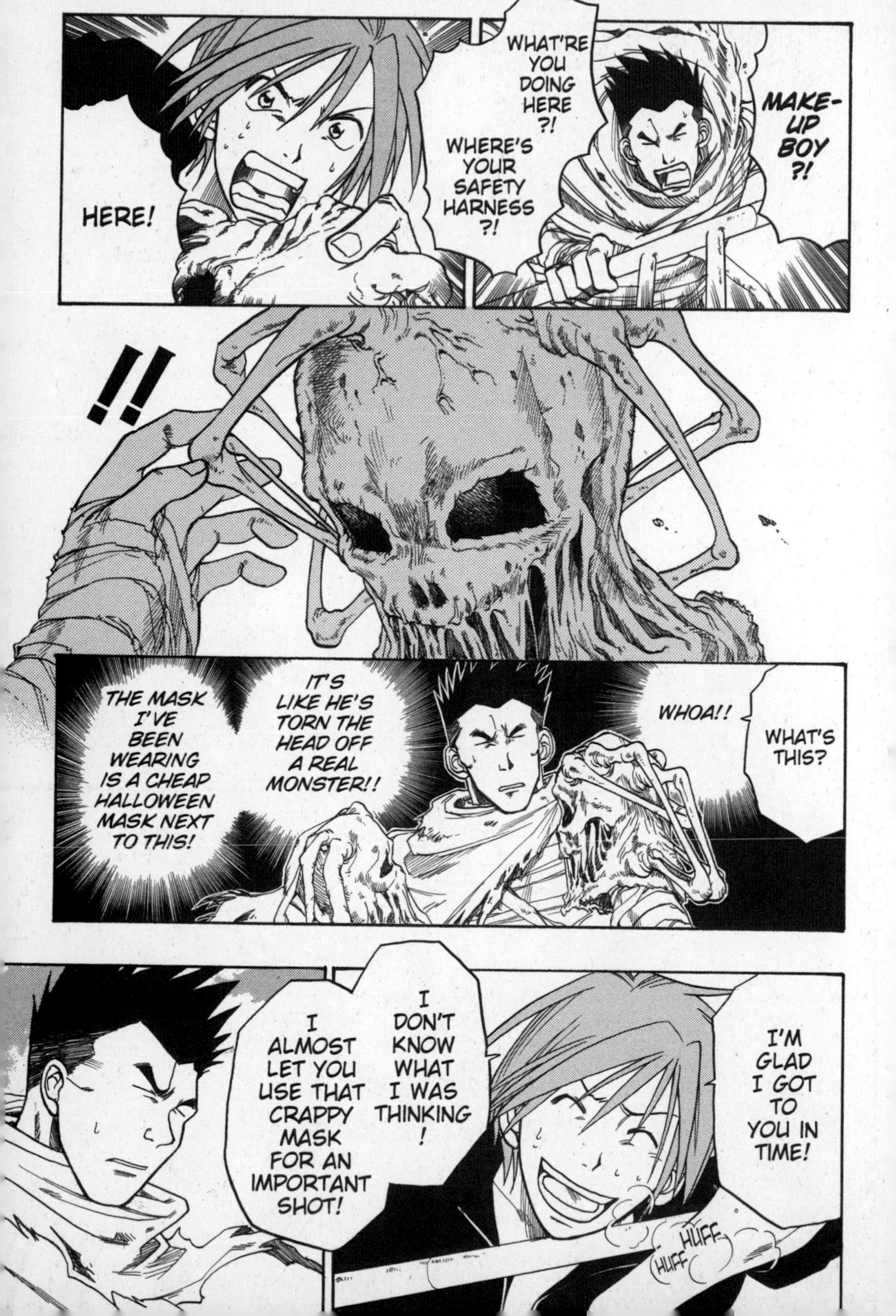
MAKE-UP BOY?!
WHAT'RE YOU DOING HERE?!
WHERE'S YOUR SAFETY HARNESS?!
HERE!
!!
WHAT'S THIS?
WHOA!!
IT'S LIKE HE'S TORN THE HEAD OFF A REAL MONSTER!!
THE MASK I'VE BEEN WEARING IS A CHEAP HALLOWEEN MASK NEXT TO THIS!
I'M GLAD I GOT TO YOU IN TIME!
HUFF HUFF
I DON'T KNOW WHAT I WAS THINKING!
I ALMOST LET YOU USE THAT CRAPPY MASK FOR AN IMPORTANT SHOT!

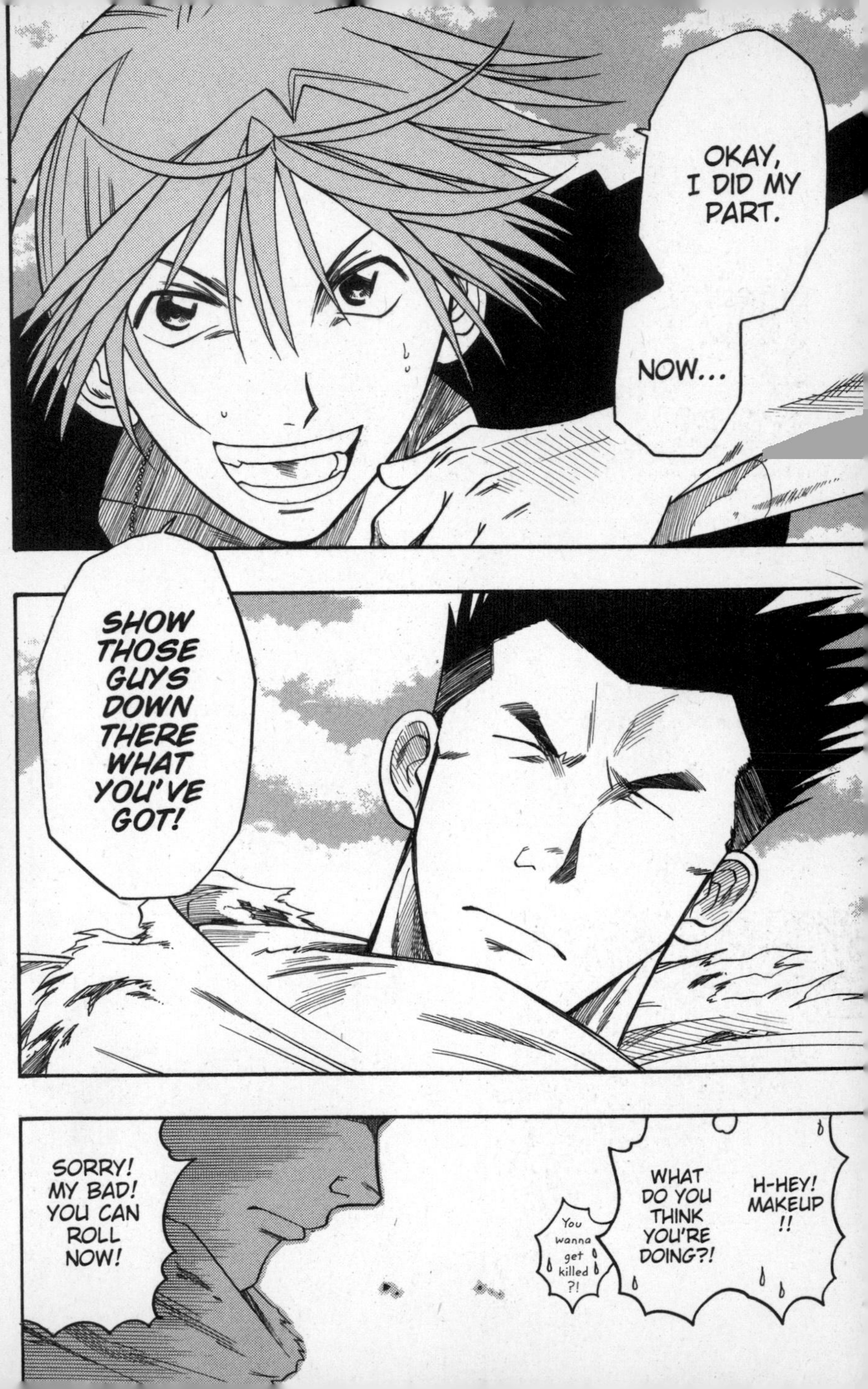
OKAY, I DID MY PART.
NOW...
SHOW THOSE GUYS DOWN THERE WHAT YOU'VE GOT!
H-HEY! MAKEUP !!
WHAT DO YOU THINK YOU'RE DOING?!
You wanna get killed ?!
SORRY! MY BAD! YOU CAN ROLL NOW!

SWUP

WE'RE READY!

CAMERAS!!

KLANK

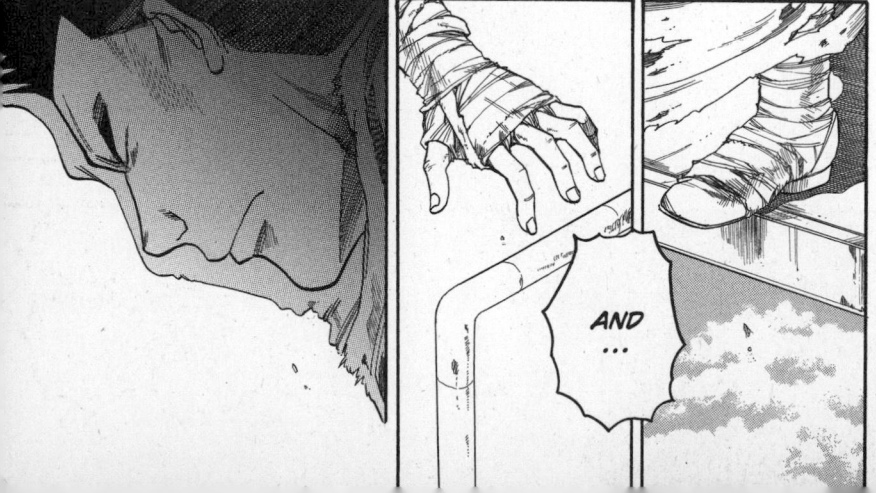

AND...

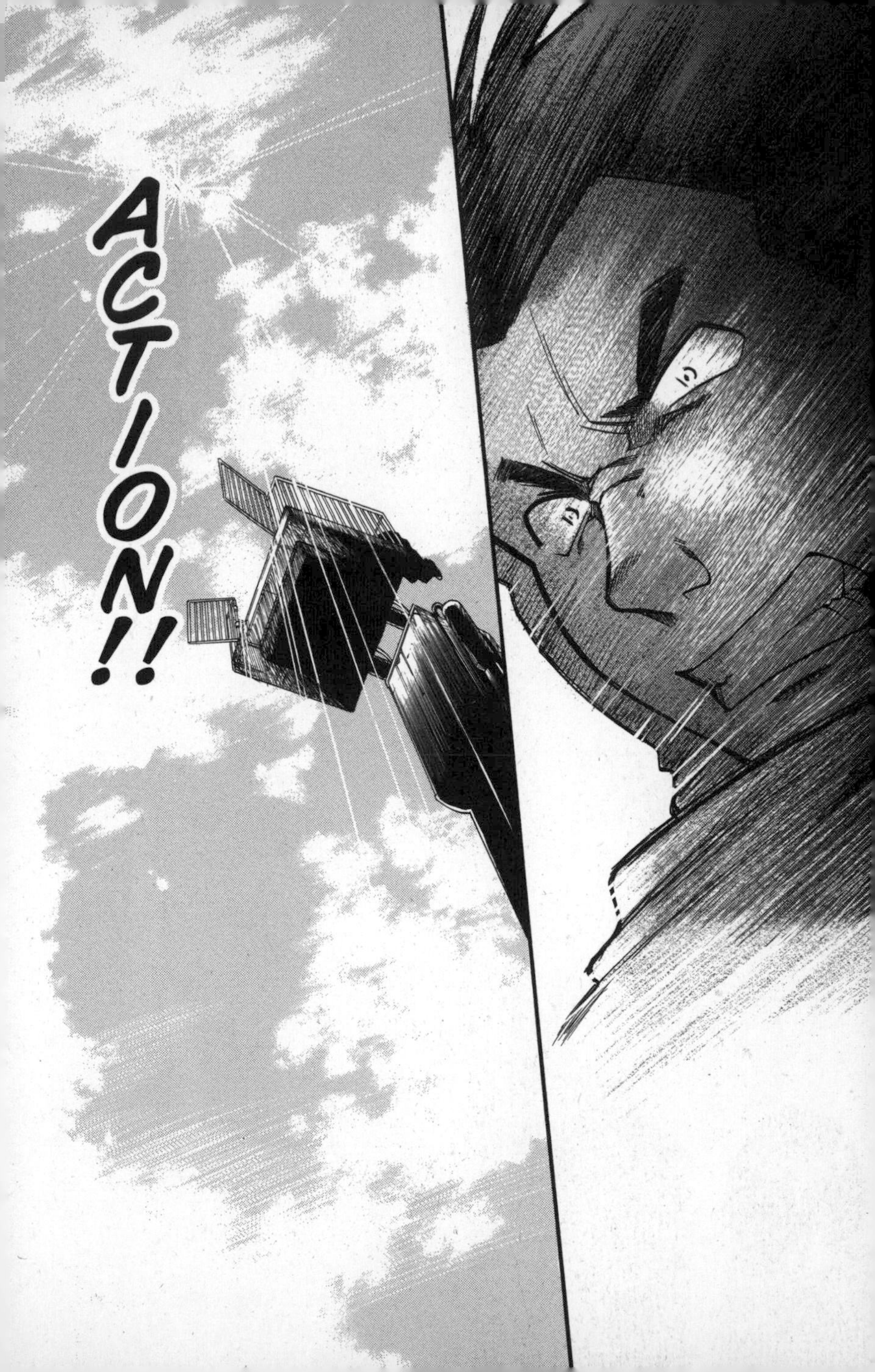
ACTION!!

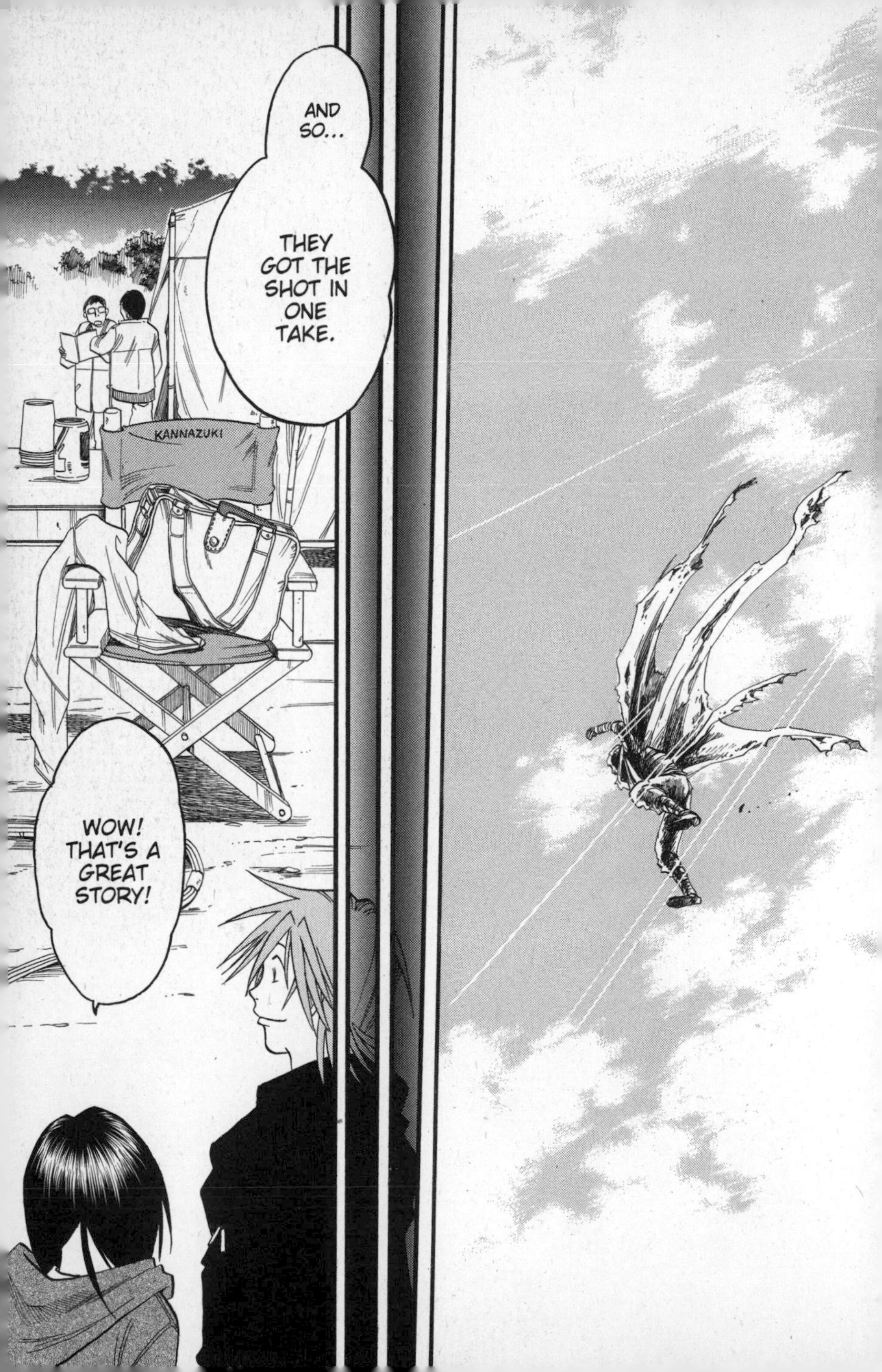
AND SO...
THEY GOT THE SHOT IN ONE TAKE.
KANNAZUKI
WOW! THAT'S A GREAT STORY!

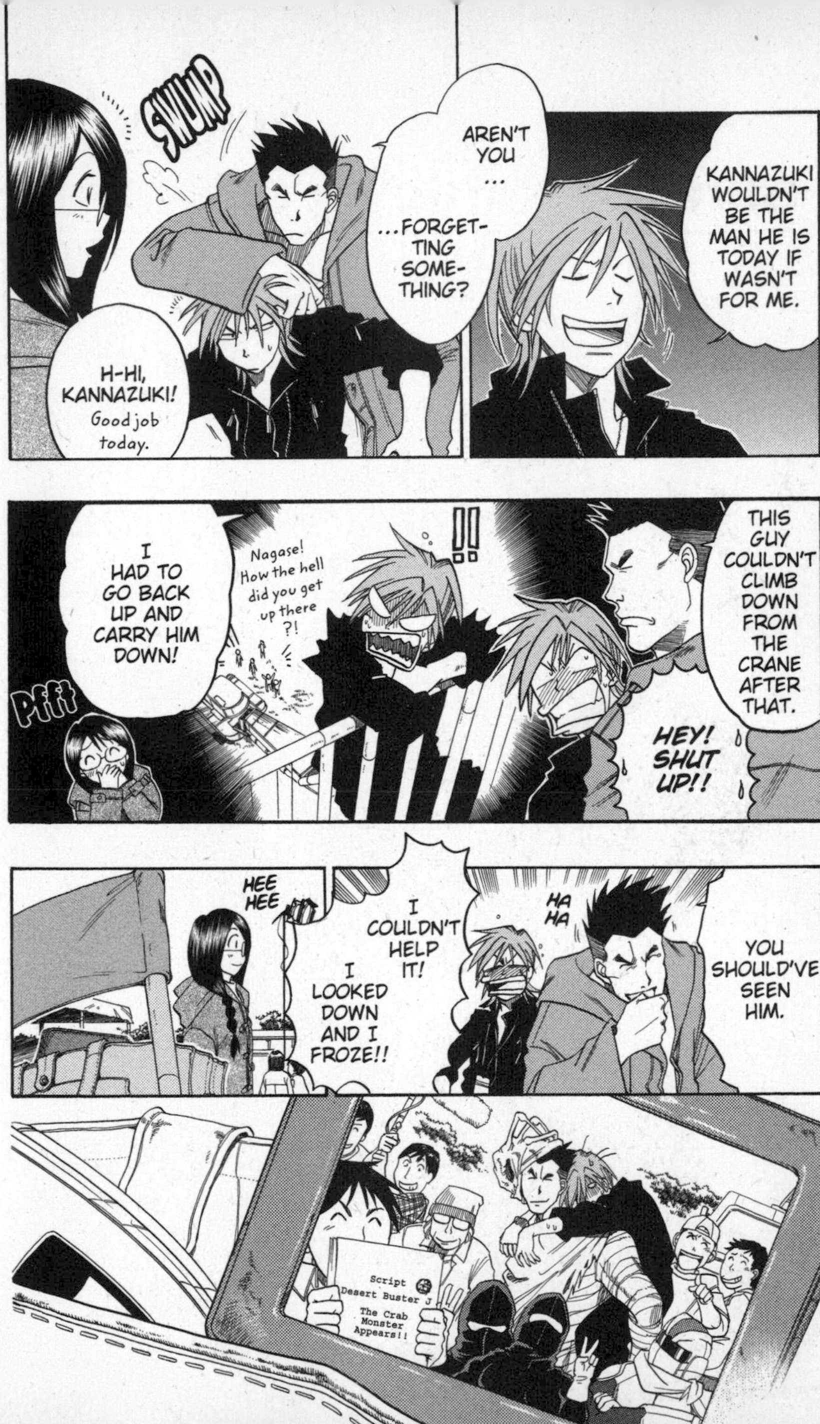
KANNAZUKI WOULDN'T BE THE MAN HE IS TODAY IF WASN'T FOR ME.
AREN'T YOU ...
...FORGET-TING SOME-THING?
SWUMP
H-HI, KANNAZUKI! Good job today.
THIS GUY COULDN'T CLIMB DOWN FROM THE CRANE AFTER THAT.
HEY! SHUT UP!!
!!
Nagase! How the hell did you get up there?!
I HAD TO GO BACK UP AND CARRY HIM DOWN!
Pfft
YOU SHOULD'VE SEEN HIM.
HA HA
I COULDN'T HELP IT!
I LOOKED DOWN AND I FROZE!!
HEE HEE
Script
Desert Buster J
The Crab Monster Appears!!

Scene 30:
Sunrise Boulevard (Part 1)

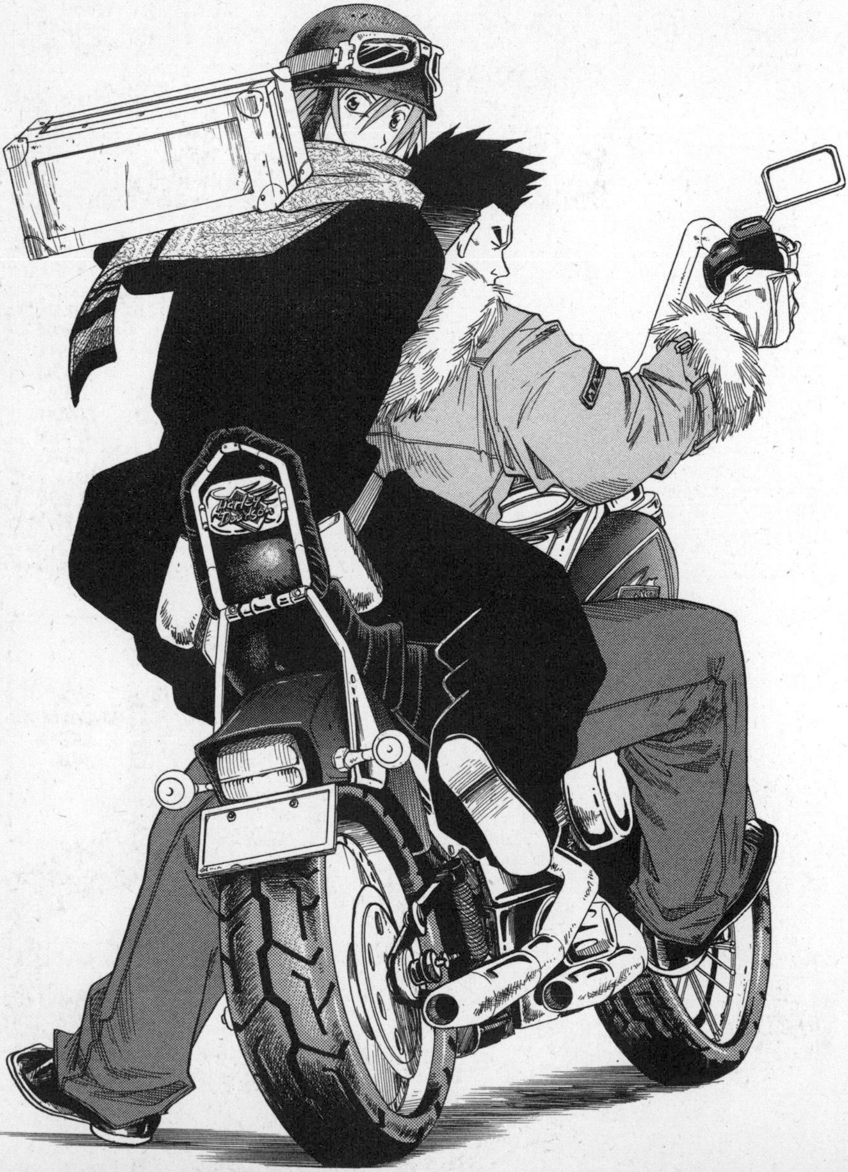

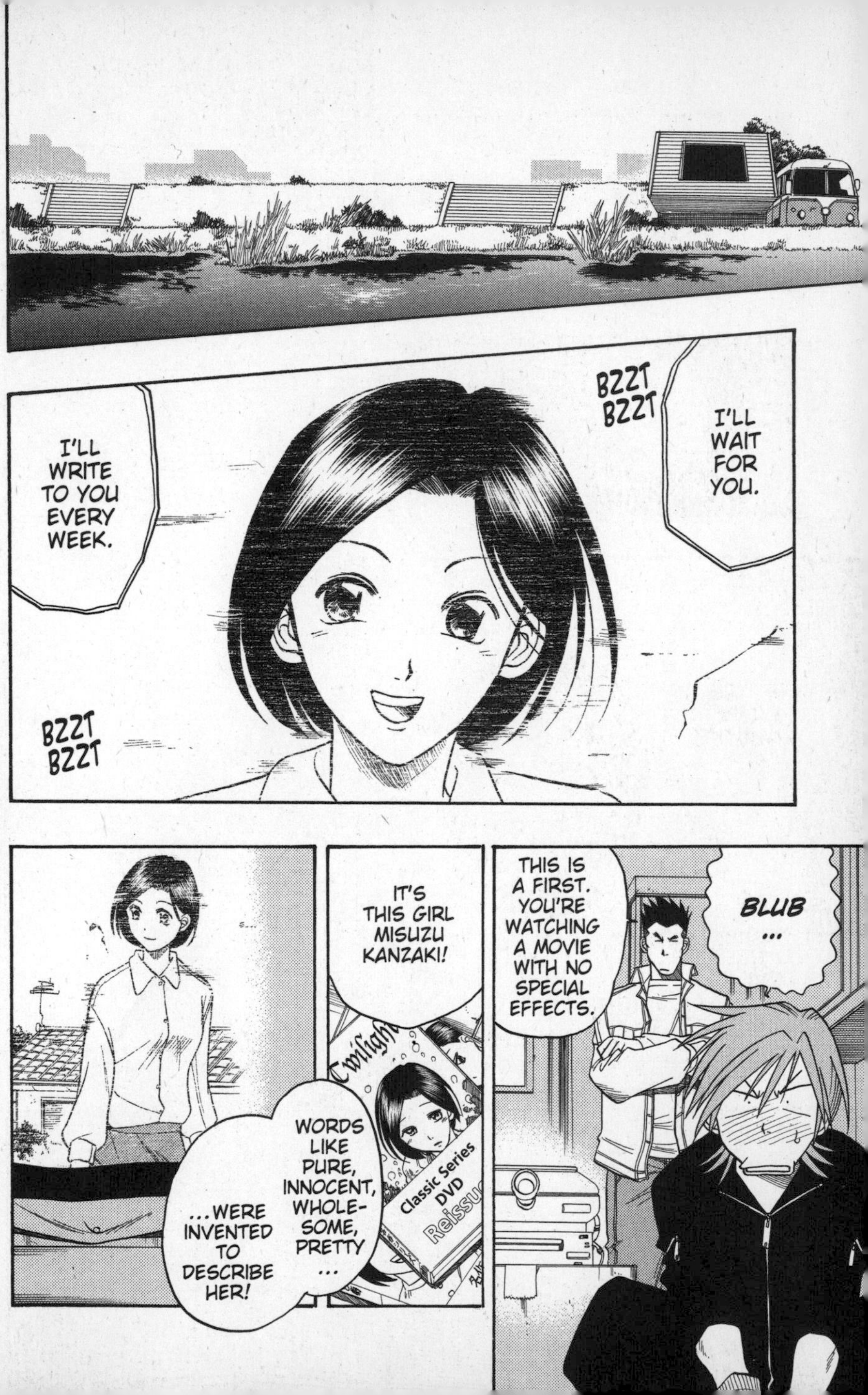
I'LL WAIT FOR YOU.
BZZT BZZT
I'LL WRITE TO YOU EVERY WEEK.
BZZT BZZT
BLUB ...
THIS IS A FIRST. YOU'RE WATCHING A MOVIE WITH NO SPECIAL EFFECTS.
IT'S THIS GIRL MISUZU KANZAKI!
Classic Series DVD
WORDS LIKE PURE, INNOCENT, WHOLE-SOME, PRETTY ...
...WERE INVENTED TO DESCRIBE HER!

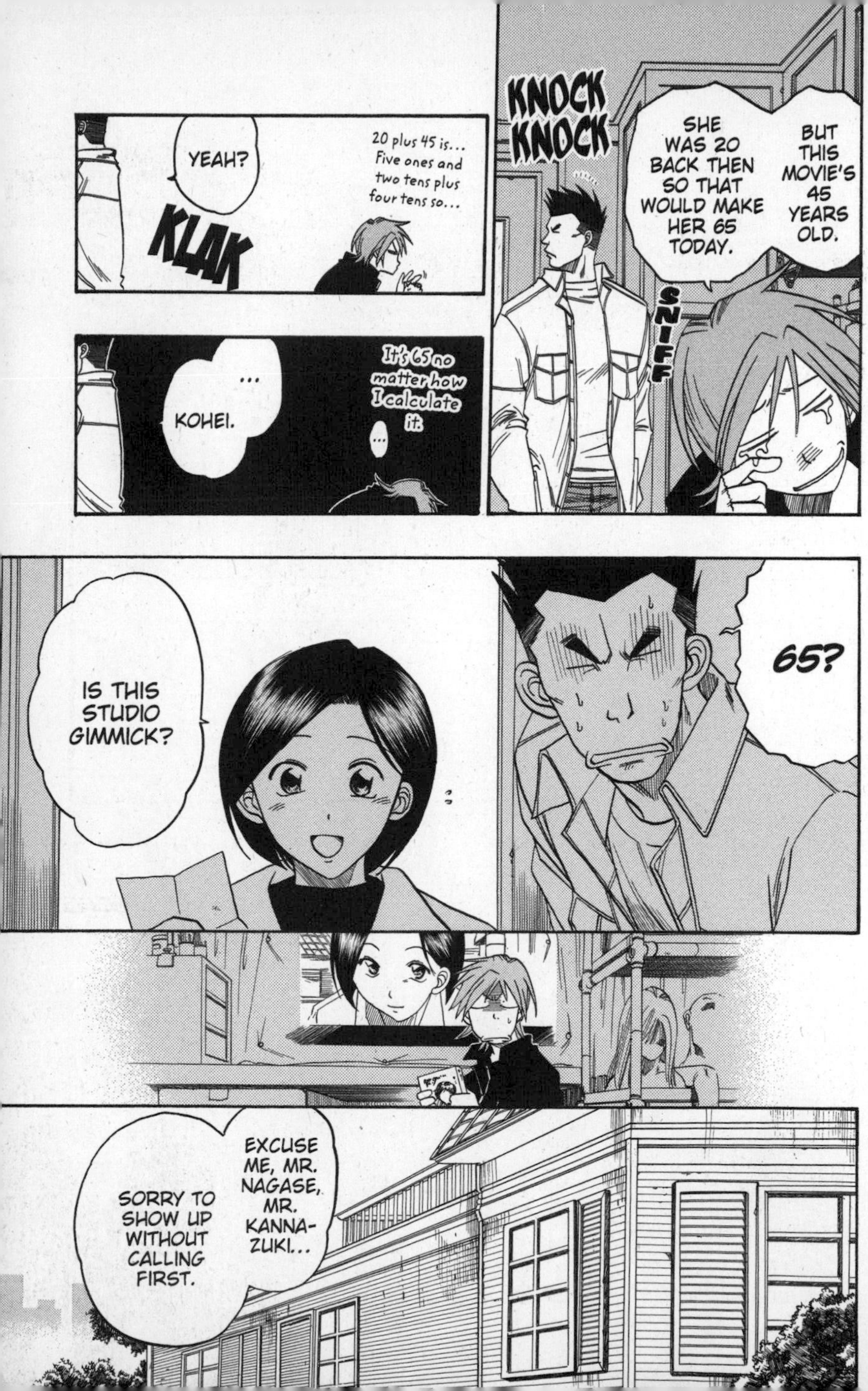
BUT THIS MOVIE'S 45 YEARS OLD.
SHE WAS 20 BACK THEN SO THAT WOULD MAKE HER 65 TODAY.
KNOCK KNOCK
SNIFF
20 plus 45 is... Five ones and two tens plus four tens so...
YEAH?
KLAK
It's 65 no matter how I calculate it.
...
... KOHEI.
65?
IS THIS STUDIO GIMMICK?
EXCUSE ME, MR. NAGASE, MR. KANNAZUKI...
SORRY TO SHOW UP WITHOUT CALLING FIRST.

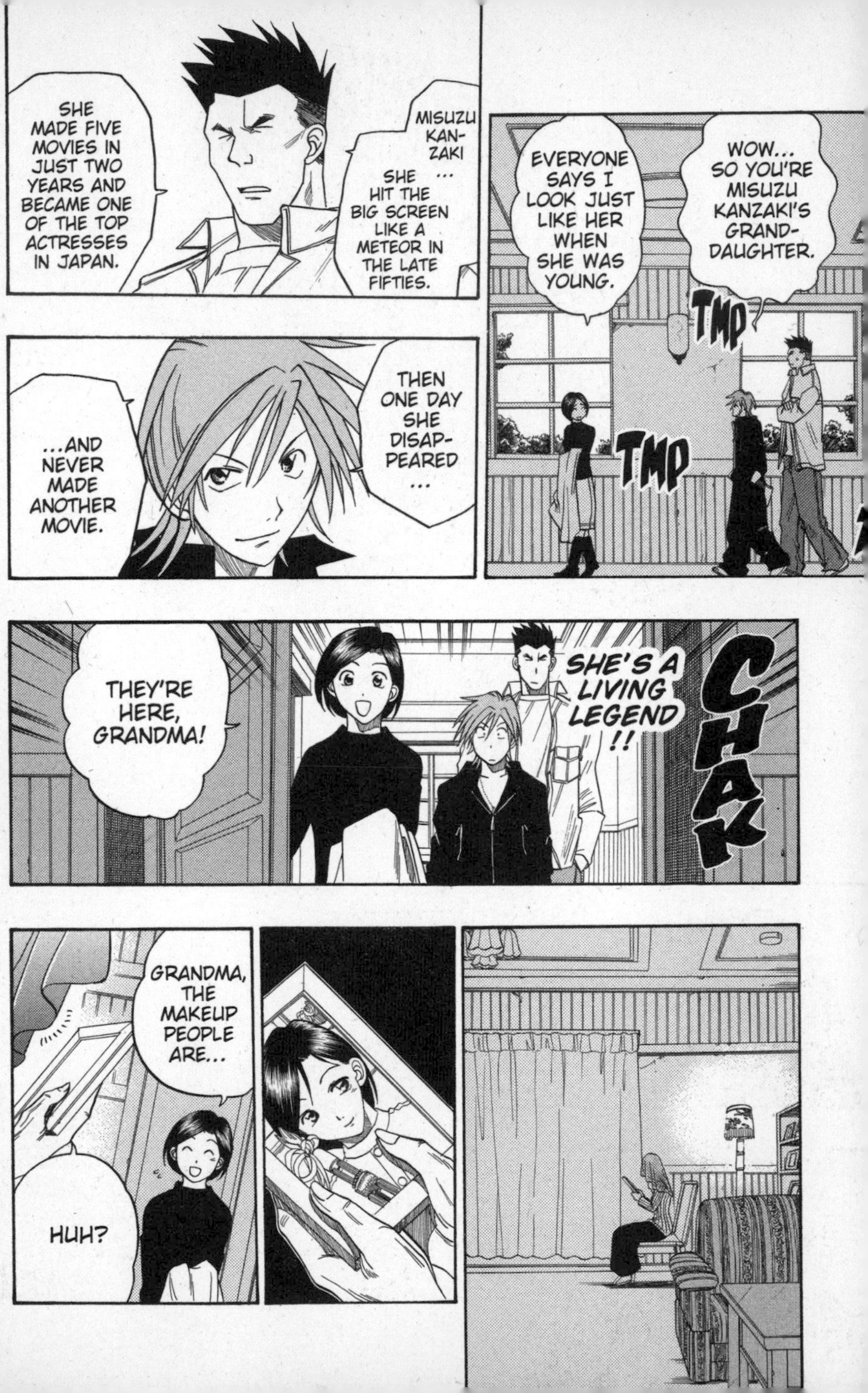
WOW... SO YOU'RE MISUZU KANZAKI'S GRAND-DAUGHTER.
EVERYONE SAYS I LOOK JUST LIKE HER WHEN SHE WAS YOUNG.
TMP
TMP
MISUZU KAN-ZAKI ...
SHE HIT THE BIG SCREEN LIKE A METEOR IN THE LATE FIFTIES.
SHE MADE FIVE MOVIES IN JUST TWO YEARS AND BECAME ONE OF THE TOP ACTRESSES IN JAPAN.
THEN ONE DAY SHE DISAP-PEARED ...
...AND NEVER MADE ANOTHER MOVIE.
CHAK
SHE'S A LIVING LEGEND !!
THEY'RE HERE, GRANDMA!
GRANDMA, THE MAKEUP PEOPLE ARE...
HUH?

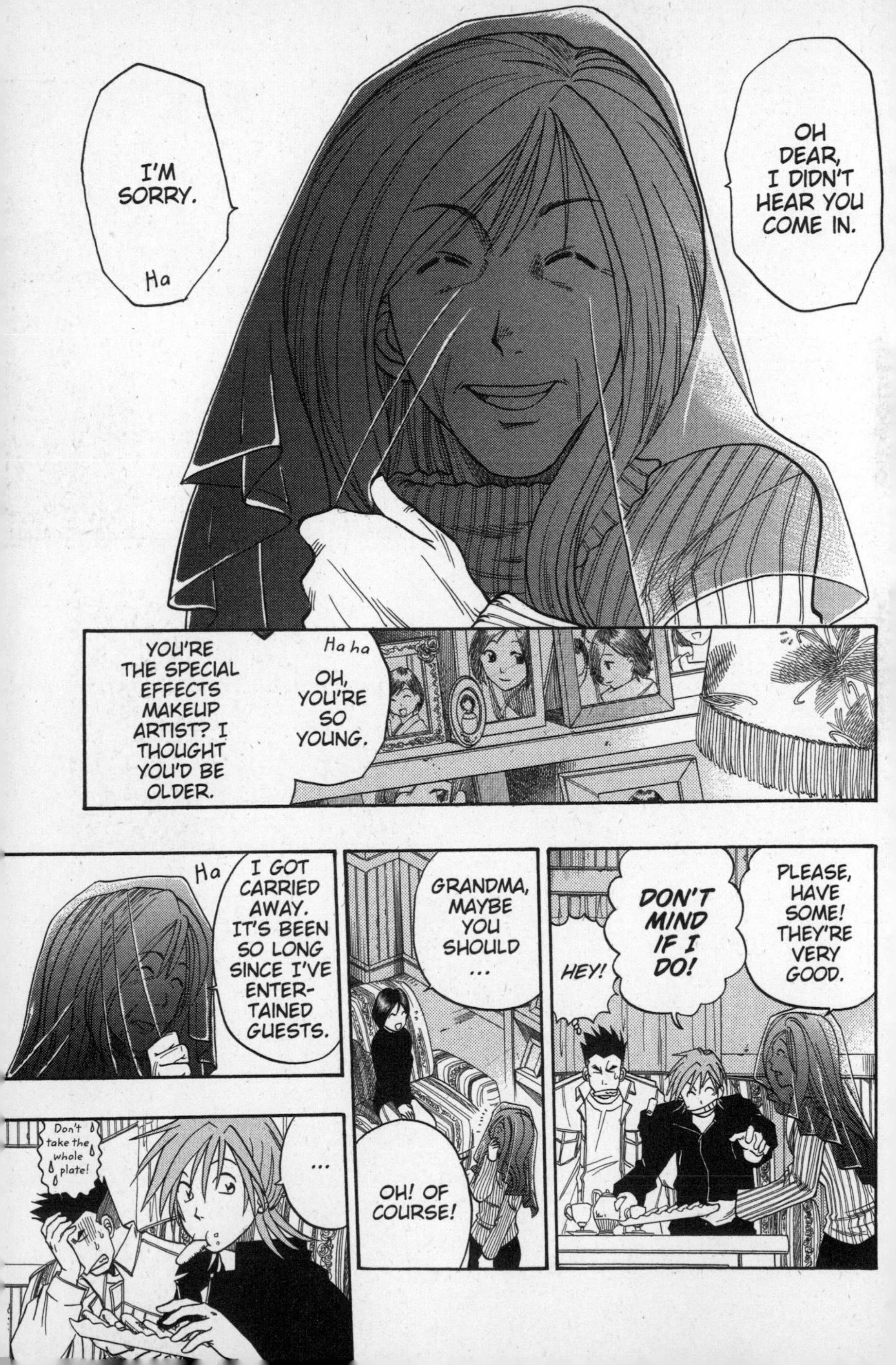
OH DEAR, I DIDN'T HEAR YOU COME IN.
I'M SORRY.
Ha
Ha ha
OH, YOU'RE SO YOUNG.
YOU'RE THE SPECIAL EFFECTS MAKEUP ARTIST? I THOUGHT YOU'D BE OLDER.
PLEASE, HAVE SOME! THEY'RE VERY GOOD.
DON'T MIND IF I DO!
HEY!
GRANDMA, MAYBE YOU SHOULD ...
OH! OF COURSE!
Ha
I GOT CARRIED AWAY. IT'S BEEN SO LONG SINCE I'VE ENTER-TAINED GUESTS.
...
Don't take the whole plate!

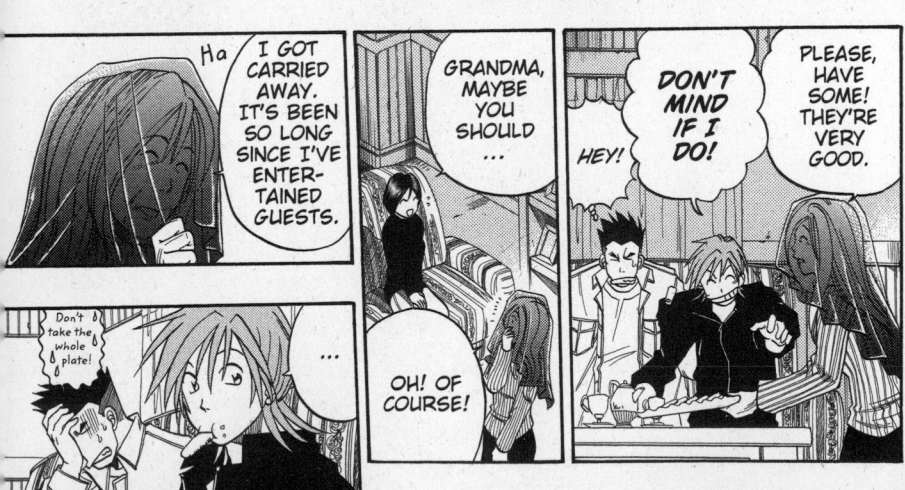

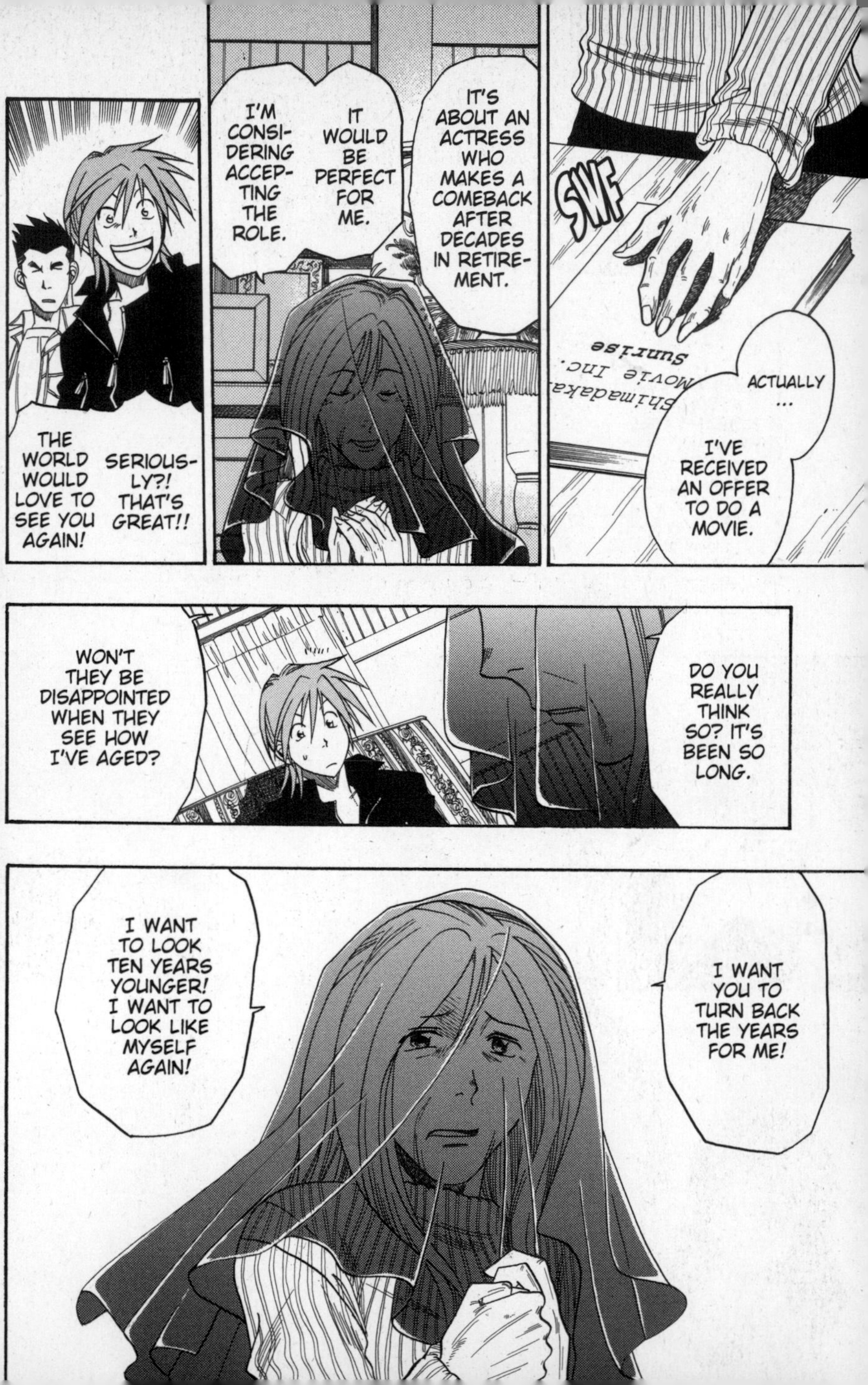
SWF
Shimadaka
Movie Inc.
Sunrise
ACTUALLY ...
I'VE RECEIVED AN OFFER TO DO A MOVIE.
IT'S ABOUT AN ACTRESS WHO MAKES A COMEBACK AFTER DECADES IN RETIREMENT.
IT WOULD BE PERFECT FOR ME.
I'M CONSIDERING ACCEPTING THE ROLE.
SERIOUSLY?! THAT'S GREAT!!
THE WORLD WOULD LOVE TO SEE YOU AGAIN!
DO YOU REALLY THINK SO? IT'S BEEN SO LONG.
WON'T THEY BE DISAPPOINTED WHEN THEY SEE HOW I'VE AGED?
I WANT YOU TO TURN BACK THE YEARS FOR ME!
I WANT TO LOOK TEN YEARS YOUNGER! I WANT TO LOOK LIKE MYSELF AGAIN!

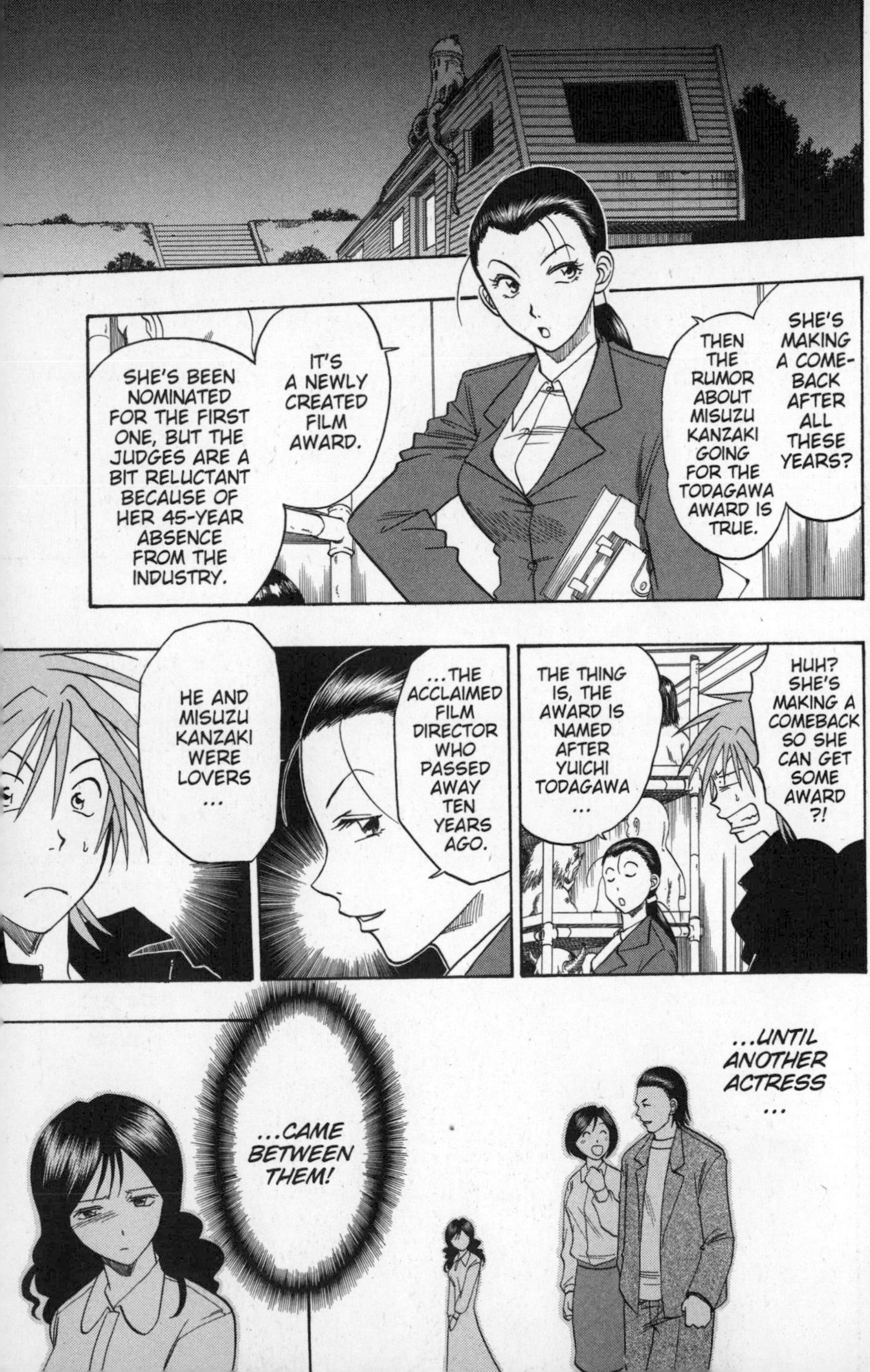
SHE'S MAKING A COME-BACK AFTER ALL THESE YEARS?
THEN THE RUMOR ABOUT MISUZU KANZAKI GOING FOR THE TODAGAWA AWARD IS TRUE.
IT'S A NEWLY CREATED FILM AWARD.
SHE'S BEEN NOMINATED FOR THE FIRST ONE, BUT THE JUDGES ARE A BIT RELUCTANT BECAUSE OF HER 45-YEAR ABSENCE FROM THE INDUSTRY.
HUH? SHE'S MAKING A COMEBACK SO SHE CAN GET SOME AWARD ?!
THE THING IS, THE AWARD IS NAMED AFTER YUICHI TODAGAWA ...
...THE ACCLAIMED FILM DIRECTOR WHO PASSED AWAY TEN YEARS AGO.
HE AND MISUZU KANZAKI WERE LOVERS ...
...UNTIL ANOTHER ACTRESS ...
...CAME BETWEEN THEM!

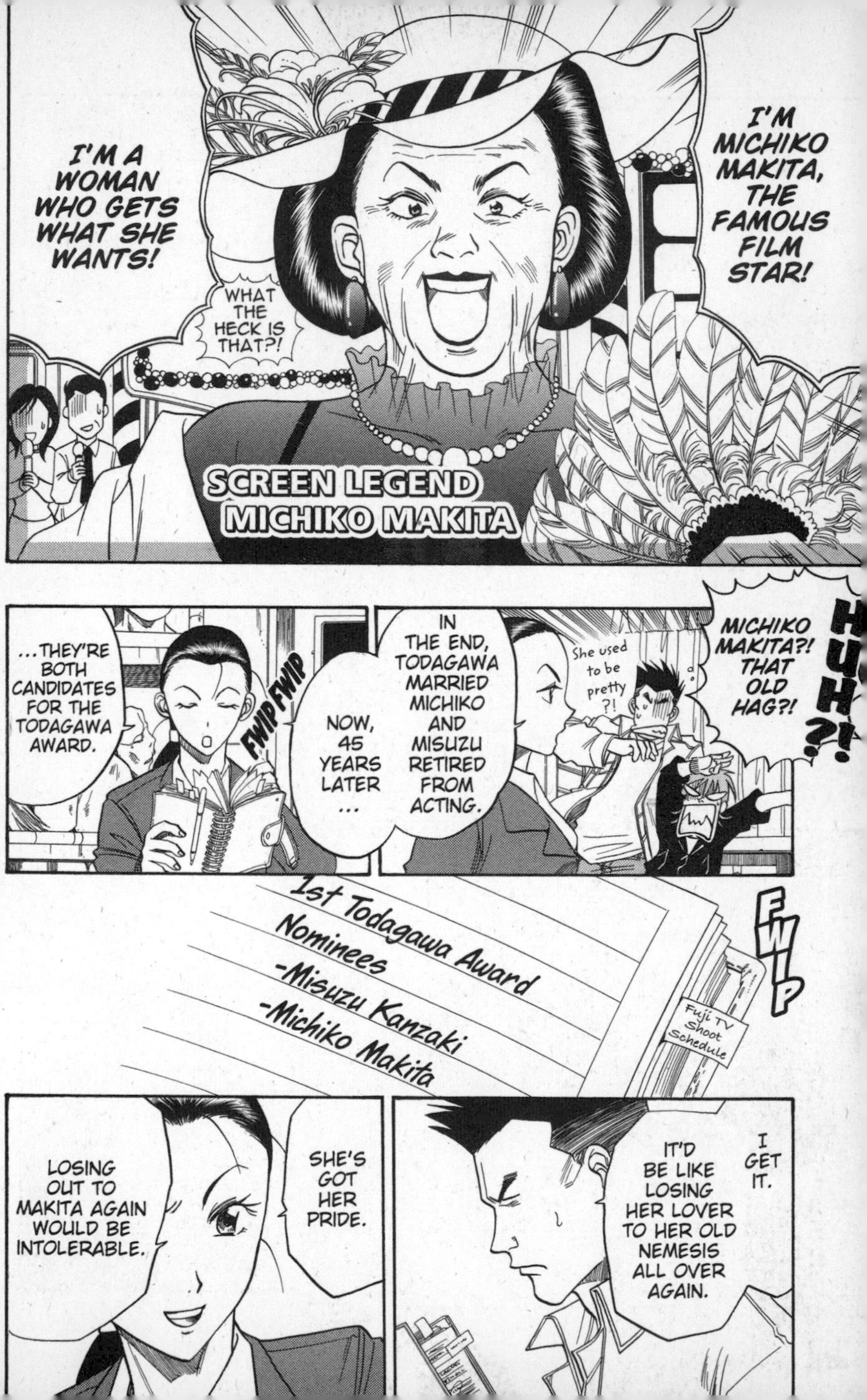
I'M MICHIKO MAKITA, THE FAMOUS FILM STAR!
I'M A WOMAN WHO GETS WHAT SHE WANTS!
WHAT THE HECK IS THAT?!
SCREEN LEGEND MICHIKO MAKITA
HUH?!
MICHIKO MAKITA?! THAT OLD HAG?!
She used to be pretty?!
IN THE END, TODAGAWA MARRIED MICHIKO AND MISUZU RETIRED FROM ACTING.
NOW, 45 YEARS LATER...
FWIP FWIP
...THEY'RE BOTH CANDIDATES FOR THE TODAGAWA AWARD.
FWIP
Fuji TV Shoot Schedule
1st Todagawa Award Nominees
-Misuzu Kanzaki
-Michiko Makita
I GET IT.
IT'D BE LIKE LOSING HER LOVER TO HER OLD NEMESIS ALL OVER AGAIN.
SHE'S GOT HER PRIDE.
LOSING OUT TO MAKITA AGAIN WOULD BE INTOLERABLE.

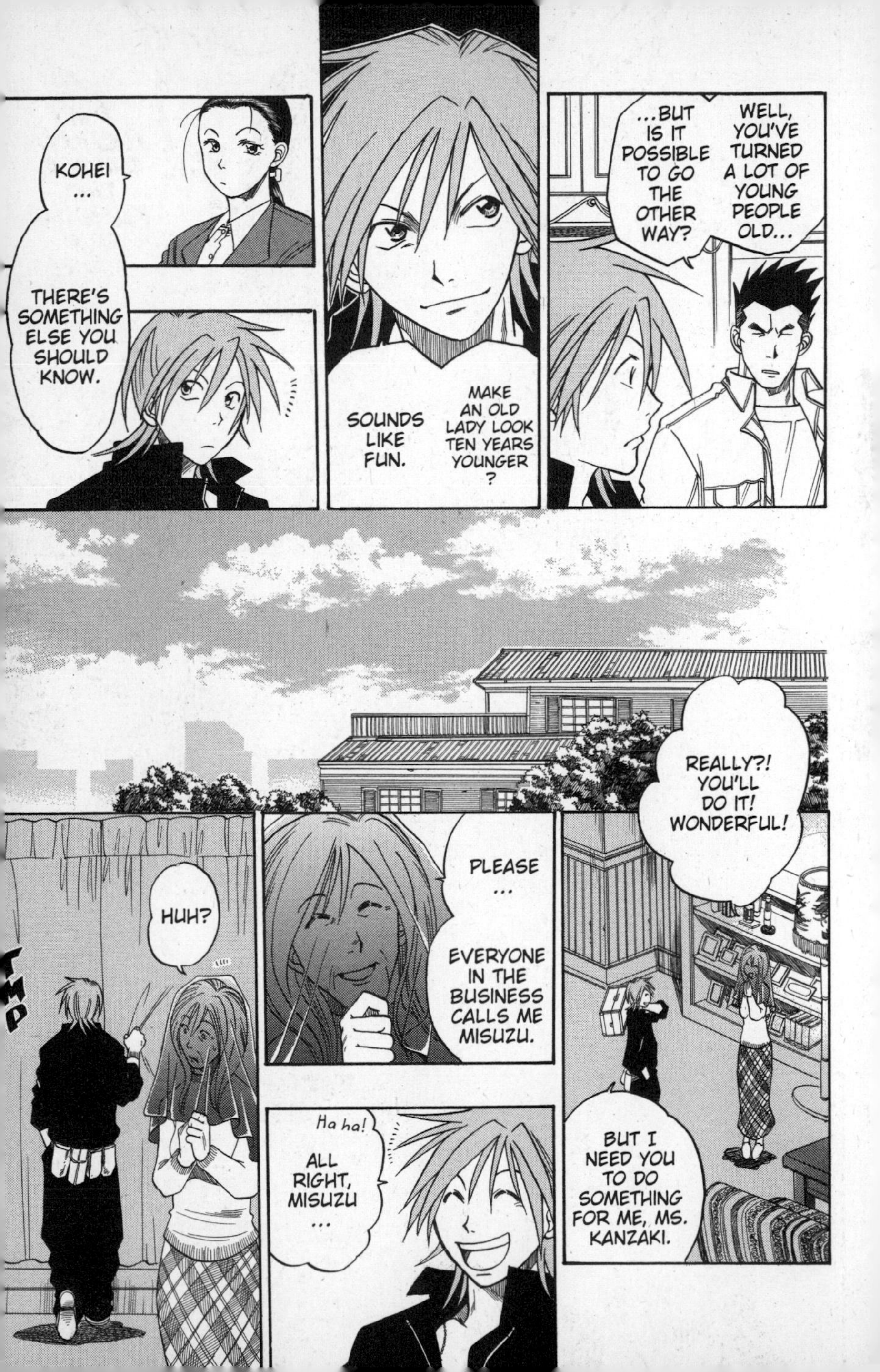
WELL, YOU'VE TURNED A LOT OF YOUNG PEOPLE OLD...
...BUT IS IT POSSIBLE TO GO THE OTHER WAY?
MAKE AN OLD LADY LOOK TEN YEARS YOUNGER?
SOUNDS LIKE FUN.
KOHEI...
THERE'S SOMETHING ELSE YOU SHOULD KNOW.
REALLY?! YOU'LL DO IT! WONDERFUL!
BUT I NEED YOU TO DO SOMETHING FOR ME, MS. KANZAKI.
PLEASE...
EVERYONE IN THE BUSINESS CALLS ME MISUZU.
Ha ha!
ALL RIGHT, MISUZU...
HUH?
TMP

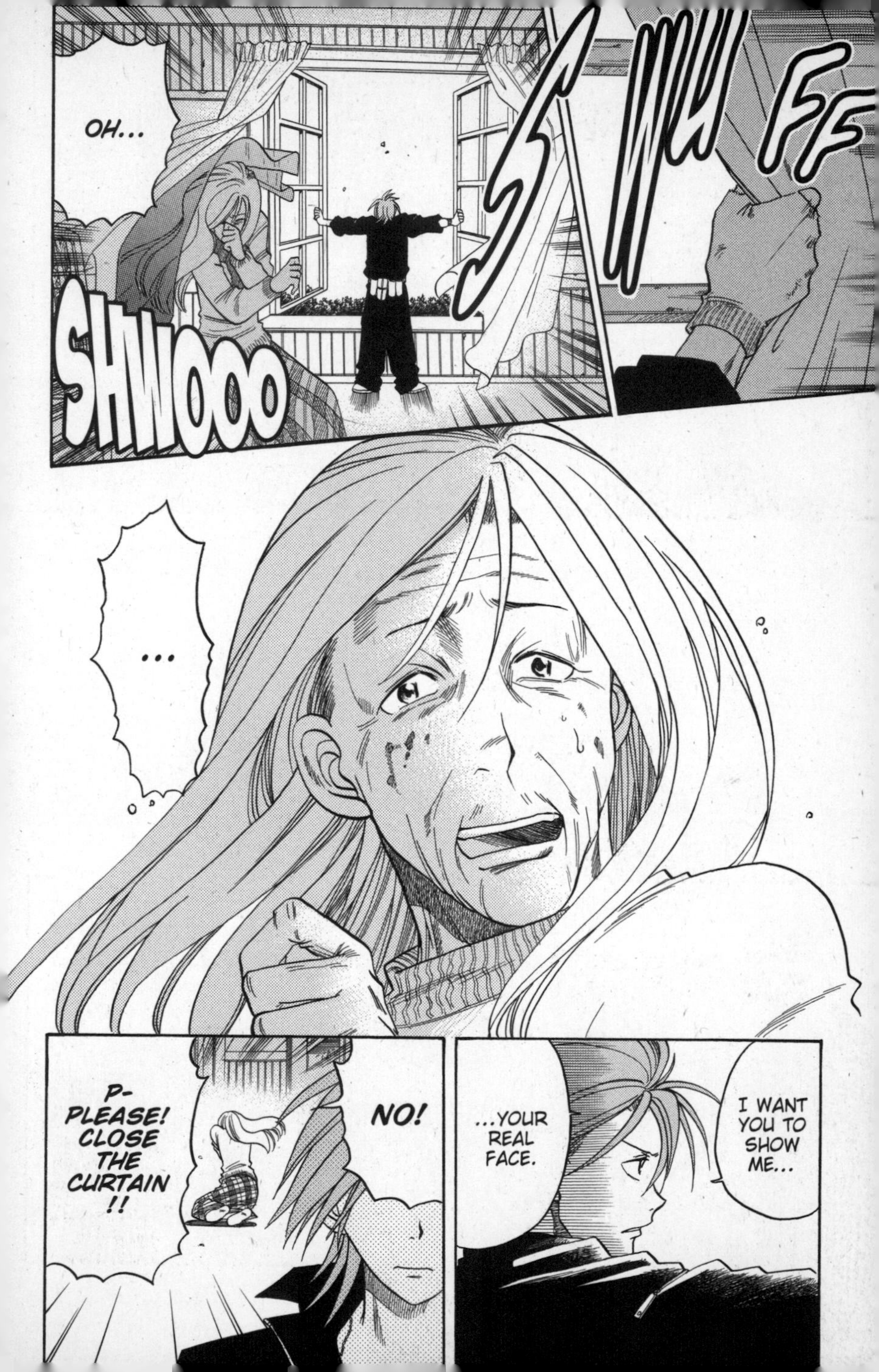
SHUFF
OH...
SHWOOO
...
I WANT YOU TO SHOW ME...
...YOUR REAL FACE.
NO!
P-PLEASE! CLOSE THE CURTAIN!!

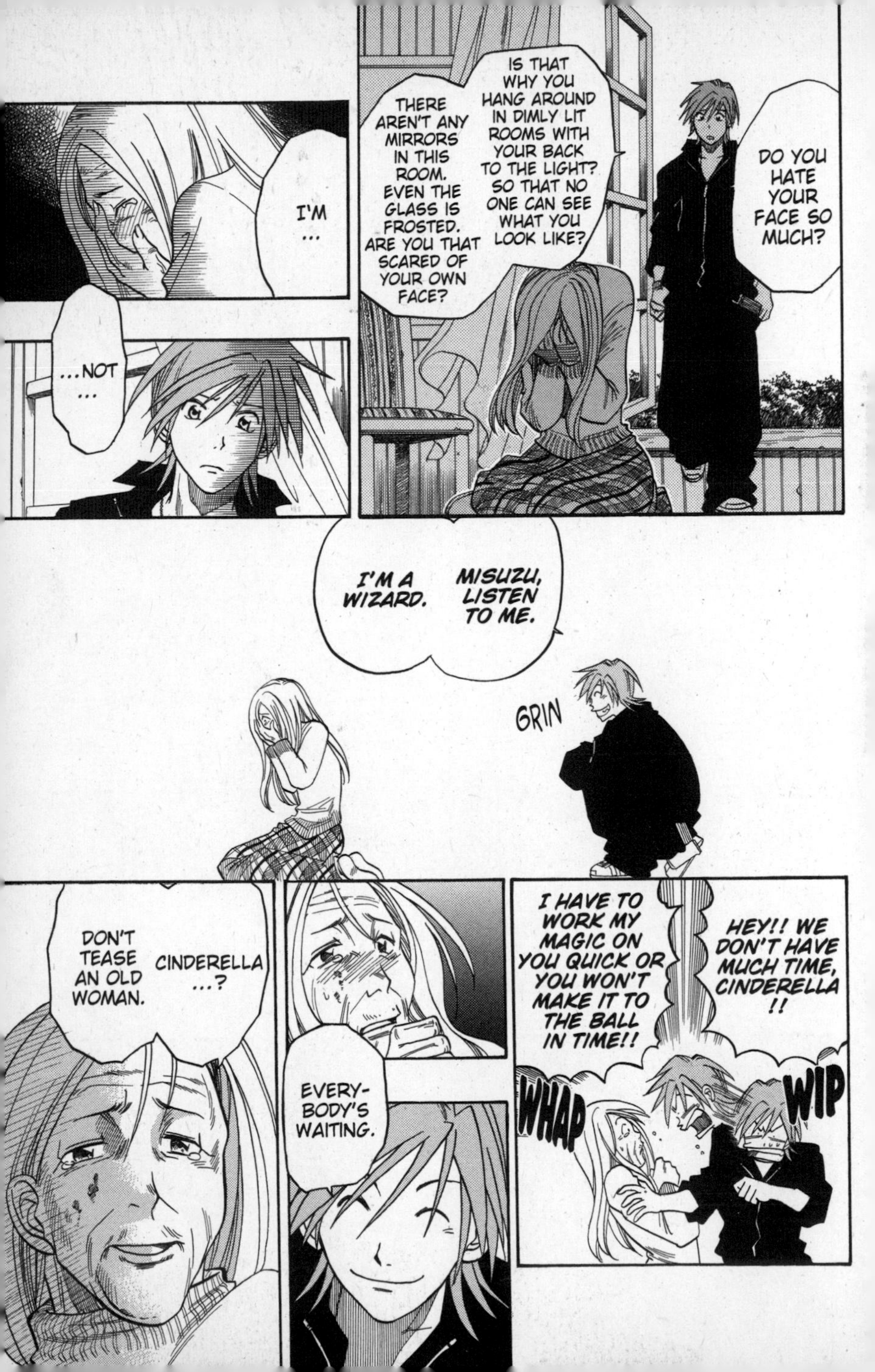
DO YOU HATE YOUR FACE SO MUCH?
IS THAT WHY YOU HANG AROUND IN DIMLY LIT ROOMS WITH YOUR BACK TO THE LIGHT? SO THAT NO ONE CAN SEE WHAT YOU LOOK LIKE?
THERE AREN'T ANY MIRRORS IN THIS ROOM. EVEN THE GLASS IS FROSTED. ARE YOU THAT SCARED OF YOUR OWN FACE?
I'M ...
...NOT ...
MISUZU, LISTEN TO ME.
I'M A WIZARD.
GRIN
HEY!! WE DON'T HAVE MUCH TIME, CINDERELLA !!
I HAVE TO WORK MY MAGIC ON YOU QUICK OR YOU WON'T MAKE IT TO THE BALL IN TIME!!
WIP
WHAP
EVERY-BODY'S WAITING.
CINDERELLA ...?
DON'T TEASE AN OLD WOMAN.

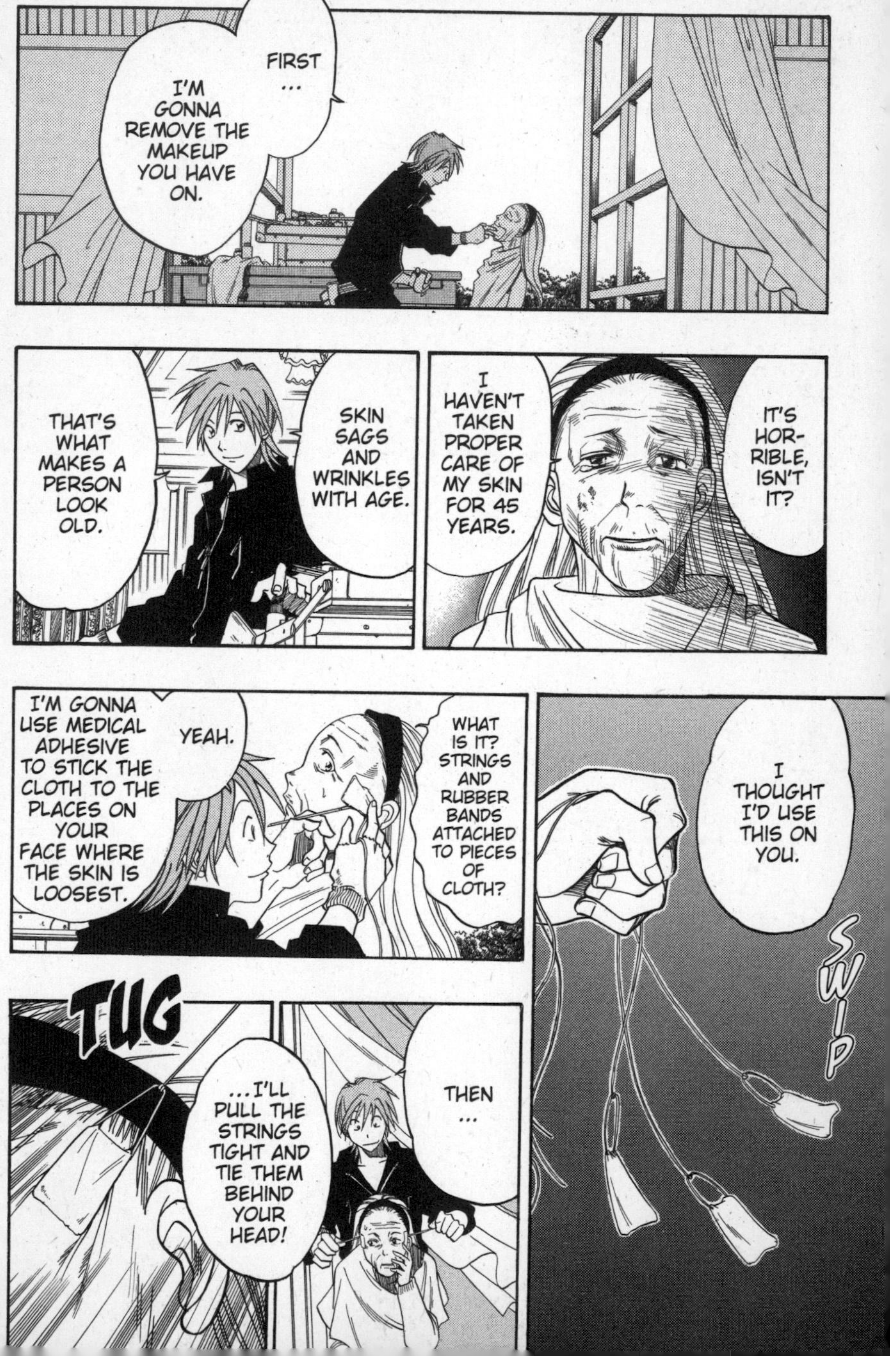
FIRST ...
I'M GONNA REMOVE THE MAKEUP YOU HAVE ON.
IT'S HOR-RIBLE, ISN'T IT?
I HAVEN'T TAKEN PROPER CARE OF MY SKIN FOR 45 YEARS.
SKIN SAGS AND WRINKLES WITH AGE.
THAT'S WHAT MAKES A PERSON LOOK OLD.
I THOUGHT I'D USE THIS ON YOU.
SWIP
WHAT IS IT? STRINGS AND RUBBER BANDS ATTACHED TO PIECES OF CLOTH?
YEAH.
I'M GONNA USE MEDICAL ADHESIVE TO STICK THE CLOTH TO THE PLACES ON YOUR FACE WHERE THE SKIN IS LOOSEST.
THEN ...
...I'LL PULL THE STRINGS TIGHT AND TIE THEM BEHIND YOUR HEAD!
TUG

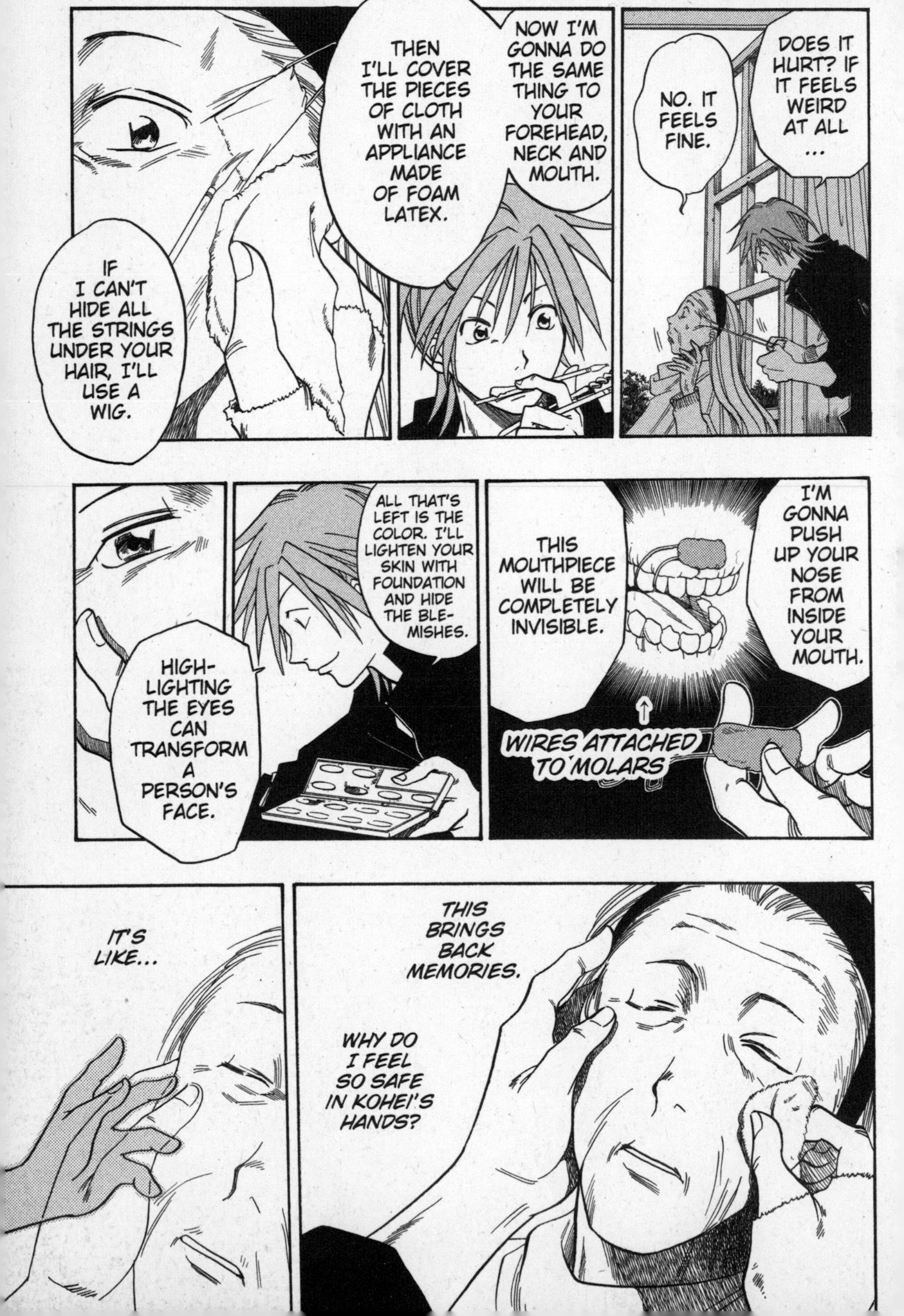
DOES IT HURT? IF IT FEELS WEIRD AT ALL ...
NO. IT FEELS FINE.
NOW I'M GONNA DO THE SAME THING TO YOUR FOREHEAD, NECK AND MOUTH.
THEN I'LL COVER THE PIECES OF CLOTH WITH AN APPLIANCE MADE OF FOAM LATEX.
IF I CAN'T HIDE ALL THE STRINGS UNDER YOUR HAIR, I'LL USE A WIG.
I'M GONNA PUSH UP YOUR NOSE FROM INSIDE YOUR MOUTH.
THIS MOUTHPIECE WILL BE COMPLETELY INVISIBLE.
WIRES ATTACHED TO MOLARS
ALL THAT'S LEFT IS THE COLOR. I'LL LIGHTEN YOUR SKIN WITH FOUNDATION AND HIDE THE BLE-MISHES.
HIGH-LIGHTING THE EYES CAN TRANSFORM A PERSON'S FACE.
THIS BRINGS BACK MEMORIES.
WHY DO I FEEL SO SAFE IN KOHEI'S HANDS?
IT'S LIKE...

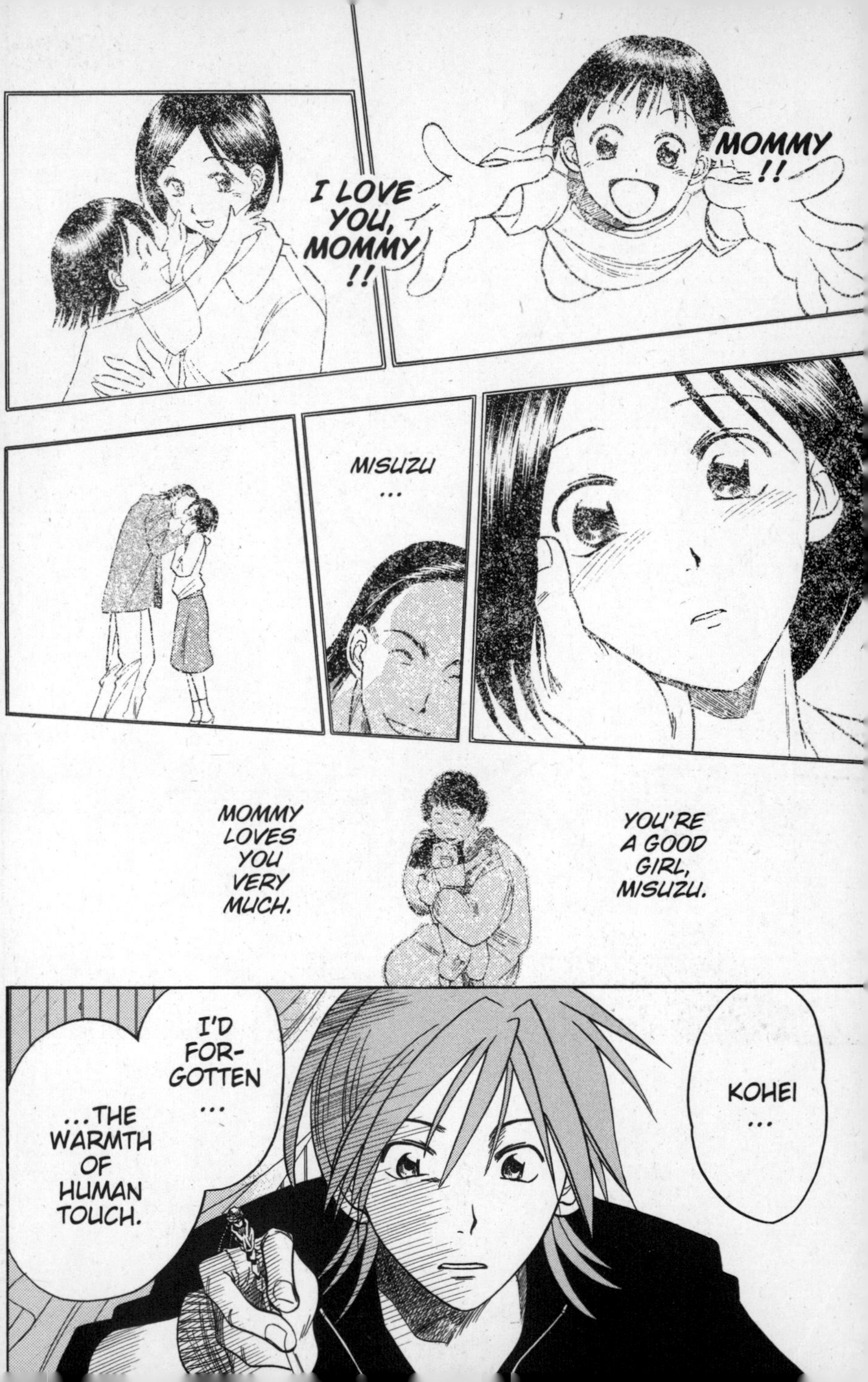
MOMMY !!
I LOVE YOU, MOMMY !!
MISUZU ...
YOU'RE A GOOD GIRL, MISUZU.
MOMMY LOVES YOU VERY MUCH.
KOHEI ...
I'D FOR-GOTTEN ...
...THE WARMTH OF HUMAN TOUCH.

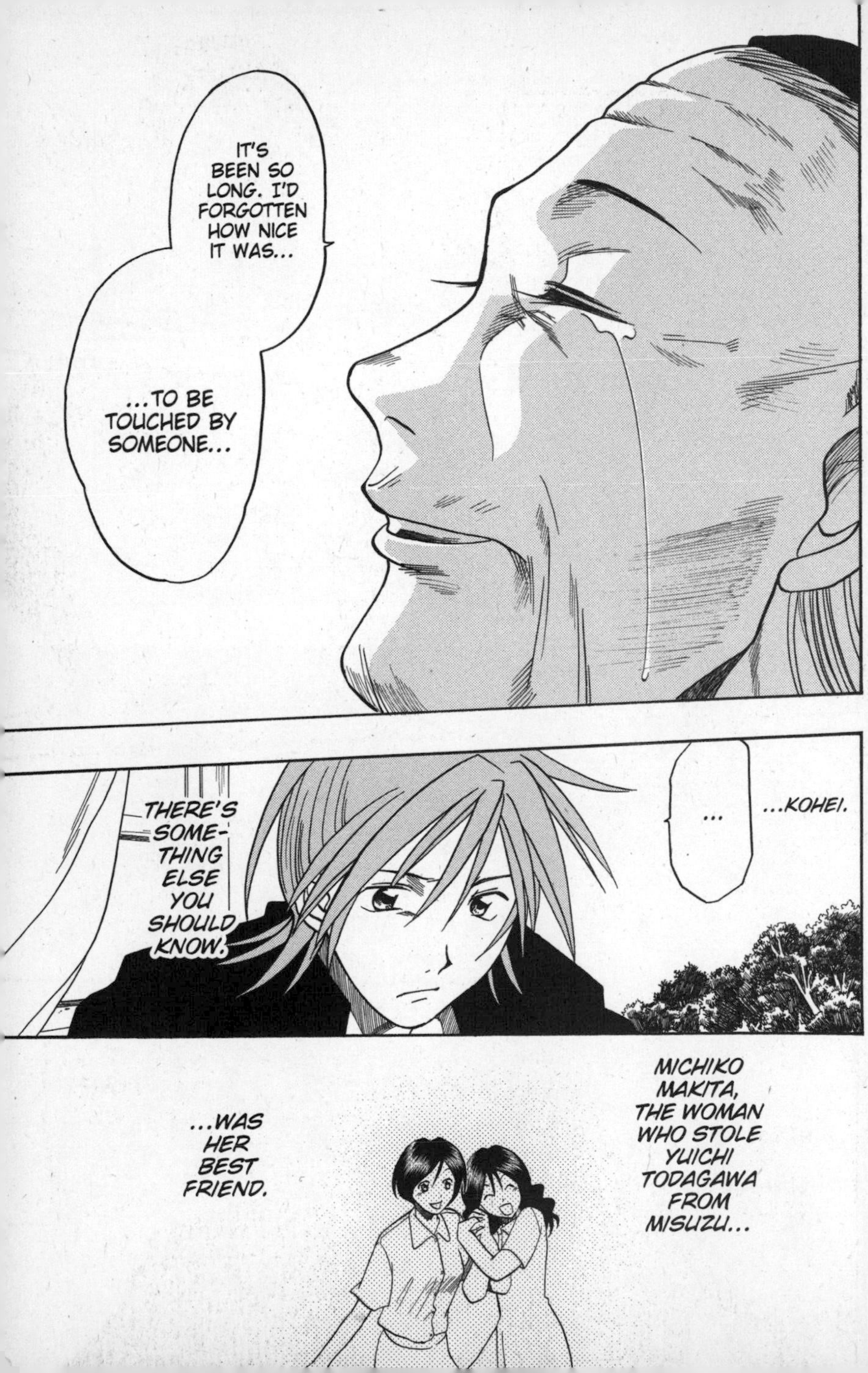
IT'S BEEN SO LONG. I'D FORGOTTEN HOW NICE IT WAS...
...TO BE TOUCHED BY SOMEONE...
...KOHEI.
...
THERE'S SOME-THING ELSE YOU SHOULD KNOW.
MICHIKO MAKITA, THE WOMAN WHO STOLE YUICHI TODAGAWA FROM MISUZU...
...WAS HER BEST FRIEND.

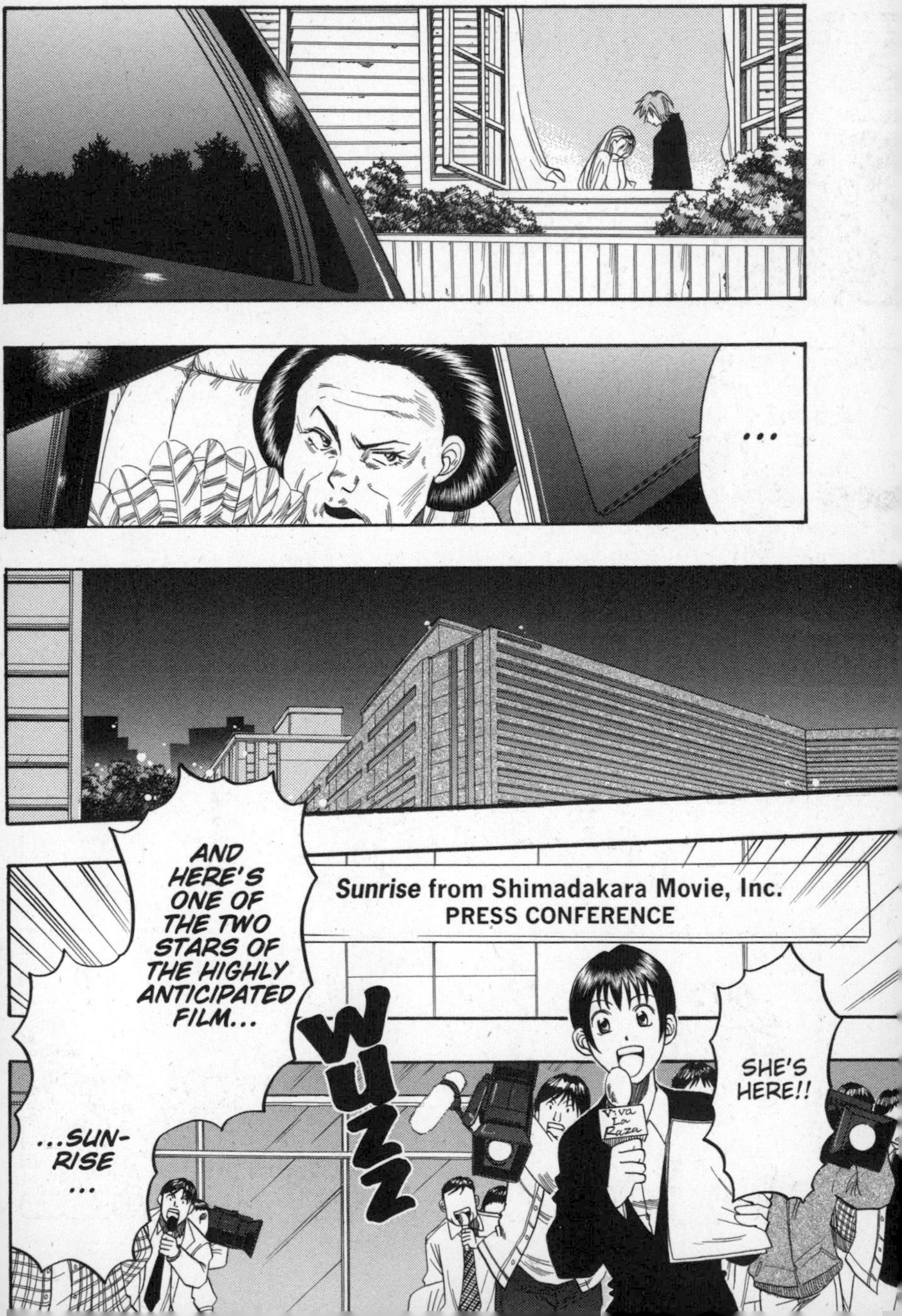
...
Sunrise from Shimadakara Movie, Inc.
PRESS CONFERENCE
SHE'S HERE!!
AND HERE'S ONE OF THE TWO STARS OF THE HIGHLY ANTICIPATED FILM...
WUZZ
...SUN-RISE...
Viva La Raza

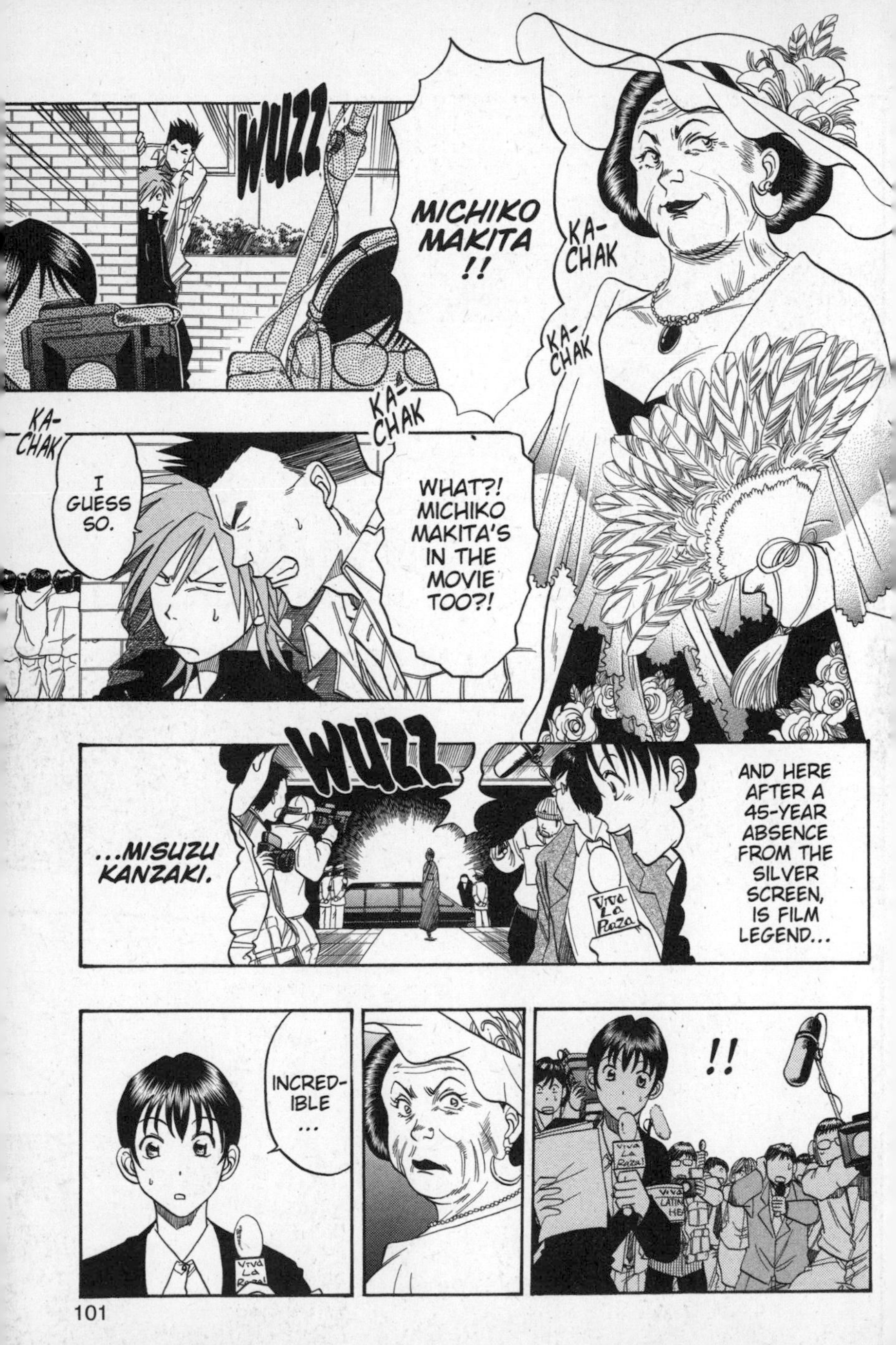

MICHIKO MAKITA !!
KA-CHAK
KA-CHAK
WUZZ
KA-CHAK
WHAT?! MICHIKO MAKITA'S IN THE MOVIE TOO?!
KA-CHAK
I GUESS SO.
AND HERE AFTER A 45-YEAR ABSENCE FROM THE SILVER SCREEN, IS FILM LEGEND...
WUZZ
...MISUZU KANZAKI.
!!
INCRED-IBLE ...

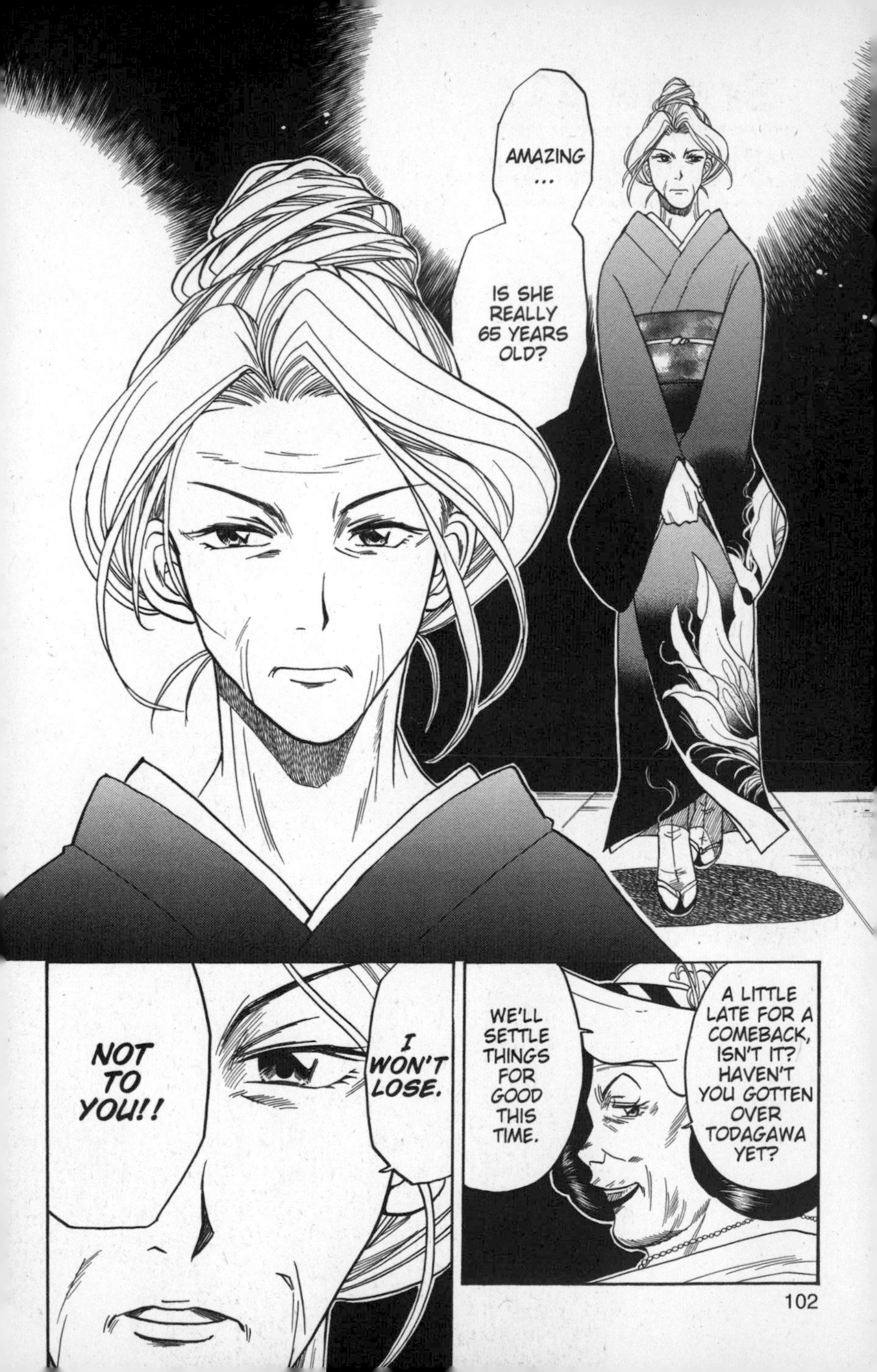
AMAZING ...
IS SHE REALLY 65 YEARS OLD?
A LITTLE LATE FOR A COMEBACK, ISN'T IT? HAVEN'T YOU GOTTEN OVER TODAGAWA YET?
WE'LL SETTLE THINGS FOR GOOD THIS TIME.
I WON'T LOSE.
NOT TO YOU!!

Scene 31: Sunrise Boulevard (Part 2)

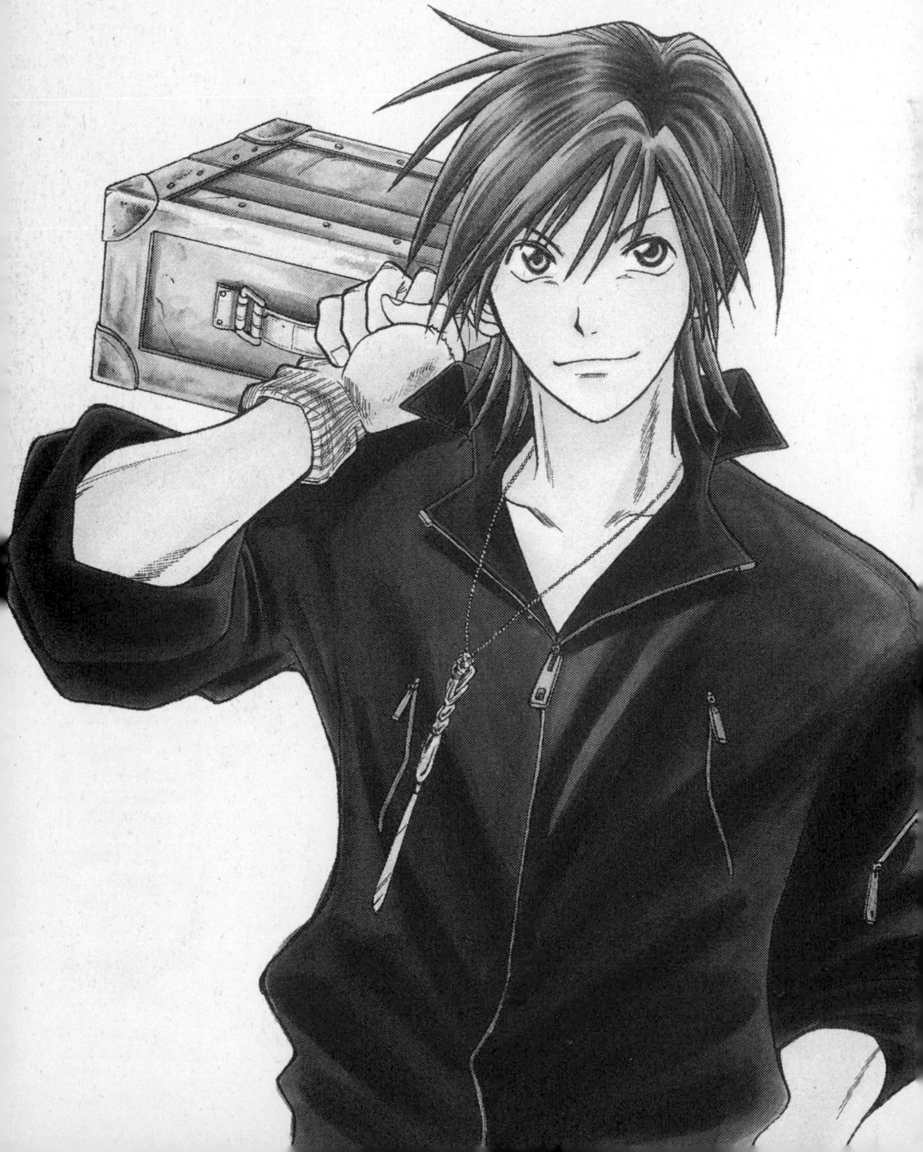

GIMMICK!

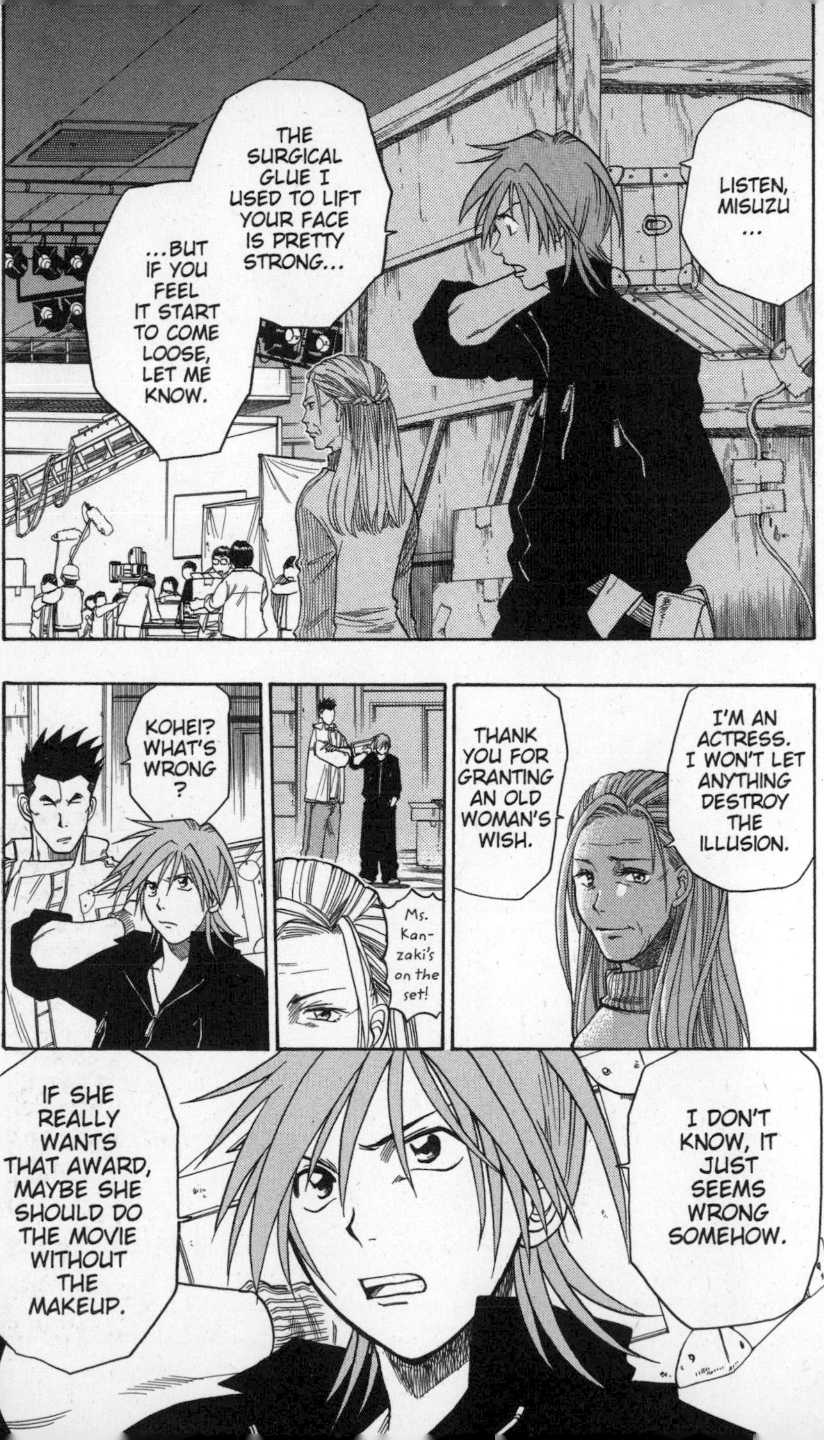
LISTEN, MISUZU...
THE SURGICAL GLUE I USED TO LIFT YOUR FACE IS PRETTY STRONG...
...BUT IF YOU FEEL IT START TO COME LOOSE, LET ME KNOW.
I'M AN ACTRESS. I WON'T LET ANYTHING DESTROY THE ILLUSION.
THANK YOU FOR GRANTING AN OLD WOMAN'S WISH.
Ms. Kanzaki's on the set!
KOHEI? WHAT'S WRONG?
I DON'T KNOW, IT JUST SEEMS WRONG SOMEHOW.
IF SHE REALLY WANTS THAT AWARD, MAYBE SHE SHOULD DO THE MOVIE WITHOUT THE MAKEUP.

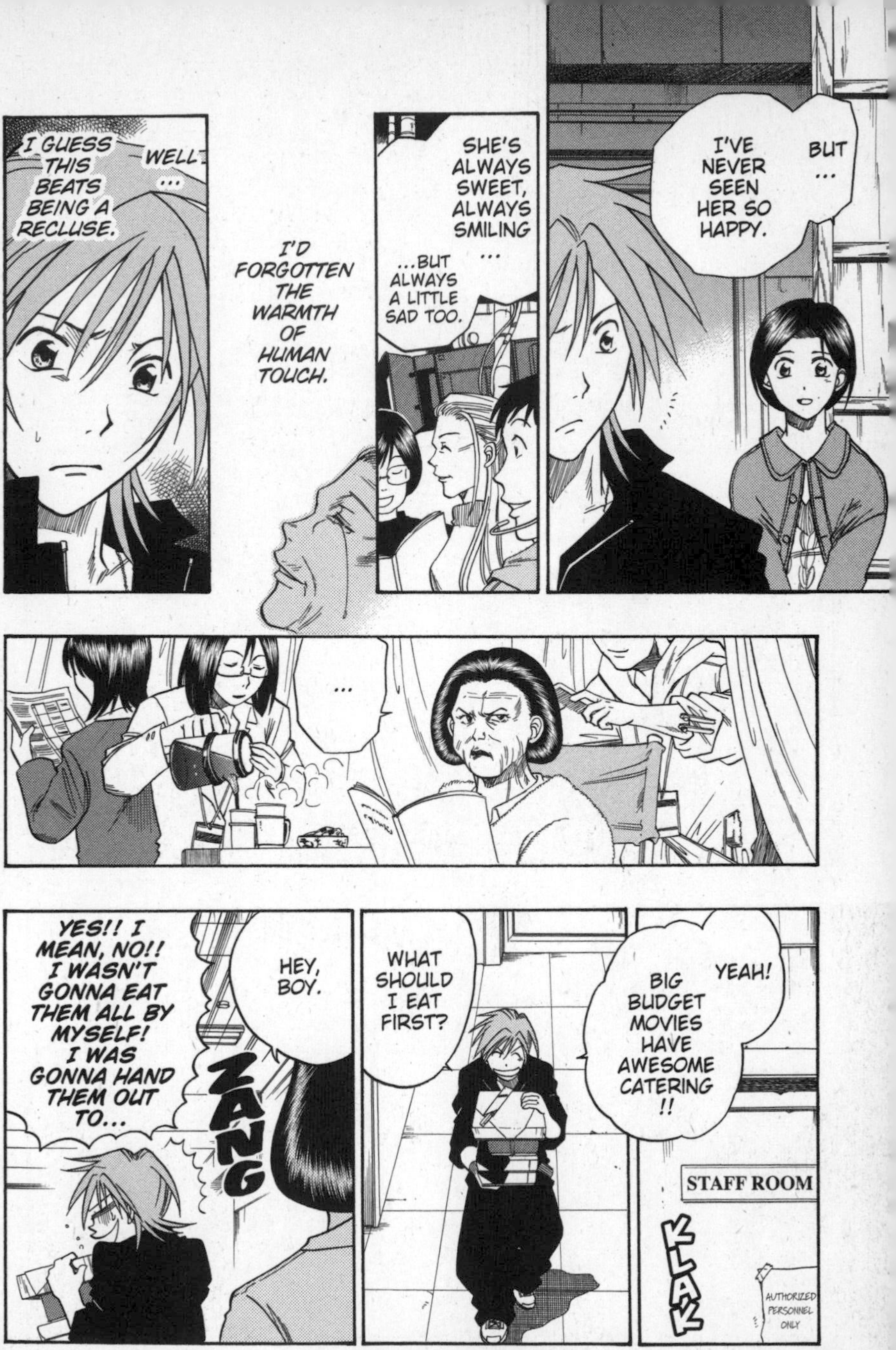
BUT ...
I'VE NEVER SEEN HER SO HAPPY.
SHE'S ALWAYS SWEET, ALWAYS SMILING ...
...BUT ALWAYS A LITTLE SAD TOO.
I'D FORGOTTEN THE WARMTH OF HUMAN TOUCH.
WELL ...
I GUESS THIS BEATS BEING A RECLUSE.
...
YEAH!
BIG BUDGET MOVIES HAVE AWESOME CATERING !!
STAFF ROOM
KLAK
AUTHORIZED PERSONNEL ONLY
WHAT SHOULD I EAT FIRST?
HEY, BOY.
ZANG
YES!! I MEAN, NO!! I WASN'T GONNA EAT THEM ALL BY MYSELF! I WAS GONNA HAND THEM OUT TO...

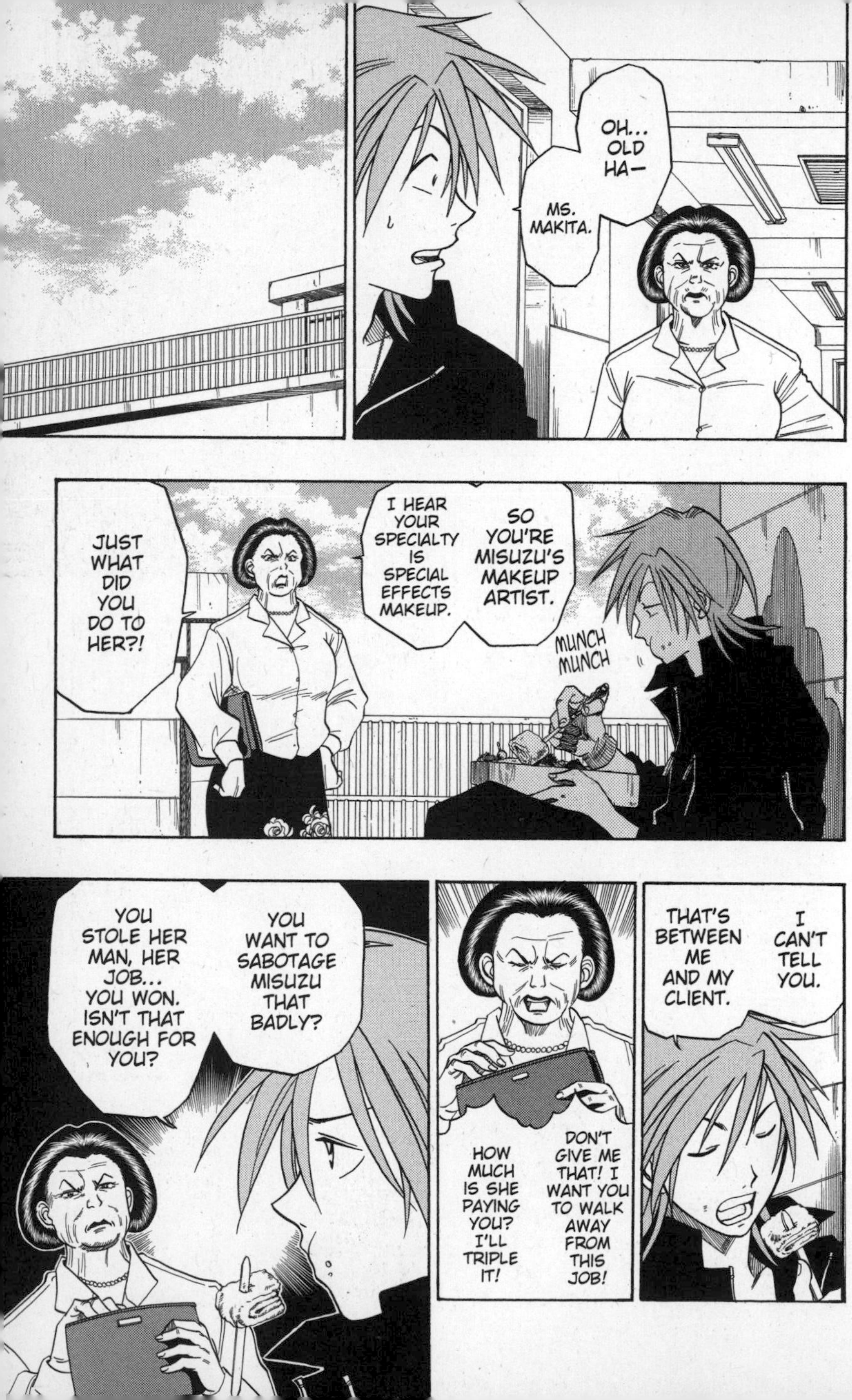
OH... OLD HA—
MS. MAKITA.
SO YOU'RE MISUZU'S MAKEUP ARTIST.
I HEAR YOUR SPECIALTY IS SPECIAL EFFECTS MAKEUP.
MUNCH MUNCH
JUST WHAT DID YOU DO TO HER?!
I CAN'T TELL YOU.
THAT'S BETWEEN ME AND MY CLIENT.
DON'T GIVE ME THAT! I WANT YOU TO WALK AWAY FROM THIS JOB!
HOW MUCH IS SHE PAYING YOU? I'LL TRIPLE IT!
YOU WANT TO SABOTAGE MISUZU THAT BADLY?
YOU STOLE HER MAN, HER JOB... YOU WON. ISN'T THAT ENOUGH FOR YOU?

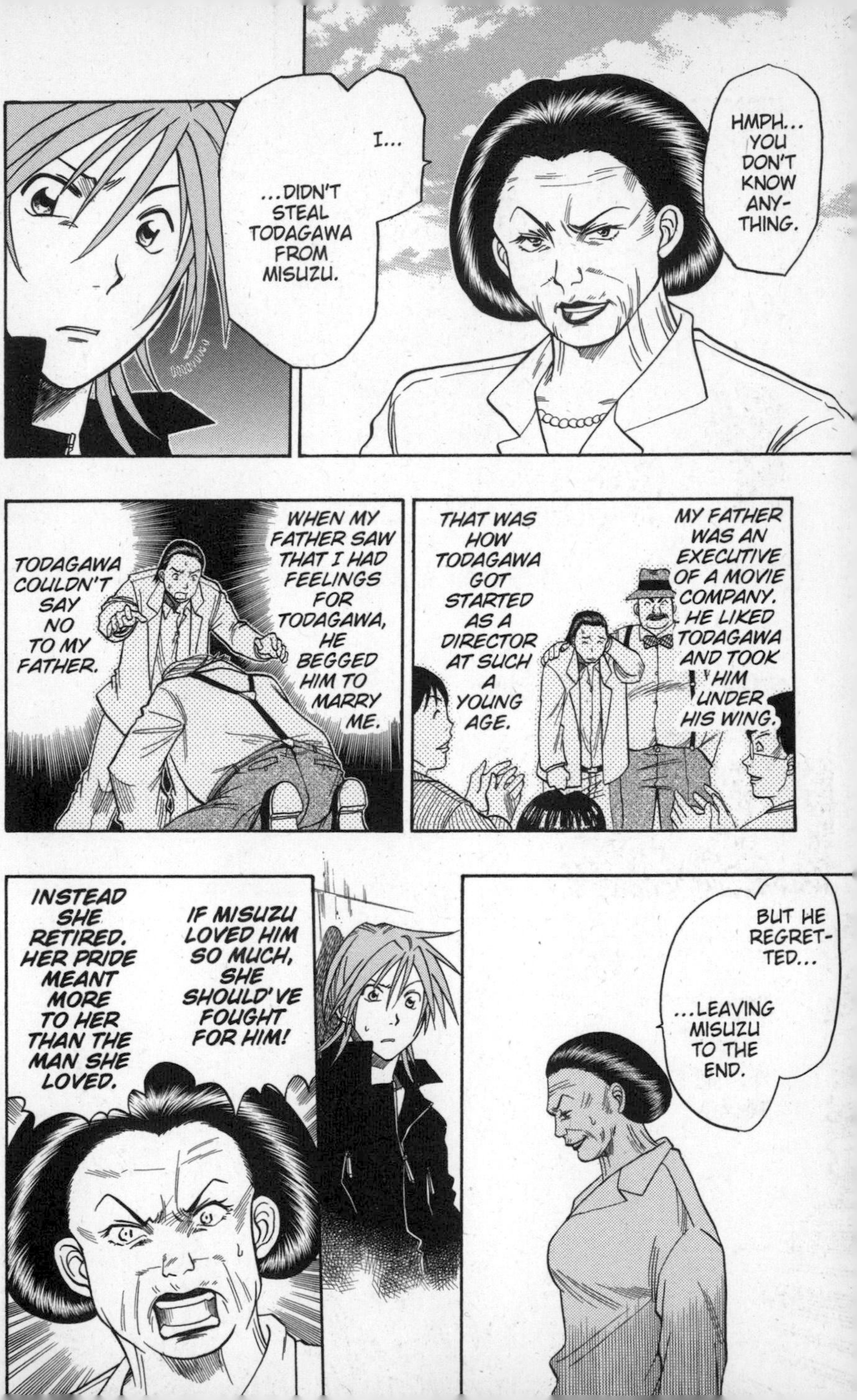
HMPH... YOU DON'T KNOW ANYTHING.
I...
...DIDN'T STEAL TODAGAWA FROM MISUZU.
MY FATHER WAS AN EXECUTIVE OF A MOVIE COMPANY. HE LIKED TODAGAWA AND TOOK HIM UNDER HIS WING.
THAT WAS HOW TODAGAWA GOT STARTED AS A DIRECTOR AT SUCH A YOUNG AGE.
WHEN MY FATHER SAW THAT I HAD FEELINGS FOR TODAGAWA, HE BEGGED HIM TO MARRY ME.
TODAGAWA COULDN'T SAY NO TO MY FATHER.
BUT HE REGRETTED...
...LEAVING MISUZU TO THE END.
IF MISUZU LOVED HIM SO MUCH, SHE SHOULD'VE FOUGHT FOR HIM!
INSTEAD SHE RETIRED. HER PRIDE MEANT MORE TO HER THAN THE MAN SHE LOVED.

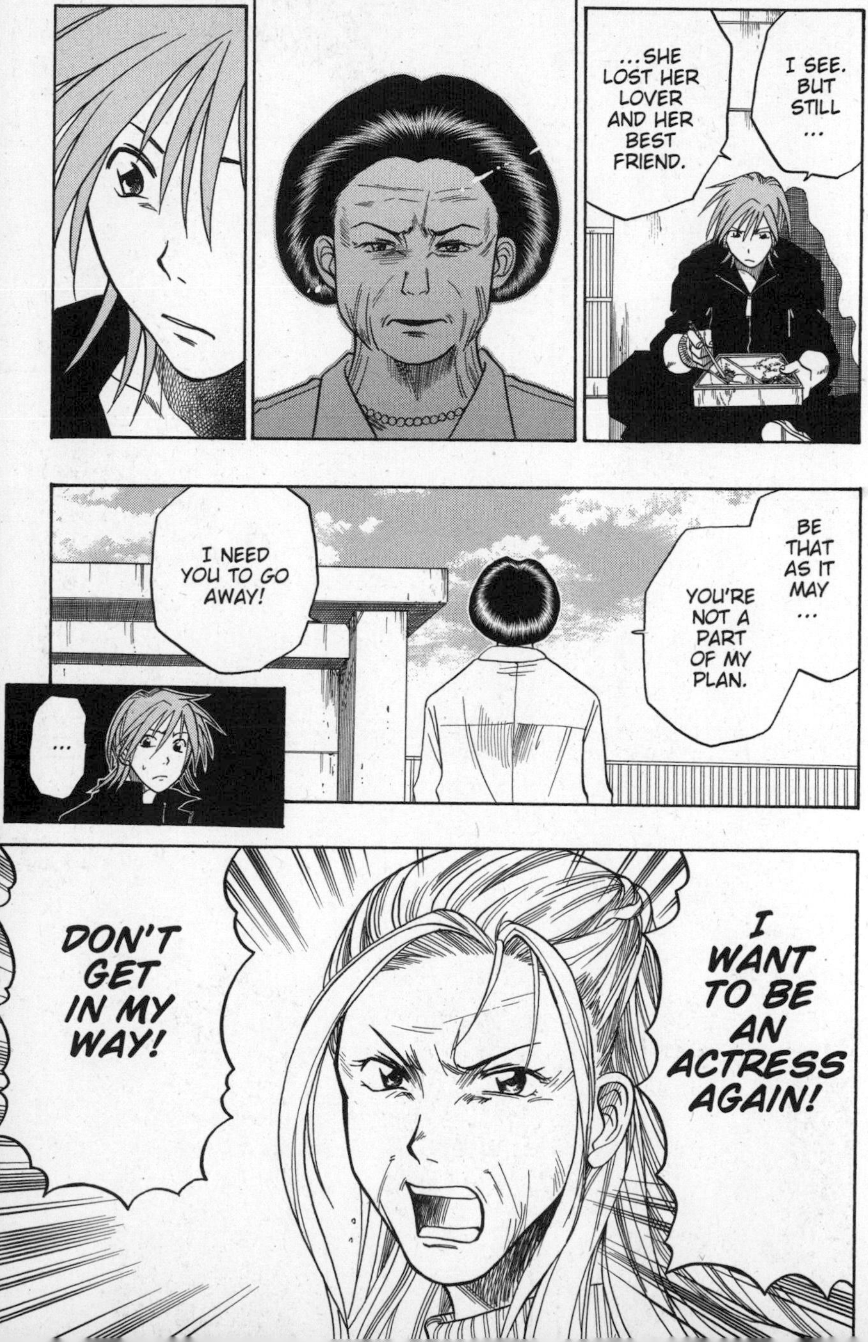
I SEE. BUT STILL ...
...SHE LOST HER LOVER AND HER BEST FRIEND.
BE THAT AS IT MAY ...
YOU'RE NOT A PART OF MY PLAN.
I NEED YOU TO GO AWAY!
...
I WANT TO BE AN ACTRESS AGAIN!
DON'T GET IN MY WAY!

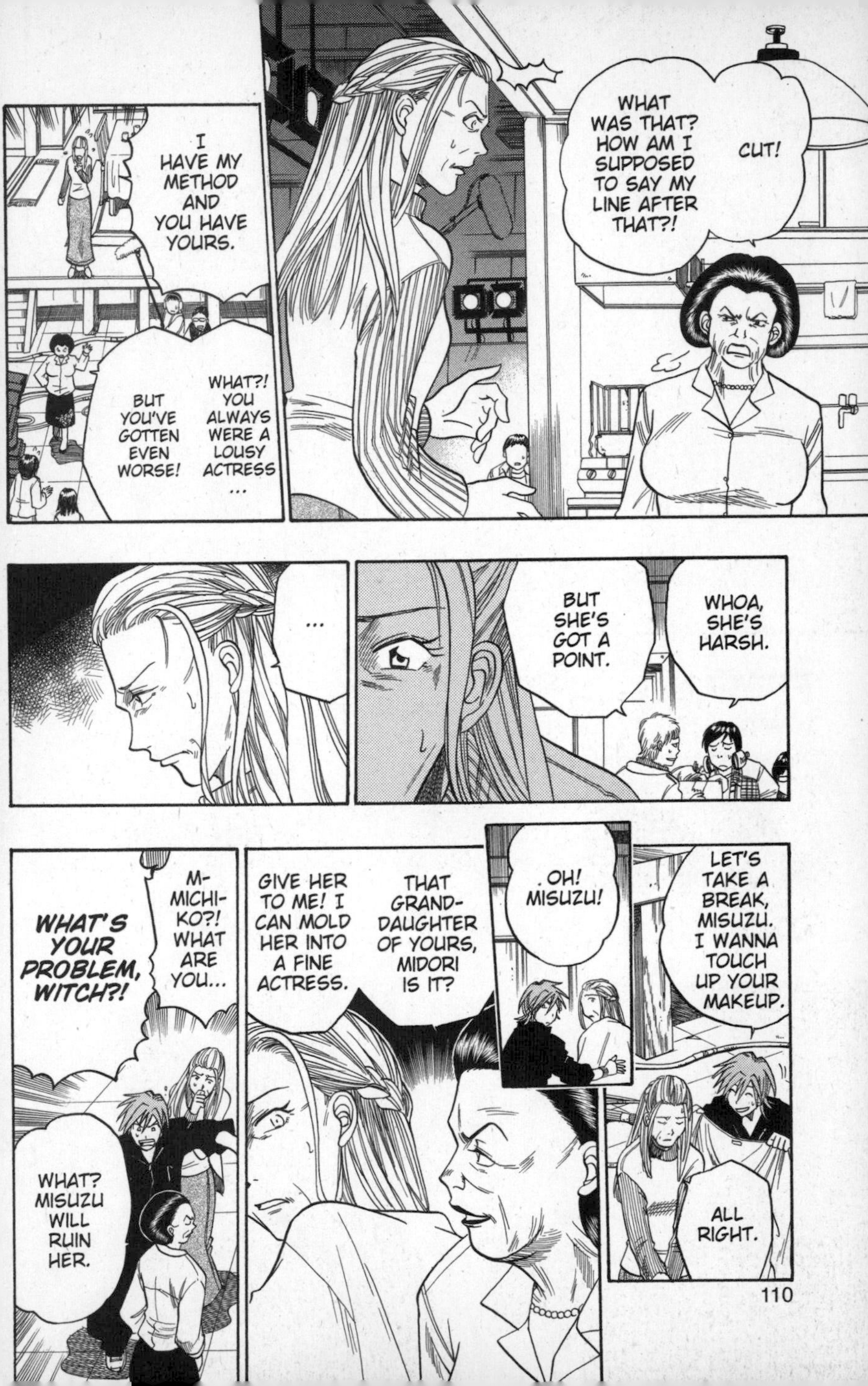
CUT!
WHAT WAS THAT? HOW AM I SUPPOSED TO SAY MY LINE AFTER THAT?!
I HAVE MY METHOD AND YOU HAVE YOURS.
WHAT?! YOU ALWAYS WERE A LOUSY ACTRESS...
BUT YOU'VE GOTTEN EVEN WORSE!
WHOA, SHE'S HARSH.
BUT SHE'S GOT A POINT.
...
LET'S TAKE A BREAK, MISUZU. I WANNA TOUCH UP YOUR MAKEUP.
ALL RIGHT.
OH! MISUZU!
THAT GRAND-DAUGHTER OF YOURS, MIDORI IS IT?
GIVE HER TO ME! I CAN MOLD HER INTO A FINE ACTRESS.
M-MICHIKO?! WHAT ARE YOU...
WHAT'S YOUR PROBLEM, WITCH?!
WHAT? MISUZU WILL RUIN HER.

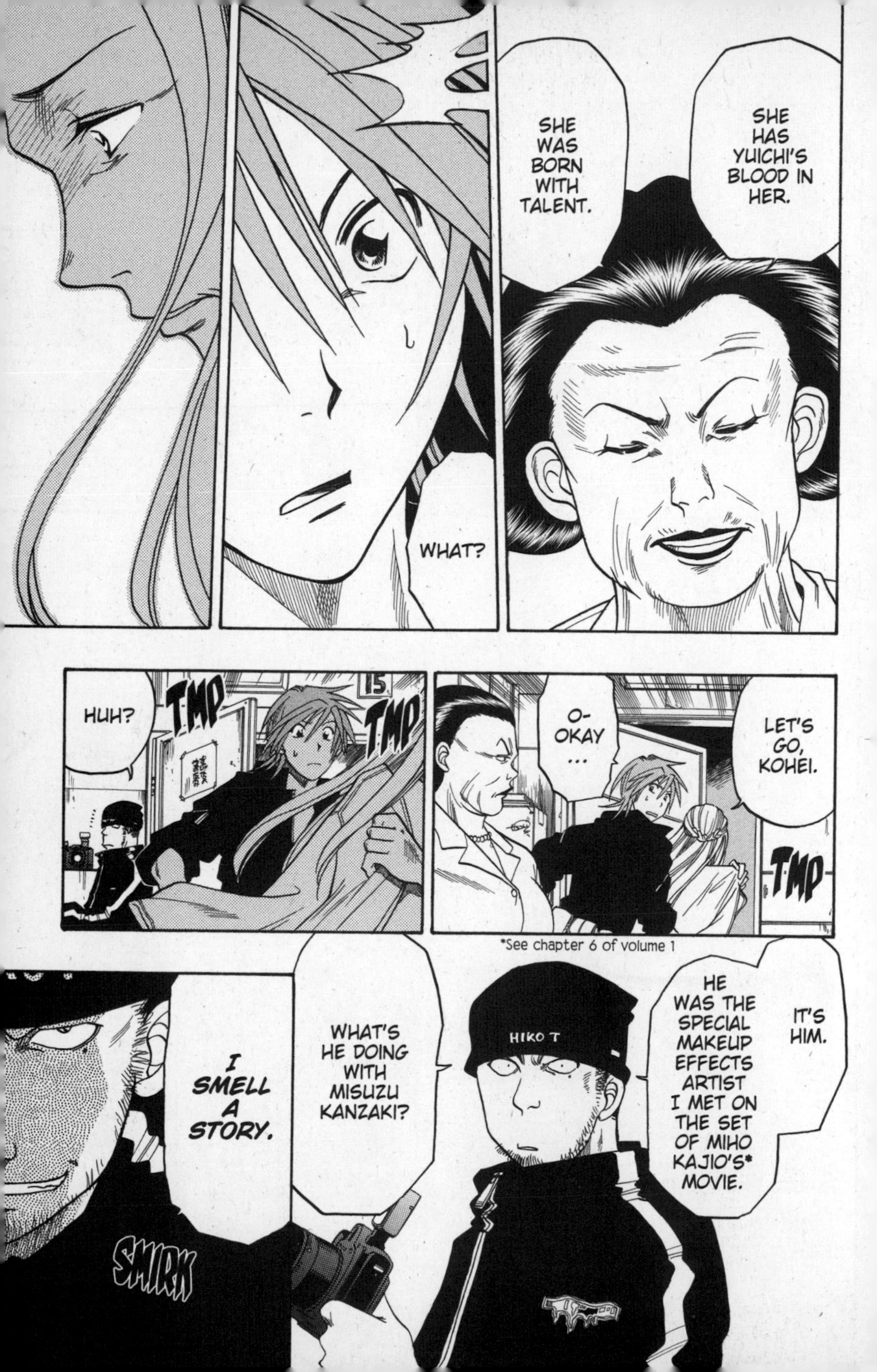
SHE HAS YUICHI'S BLOOD IN HER.
SHE WAS BORN WITH TALENT.
WHAT?
LET'S GO, KOHEI.
TMP
O-OKAY ...
TMP
TMP
HUH?
IT'S HIM.
HE WAS THE SPECIAL MAKEUP EFFECTS ARTIST I MET ON THE SET OF MIHO KAJIO'S* MOVIE.
HIKO T
WHAT'S HE DOING WITH MISUZU KANZAKI?
I SMELL A STORY.
SMIRK
*See chapter 6 of volume 1

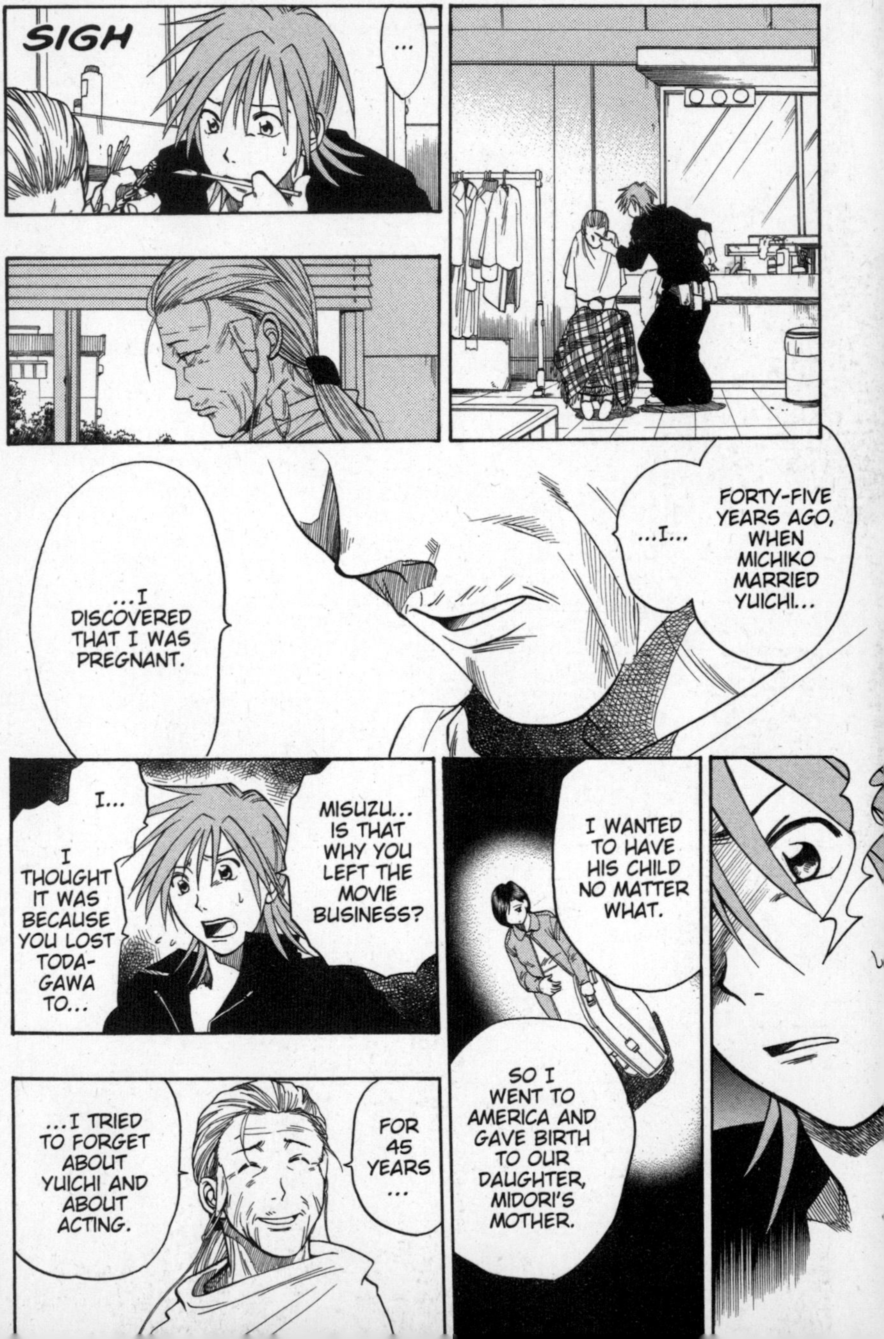
SIGH
...
...I...
FORTY-FIVE YEARS AGO, WHEN MICHIKO MARRIED YUICHI...
...I DISCOVERED THAT I WAS PREGNANT.
I WANTED TO HAVE HIS CHILD NO MATTER WHAT.
SO I WENT TO AMERICA AND GAVE BIRTH TO OUR DAUGHTER, MIDORI'S MOTHER.
MISUZU... IS THAT WHY YOU LEFT THE MOVIE BUSINESS?
I...
I THOUGHT IT WAS BECAUSE YOU LOST TODA-GAWA TO...
FOR 45 YEARS...
...I TRIED TO FORGET ABOUT YUICHI AND ABOUT ACTING.

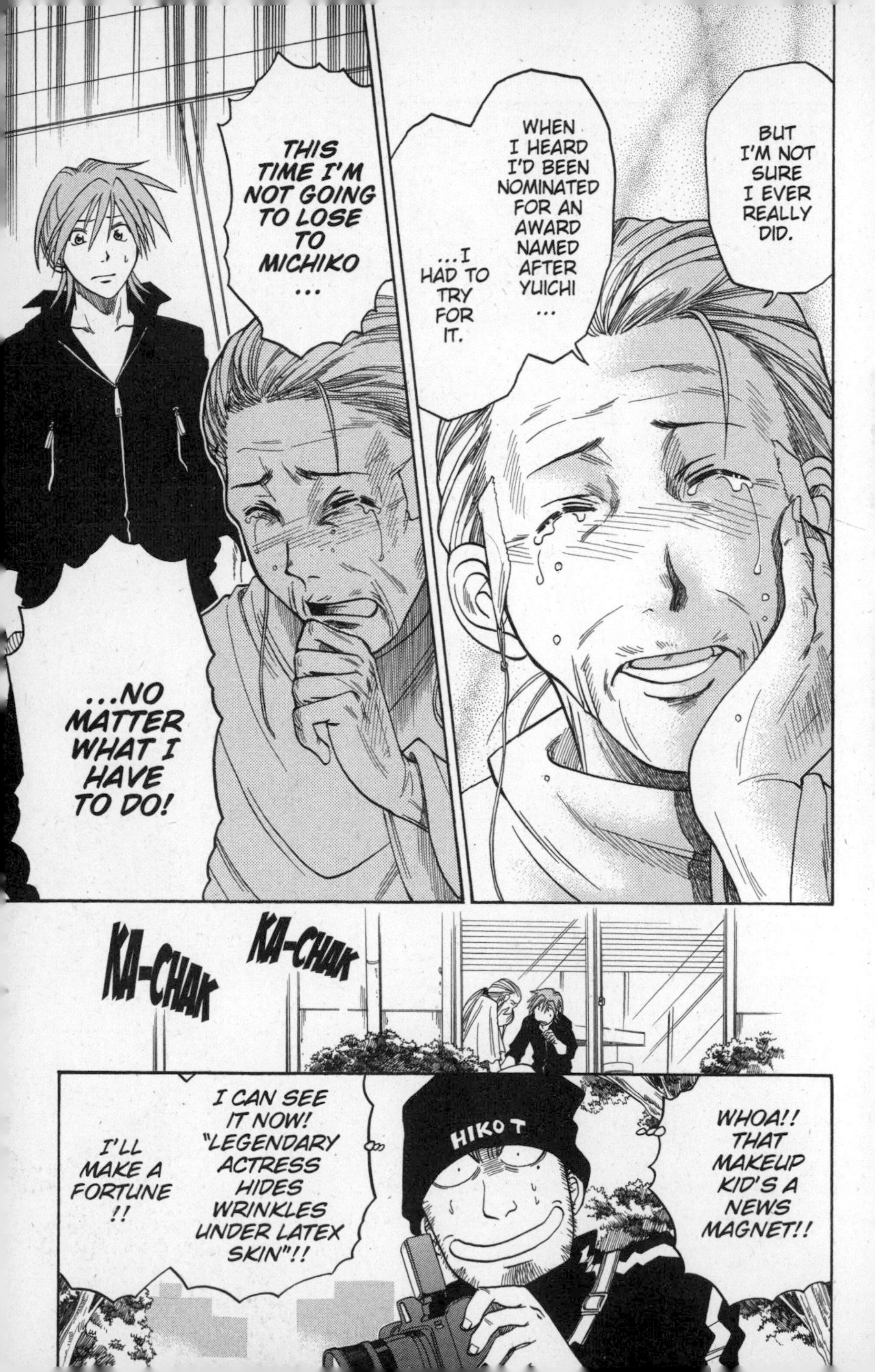
BUT I'M NOT SURE I EVER REALLY DID.
WHEN I HEARD I'D BEEN NOMINATED FOR AN AWARD NAMED AFTER YUICHI...
...I HAD TO TRY FOR IT.
THIS TIME I'M NOT GOING TO LOSE TO MICHIKO...
...NO MATTER WHAT I HAVE TO DO!
KA-CHAK
KA-CHAK
HIKO T.
WHOA!! THAT MAKEUP KID'S A NEWS MAGNET!!
I CAN SEE IT NOW! "LEGENDARY ACTRESS HIDES WRINKLES UNDER LATEX SKIN"!!
I'LL MAKE A FORTUNE!!

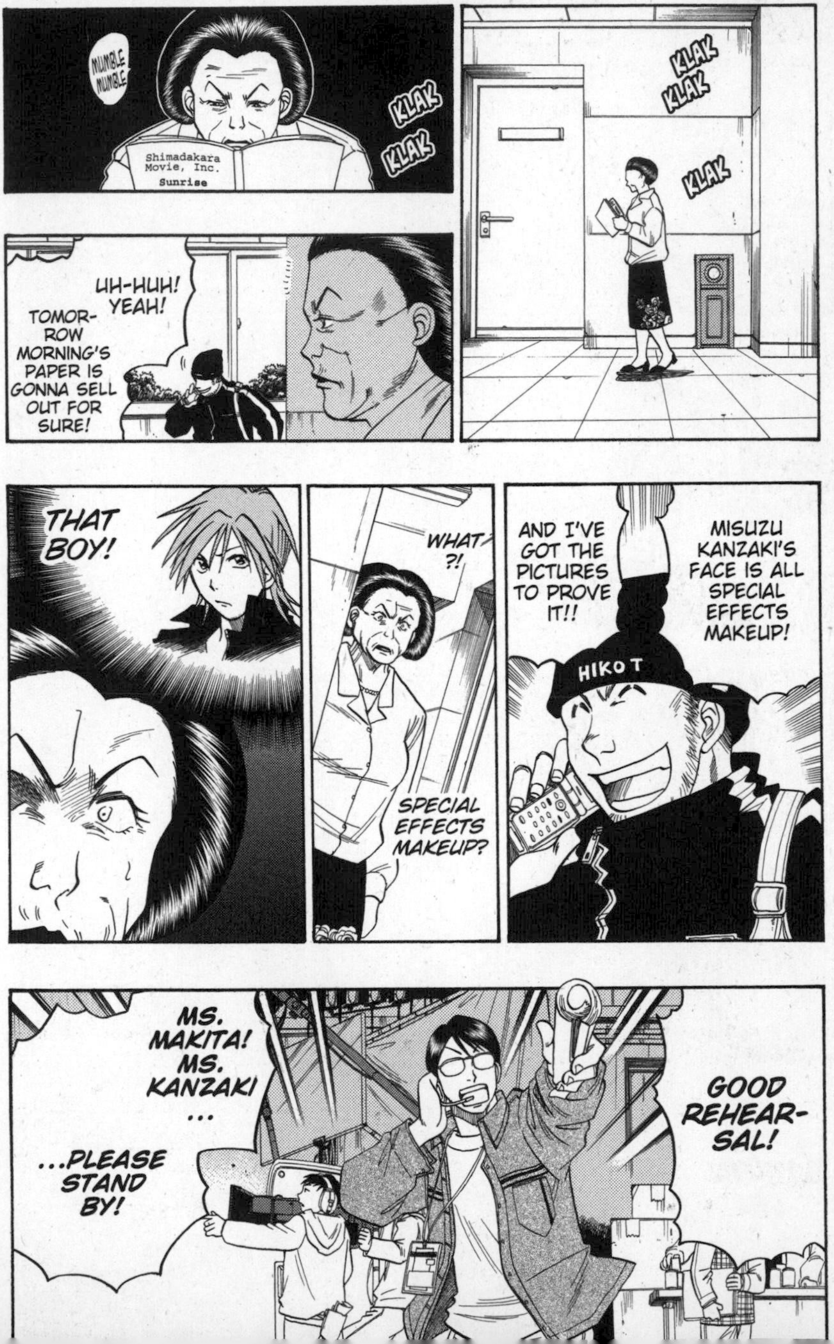
KLAK KLAK
KLAK
MUMBLE MUMBLE
Shimadakara Movie, Inc. Sunrise
KLAK KLAK
UH-HUH! YEAH!
TOMORROW MORNING'S PAPER IS GONNA SELL OUT FOR SURE!
MISUZU KANZAKI'S FACE IS ALL SPECIAL EFFECTS MAKEUP!
AND I'VE GOT THE PICTURES TO PROVE IT!!
HIKOT
WHAT?!
SPECIAL EFFECTS MAKEUP?
THAT BOY!
GOOD REHEARSAL!
MS. MAKITA! MS. KANZAKI ...
...PLEASE STAND BY!

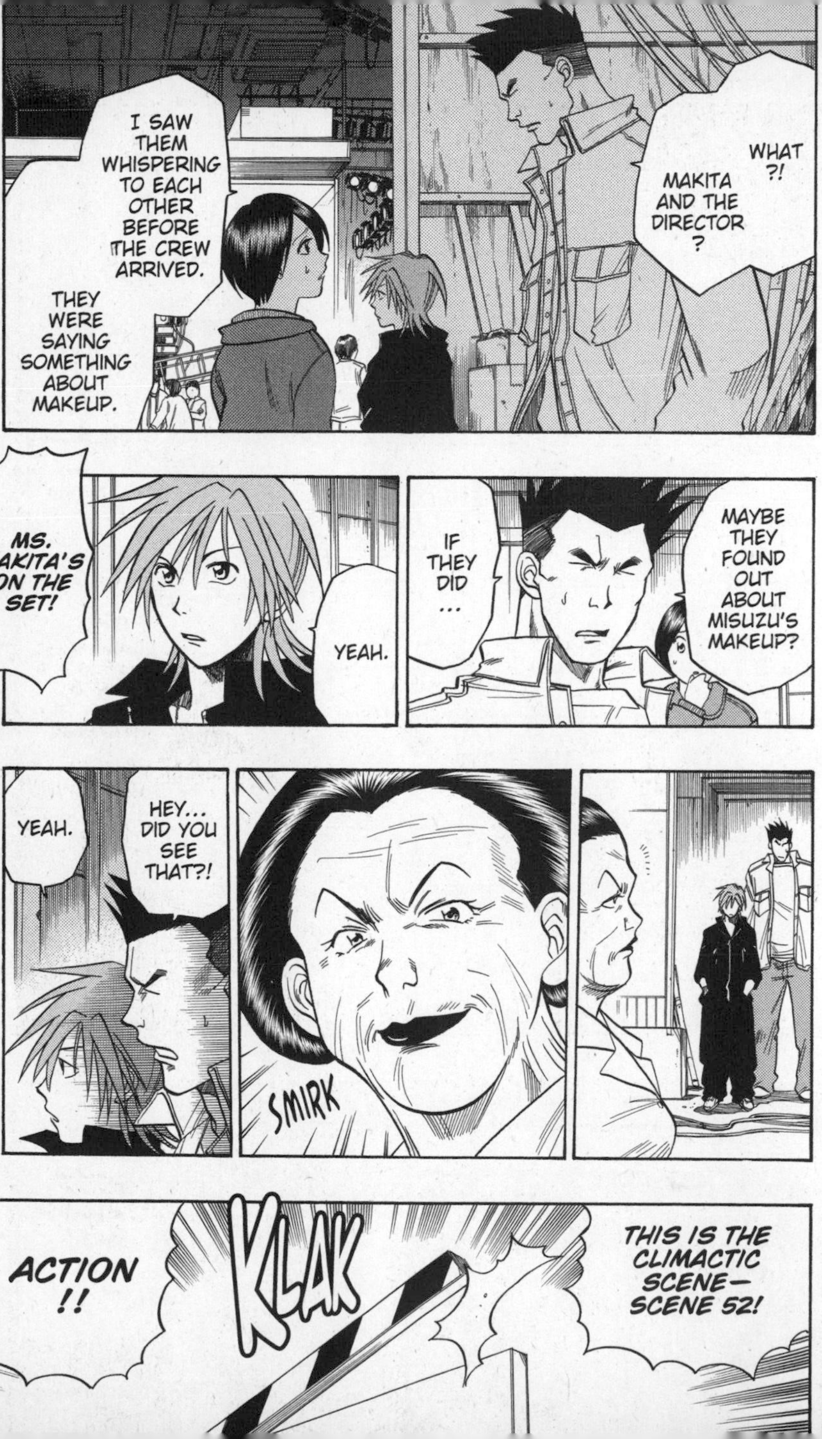
WHAT?!
MAKITA AND THE DIRECTOR?
I SAW THEM WHISPERING TO EACH OTHER BEFORE THE CREW ARRIVED.
THEY WERE SAYING SOMETHING ABOUT MAKEUP.
MAYBE THEY FOUND OUT ABOUT MISUZU'S MAKEUP?
IF THEY DID...
YEAH.
MS. MAKITA'S ON THE SET!
SMIRK
HEY... DID YOU SEE THAT?!
YEAH.
THIS IS THE CLIMACTIC SCENE— SCENE 52!
KLAK
ACTION!!

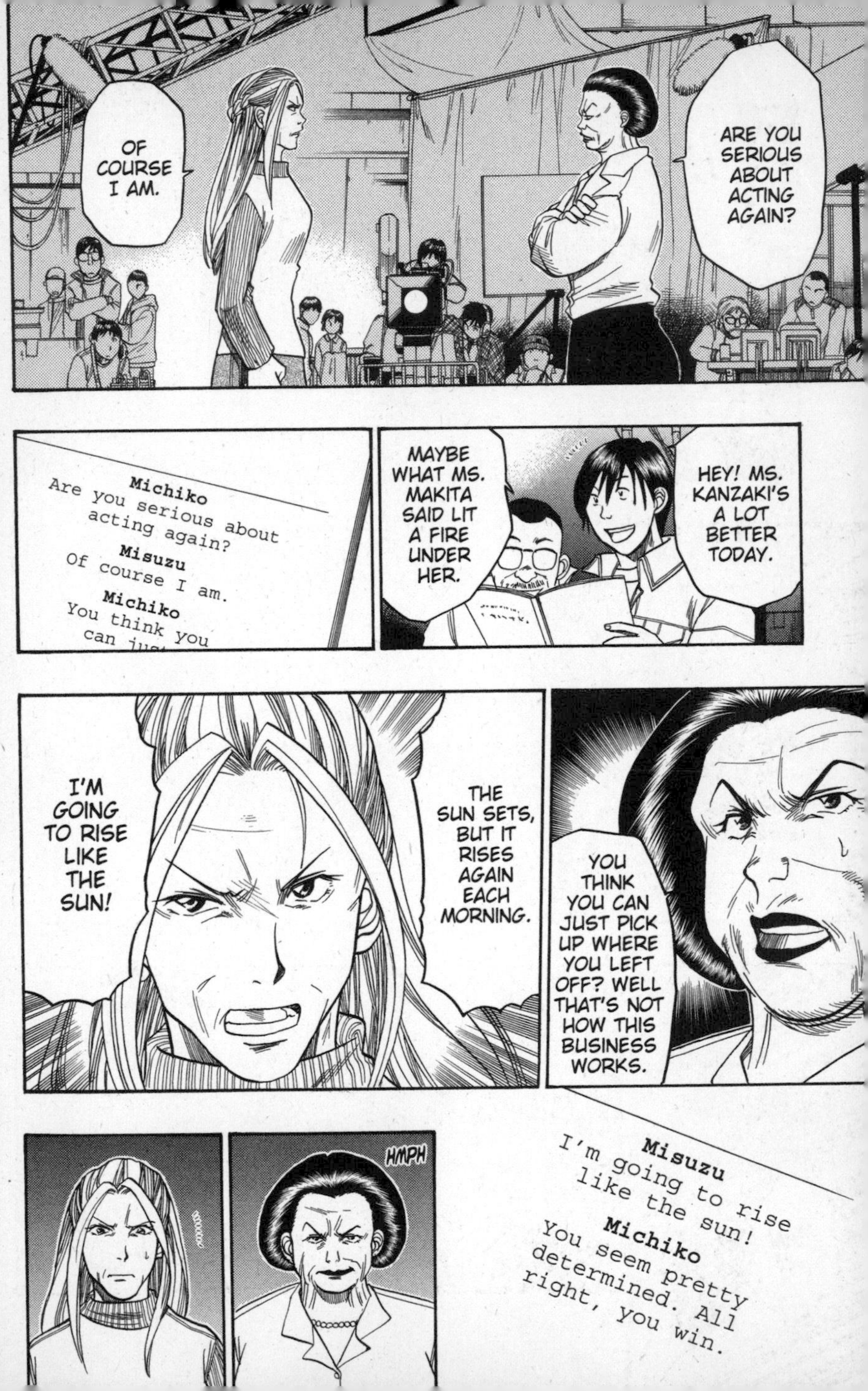
ARE YOU SERIOUS ABOUT ACTING AGAIN?
OF COURSE I AM.
HEY! MS. KANZAKI'S A LOT BETTER TODAY.
MAYBE WHAT MS. MAKITA SAID LIT A FIRE UNDER HER.
Michiko
Are you serious about acting again?
Misuzu
Of course I am.
Michiko
You think you
YOU THINK YOU CAN JUST PICK UP WHERE YOU LEFT OFF? WELL THAT'S NOT HOW THIS BUSINESS WORKS.
THE SUN SETS, BUT IT RISES AGAIN EACH MORNING.
I'M GOING TO RISE LIKE THE SUN!
Misuzu
I'm going to rise like the sun!
Michiko
You seem pretty determined. All right, you win.
HMPH

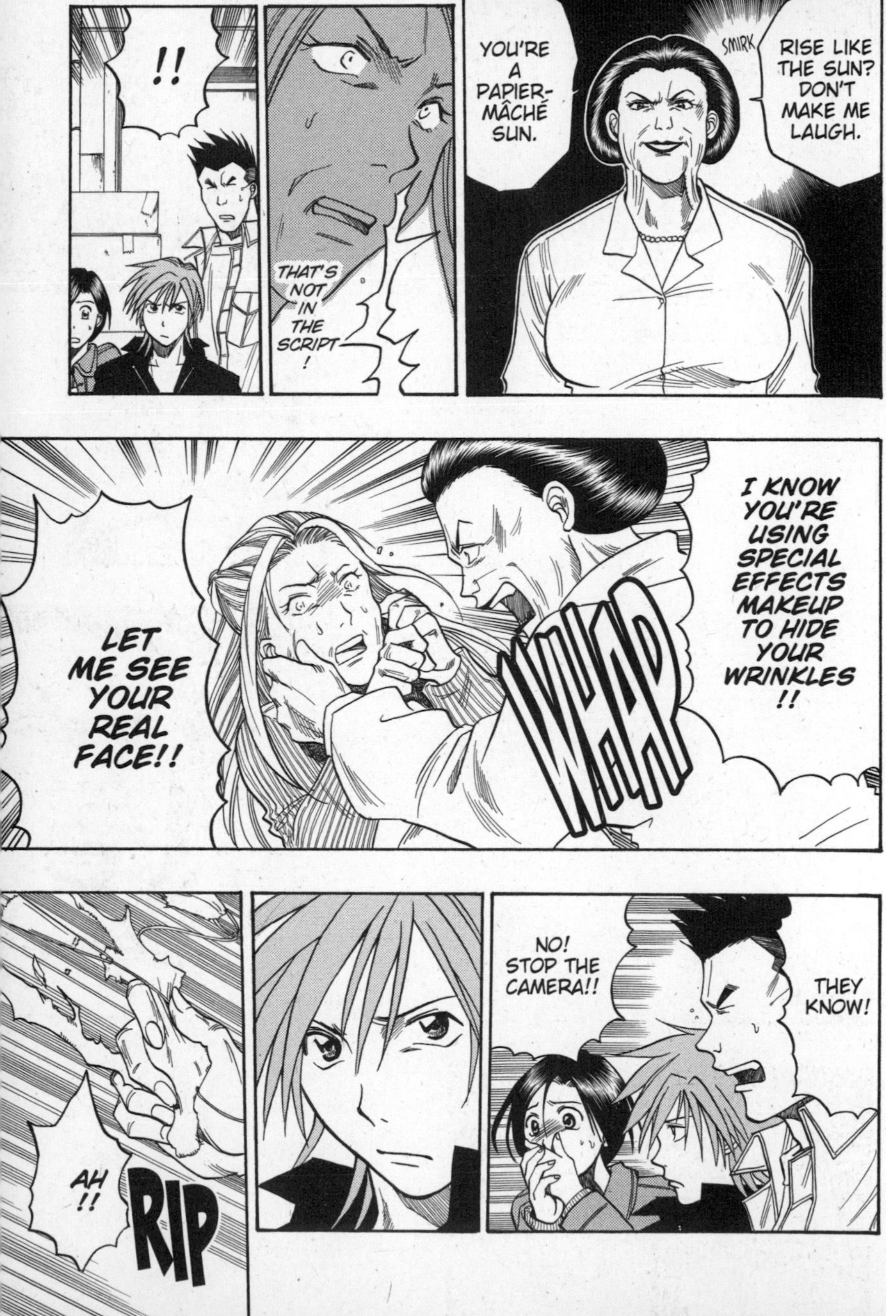
RISE LIKE THE SUN? DON'T MAKE ME LAUGH.
SMIRK
YOU'RE A PAPIER-MÂCHÉ SUN.
THAT'S NOT IN THE SCRIPT!
!!
I KNOW YOU'RE USING SPECIAL EFFECTS MAKEUP TO HIDE YOUR WRINKLES!!
WHAP
LET ME SEE YOUR REAL FACE!!
THEY KNOW!
NO! STOP THE CAMERA!!
AH!!
RIP

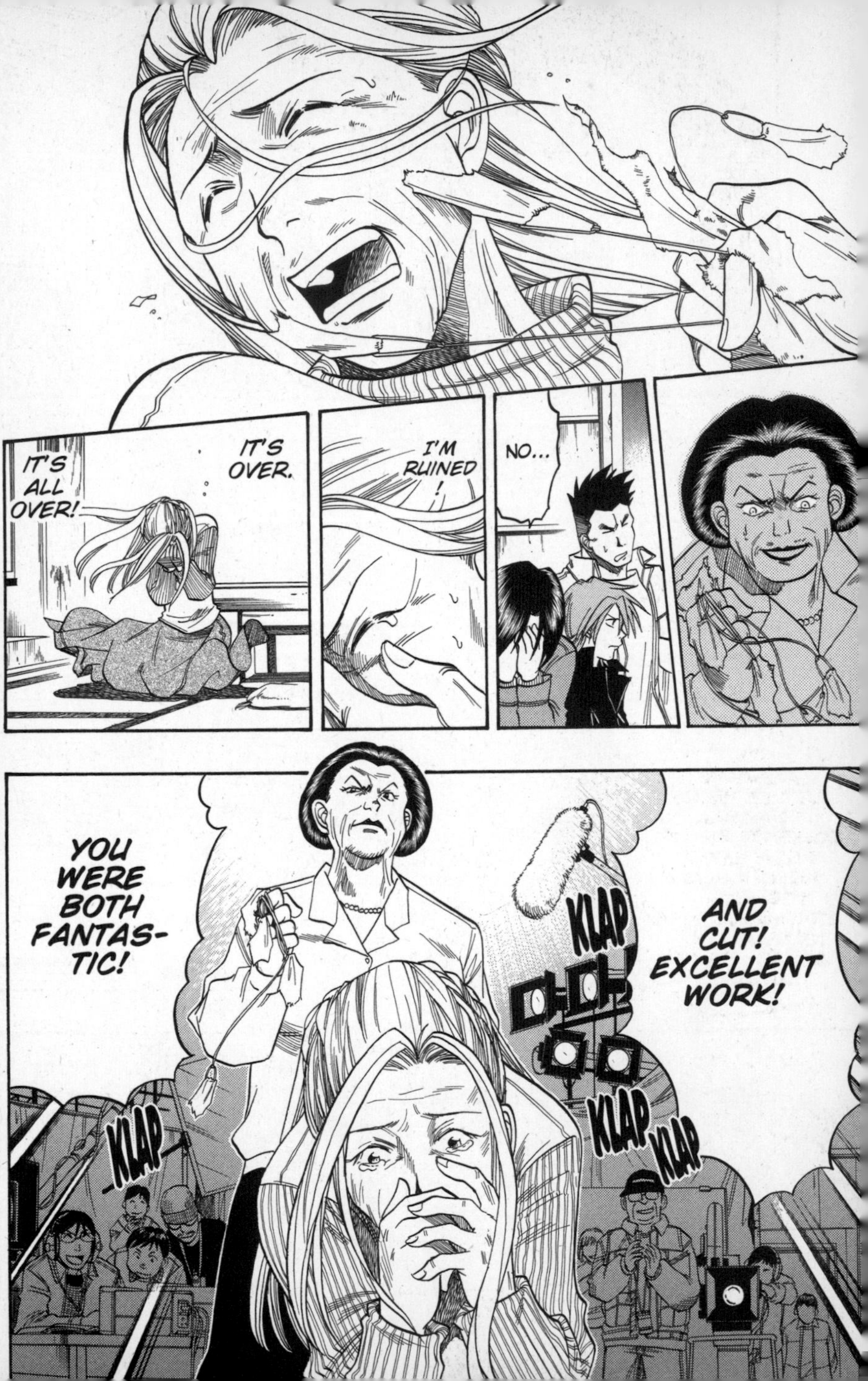
NO...
I'M RUINED!
IT'S OVER.
IT'S ALL OVER!
AND CUT! EXCELLENT WORK!
KLAP
YOU WERE BOTH FANTASTIC!
KLAP KLAP
KLAP

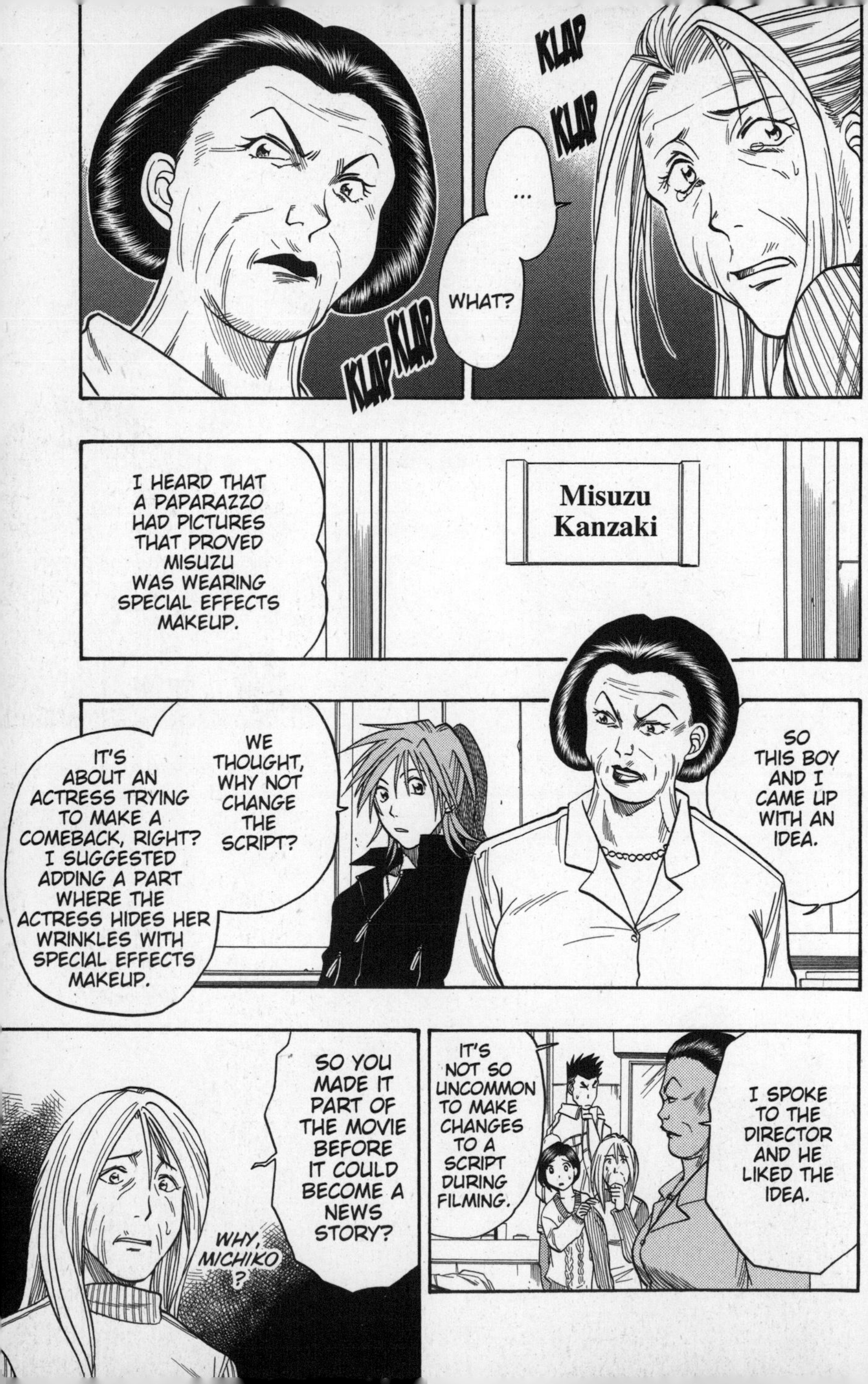
KLAP
KLAP
...
WHAT?
KLAP KLAP
Misuzu Kanzaki
I HEARD THAT A PAPARAZZO HAD PICTURES THAT PROVED MISUZU WAS WEARING SPECIAL EFFECTS MAKEUP.
SO THIS BOY AND I CAME UP WITH AN IDEA.
WE THOUGHT, WHY NOT CHANGE THE SCRIPT?
IT'S ABOUT AN ACTRESS TRYING TO MAKE A COMEBACK, RIGHT? I SUGGESTED ADDING A PART WHERE THE ACTRESS HIDES HER WRINKLES WITH SPECIAL EFFECTS MAKEUP.
I SPOKE TO THE DIRECTOR AND HE LIKED THE IDEA.
IT'S NOT SO UNCOMMON TO MAKE CHANGES TO A SCRIPT DURING FILMING.
SO YOU MADE IT PART OF THE MOVIE BEFORE IT COULD BECOME A NEWS STORY?
WHY, MICHIKO?

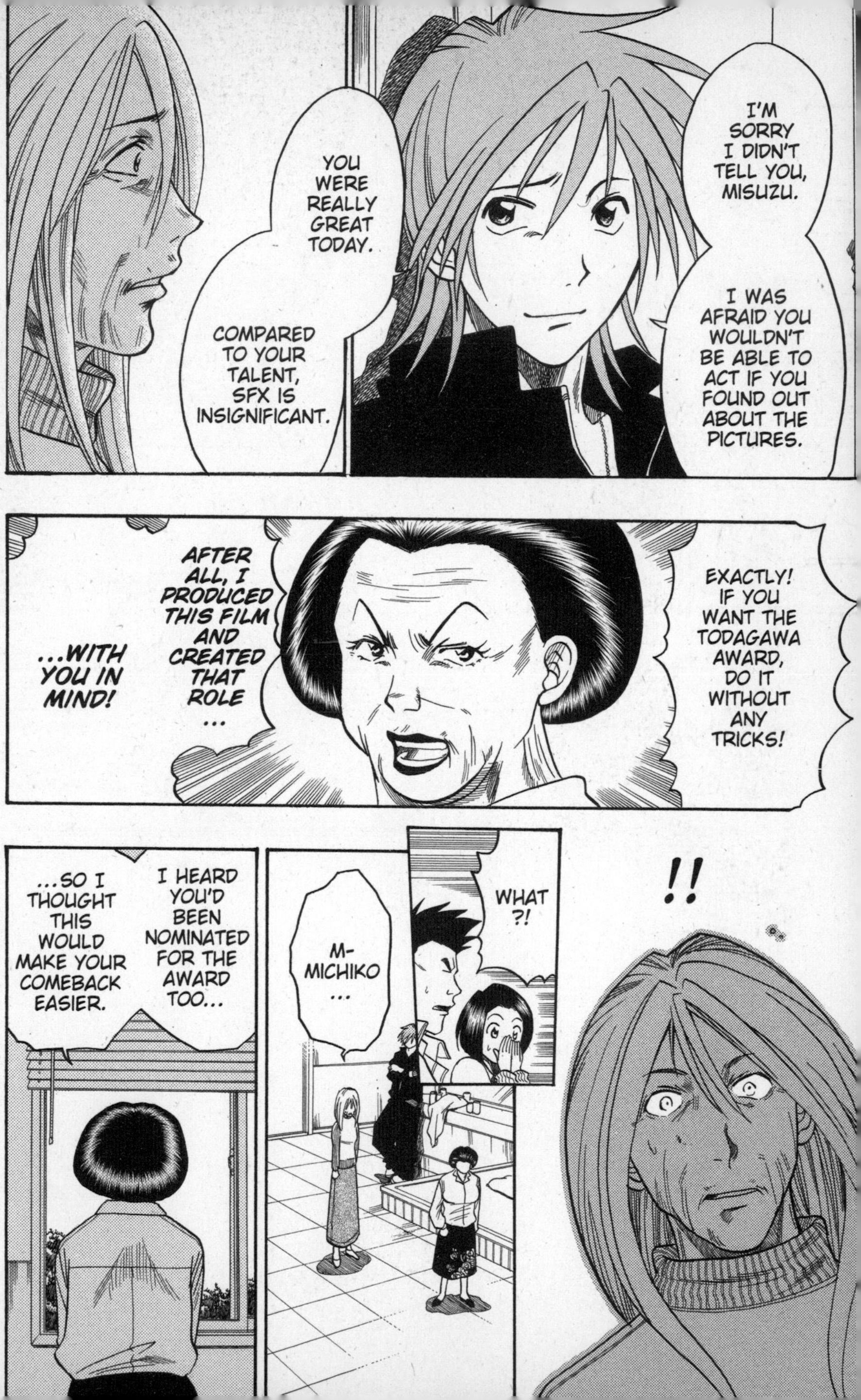
I'M SORRY I DIDN'T TELL YOU, MISUZU.
I WAS AFRAID YOU WOULDN'T BE ABLE TO ACT IF YOU FOUND OUT ABOUT THE PICTURES.
YOU WERE REALLY GREAT TODAY.
COMPARED TO YOUR TALENT, SFX IS INSIGNIFICANT.
EXACTLY! IF YOU WANT THE TODAGAWA AWARD, DO IT WITHOUT ANY TRICKS!
AFTER ALL, I PRODUCED THIS FILM AND CREATED THAT ROLE...
...WITH YOU IN MIND!
!!
WHAT ?!
M-MICHIKO...
I HEARD YOU'D BEEN NOMINATED FOR THE AWARD TOO...
...SO I THOUGHT THIS WOULD MAKE YOUR COMEBACK EASIER.

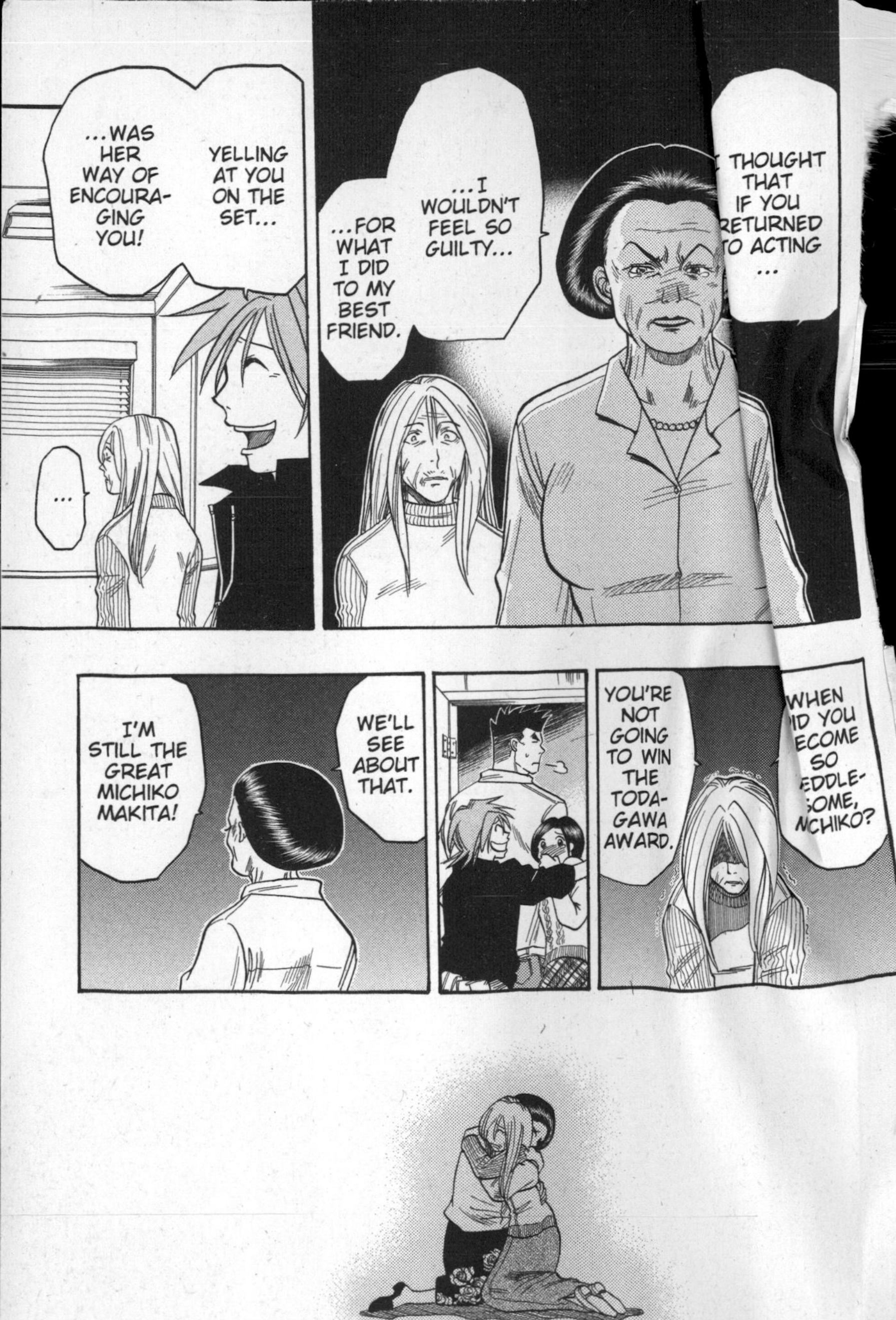
THOUGHT THAT IF YOU RETURNED TO ACTING...
...I WOULDN'T FEEL SO GUILTY...
...FOR WHAT I DID TO MY BEST FRIEND.
YELLING AT YOU ON THE SET...
...WAS HER WAY OF ENCOURAGING YOU!
...
WHEN ID YOU ECOME SO EDDLE-SOME, NCHIKO?
YOU'RE NOT GOING TO WIN THE TODA-GAWA AWARD.
WE'LL SEE ABOUT THAT.
I'M STILL THE GREAT MICHIKO MAKITA!

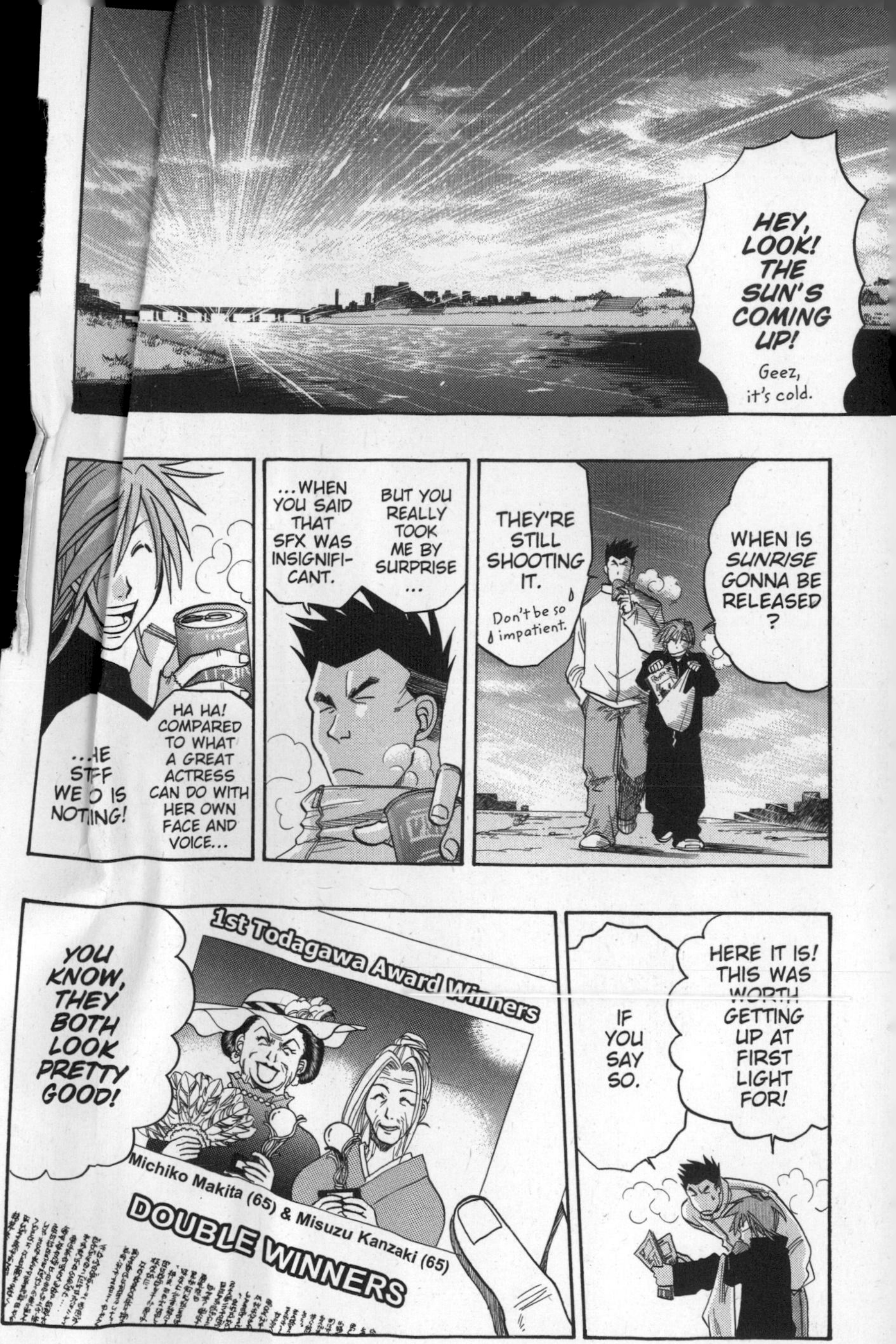
HEY, LOOK! THE SUN'S COMING UP!
Geez, it's cold.
WHEN IS SUNRISE GONNA BE RELEASED?
THEY'RE STILL SHOOTING IT.
Don't be so impatient.
BUT YOU REALLY TOOK ME BY SURPRISE...
...WHEN YOU SAID THAT SFX WAS INSIGNIFICANT.
HA HA! COMPARED TO WHAT A GREAT ACTRESS CAN DO WITH HER OWN FACE AND VOICE...
...HE STFF WE O IS NOTING!
HERE IT IS! THIS WAS WORTH GETTING UP AT FIRST LIGHT FOR!
IF YOU SAY SO.
YOU KNOW, THEY BOTH LOOK PRETTY GOOD!
1st Todagawa Award Winners
Michiko Makita (65) & Misuzu Kanzaki (65)
DOUBLE WINNERS

Scene 32: Miracle in 35-Chome

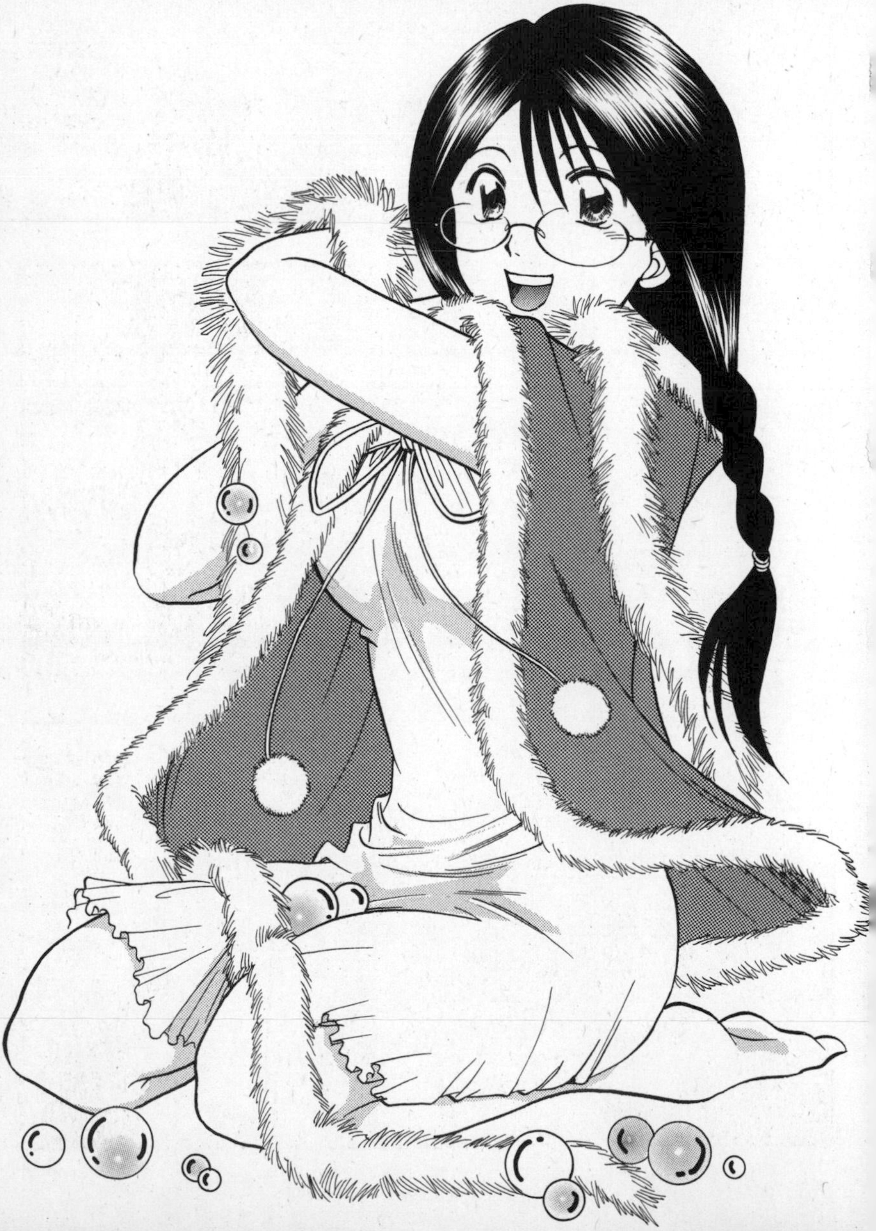

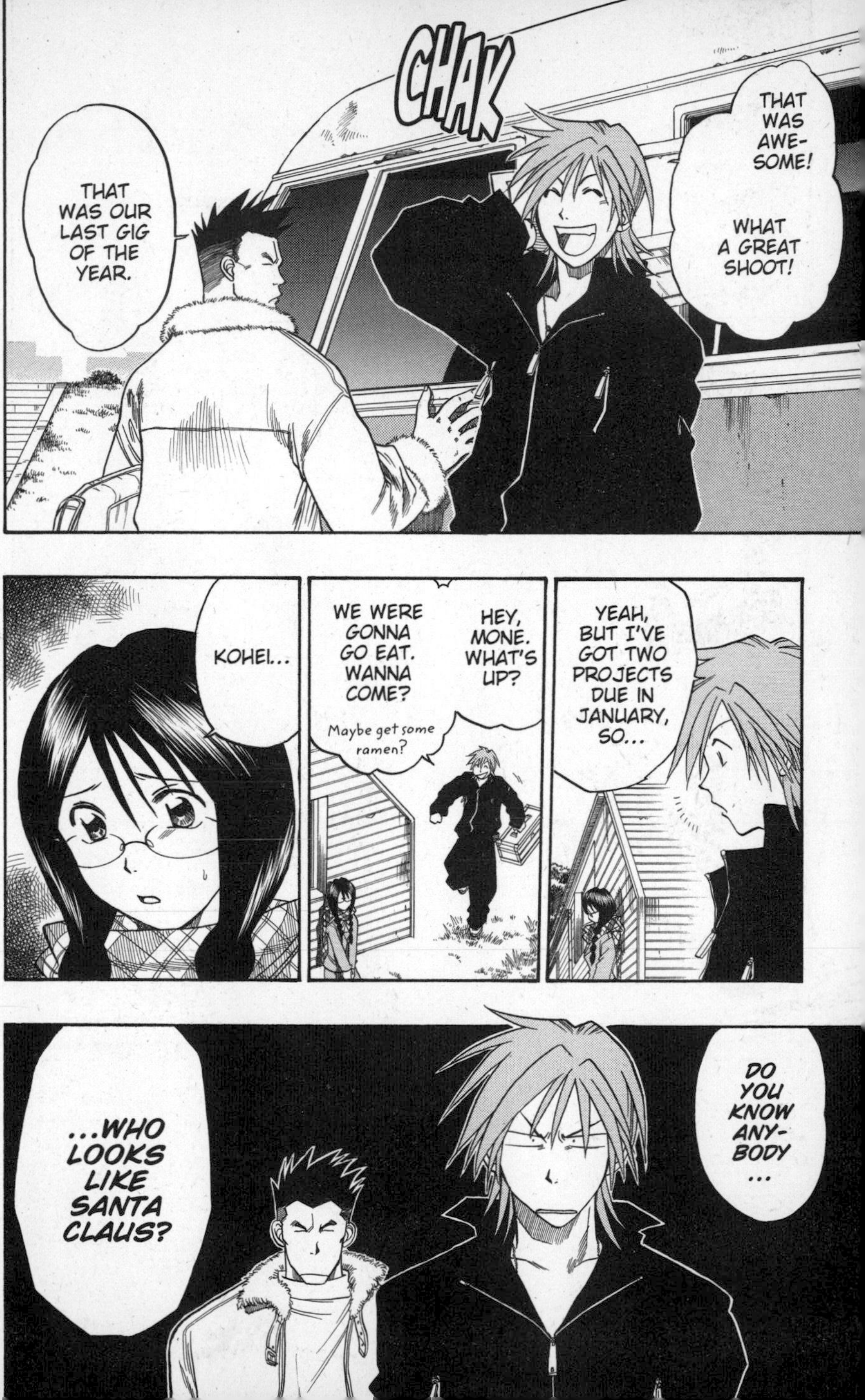
CHAK
THAT WAS AWESOME!
WHAT A GREAT SHOOT!
THAT WAS OUR LAST GIG OF THE YEAR.
YEAH, BUT I'VE GOT TWO PROJECTS DUE IN JANUARY, SO...
HEY, MONE. WHAT'S UP?
WE WERE GONNA GO EAT. WANNA COME?
Maybe get some ramen?
KOHEI...
DO YOU KNOW ANYBODY...
...WHO LOOKS LIKE SANTA CLAUS?

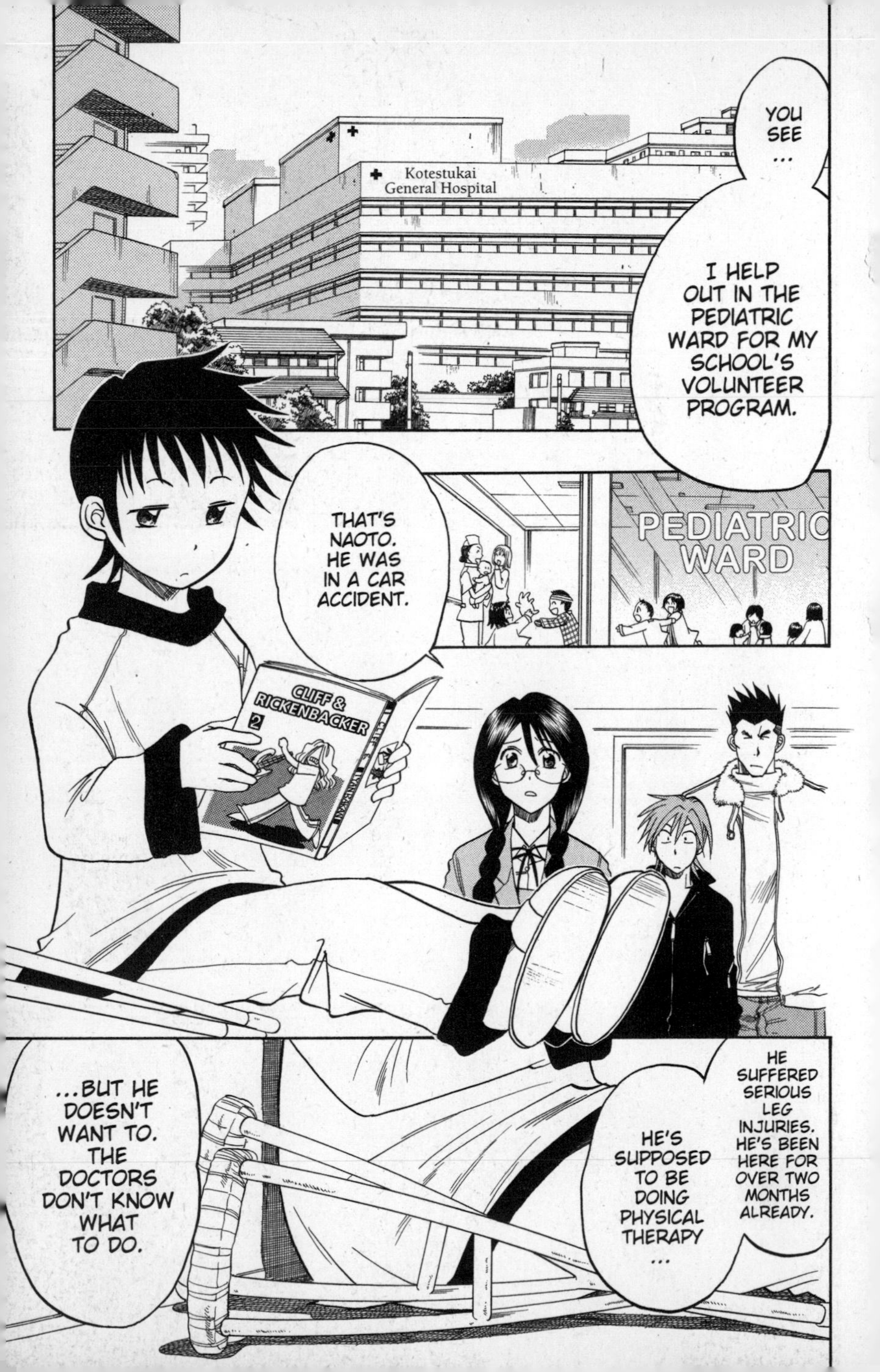
Kotestukai General Hospital
YOU SEE ...
I HELP OUT IN THE PEDIATRIC WARD FOR MY SCHOOL'S VOLUNTEER PROGRAM.
PEDIATRIC WARD
THAT'S NAOTO. HE WAS IN A CAR ACCIDENT.
CLIFF & RICKENBACKER 2
HE SUFFERED SERIOUS LEG INJURIES. HE'S BEEN HERE FOR OVER TWO MONTHS ALREADY.
HE'S SUPPOSED TO BE DOING PHYSICAL THERAPY ...
...BUT HE DOESN'T WANT TO. THE DOCTORS DON'T KNOW WHAT TO DO.

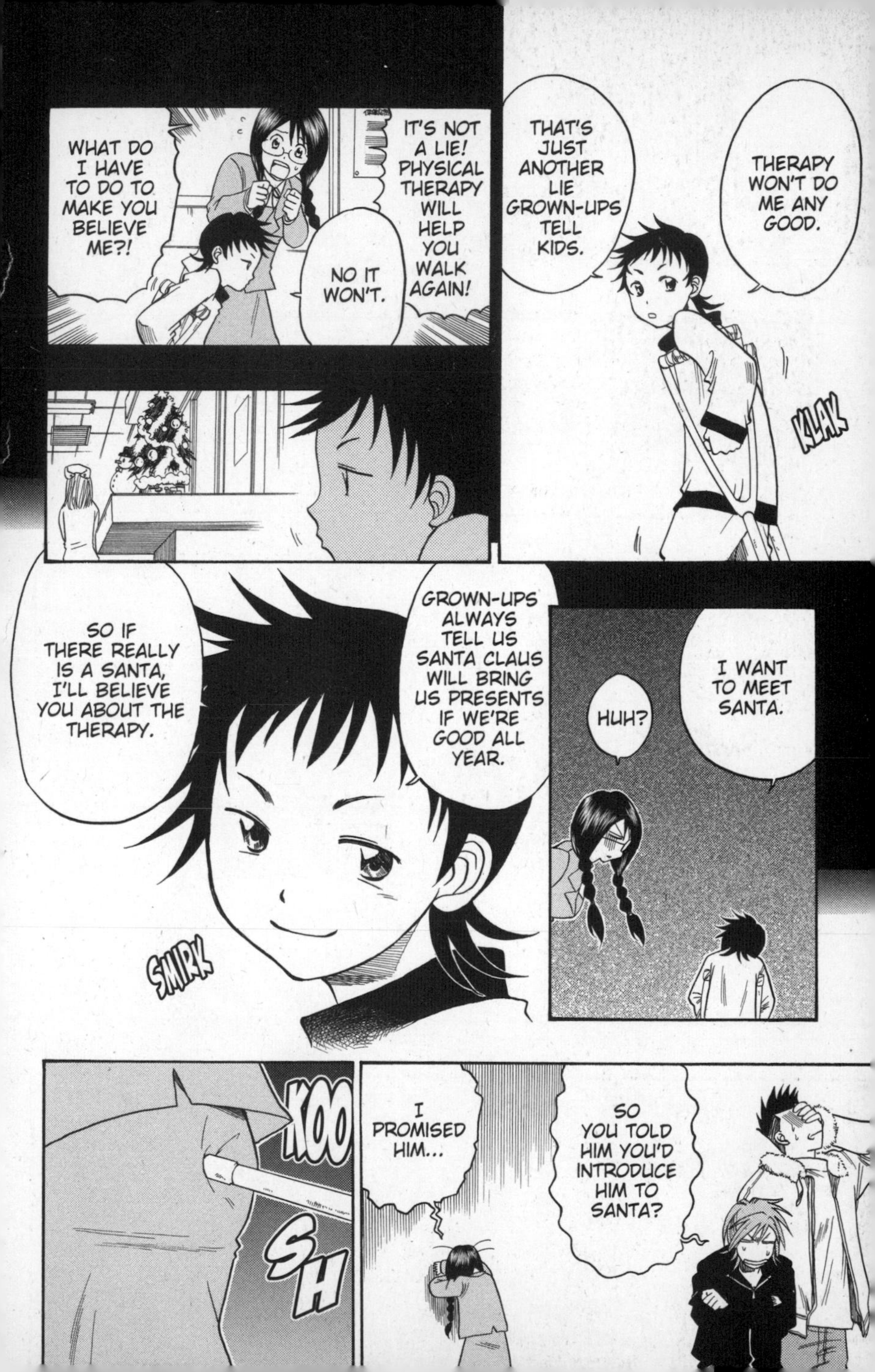
THERAPY WON'T DO ME ANY GOOD.
THAT'S JUST ANOTHER LIE GROWN-UPS TELL KIDS.
KLAK
IT'S NOT A LIE! PHYSICAL THERAPY WILL HELP YOU WALK AGAIN!
NO IT WON'T.
WHAT DO I HAVE TO DO TO MAKE YOU BELIEVE ME?!
I WANT TO MEET SANTA.
HUH?
GROWN-UPS ALWAYS TELL US SANTA CLAUS WILL BRING US PRESENTS IF WE'RE GOOD ALL YEAR.
SO IF THERE REALLY IS A SANTA, I'LL BELIEVE YOU ABOUT THE THERAPY.
SMIRK
SO YOU TOLD HIM YOU'D INTRODUCE HIM TO SANTA?
I PROMISED HIM...
KOO
SH

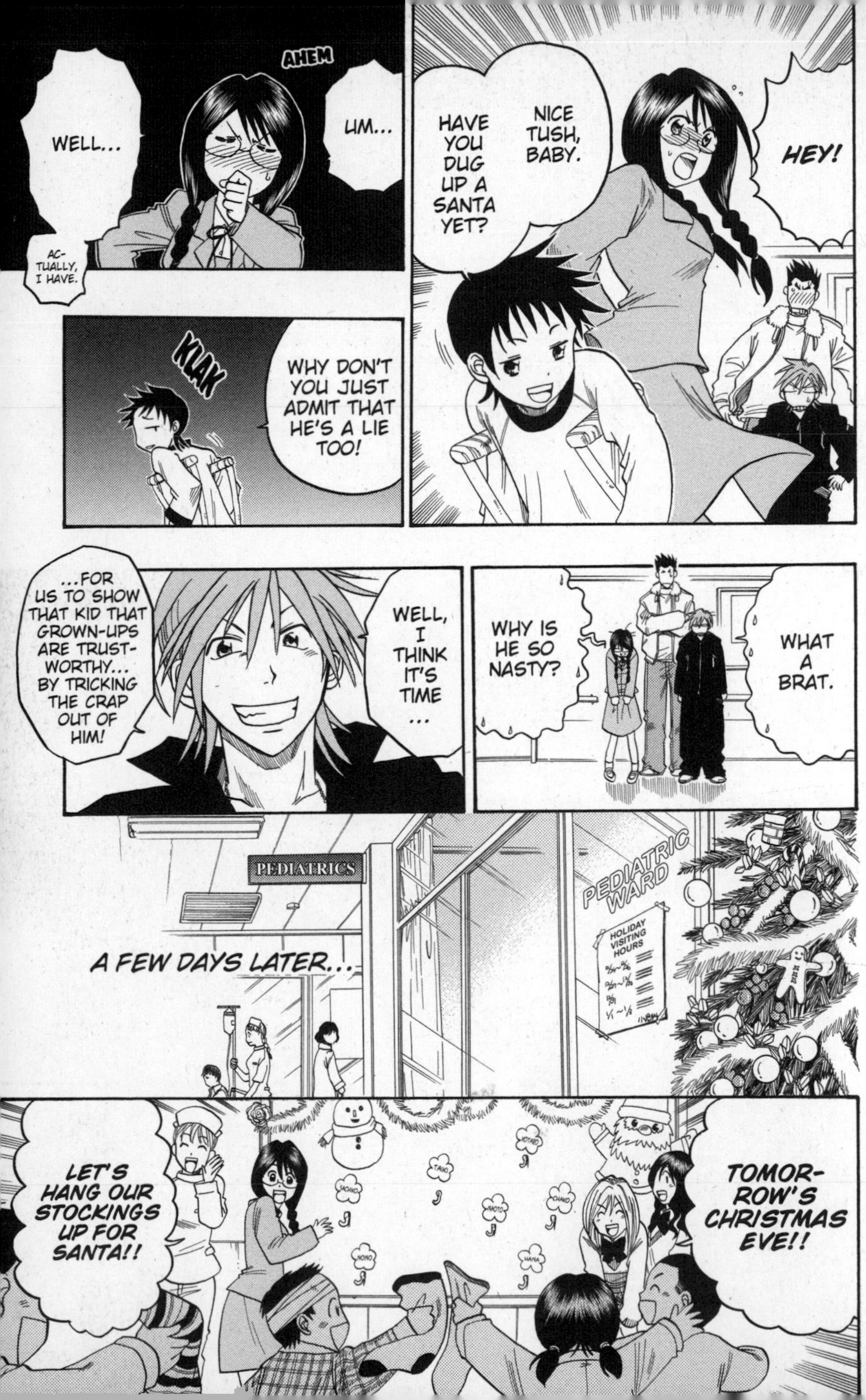
HEY!
NICE TUSH, BABY.
HAVE YOU DUG UP A SANTA YET?
UM...
AHEM
WELL...
AC-TUALLY, I HAVE.
WHY DON'T YOU JUST ADMIT THAT HE'S A LIE TOO!
KLAK
WHAT A BRAT.
WHY IS HE SO NASTY?
WELL, I THINK IT'S TIME...
...FOR US TO SHOW THAT KID THAT GROWN-UPS ARE TRUST-WORTHY... BY TRICKING THE CRAP OUT OF HIM!
PEDIATRIC WARD
HOLIDAY VISITING HOURS
PEDIATRICS
A FEW DAYS LATER...
TOMOR-ROW'S CHRISTMAS EVE!!
LET'S HANG OUR STOCKINGS UP FOR SANTA!!

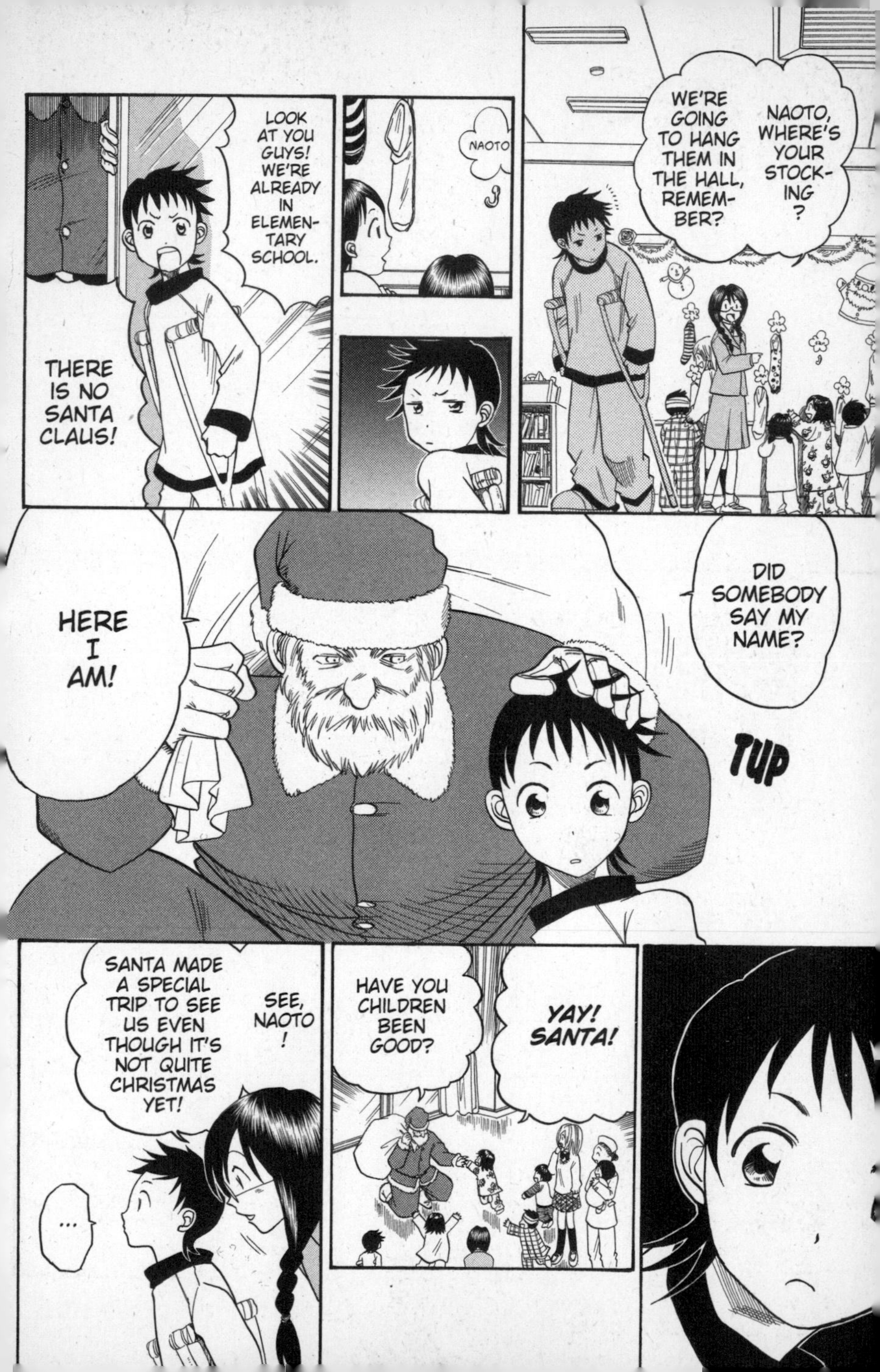
NAOTO, WHERE'S YOUR STOCKING?
WE'RE GOING TO HANG THEM IN THE HALL, REMEMBER?
NAOTO
LOOK AT YOU GUYS! WE'RE ALREADY IN ELEMENTARY SCHOOL.
THERE IS NO SANTA CLAUS!
DID SOMEBODY SAY MY NAME?
TUP
HERE I AM!
YAY! SANTA!
HAVE YOU CHILDREN BEEN GOOD?
SEE, NAOTO!
SANTA MADE A SPECIAL TRIP TO SEE US EVEN THOUGH IT'S NOT QUITE CHRISTMAS YET!
...

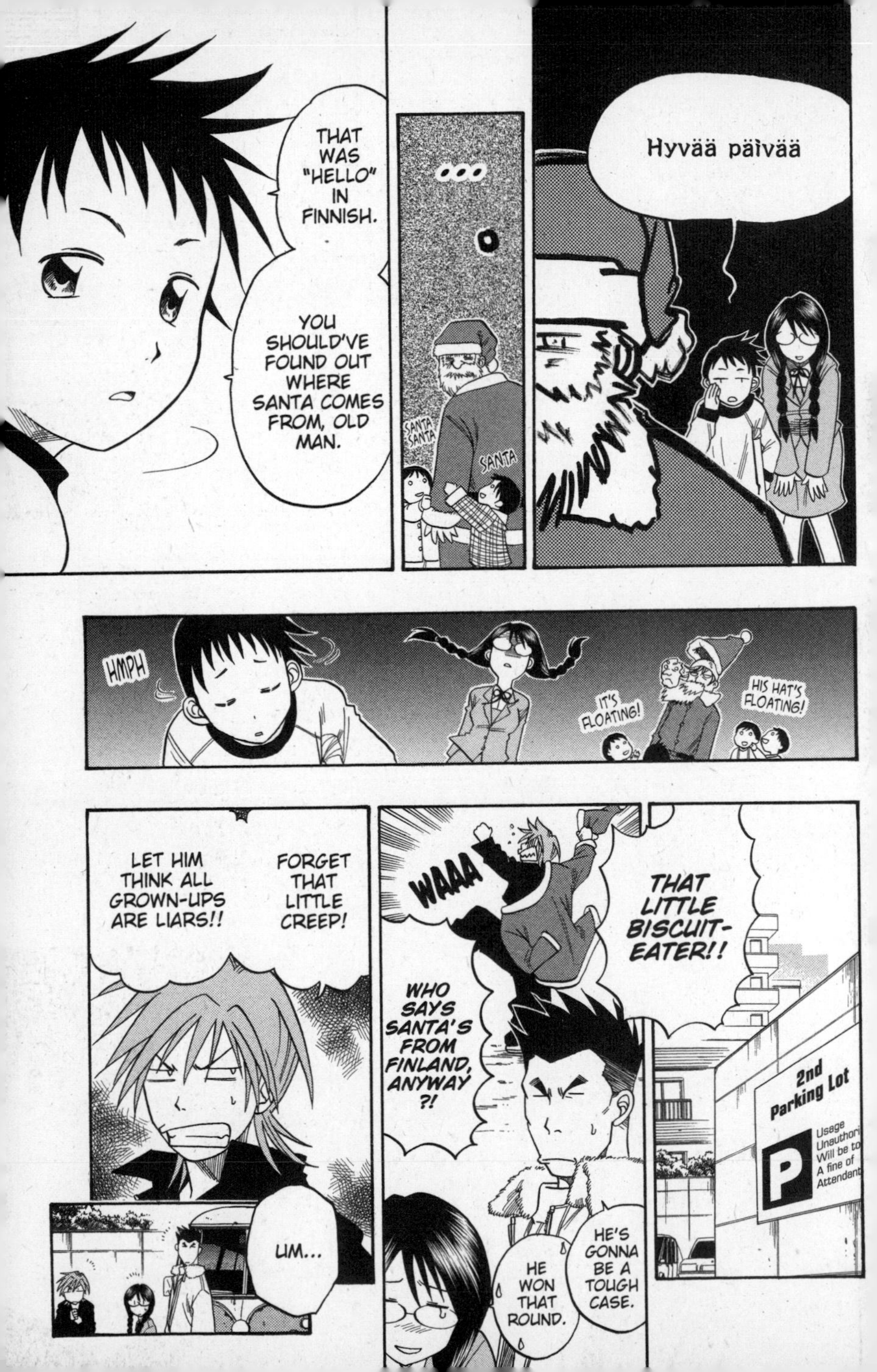
Hyvää päivää
...
SANTA SANTA
SANTA
THAT WAS "HELLO" IN FINNISH.
YOU SHOULD'VE FOUND OUT WHERE SANTA COMES FROM, OLD MAN.
HIS HAT'S FLOATING!
IT'S FLOATING!
HMPH
THAT LITTLE BISCUIT-EATER!!
WAAA
WHO SAYS SANTA'S FROM FINLAND, ANYWAY?!
2nd Parking Lot
P
FORGET THAT LITTLE CREEP!
LET HIM THINK ALL GROWN-UPS ARE LIARS!!
HE'S GONNA BE A TOUGH CASE.
HE WON THAT ROUND.
UM...

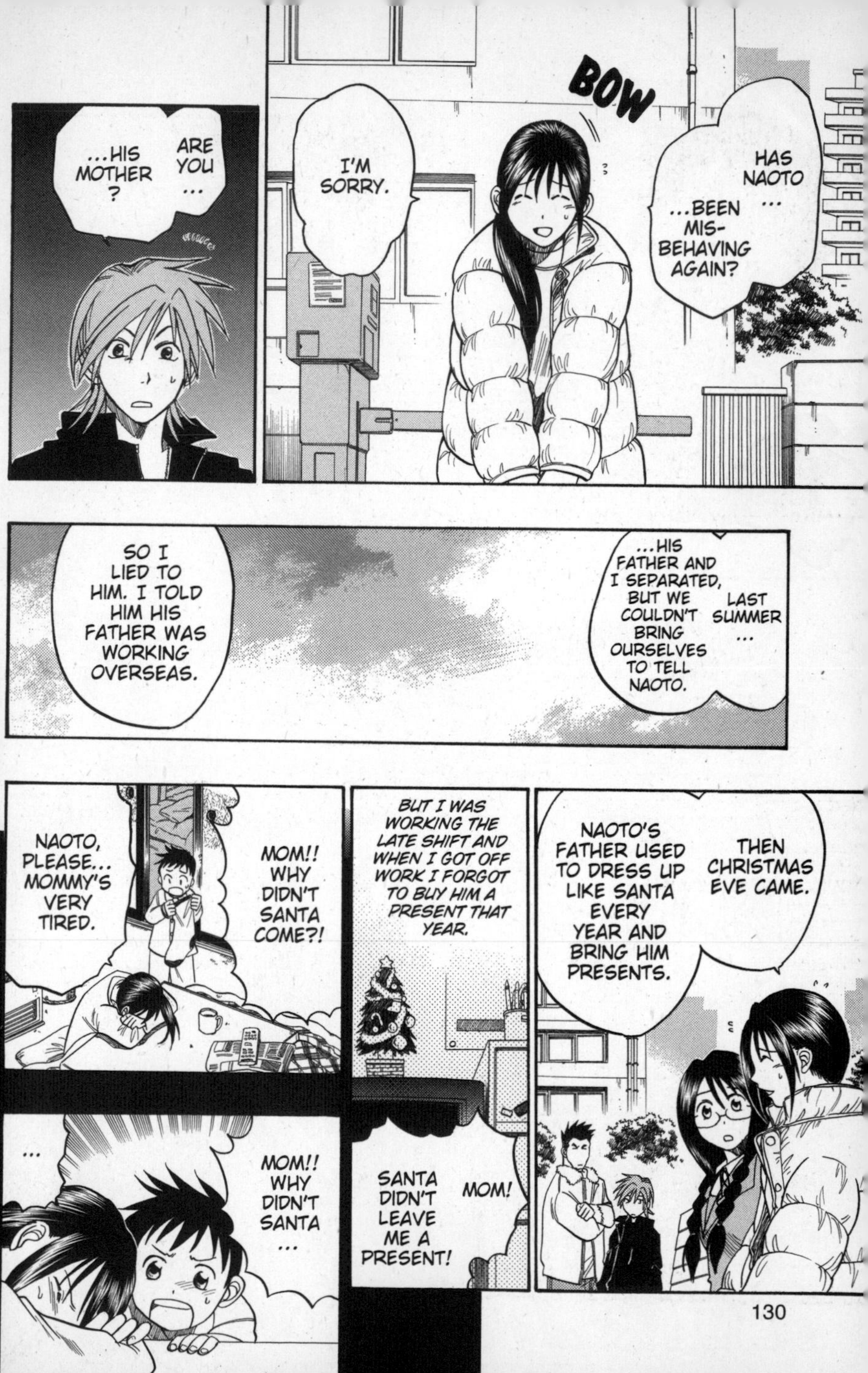
BOW
HAS NAOTO ... ...BEEN MIS-BEHAVING AGAIN?
I'M SORRY.
ARE YOU ...
...HIS MOTHER ?
LAST SUMMER ...
...HIS FATHER AND I SEPARATED, BUT WE COULDN'T BRING OURSELVES TO TELL NAOTO.
SO I LIED TO HIM. I TOLD HIM HIS FATHER WAS WORKING OVERSEAS.
THEN CHRISTMAS EVE CAME.
NAOTO'S FATHER USED TO DRESS UP LIKE SANTA EVERY YEAR AND BRING HIM PRESENTS.
BUT I WAS WORKING THE LATE SHIFT AND WHEN I GOT OFF WORK I FORGOT TO BUY HIM A PRESENT THAT YEAR.
MOM!! WHY DIDN'T SANTA COME?!
NAOTO, PLEASE... MOMMY'S VERY TIRED.
MOM!
SANTA DIDN'T LEAVE ME A PRESENT!
MOM!! WHY DIDN'T SANTA ...
...

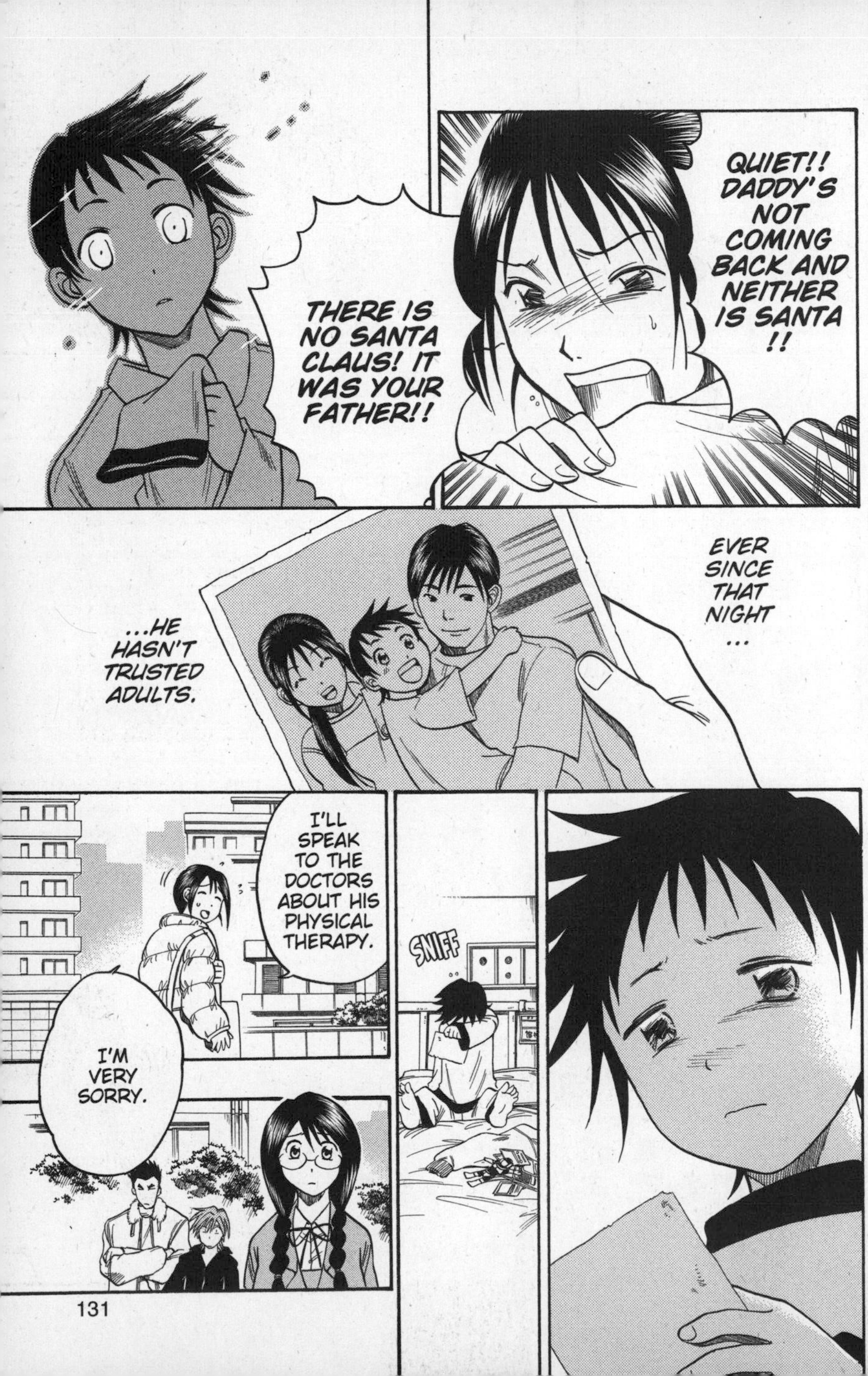
QUIET!! DADDY'S NOT COMING BACK AND NEITHER IS SANTA !!
THERE IS NO SANTA CLAUS! IT WAS YOUR FATHER!!
EVER SINCE THAT NIGHT...
...HE HASN'T TRUSTED ADULTS.
SNIFF
I'LL SPEAK TO THE DOCTORS ABOUT HIS PHYSICAL THERAPY.
I'M VERY SORRY.

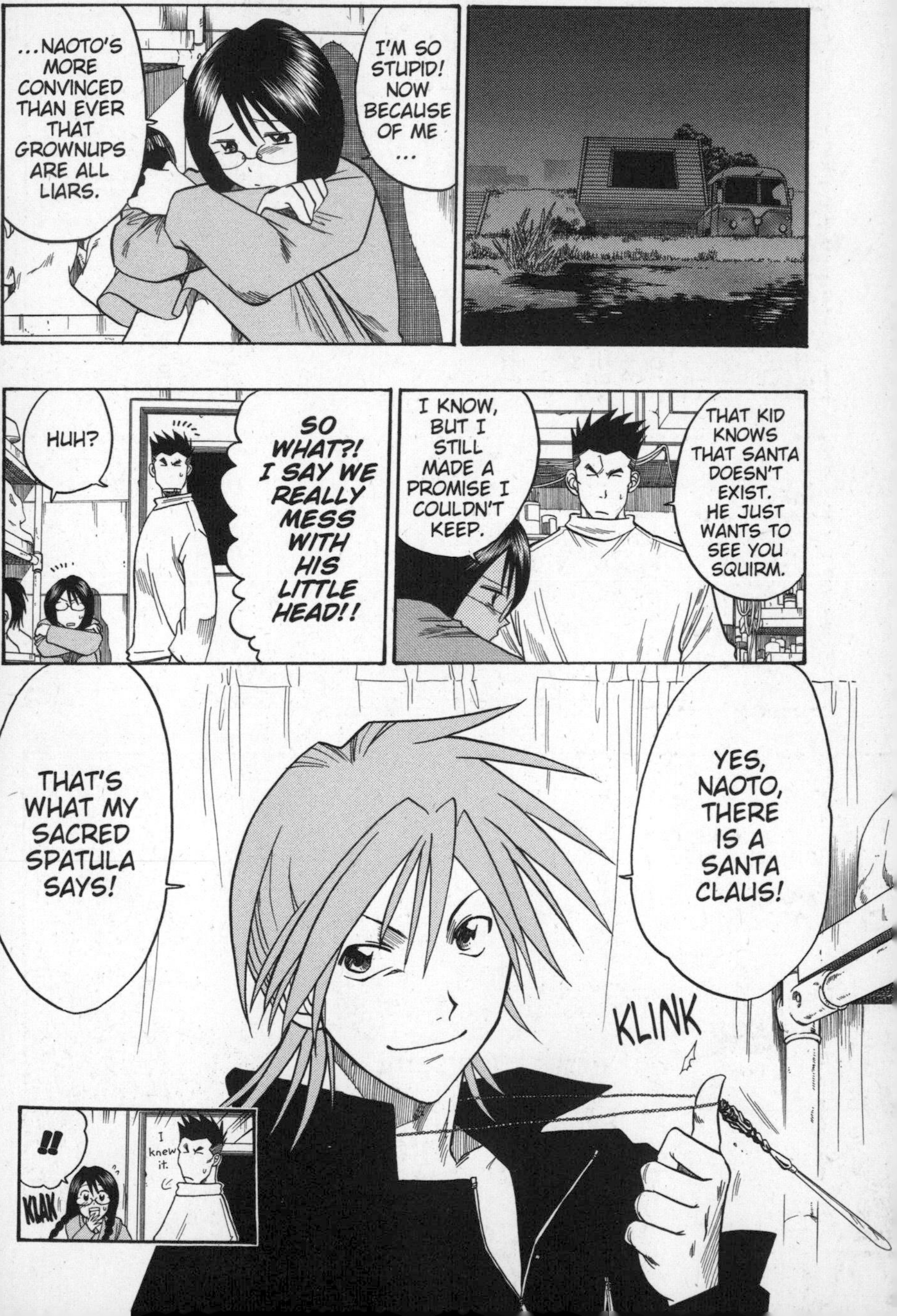
I'M SO STUPID! NOW BECAUSE OF ME ...
...NAOTO'S MORE CONVINCED THAN EVER THAT GROWNUPS ARE ALL LIARS.
THAT KID KNOWS THAT SANTA DOESN'T EXIST. HE JUST WANTS TO SEE YOU SQUIRM.
I KNOW, BUT I STILL MADE A PROMISE I COULDN'T KEEP.
SO WHAT?! I SAY WE REALLY MESS WITH HIS LITTLE HEAD!!
HUH?
YES, NAOTO, THERE IS A SANTA CLAUS!
THAT'S WHAT MY SACRED SPATULA SAYS!
KLINK
I knew it.
!!
KLAK

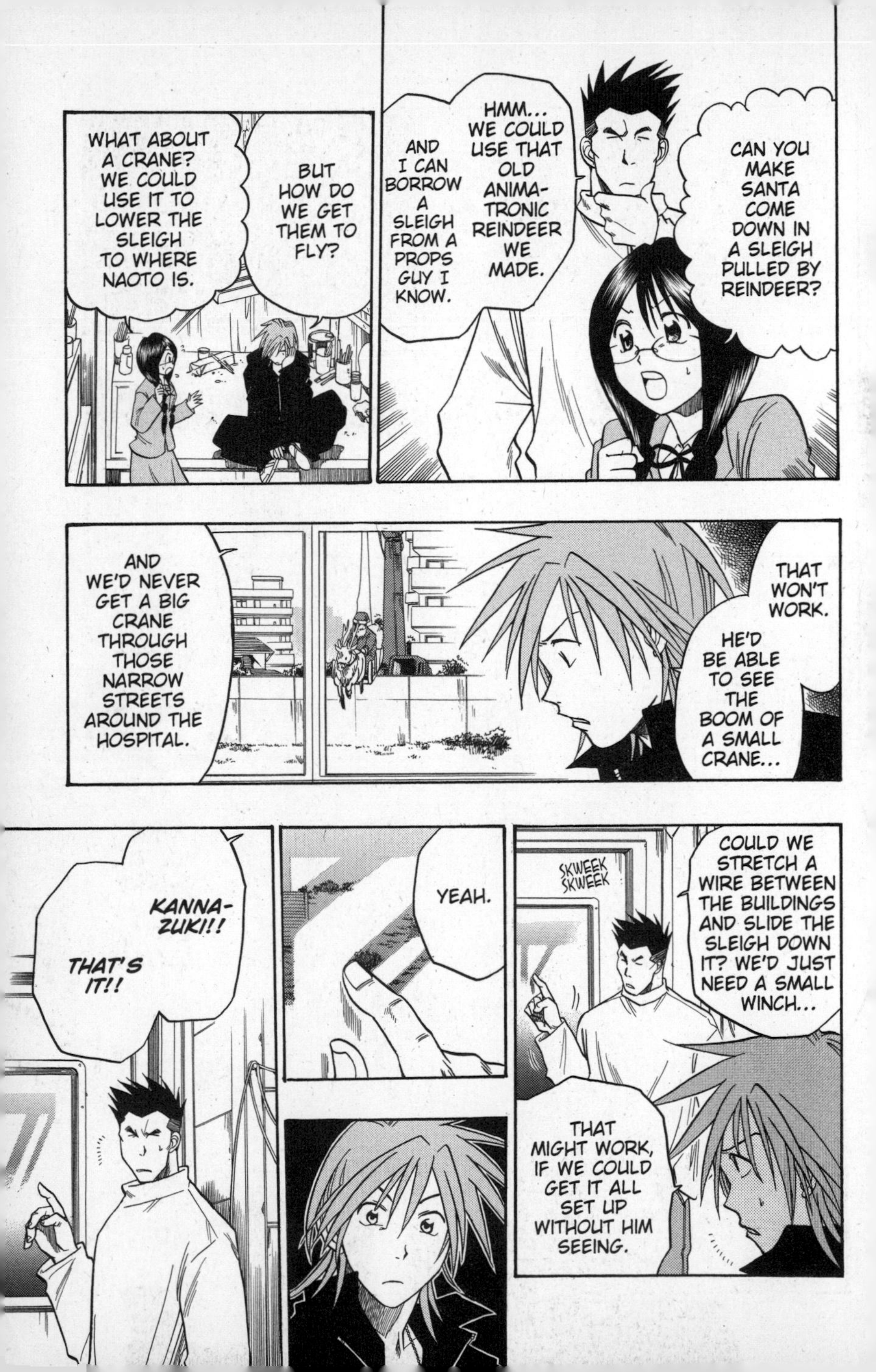
CAN YOU MAKE SANTA COME DOWN IN A SLEIGH PULLED BY REINDEER?
HMM... WE COULD USE THAT OLD ANIMA-TRONIC REINDEER WE MADE.
AND I CAN BORROW A SLEIGH FROM A PROPS GUY I KNOW.
BUT HOW DO WE GET THEM TO FLY?
WHAT ABOUT A CRANE? WE COULD USE IT TO LOWER THE SLEIGH TO WHERE NAOTO IS.
THAT WON'T WORK.
HE'D BE ABLE TO SEE THE BOOM OF A SMALL CRANE...
AND WE'D NEVER GET A BIG CRANE THROUGH THOSE NARROW STREETS AROUND THE HOSPITAL.
SKWEEK SKWEEK
COULD WE STRETCH A WIRE BETWEEN THE BUILDINGS AND SLIDE THE SLEIGH DOWN IT? WE'D JUST NEED A SMALL WINCH...
THAT MIGHT WORK, IF WE COULD GET IT ALL SET UP WITHOUT HIM SEEING.
YEAH.
KANNA-ZUKI!!
THAT'S IT!!

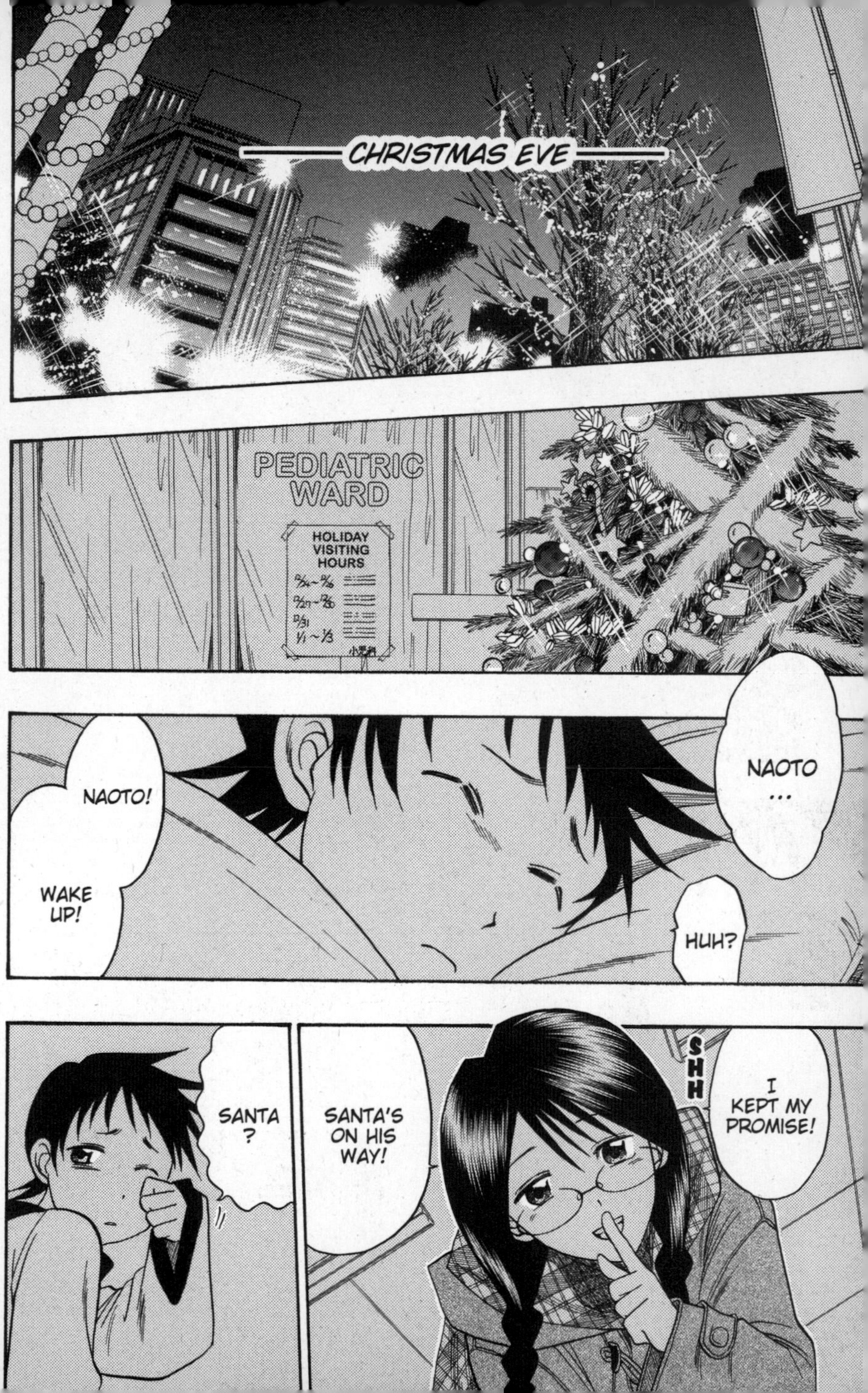
CHRISTMAS EVE
PEDIATRIC WARD
HOLIDAY VISITING HOURS
NAOTO ...
NAOTO!
WAKE UP!
HUH?
SHH
I KEPT MY PROMISE!
SANTA'S ON HIS WAY!
SANTA ?

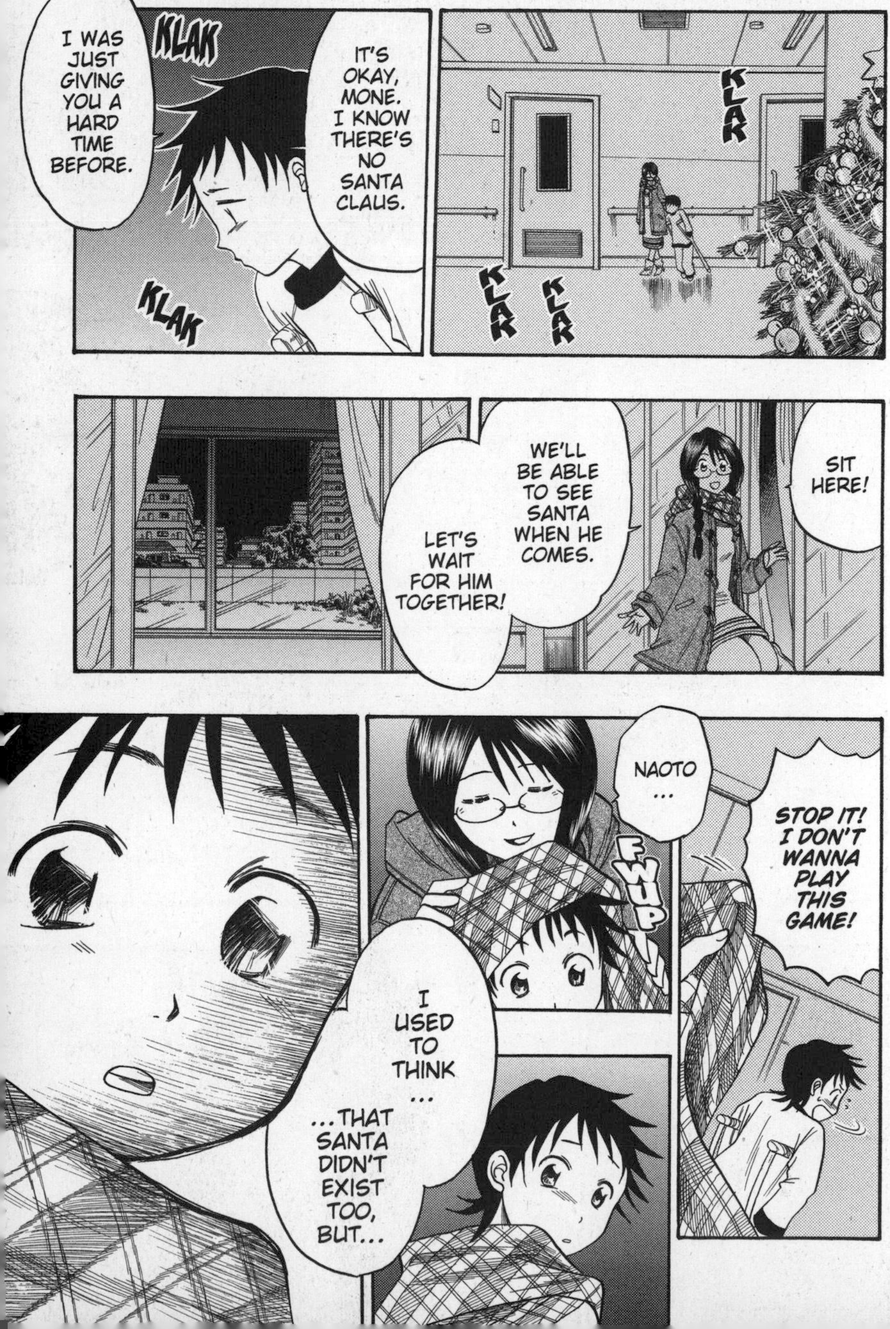
KLAK
KLAK
KLAK
IT'S OKAY, MONE. I KNOW THERE'S NO SANTA CLAUS.
KLAK
I WAS JUST GIVING YOU A HARD TIME BEFORE.
KLAK
SIT HERE!
WE'LL BE ABLE TO SEE SANTA WHEN HE COMES.
LET'S WAIT FOR HIM TOGETHER!
STOP IT! I DON'T WANNA PLAY THIS GAME!
NAOTO...
FWUP
I USED TO THINK...
...THAT SANTA DIDN'T EXIST TOO, BUT...

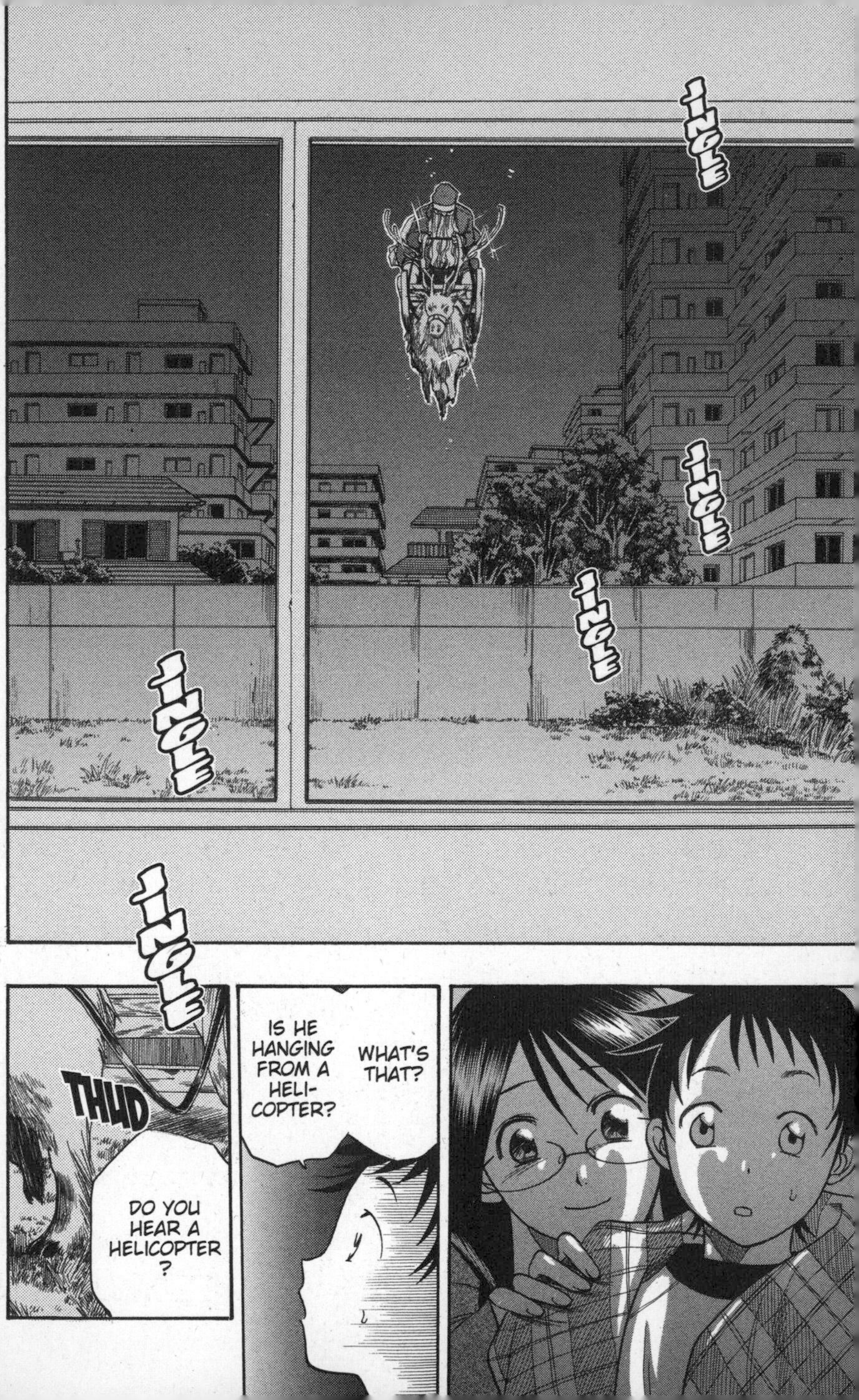
JINGLE
JINGLE
JINGLE
JINGLE
JINGLE
WHAT'S THAT?
IS HE HANGING FROM A HELI-COPTER?
THUD
DO YOU HEAR A HELICOPTER ?

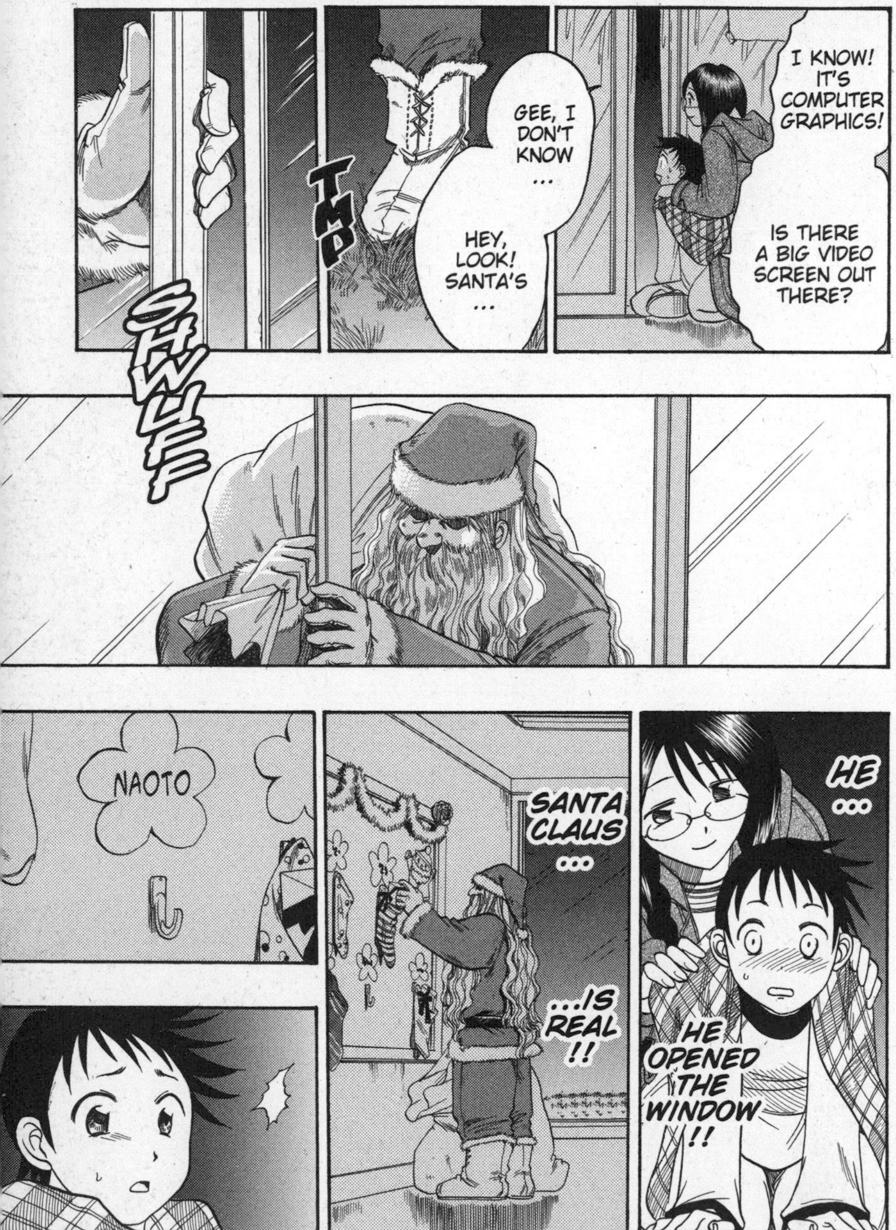
I KNOW! IT'S COMPUTER GRAPHICS!
IS THERE A BIG VIDEO SCREEN OUT THERE?
GEE, I DON'T KNOW ...
HEY, LOOK! SANTA'S ...
TMP
SHWUFF
HE ...
HE OPENED THE WINDOW !!
SANTA CLAUS ...
...IS REAL !!
NAOTO

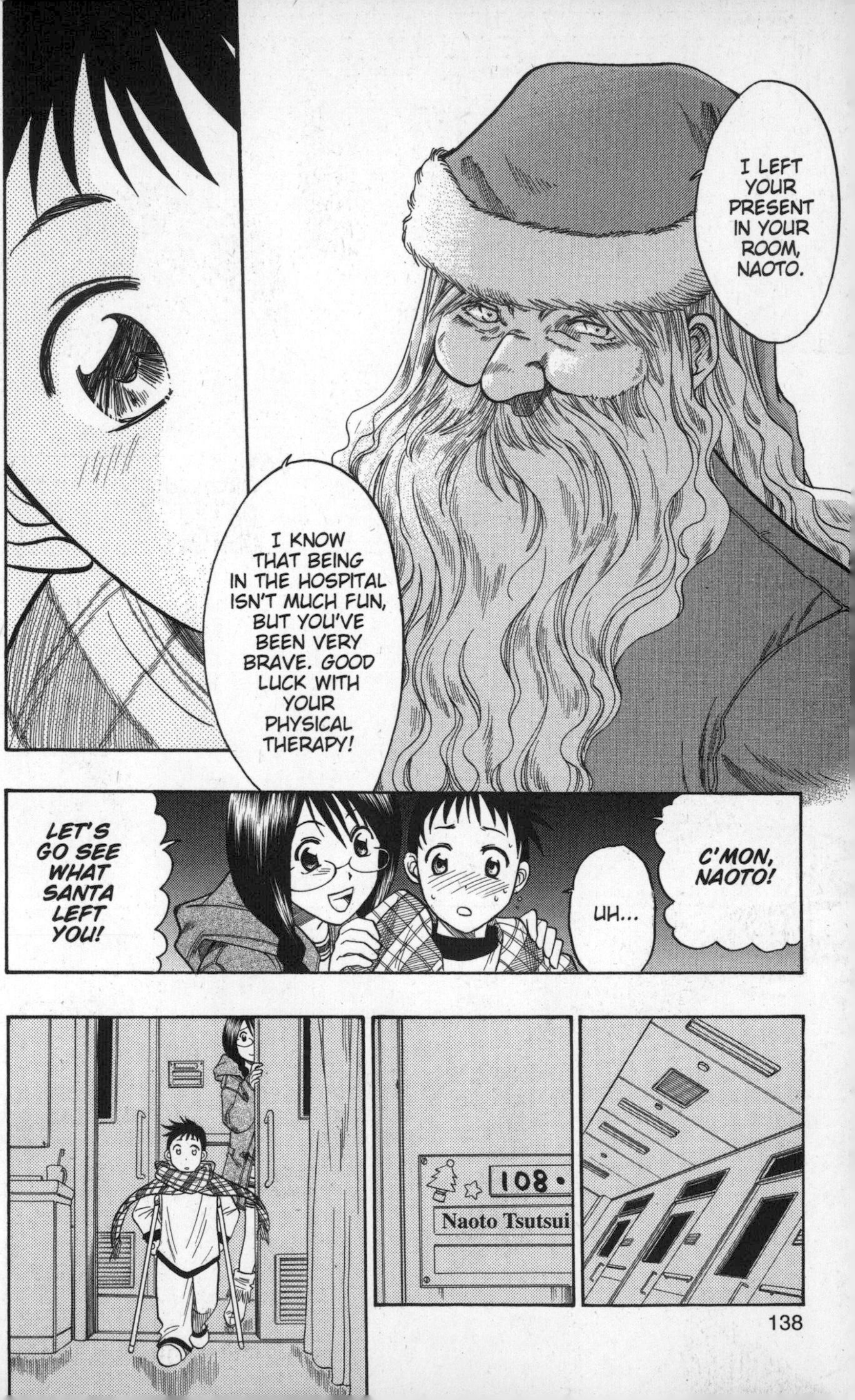
I LEFT YOUR PRESENT IN YOUR ROOM, NAOTO.
I KNOW THAT BEING IN THE HOSPITAL ISN'T MUCH FUN, BUT YOU'VE BEEN VERY BRAVE. GOOD LUCK WITH YOUR PHYSICAL THERAPY!
C'MON, NAOTO!
UH...
LET'S GO SEE WHAT SANTA LEFT YOU!
108・
Naoto Tsutsui

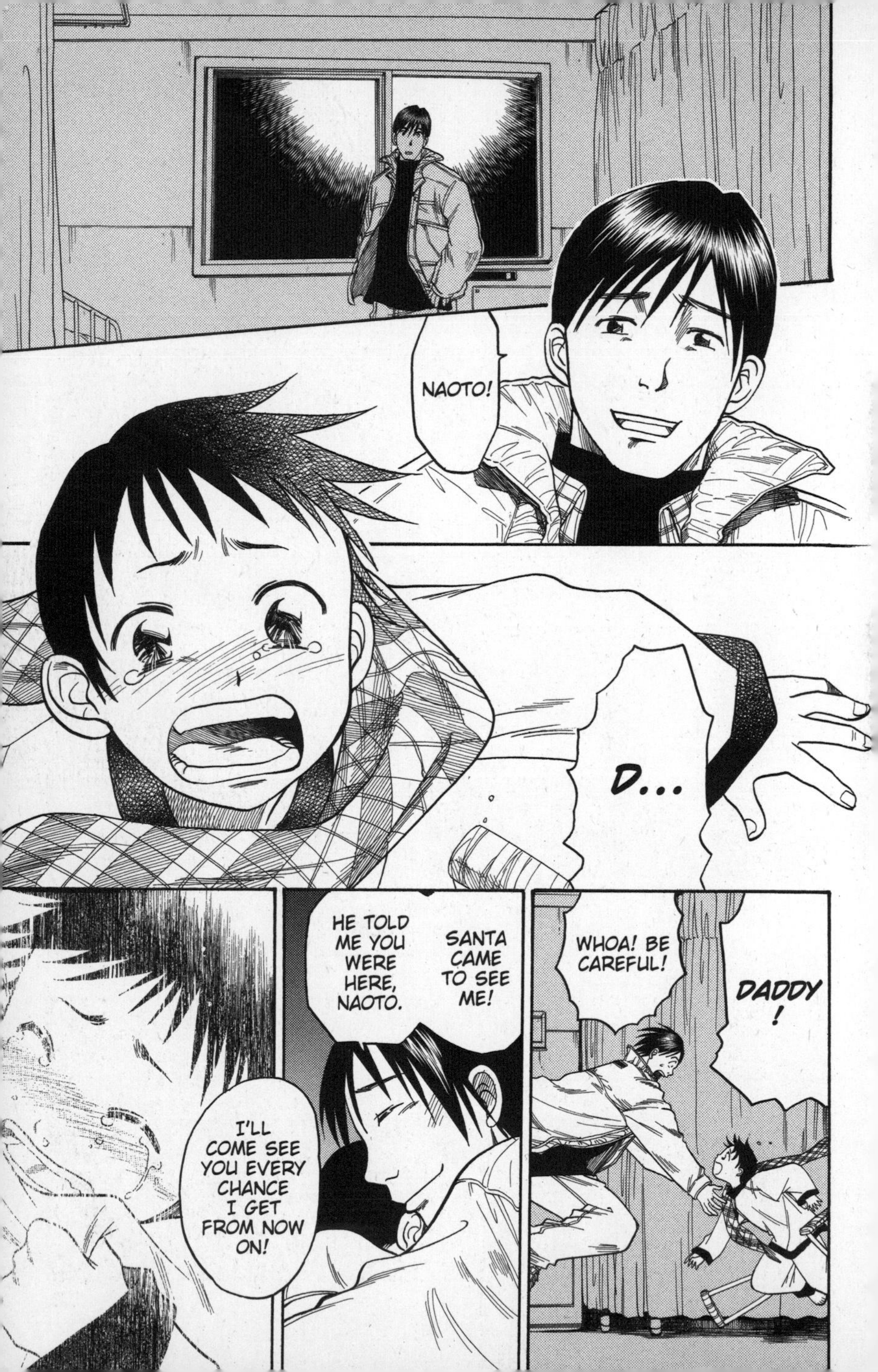
NAOTO!
D...
DADDY!
WHOA! BE CAREFUL!
SANTA CAME TO SEE ME!
HE TOLD ME YOU WERE HERE, NAOTO.
I'LL COME SEE YOU EVERY CHANCE I GET FROM NOW ON!

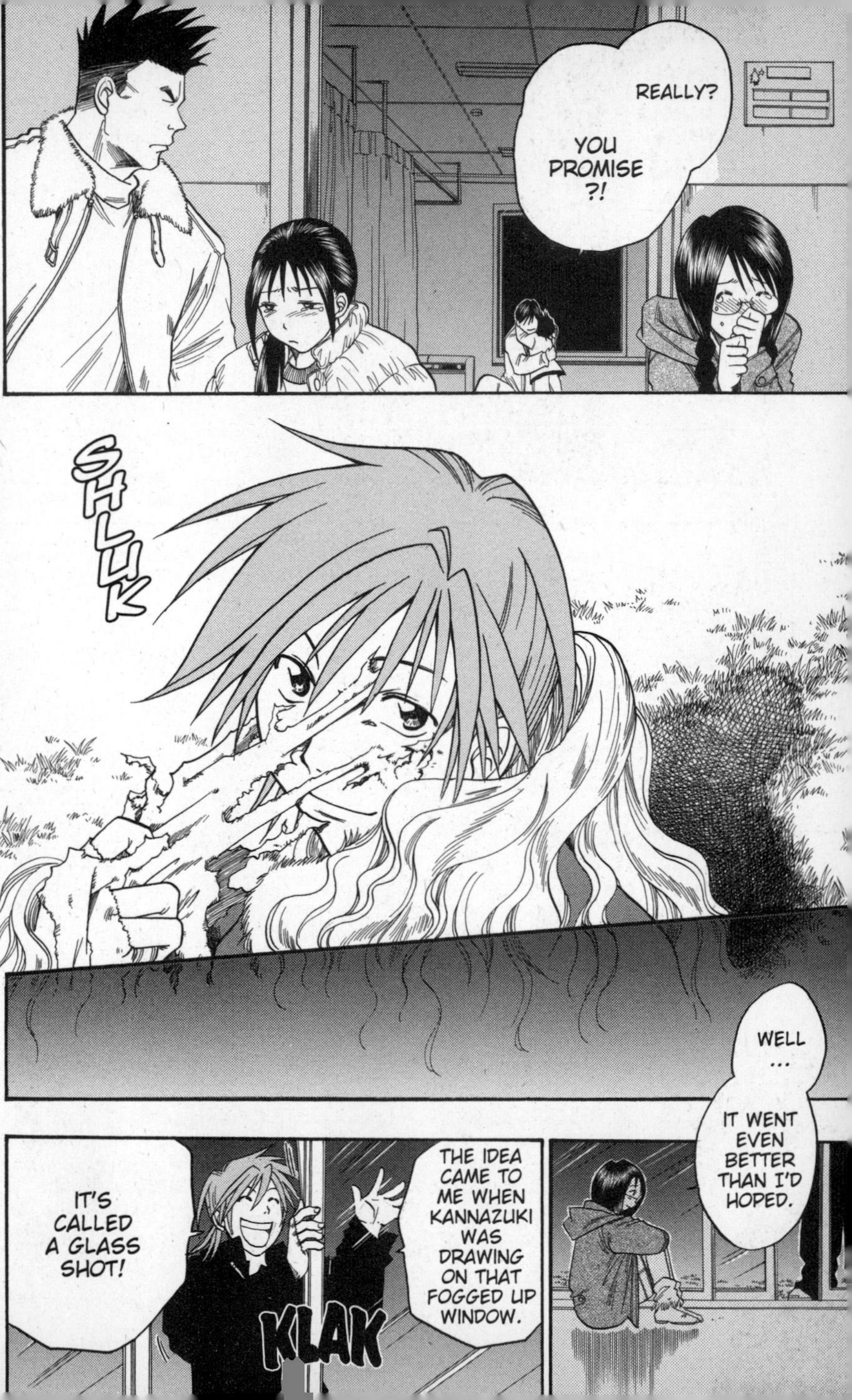
REALLY?
YOU PROMISE ?!
SHLUK
WELL ...
IT WENT EVEN BETTER THAN I'D HOPED.
THE IDEA CAME TO ME WHEN KANNAZUKI WAS DRAWING ON THAT FOGGED UP WINDOW.
IT'S CALLED A GLASS SHOT!
KLAK

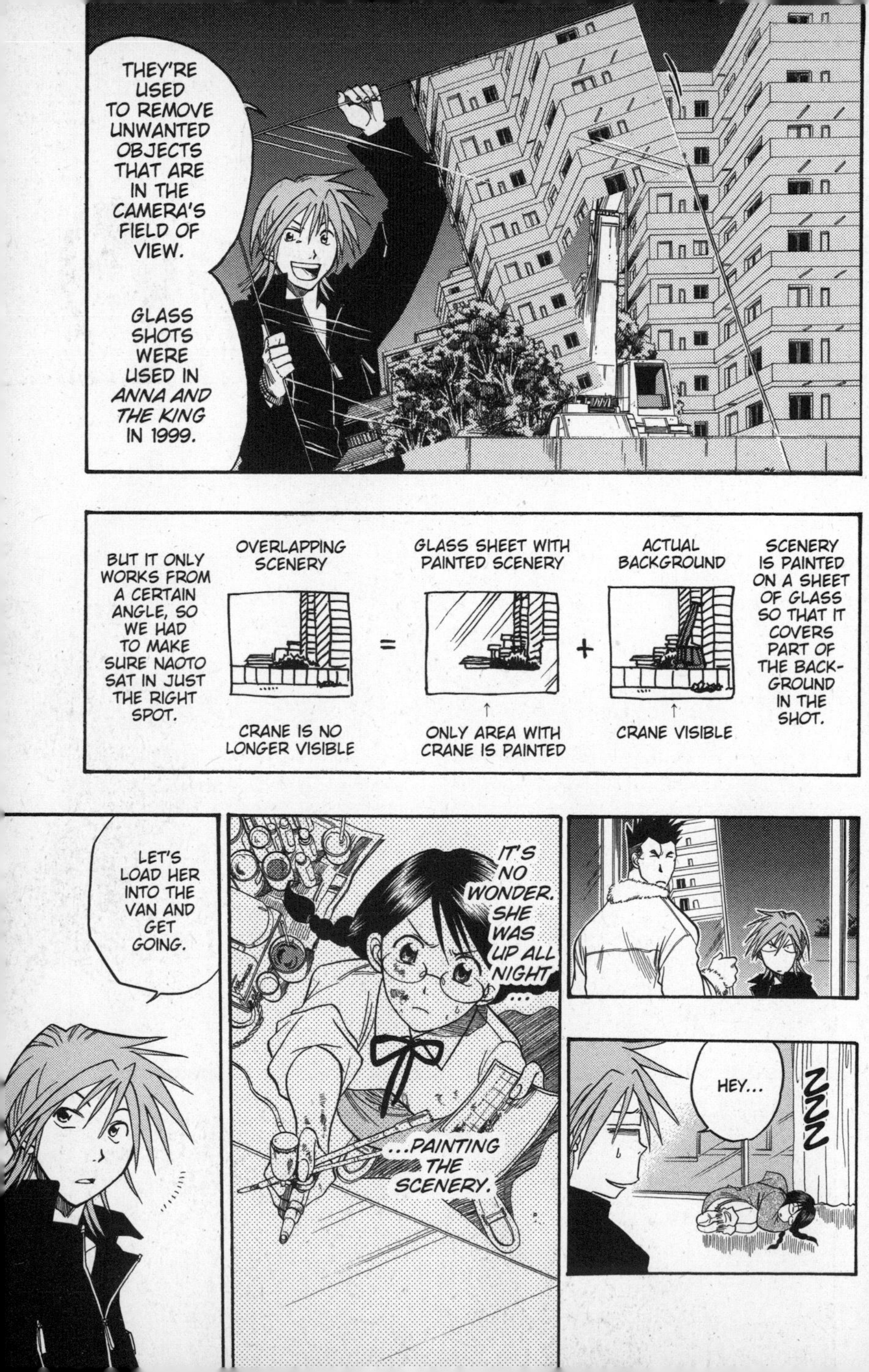
THEY'RE USED TO REMOVE UNWANTED OBJECTS THAT ARE IN THE CAMERA'S FIELD OF VIEW.
GLASS SHOTS WERE USED IN *ANNA AND THE KING* IN 1999.
SCENERY IS PAINTED ON A SHEET OF GLASS SO THAT IT COVERS PART OF THE BACK-GROUND IN THE SHOT.
ACTUAL BACKGROUND
GLASS SHEET WITH PAINTED SCENERY
OVERLAPPING SCENERY
BUT IT ONLY WORKS FROM A CERTAIN ANGLE, SO WE HAD TO MAKE SURE NAOTO SAT IN JUST THE RIGHT SPOT.
CRANE VISIBLE
ONLY AREA WITH CRANE IS PAINTED
CRANE IS NO LONGER VISIBLE
HEY...
ZZZZ
IT'S NO WONDER. SHE WAS UP ALL NIGHT...
...PAINTING THE SCENERY.
LET'S LOAD HER INTO THE VAN AND GET GOING.

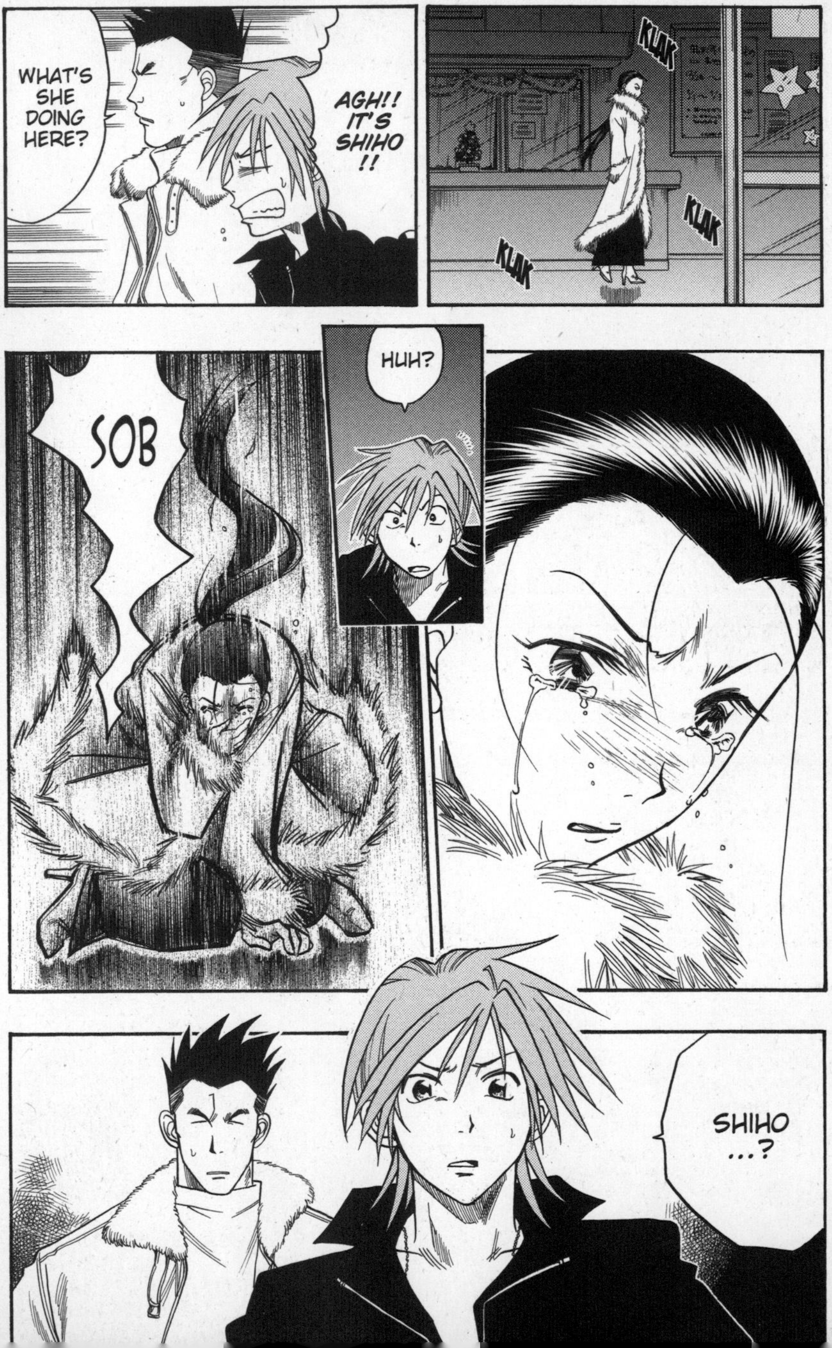
KLAK
KLAK
KLAK
AGH!! IT'S SHIHO !!
WHAT'S SHE DOING HERE?
HUH?
SOB
SHIHO ...?

Scene 33: Rosebud

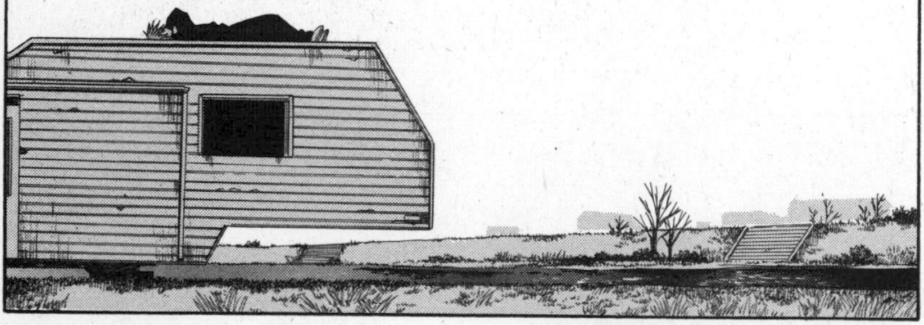

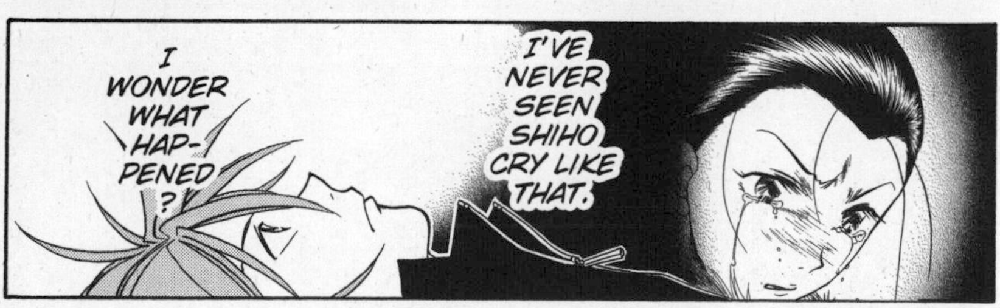
I'VE NEVER SEEN SHIHO CRY LIKE THAT.
I WONDER WHAT HAP-PENED?

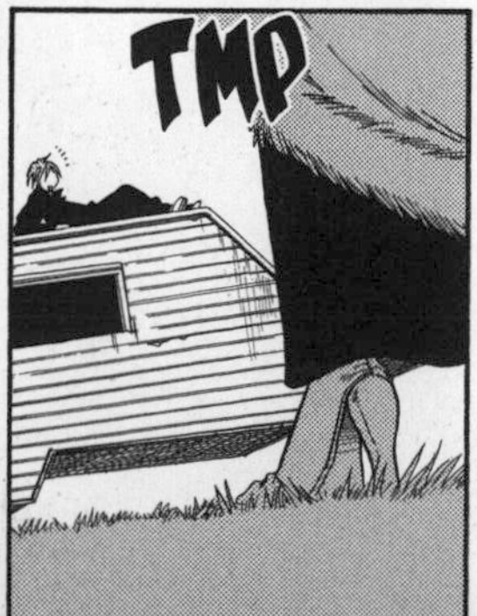
TMP

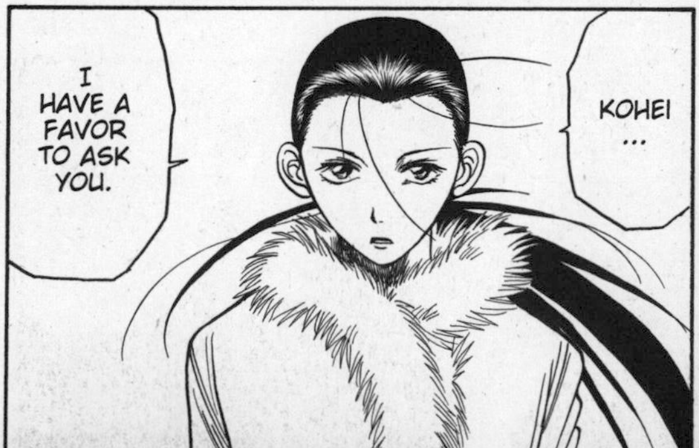
KOHEI ...
I HAVE A FAVOR TO ASK YOU.

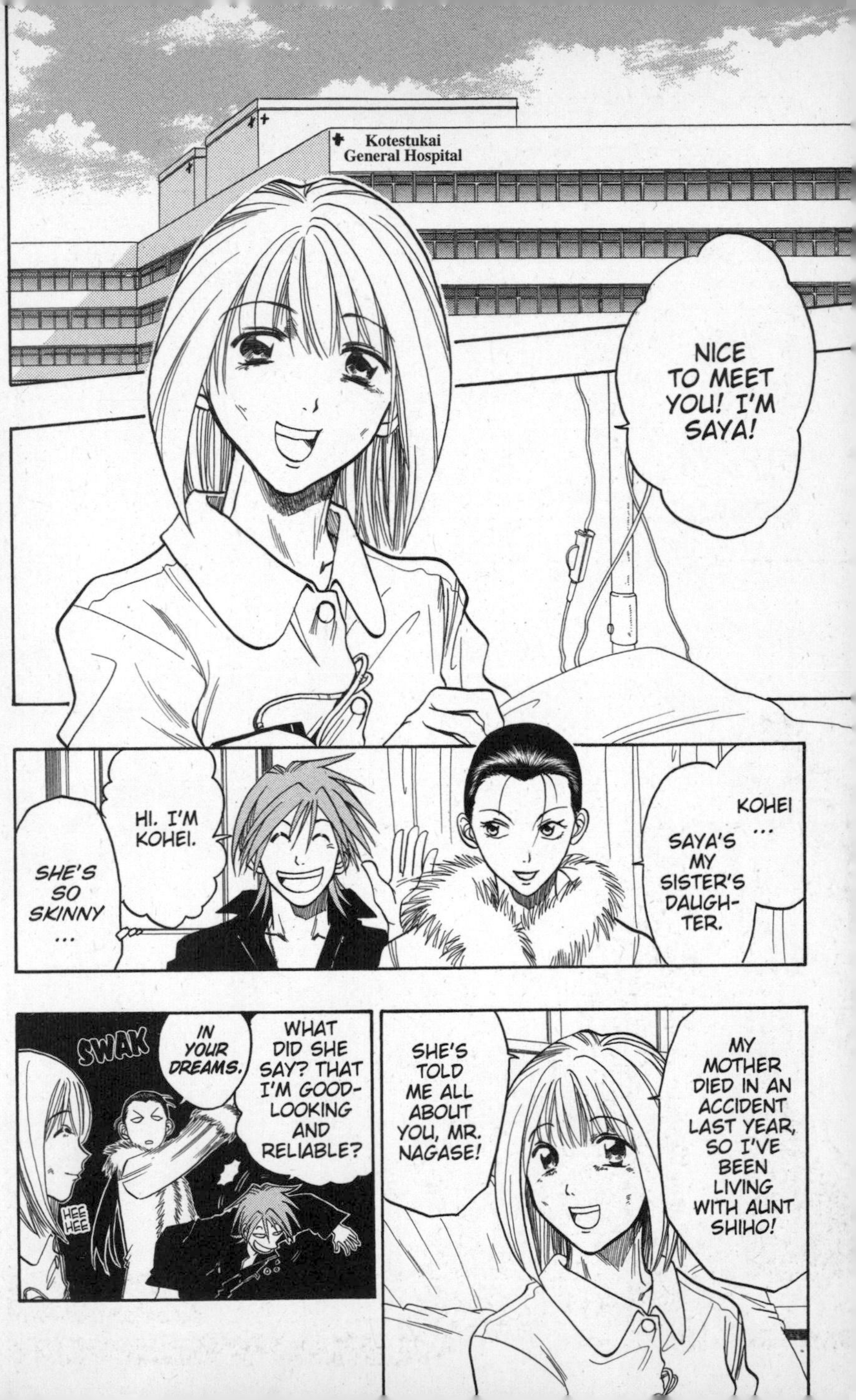
Kotestukai General Hospital
NICE TO MEET YOU! I'M SAYA!
KOHEI ...
SAYA'S MY SISTER'S DAUGHTER.
HI. I'M KOHEI.
SHE'S SO SKINNY ...
MY MOTHER DIED IN AN ACCIDENT LAST YEAR, SO I'VE BEEN LIVING WITH AUNT SHIHO!
SHE'S TOLD ME ALL ABOUT YOU, MR. NAGASE!
WHAT DID SHE SAY? THAT I'M GOOD-LOOKING AND RELIABLE?
IN YOUR DREAMS.
SWAK
HEE HEE

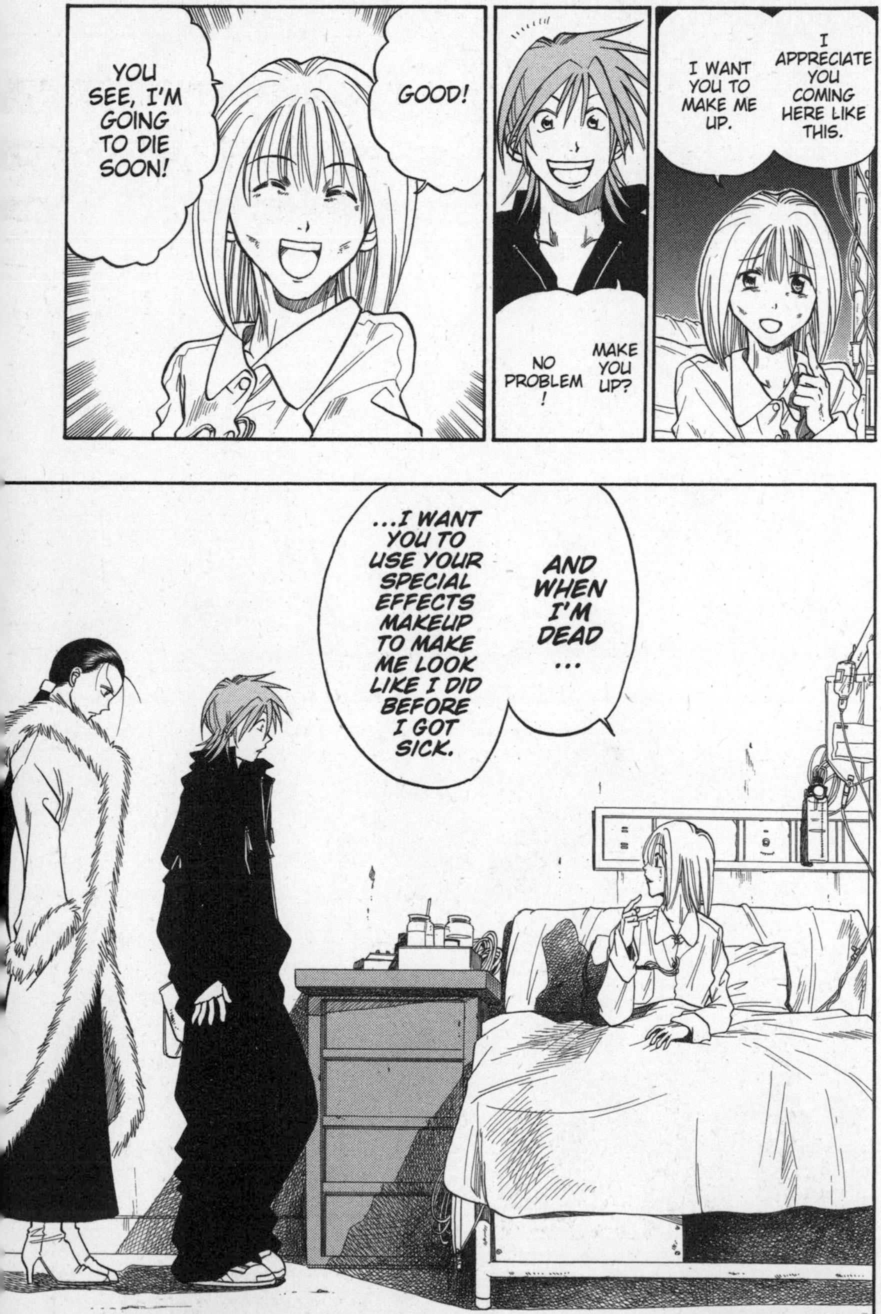
I APPRECIATE YOU COMING HERE LIKE THIS.
I WANT YOU TO MAKE ME UP.
MAKE YOU UP?
NO PROBLEM!
GOOD!
YOU SEE, I'M GOING TO DIE SOON!
AND WHEN I'M DEAD...
...I WANT YOU TO USE YOUR SPECIAL EFFECTS MAKEUP TO MAKE ME LOOK LIKE I DID BEFORE I GOT SICK.

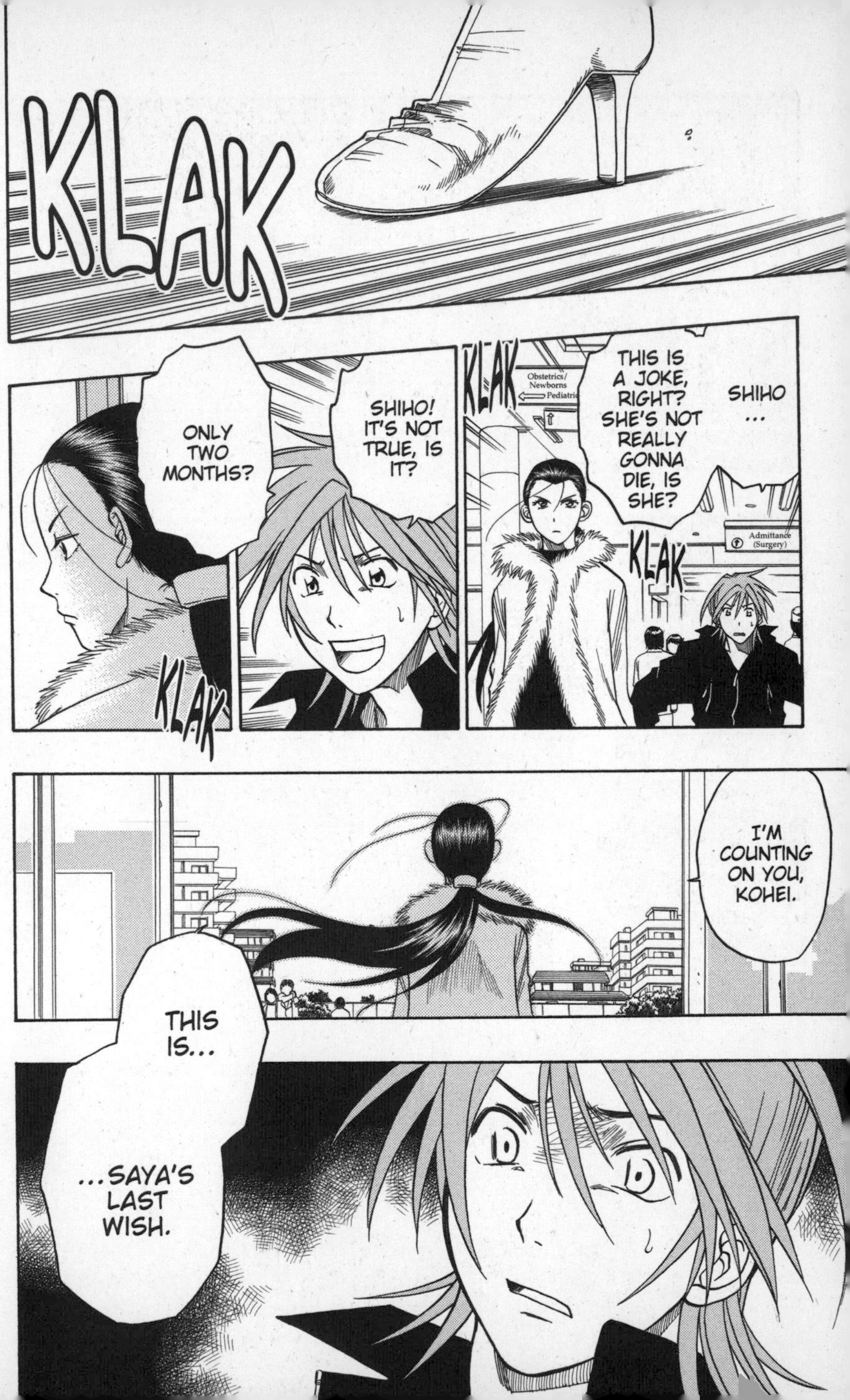
KLAK
SHIHO ...
THIS IS A JOKE, RIGHT? SHE'S NOT REALLY GONNA DIE, IS SHE?
Obstetrics/ Newborns
Pediatric
KLAK
Admittance (Surgery)
KLAK
SHIHO! IT'S NOT TRUE, IS IT?
ONLY TWO MONTHS?
KLAK
I'M COUNTING ON YOU, KOHEI.
THIS IS...
...SAYA'S LAST WISH.

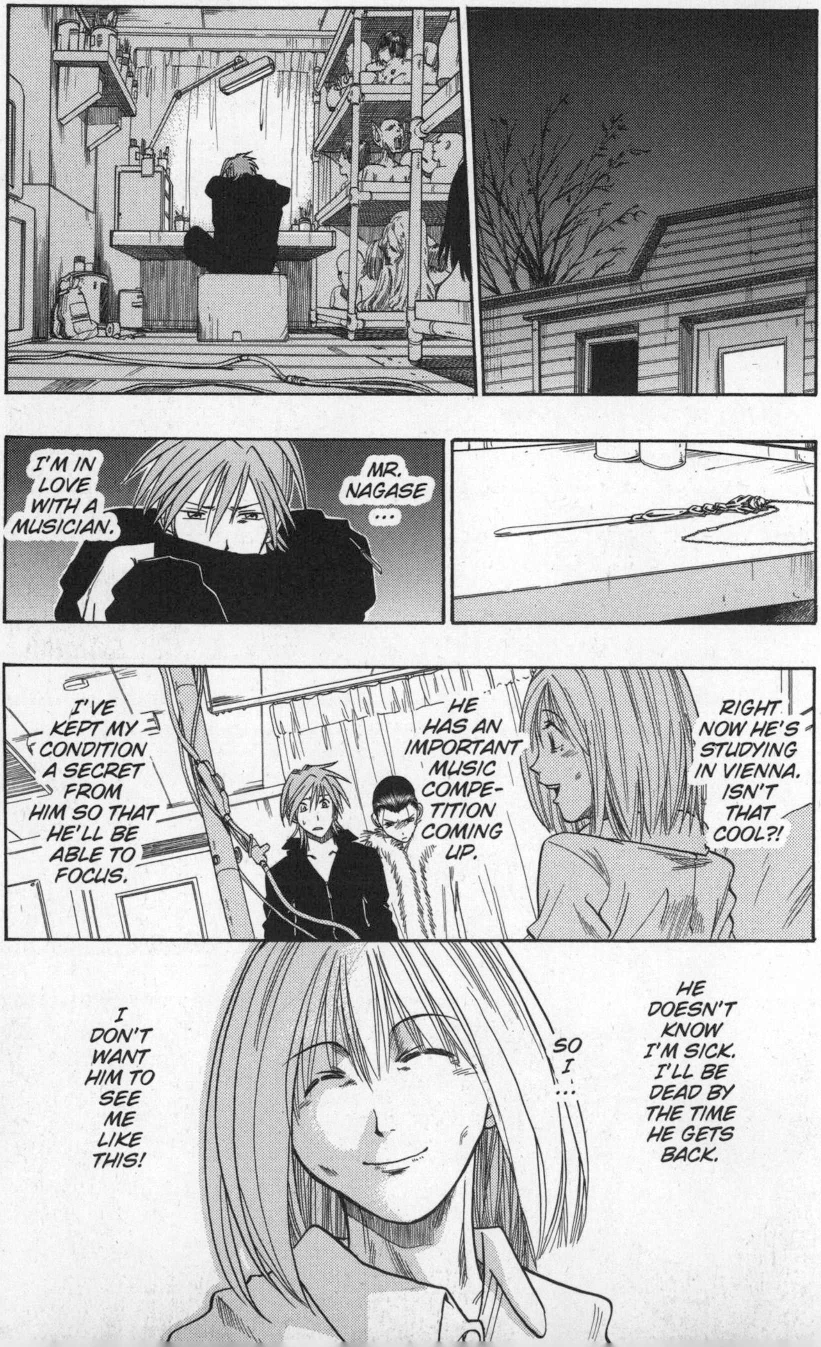
MR. NAGASE ...
I'M IN LOVE WITH A MUSICIAN.
RIGHT NOW HE'S STUDYING IN VIENNA. ISN'T THAT COOL?!
HE HAS AN IMPORTANT MUSIC COMPETITION COMING UP.
I'VE KEPT MY CONDITION A SECRET FROM HIM SO THAT HE'LL BE ABLE TO FOCUS.
HE DOESN'T KNOW I'M SICK. I'LL BE DEAD BY THE TIME HE GETS BACK.
SO I ...
I DON'T WANT HIM TO SEE ME LIKE THIS!

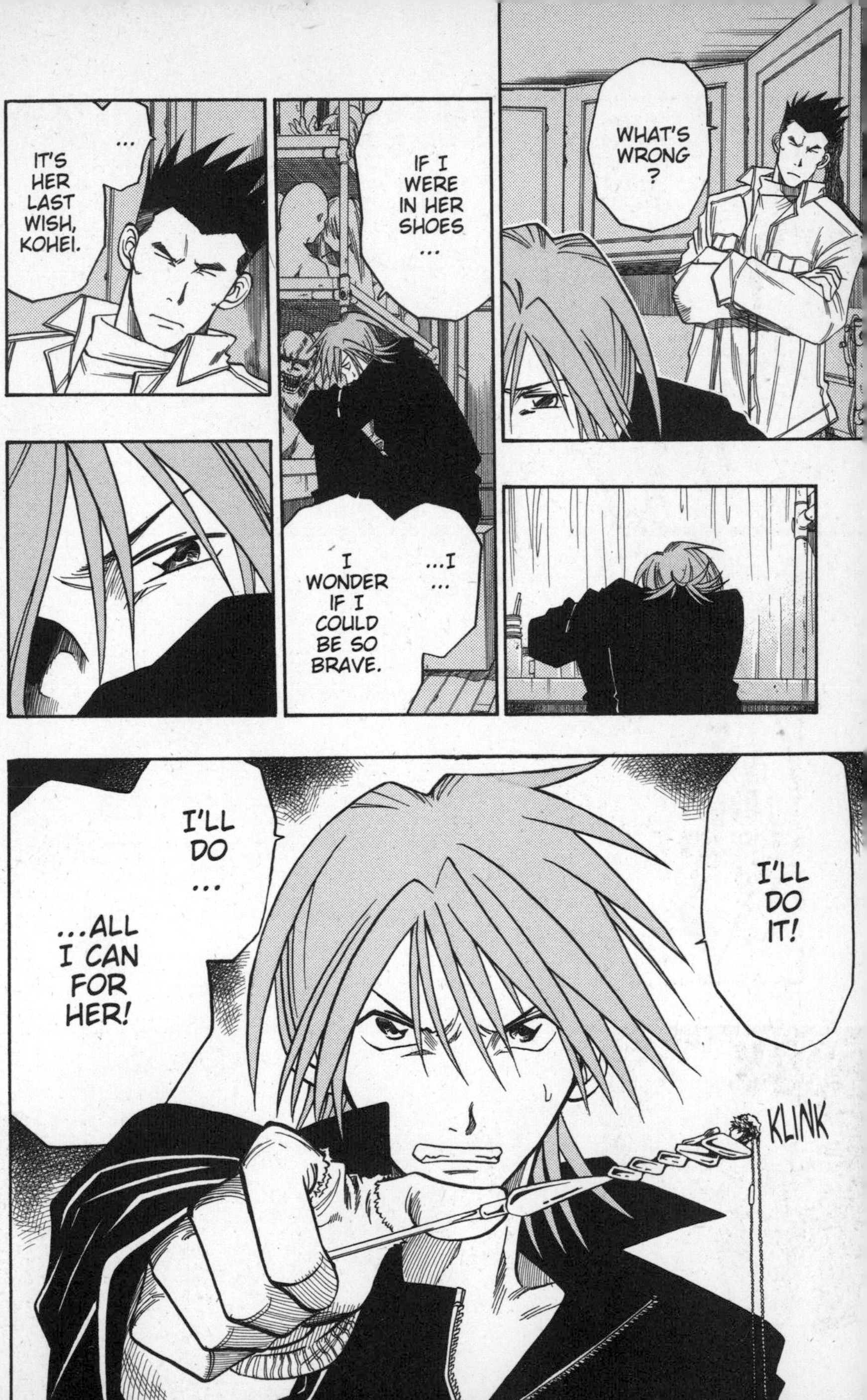
WHAT'S WRONG ?
IF I WERE IN HER SHOES ...
...
IT'S HER LAST WISH, KOHEI.
...I ...
I WONDER IF I COULD BE SO BRAVE.
I'LL DO IT!
I'LL DO ...
...ALL I CAN FOR HER!
KLINK

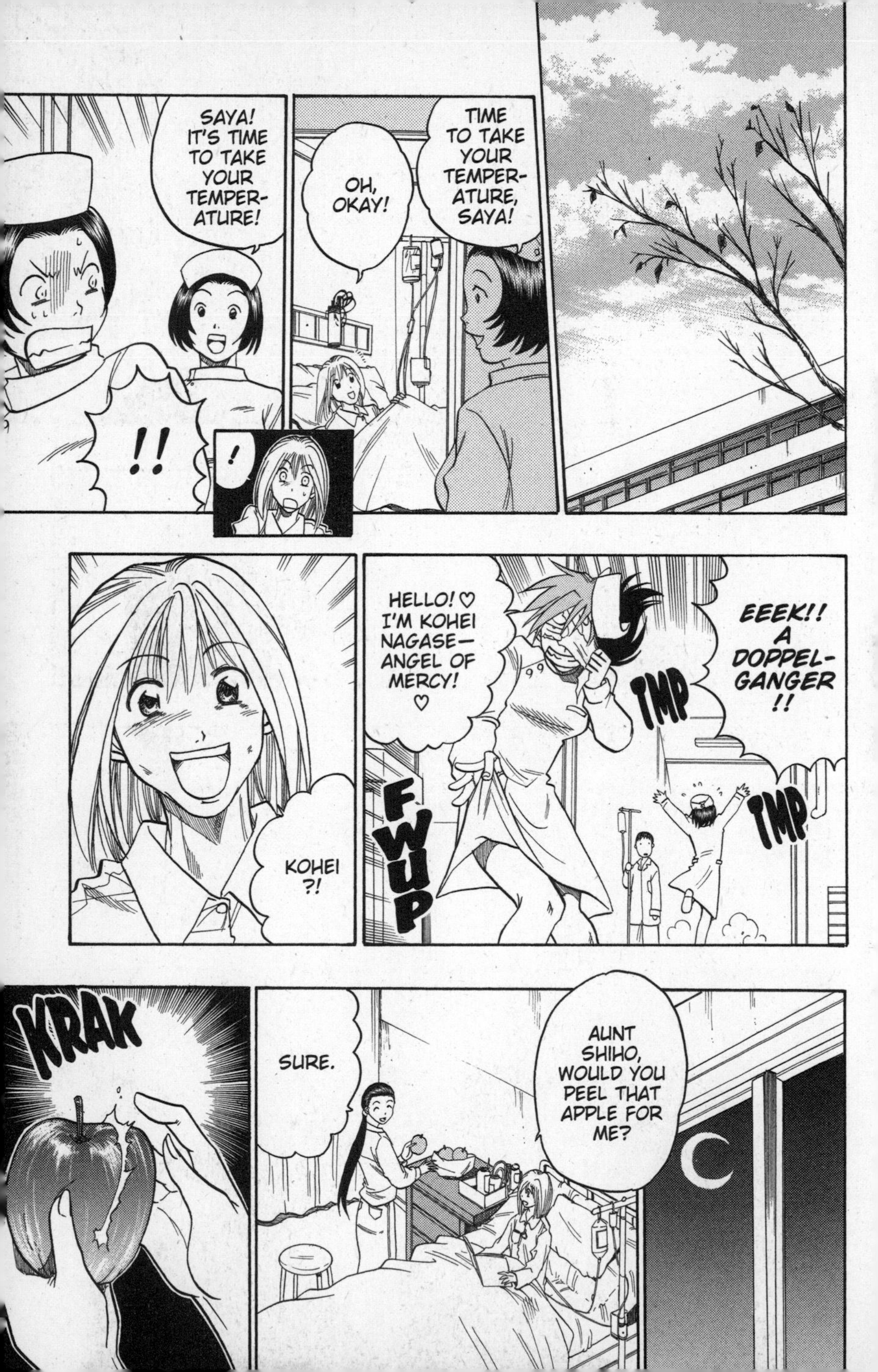
TIME TO TAKE YOUR TEMPER-ATURE, SAYA!
OH, OKAY!
SAYA! IT'S TIME TO TAKE YOUR TEMPER-ATURE!
!!
!
EEEK!! A DOPPEL-GANGER!!
TMP
TMP
HELLO! ♡ I'M KOHEI NAGASE—ANGEL OF MERCY! ♡
FWUP
KOHEI ?!
AUNT SHIHO, WOULD YOU PEEL THAT APPLE FOR ME?
SURE.
KRAK

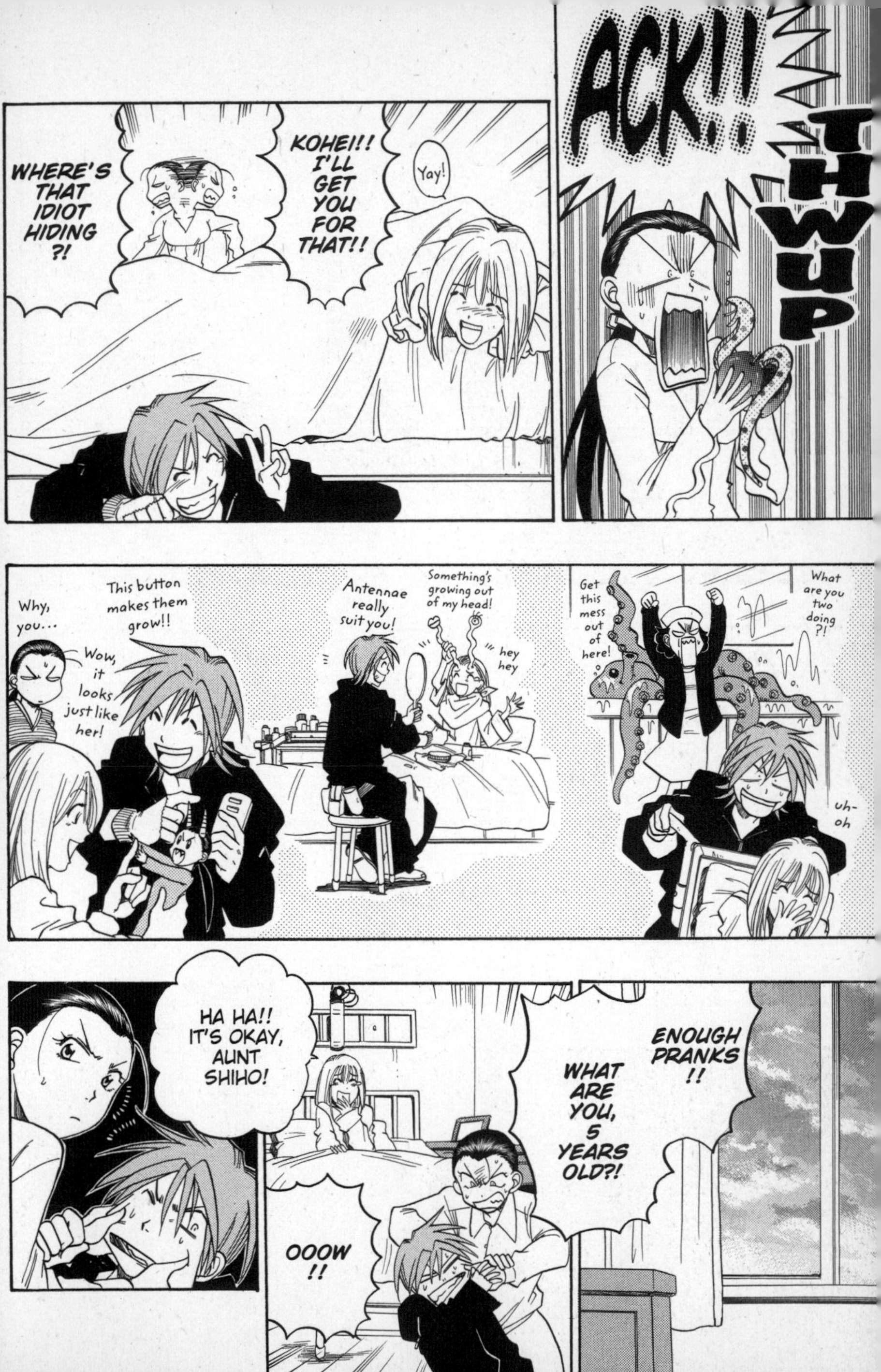
ACK!!
THWUP
Yay!
KOHEI!! I'LL GET YOU FOR THAT!!
WHERE'S THAT IDIOT HIDING?!
What are you two doing?!
Get this mess out of here!
uh-oh
Something's growing out of my head!
Antennae really suit you!
hey hey
This button makes them grow!!
Why, you...
Wow, it looks just like her!
ENOUGH PRANKS!!
WHAT ARE YOU, 5 YEARS OLD?!
OOOW!!
HA HA!! IT'S OKAY, AUNT SHIHO!

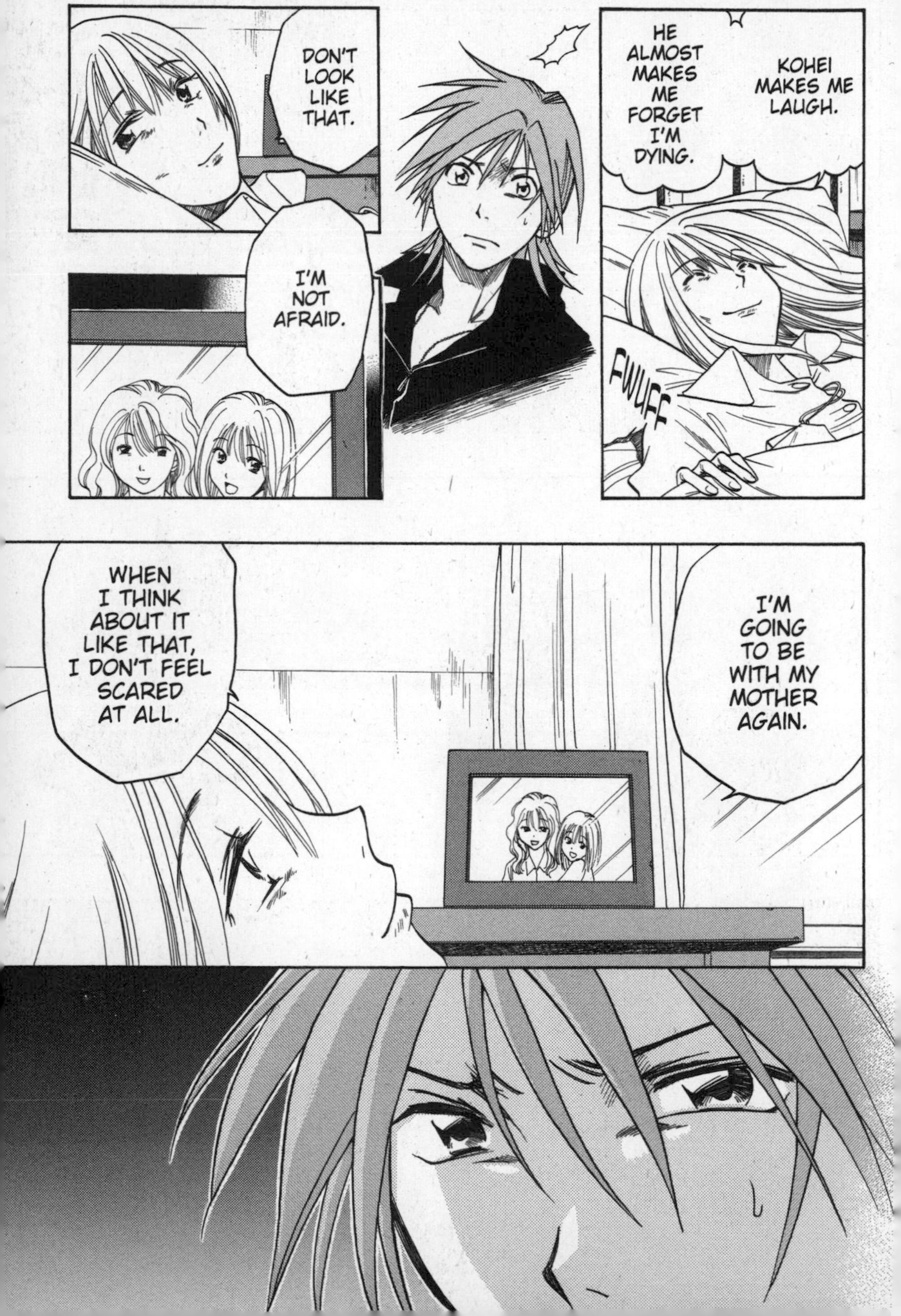
KOHEI MAKES ME LAUGH.
HE ALMOST MAKES ME FORGET I'M DYING.
FWUFF
DON'T LOOK LIKE THAT.
I'M NOT AFRAID.
I'M GOING TO BE WITH MY MOTHER AGAIN.
WHEN I THINK ABOUT IT LIKE THAT, I DON'T FEEL SCARED AT ALL.

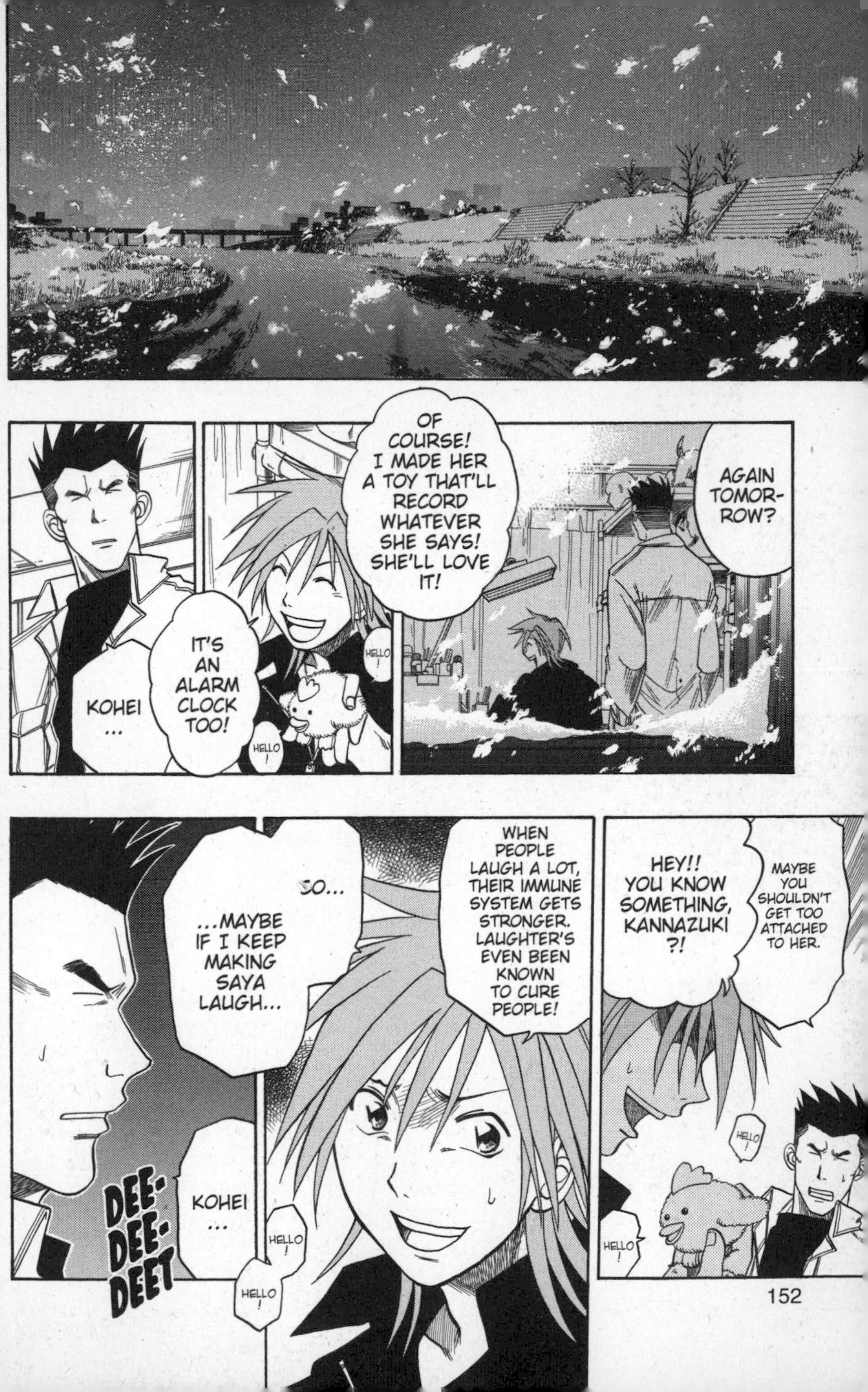
AGAIN TOMORROW?
OF COURSE! I MADE HER A TOY THAT'LL RECORD WHATEVER SHE SAYS! SHE'LL LOVE IT!
HELLO!
IT'S AN ALARM CLOCK TOO!
HELLO!
KOHEI ...
MAYBE YOU SHOULDN'T GET TOO ATTACHED TO HER.
HEY!! YOU KNOW SOMETHING, KANNAZUKI?!
HELLO!
HELLO!
WHEN PEOPLE LAUGH A LOT, THEIR IMMUNE SYSTEM GETS STRONGER. LAUGHTER'S EVEN BEEN KNOWN TO CURE PEOPLE!
SO...
HELLO!
HELLO!
...MAYBE IF I KEEP MAKING SAYA LAUGH...
KOHEI ...
DEE-DEE-DEET

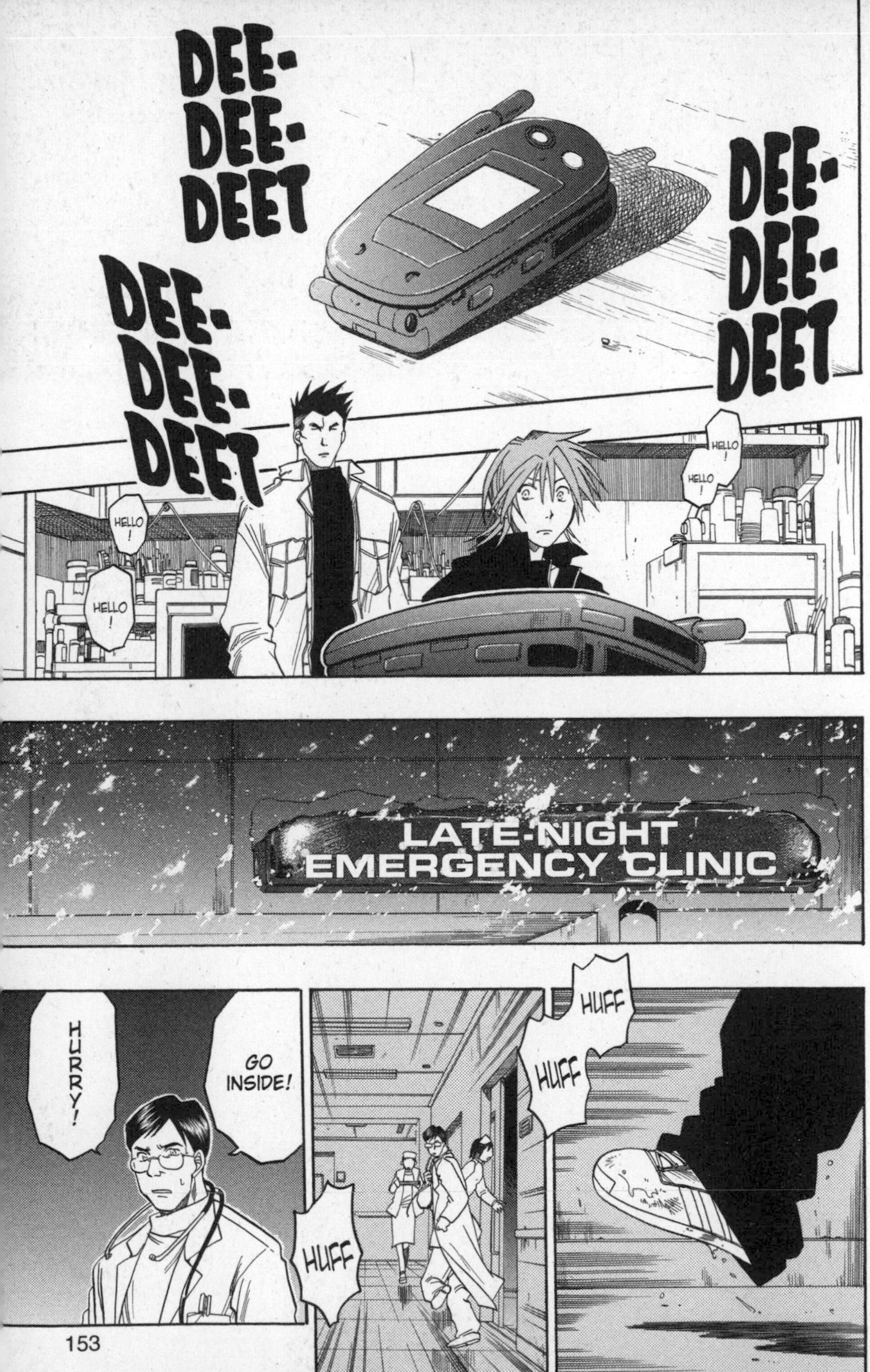
DEE-DEE-DEET
DEE-DEE-DEET
DEE-DEE-DEET
HELLO!
HELLO!
HELLO!
HELLO!
LATE-NIGHT EMERGENCY CLINIC
HUFF
HUFF
HUFF
GO INSIDE!
HURRY!

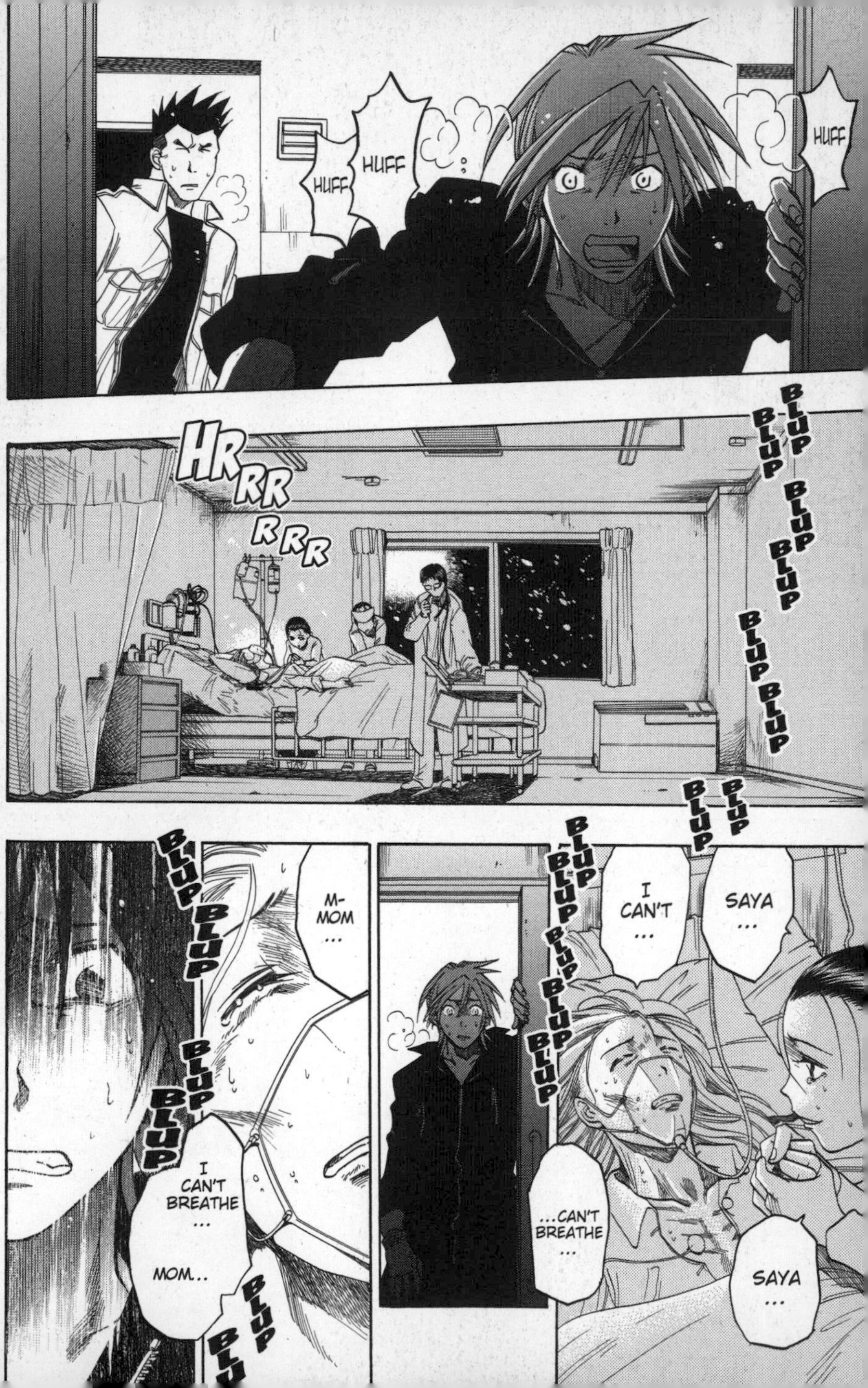
HUFF
HUFF
HUFF
BLUP BLUP
BLUP BLUP
BLUP BLUP
HRRRRRR
BLUP BLUP
SAYA...
I CAN'T...
BLUP BLUP
BLUP BLUP BLUP
...CAN'T BREATHE...
SAYA...
M-MOM...
BLUP BLUP
BLUP BLUP
I CAN'T BREATHE...
MOM...
BLUP BLU

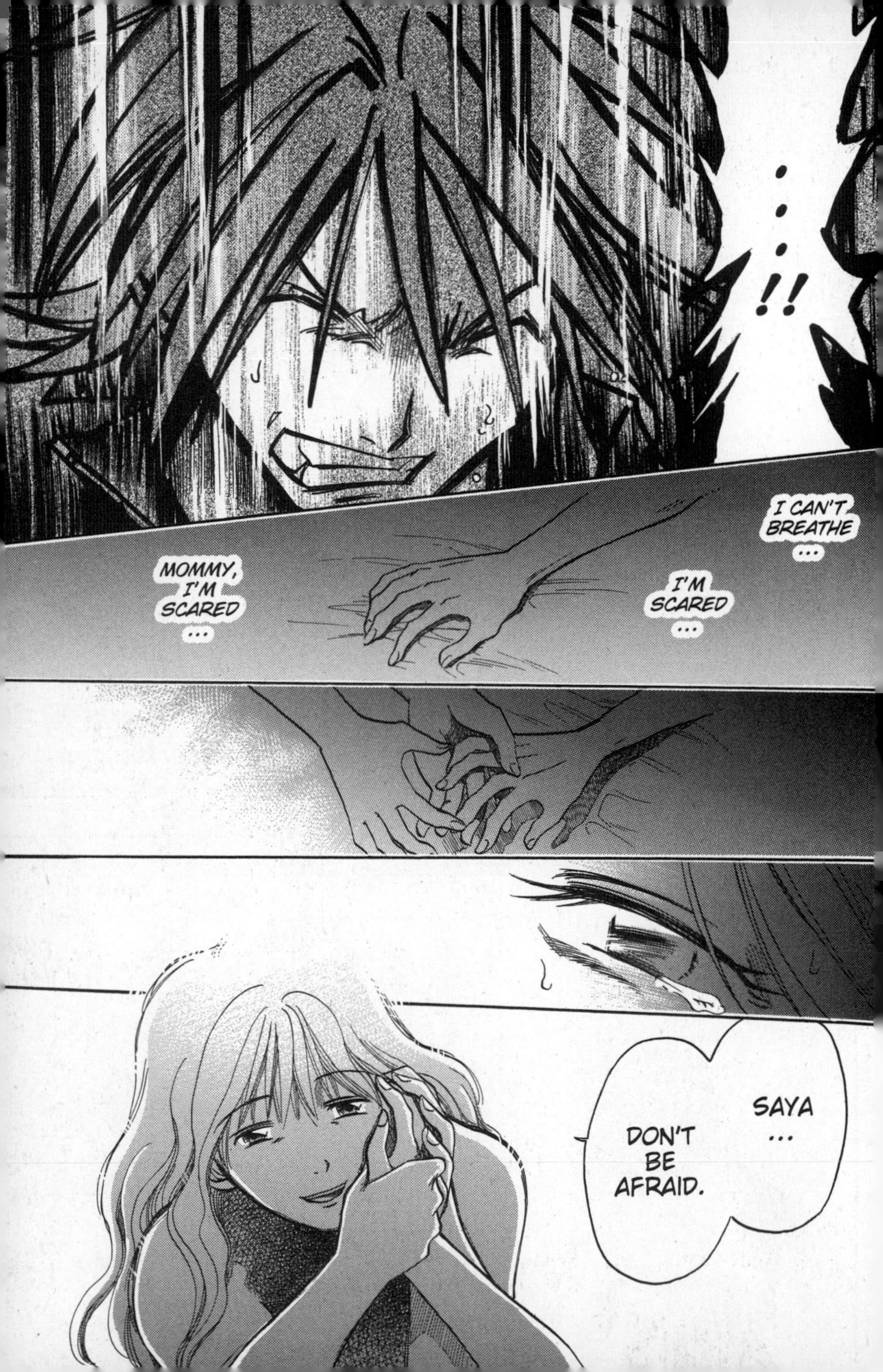
...!!
I CAN'T BREATHE ...
I'M SCARED ...
MOMMY, I'M SCARED ...
SAYA ... DON'T BE AFRAID.

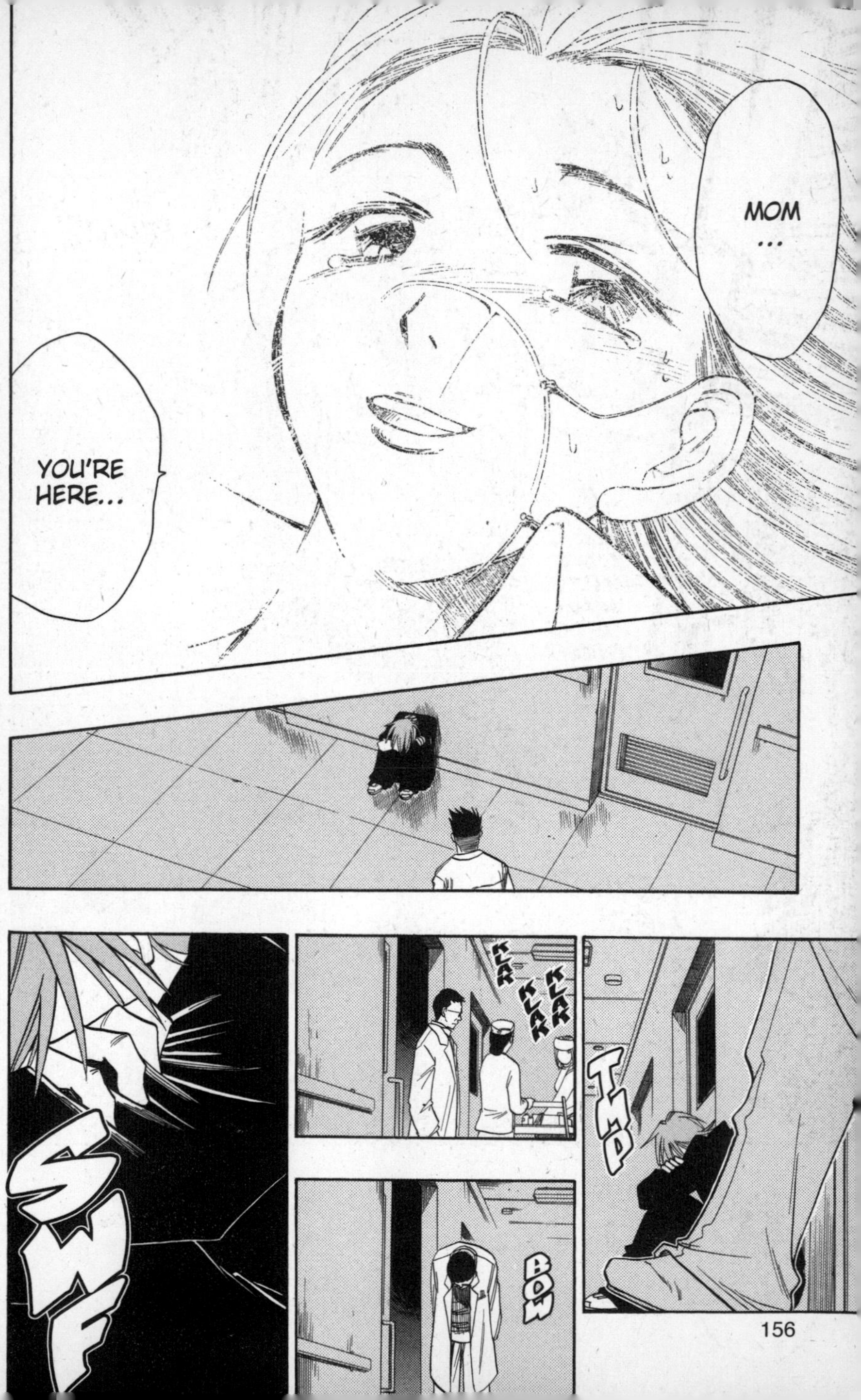
MOM ...
YOU'RE HERE...
THMP
KLAK KLAK KLAK
BOW
SWF

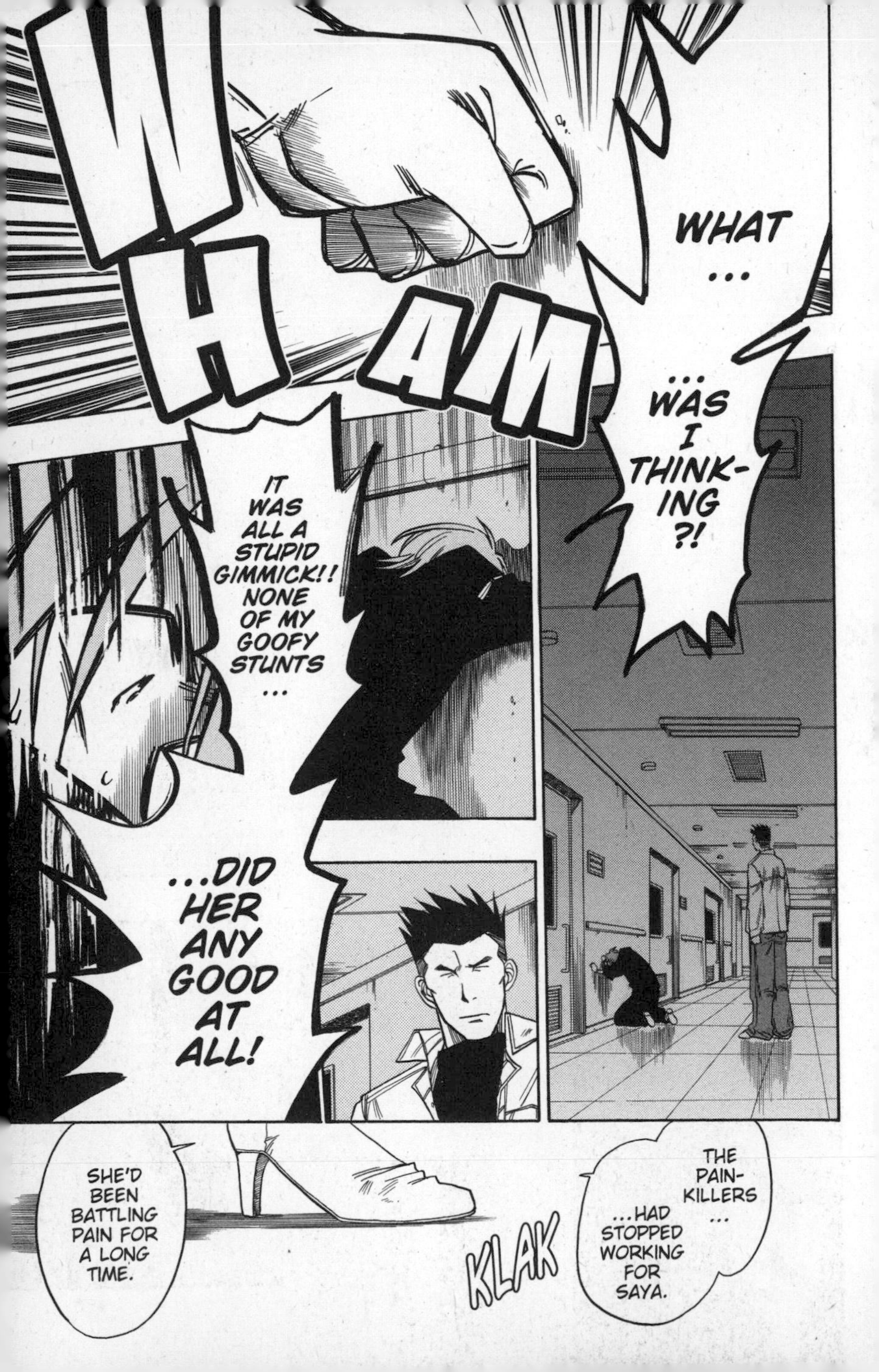
WHAT ...
... WAS I THINKING ?!
WHAM
IT WAS ALL A STUPID GIMMICK!! NONE OF MY GOOFY STUNTS ...
...DID HER ANY GOOD AT ALL!
THE PAIN-KILLERS ...
...HAD STOPPED WORKING FOR SAYA.
KLAK
SHE'D BEEN BATTLING PAIN FOR A LONG TIME.

THANK YOU.

SHE SAID...YOU MADE HER FORGET HER PAIN, KOHEI.

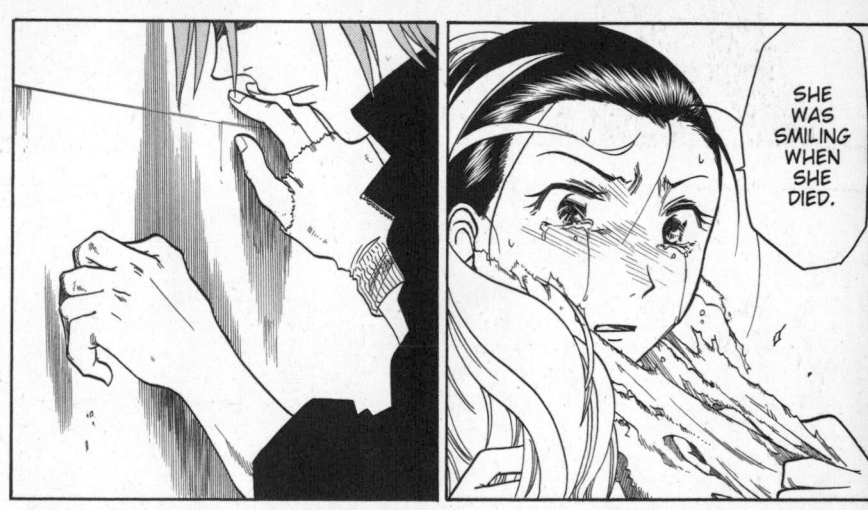

SHE WAS SMILING WHEN SHE DIED.

CHEEP

CHEEP   CHEEP

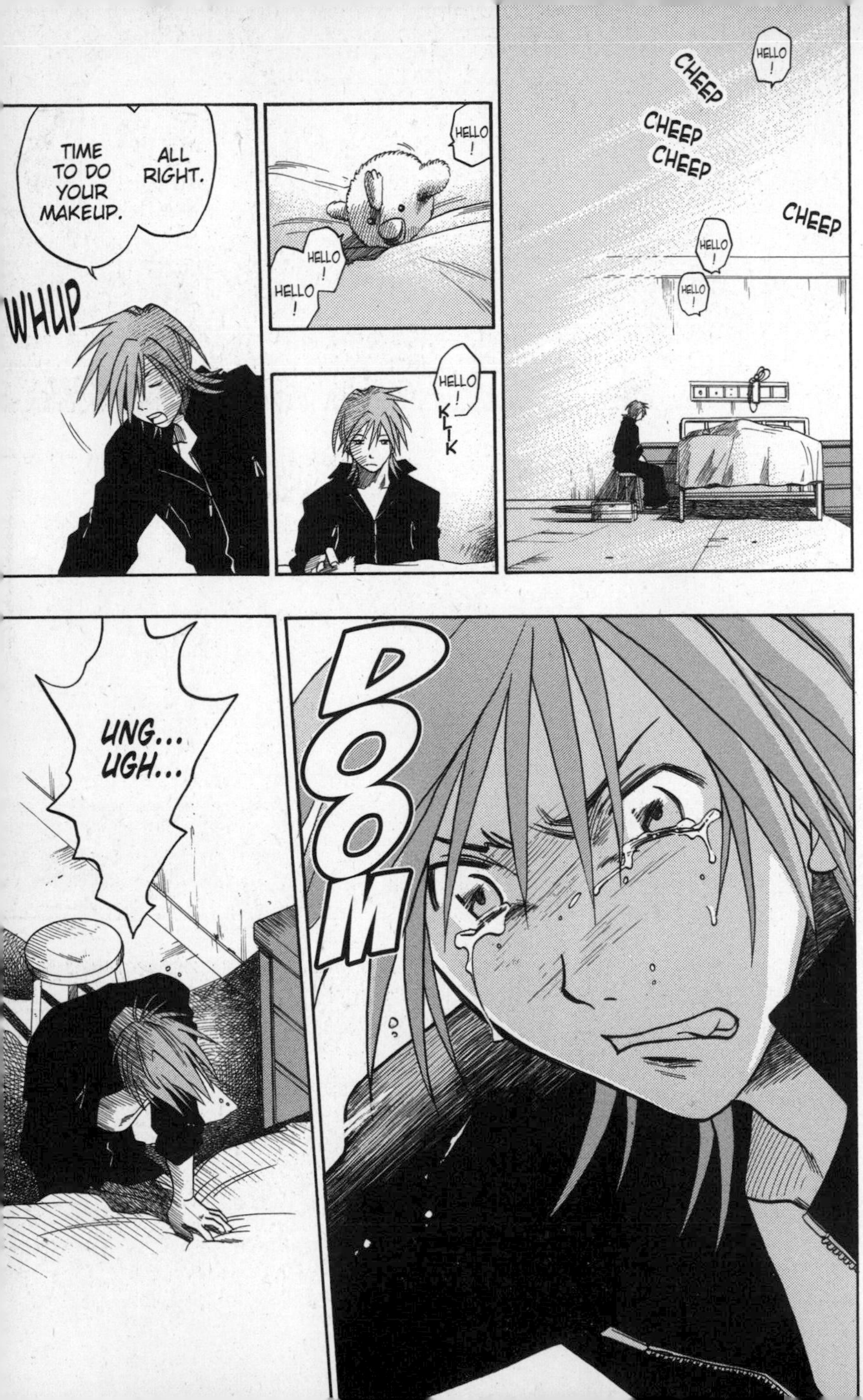
HELLO!
CHEEP
CHEEP
CHEEP
CHEEP
HELLO!
HELLO!
HELLO!
HELLO!
HELLO!
HELLO!
KLIK
ALL RIGHT.
TIME TO DO YOUR MAKEUP.
WHUP
DOOM
UNG... UGH...

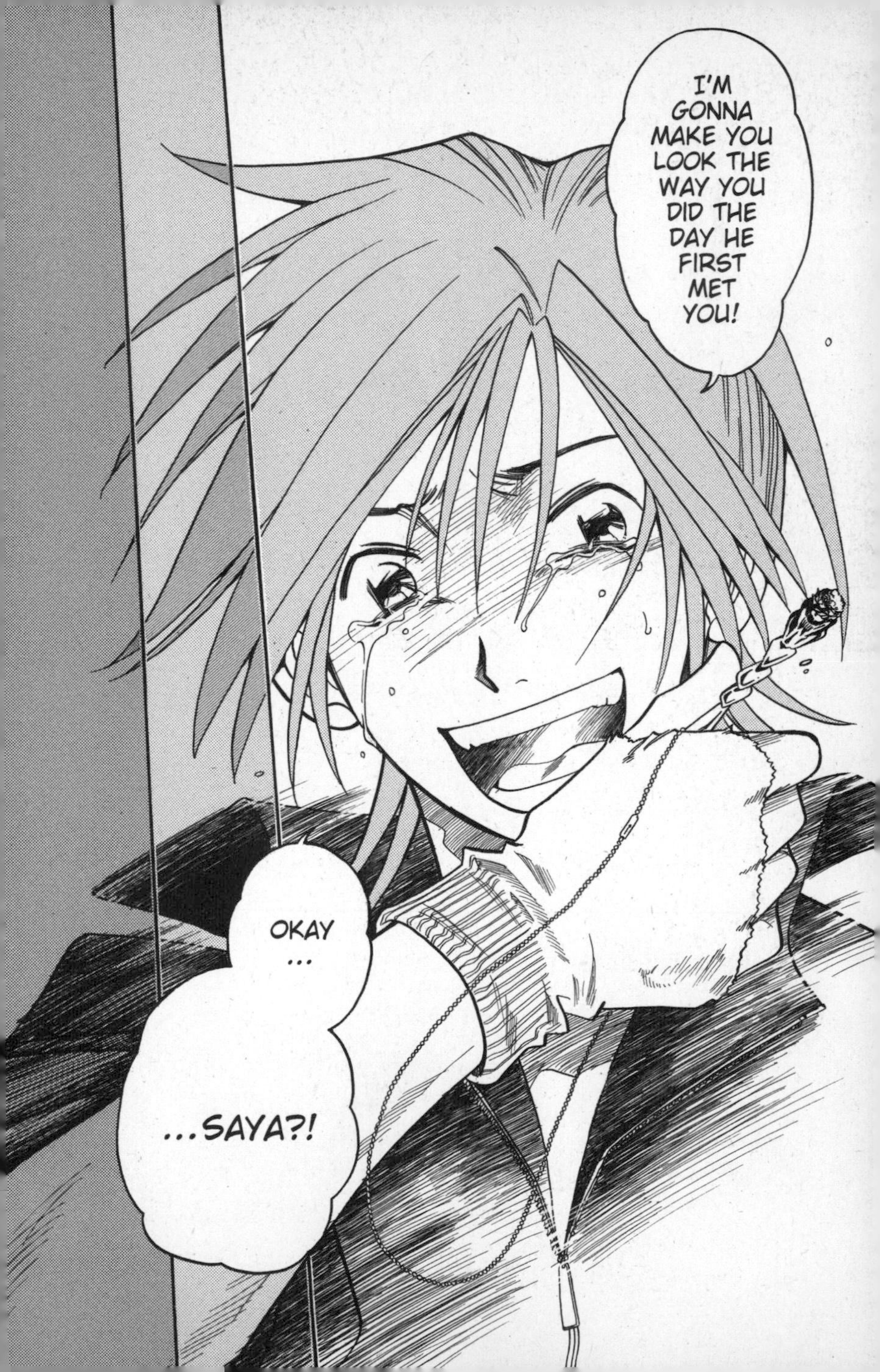
I'M GONNA MAKE YOU LOOK THE WAY YOU DID THE DAY HE FIRST MET YOU!
OKAY ...
...SAYA?!

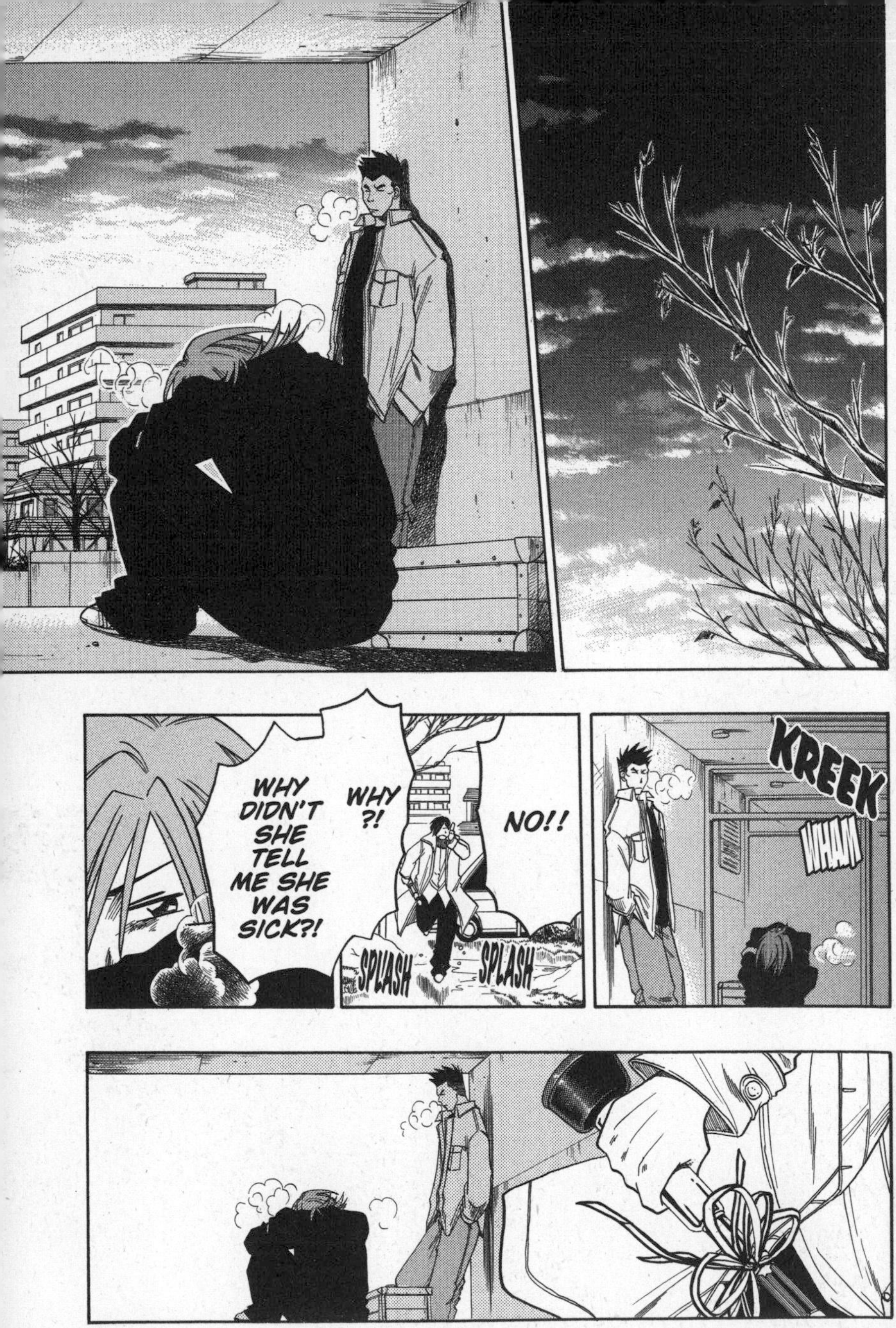
KREEK
WHAM
NO!!
SPLASH
SPLASH
WHY ?!
WHY DIDN'T SHE TELL ME SHE WAS SICK?!

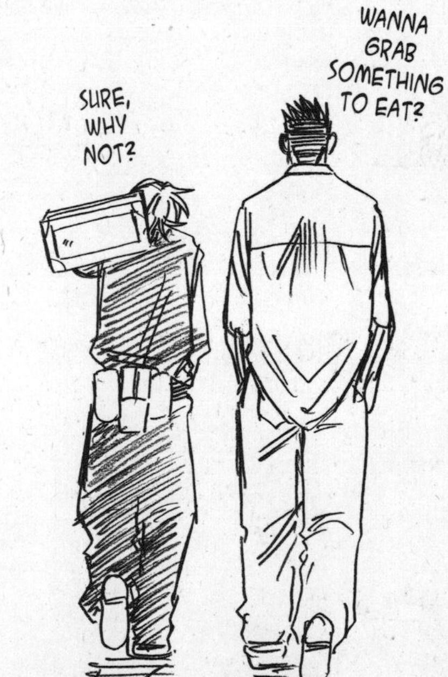
WANNA GRAB SOMETHING TO EAT?
SURE, WHY NOT?

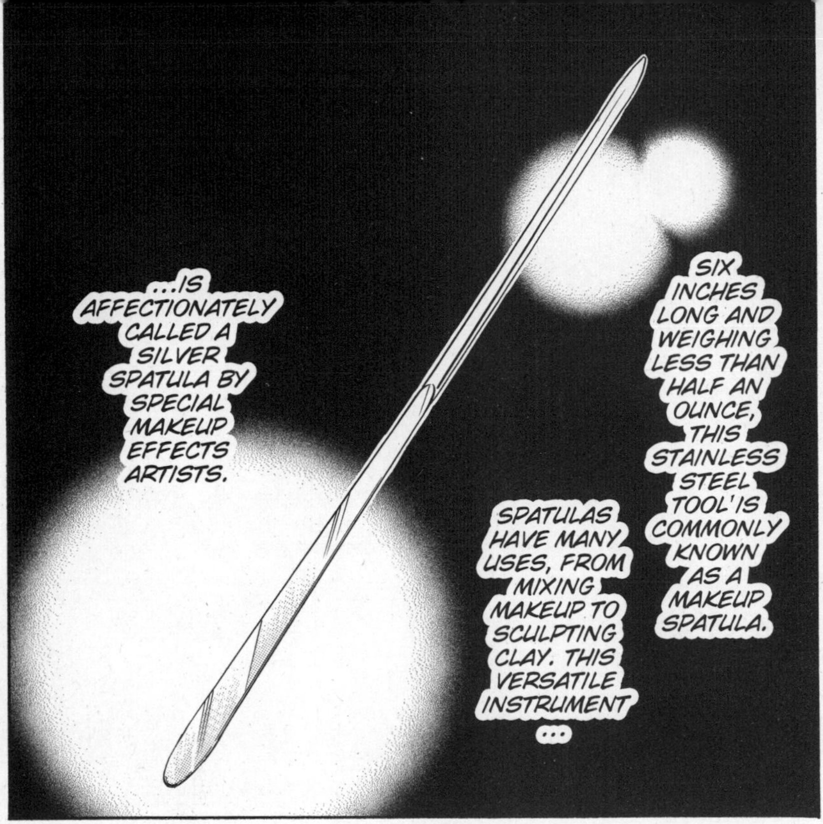
SIX INCHES LONG AND WEIGHING LESS THAN HALF AN OUNCE, THIS STAINLESS STEEL TOOL IS COMMONLY KNOWN AS A MAKEUP SPATULA.
SPATULAS HAVE MANY USES, FROM MIXING MAKEUP TO SCULPTING CLAY. THIS VERSATILE INSTRUMENT...
...IS AFFECTIONATELY CALLED A SILVER SPATULA BY SPECIAL MAKEUP EFFECTS ARTISTS.

Scene 34:

The Sorcerer's Apprentice (Part 1)

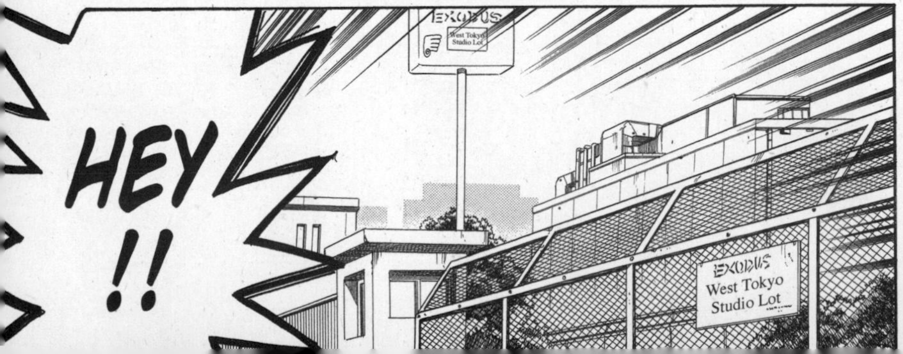
EXODUS West Tokyo Studio Lot
EXODUS West Tokyo Studio Lot
HEY!!

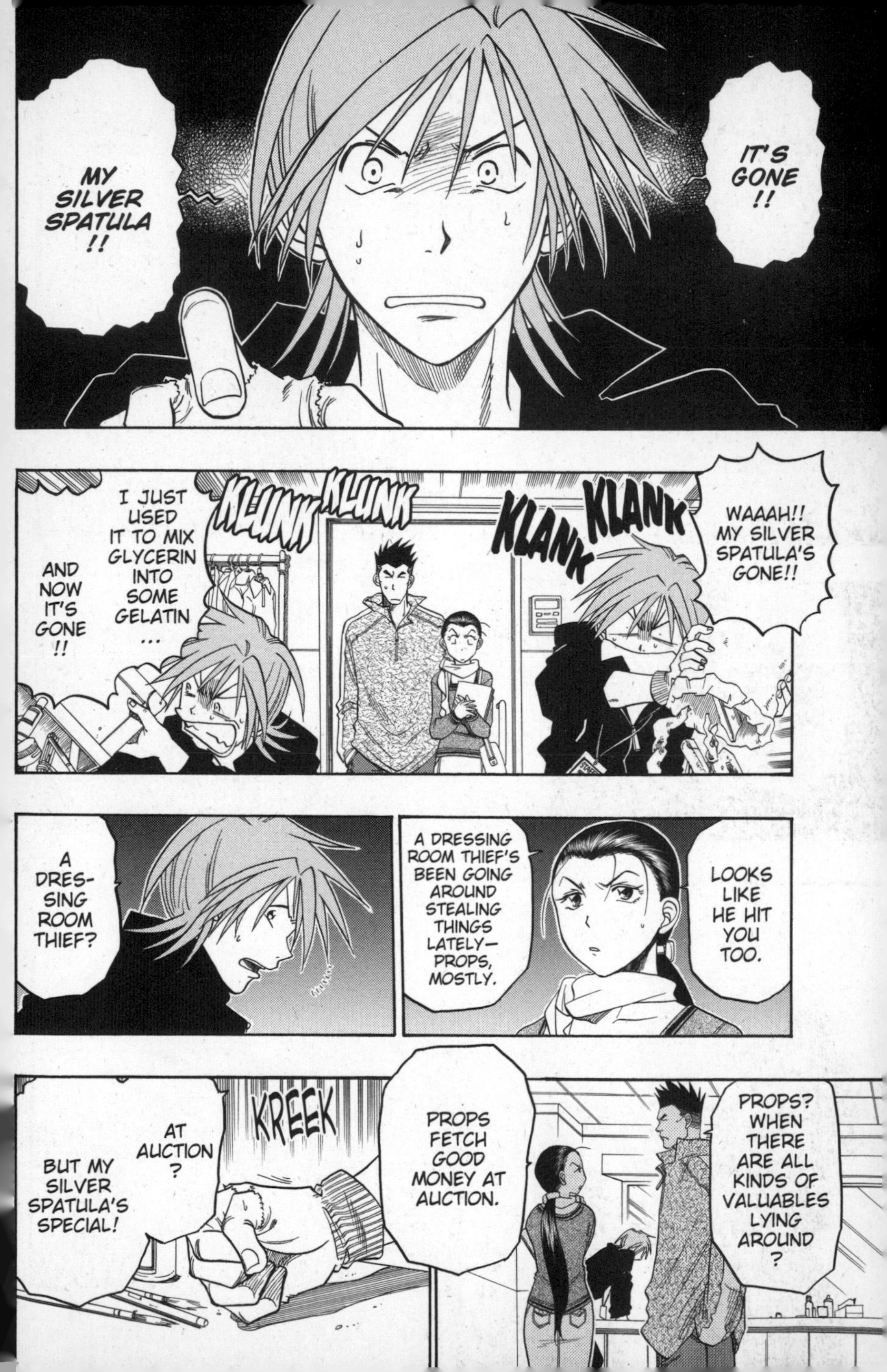
IT'S GONE!!
MY SILVER SPATULA!!
WAAAH!! MY SILVER SPATULA'S GONE!!
KLANK
KLANK
KLUNK
KLUNK
I JUST USED IT TO MIX GLYCERIN INTO SOME GELATIN...
AND NOW IT'S GONE!!
LOOKS LIKE HE HIT YOU TOO.
A DRESSING ROOM THIEF'S BEEN GOING AROUND STEALING THINGS LATELY—PROPS, MOSTLY.
A DRES-SING ROOM THIEF?
PROPS? WHEN THERE ARE ALL KINDS OF VALUABLES LYING AROUND?
PROPS FETCH GOOD MONEY AT AUCTION.
KREEK
AT AUCTION?
BUT MY SILVER SPATULA'S SPECIAL!

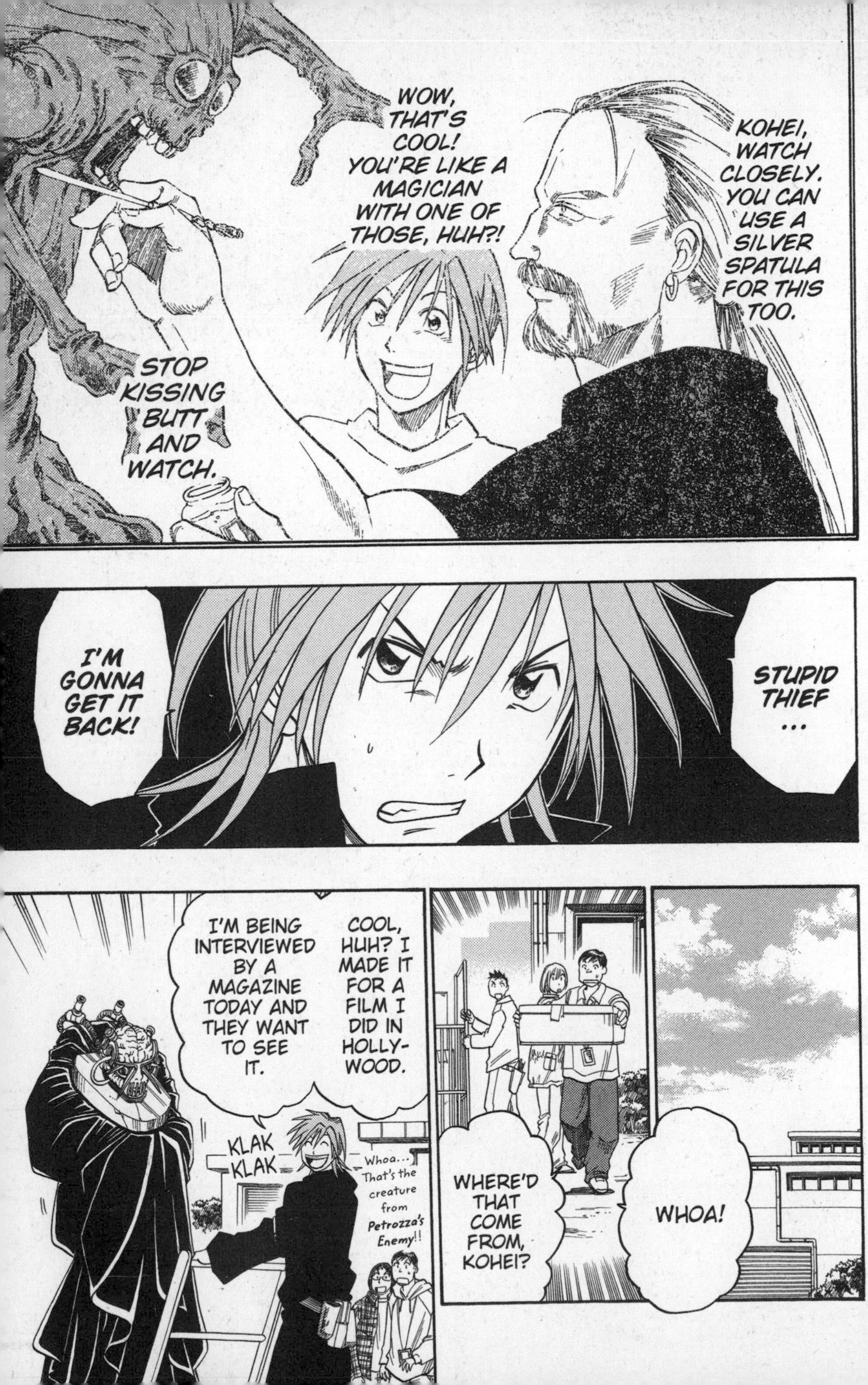
KOHEI, WATCH CLOSELY. YOU CAN USE A SILVER SPATULA FOR THIS TOO.
WOW, THAT'S COOL! YOU'RE LIKE A MAGICIAN WITH ONE OF THOSE, HUH?!
STOP KISSING BUTT AND WATCH.
STUPID THIEF...
I'M GONNA GET IT BACK!
WHOA!
WHERE'D THAT COME FROM, KOHEI?
COOL, HUH? I MADE IT FOR A FILM I DID IN HOLLYWOOD.
I'M BEING INTERVIEWED BY A MAGAZINE TODAY AND THEY WANT TO SEE IT.
KLAK KLAK
Whoa... That's the creature from *Petrozza's Enemy*!!

… | HEY! CAN I TAKE A PICTURE OF IT?! | SURE, BUT NOT NOW! | That's so cool! | YACK YACK | WOW!! THAT'S GOTTA BE WORTH A BOAT-LOAD!!

DID YOU HEAR ANY-THING? | DID YOU SEE ANYBODY SNOOPING AROUND IN THE PROPS STORE-ROOM?

MR. KAIEDA THE PROPS MANAGER! | HEY, KOHEI!! | SWFF

KLUNK KLUNK

HUH? YOU WILL? | JUST WAIT!! I'LL CATCH THE LITTLE RAT!

A THIEF? | HUH? DON'T TELL ME THE DRESSING ROOM THIEF GOT YOU TOO?!

MAKEUP ROOM A

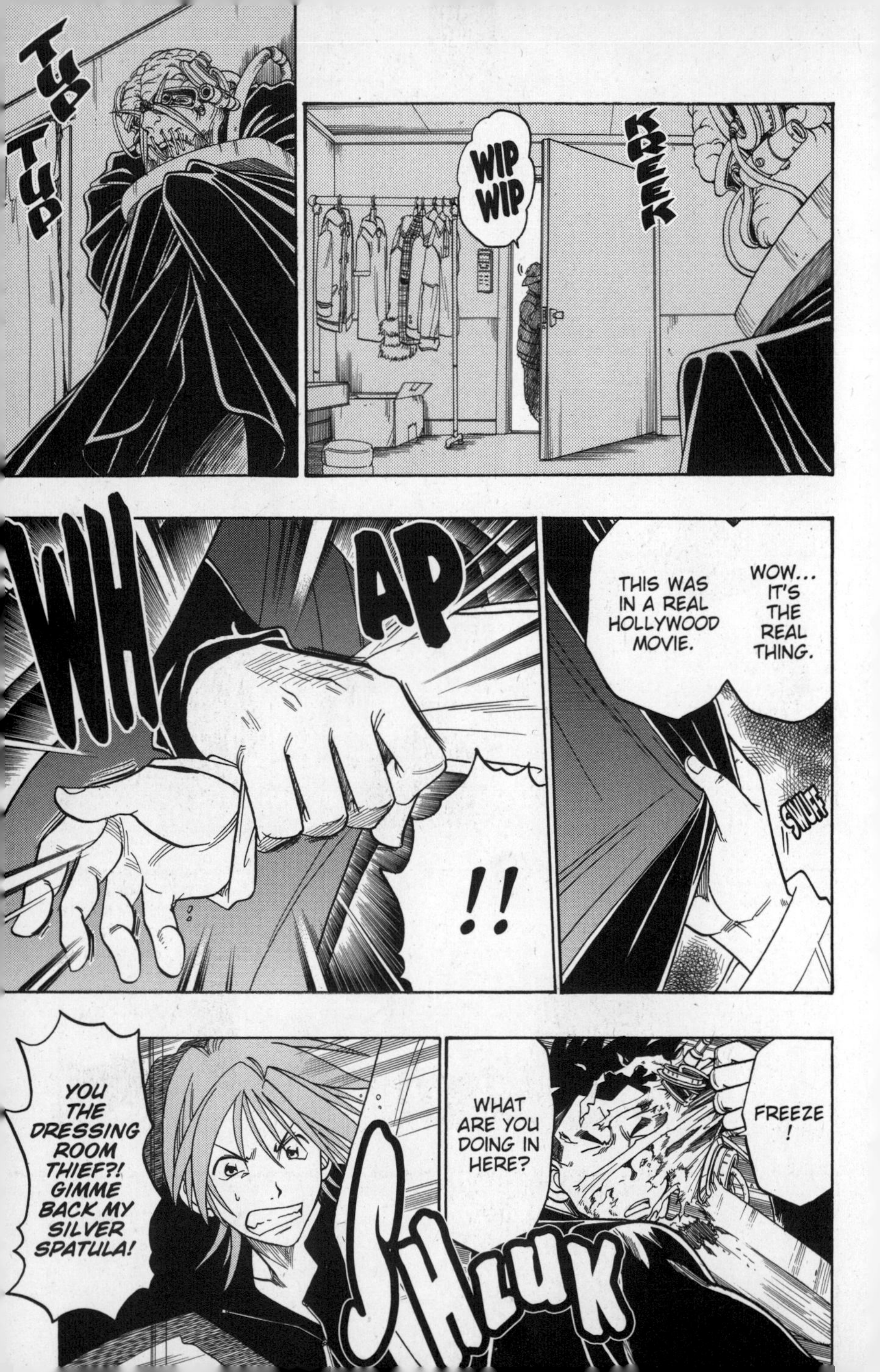
KREEK
WIP WIP
TUP TUP TUP
WOW... IT'S THE REAL THING.
THIS WAS IN A REAL HOLLYWOOD MOVIE.
SWUFF
WHAP
!!
FREEZE!
WHAT ARE YOU DOING IN HERE?
SHLUK
YOU THE DRESSING ROOM THIEF?! GIMME BACK MY SILVER SPATULA!

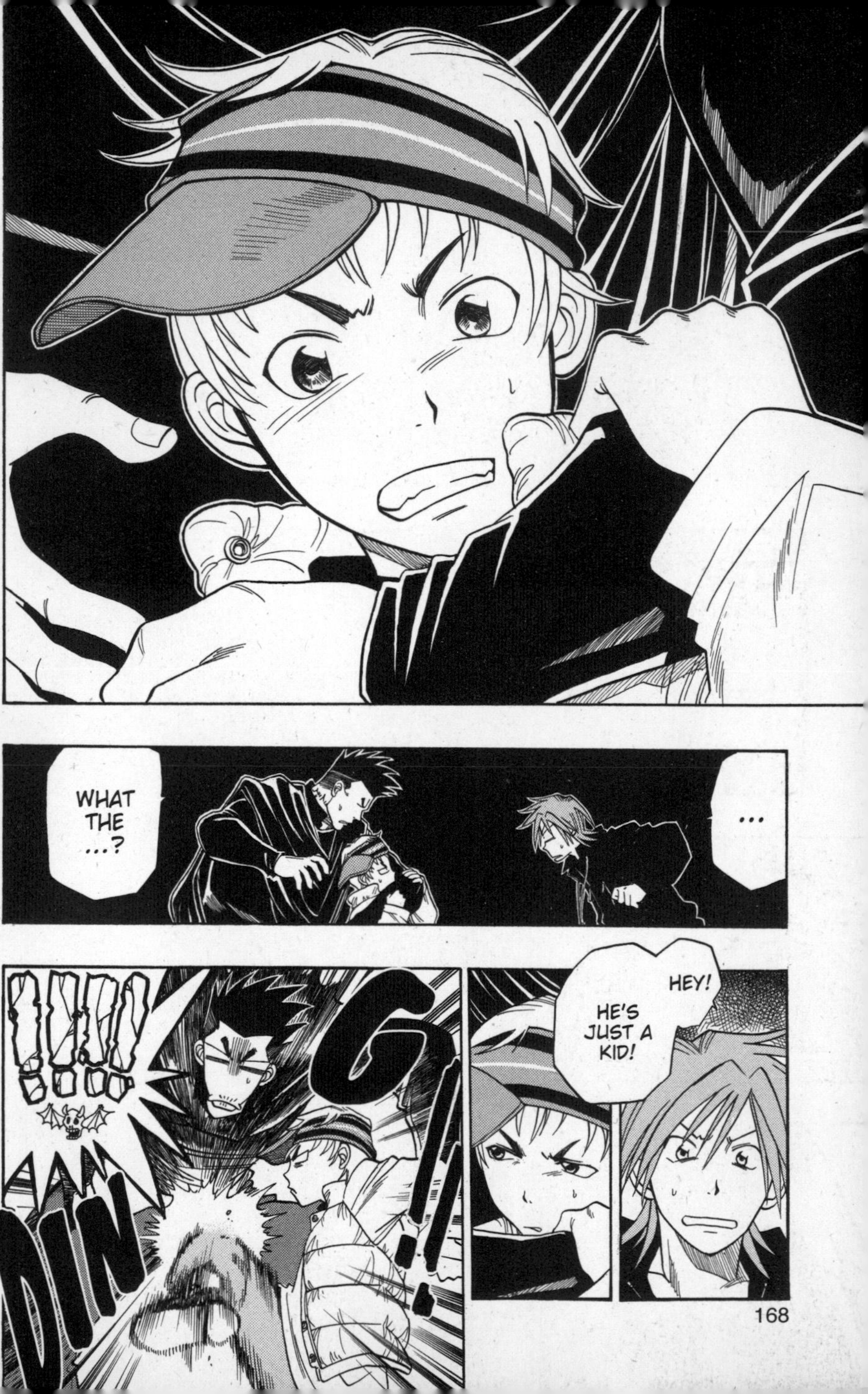
...
WHAT THE ...?
HEY! HE'S JUST A KID!

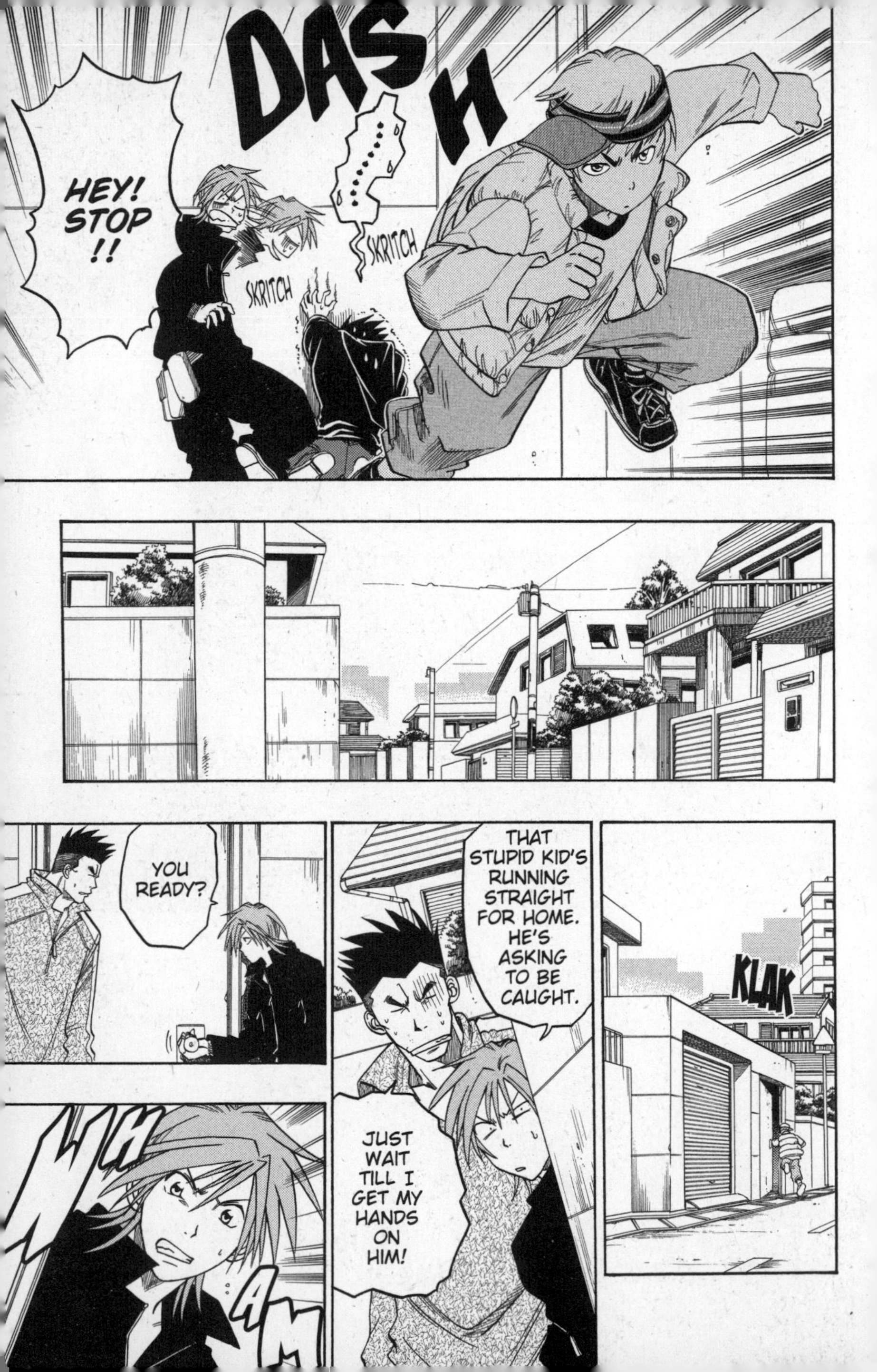
DASH
SKRITCH
HEY! STOP!!
SKRITCH
KLAK
THAT STUPID KID'S RUNNING STRAIGHT FOR HOME. HE'S ASKING TO BE CAUGHT.
JUST WAIT TILL I GET MY HANDS ON HIM!
YOU READY?
WHAM

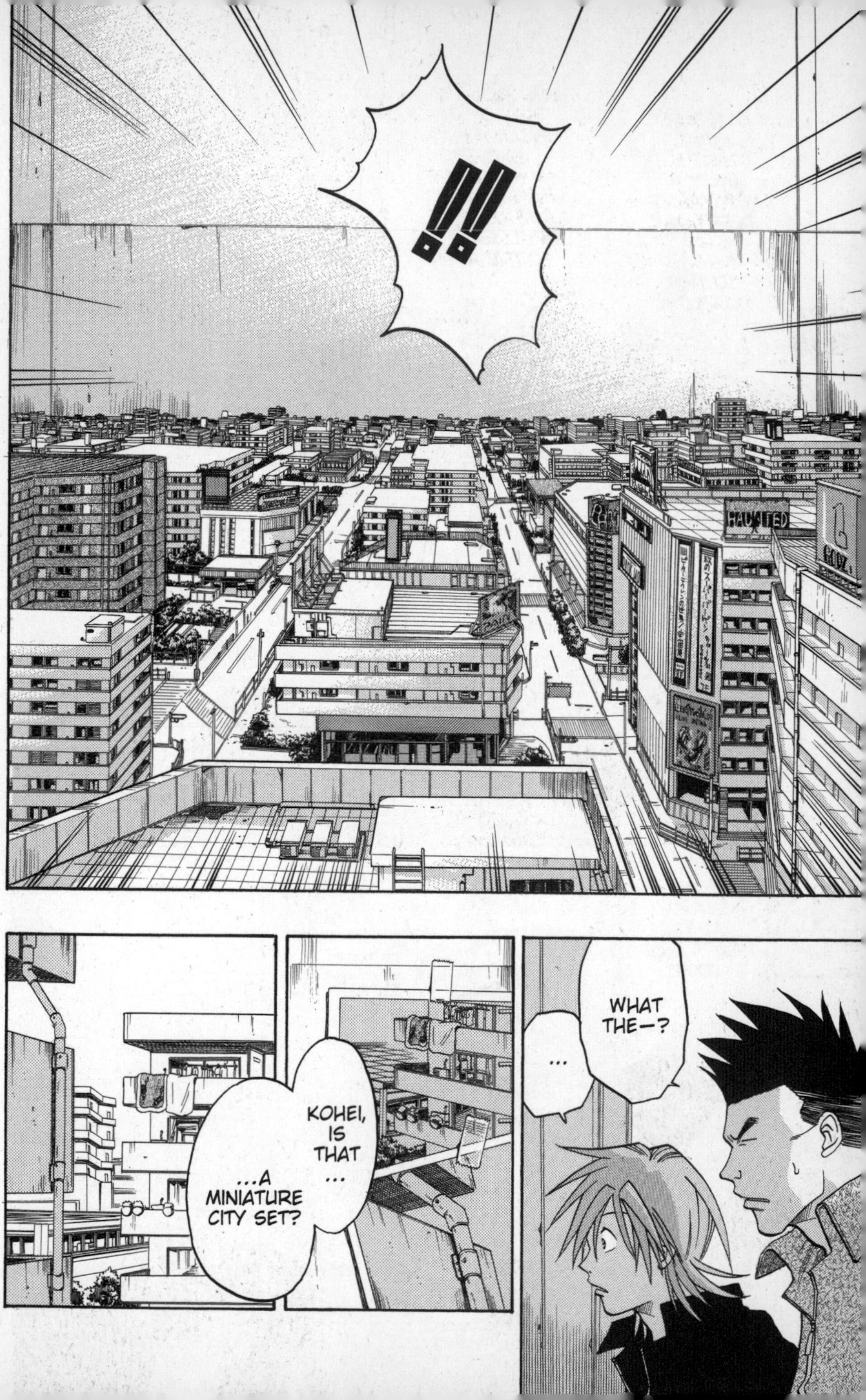
!!
HAUNTED
WHAT THE—?
...
KOHEI, IS THAT ...
...A MINIATURE CITY SET?

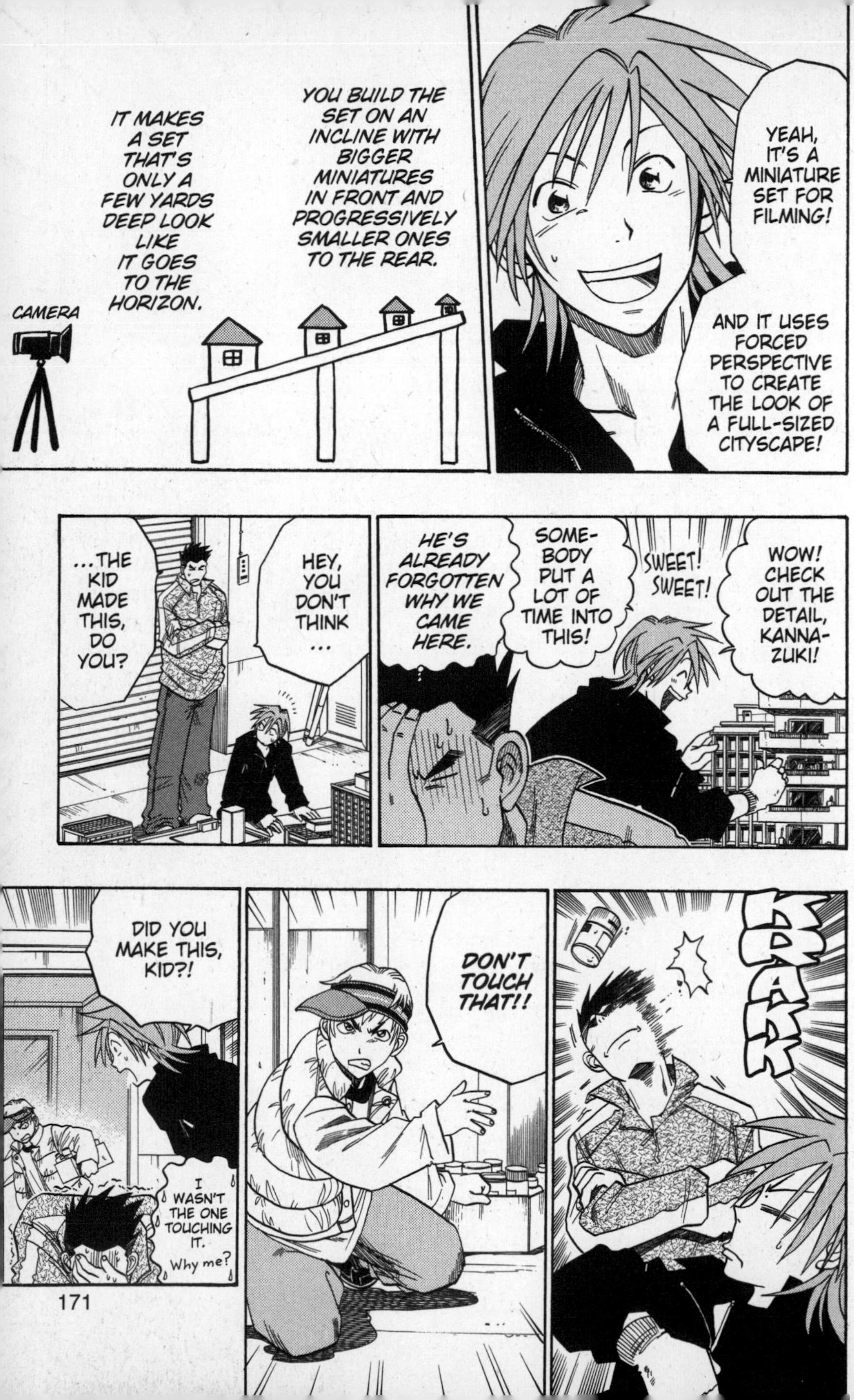
YEAH, IT'S A MINIATURE SET FOR FILMING!
AND IT USES FORCED PERSPECTIVE TO CREATE THE LOOK OF A FULL-SIZED CITYSCAPE!
YOU BUILD THE SET ON AN INCLINE WITH BIGGER MINIATURES IN FRONT AND PROGRESSIVELY SMALLER ONES TO THE REAR.
IT MAKES A SET THAT'S ONLY A FEW YARDS DEEP LOOK LIKE IT GOES TO THE HORIZON.
CAMERA
WOW! CHECK OUT THE DETAIL, KANNAZUKI!
SWEET! SWEET!
SOMEBODY PUT A LOT OF TIME INTO THIS!
HE'S ALREADY FORGOTTEN WHY WE CAME HERE.
HEY, YOU DON'T THINK...
...THE KID MADE THIS, DO YOU?
WHAK
DON'T TOUCH THAT!!
DID YOU MAKE THIS, KID?!
I WASN'T THE ONE TOUCHING IT.
Why me?

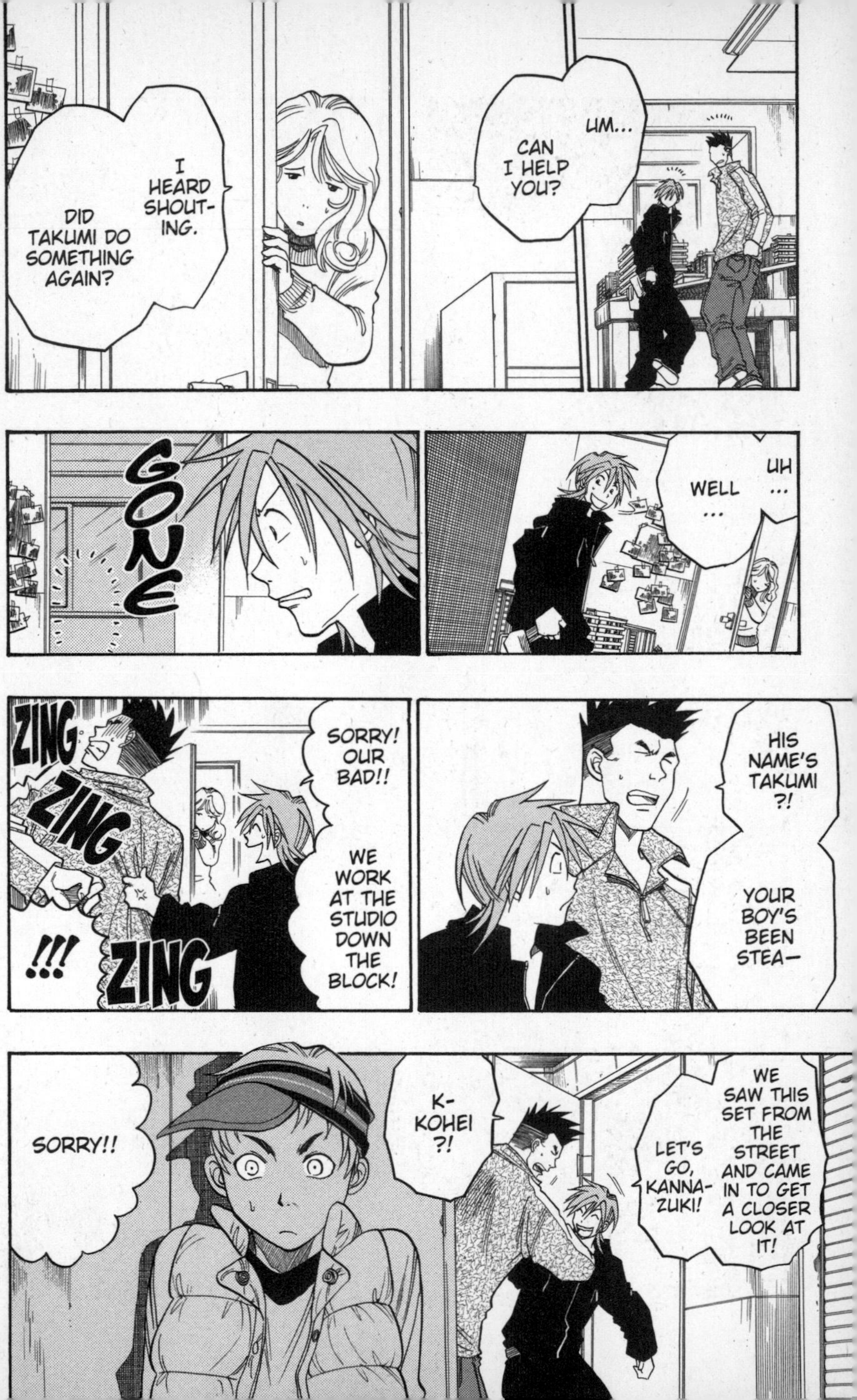
UM...
CAN I HELP YOU?
I HEARD SHOUT-ING.
DID TAKUMI DO SOMETHING AGAIN?
UH ...
WELL ...
GONE
HIS NAME'S TAKUMI ?!
YOUR BOY'S BEEN STEA—
SORRY! OUR BAD!!
WE WORK AT THE STUDIO DOWN THE BLOCK!
ZING
ZING
ZING
!!!
ZING
WE SAW THIS SET FROM THE STREET AND CAME IN TO GET A CLOSER LOOK AT IT!
LET'S GO, KANNA-ZUKI!
K-KOHEI ?!
SORRY!!

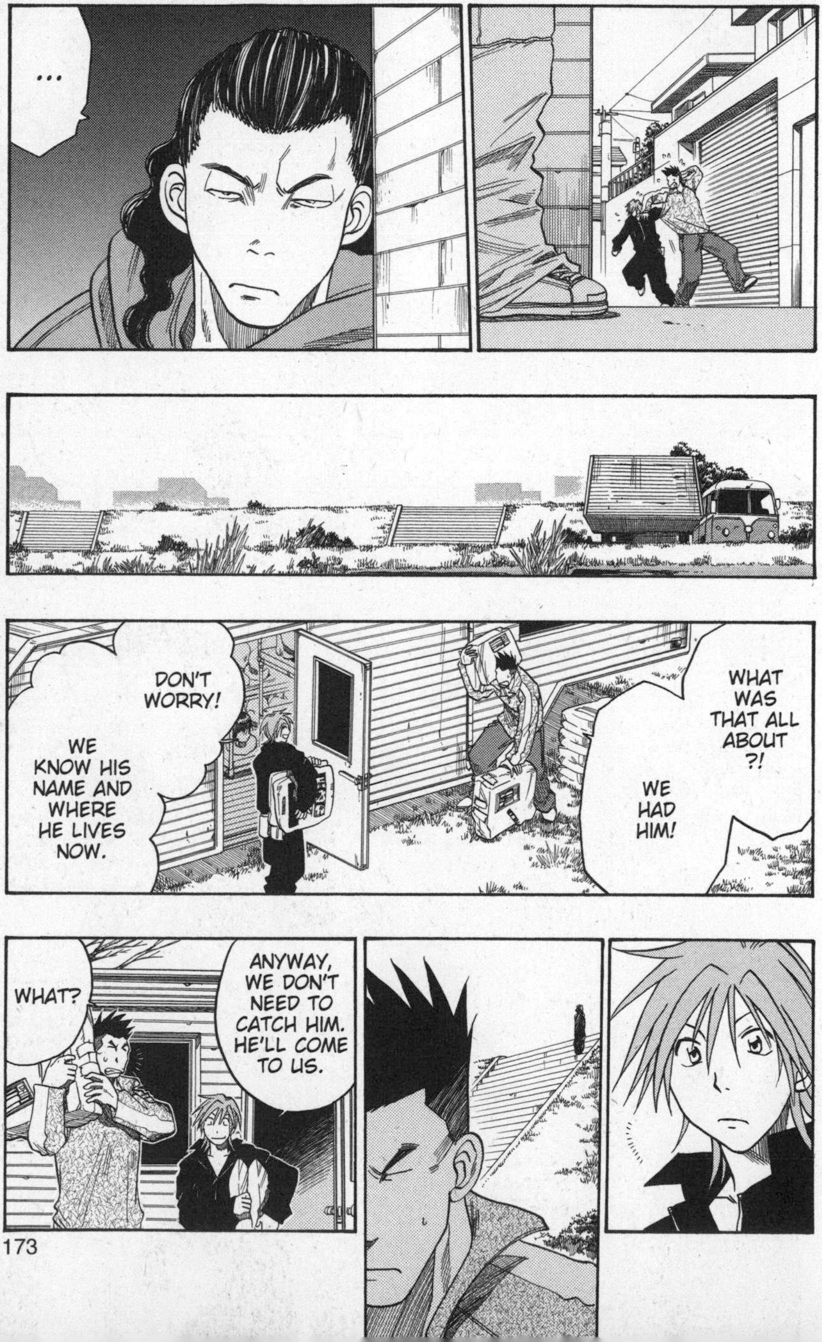
...
WHAT WAS THAT ALL ABOUT?!
WE HAD HIM!
DON'T WORRY!
WE KNOW HIS NAME AND WHERE HE LIVES NOW.
ANYWAY, WE DON'T NEED TO CATCH HIM. HE'LL COME TO US.
WHAT?

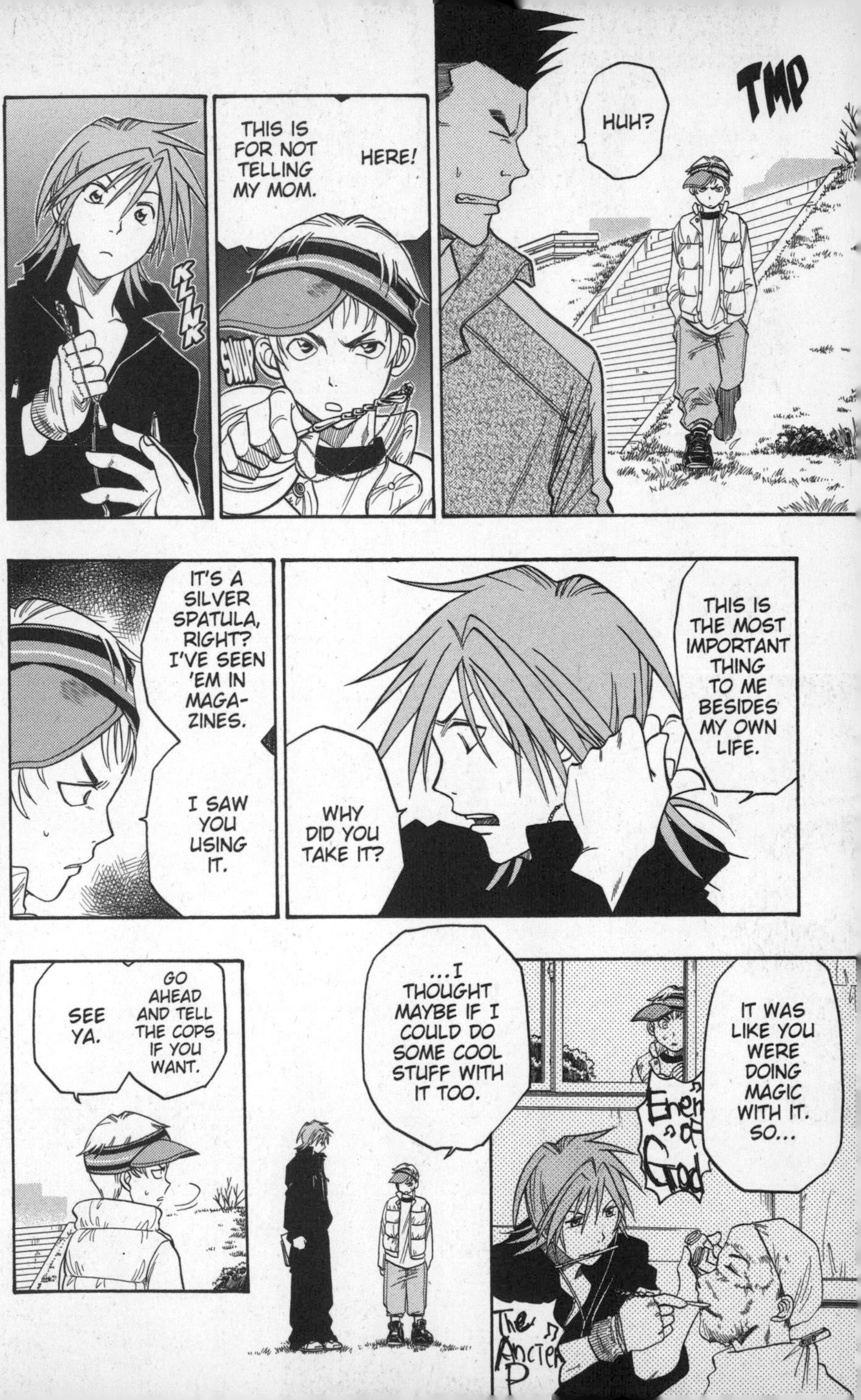
TMP
HUH?
HERE!
THIS IS FOR NOT TELLING MY MOM.
SWIP
KLINK
THIS IS THE MOST IMPORTANT THING TO ME BESIDES MY OWN LIFE.
WHY DID YOU TAKE IT?
IT'S A SILVER SPATULA, RIGHT? I'VE SEEN 'EM IN MAGAZINES.
I SAW YOU USING IT.
IT WAS LIKE YOU WERE DOING MAGIC WITH IT. SO...
...I THOUGHT MAYBE IF I COULD DO SOME COOL STUFF WITH IT TOO.
GO AHEAD AND TELL THE COPS IF YOU WANT.
SEE YA.

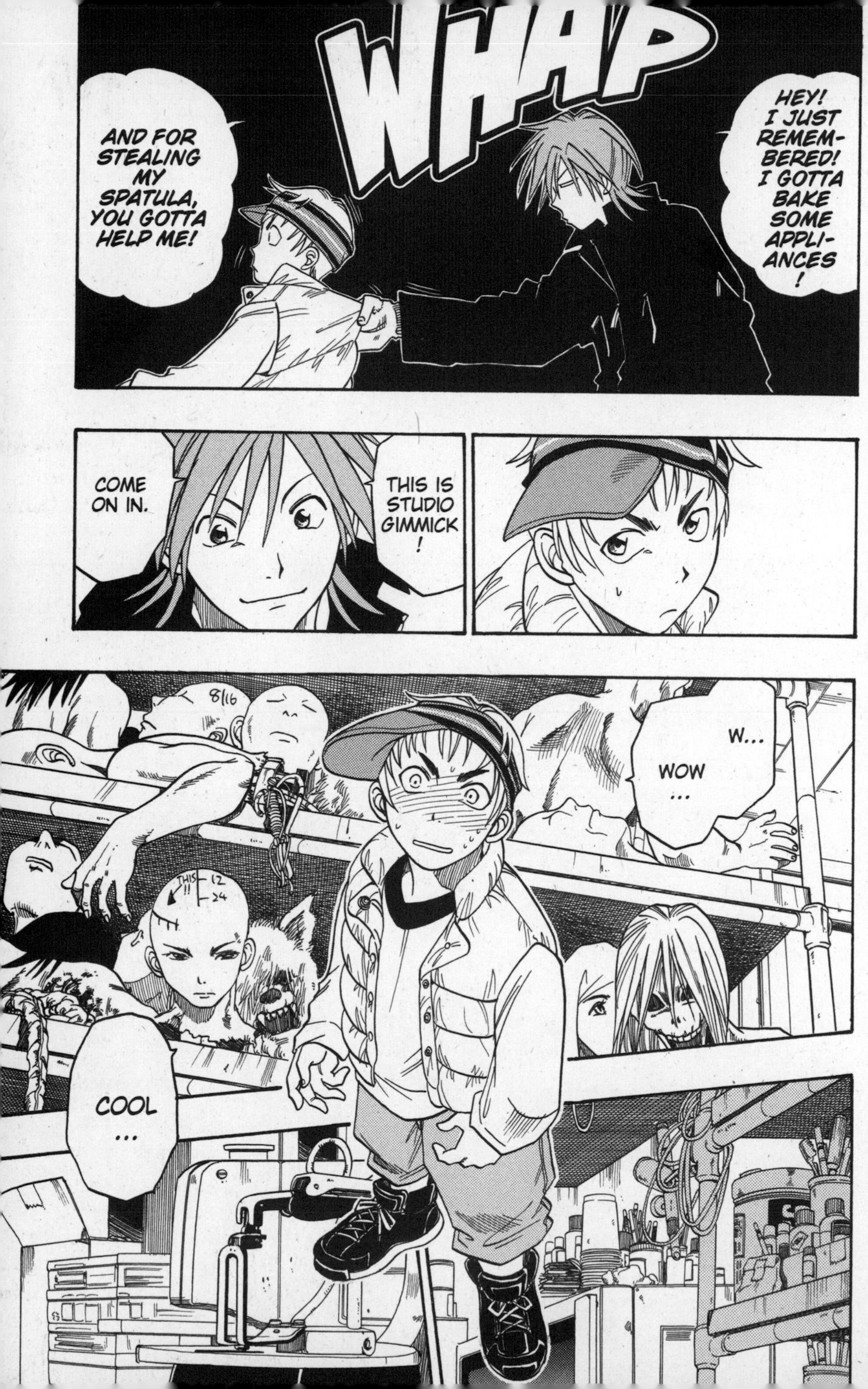
WHAP
HEY! I JUST REMEMBERED! I GOTTA BAKE SOME APPLIANCES!
AND FOR STEALING MY SPATULA, YOU GOTTA HELP ME!
THIS IS STUDIO GIMMICK!
COME ON IN.
W... WOW...
COOL...

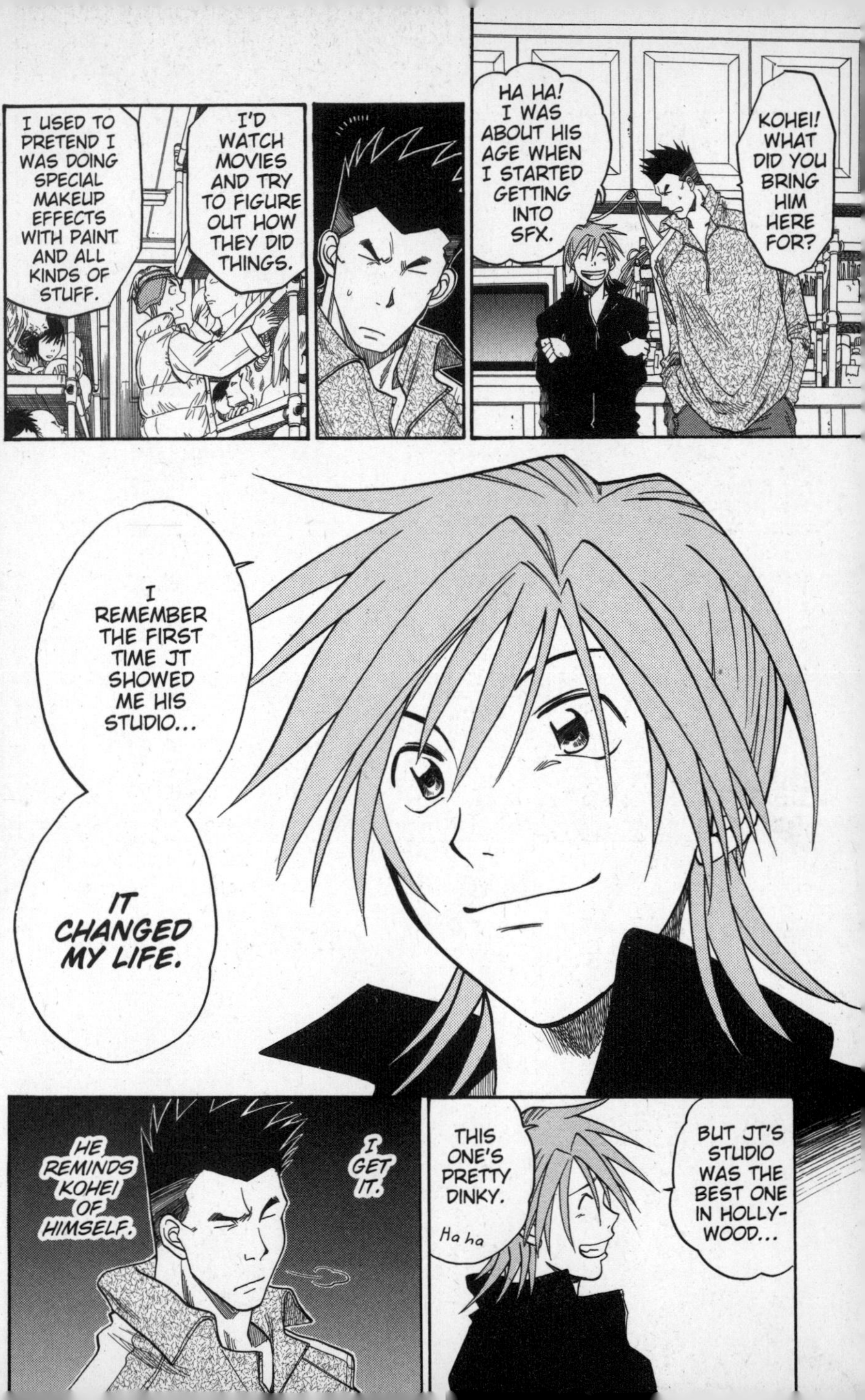
KOHEI! WHAT DID YOU BRING HIM HERE FOR?
HA HA! I WAS ABOUT HIS AGE WHEN I STARTED GETTING INTO SFX.
I'D WATCH MOVIES AND TRY TO FIGURE OUT HOW THEY DID THINGS.
I USED TO PRETEND I WAS DOING SPECIAL MAKEUP EFFECTS WITH PAINT AND ALL KINDS OF STUFF.
I REMEMBER THE FIRST TIME JT SHOWED ME HIS STUDIO...
IT CHANGED MY LIFE.
BUT JT'S STUDIO WAS THE BEST ONE IN HOLLY-WOOD...
THIS ONE'S PRETTY DINKY.
Ha ha
I GET IT.
HE REMINDS KOHEI OF HIMSELF.

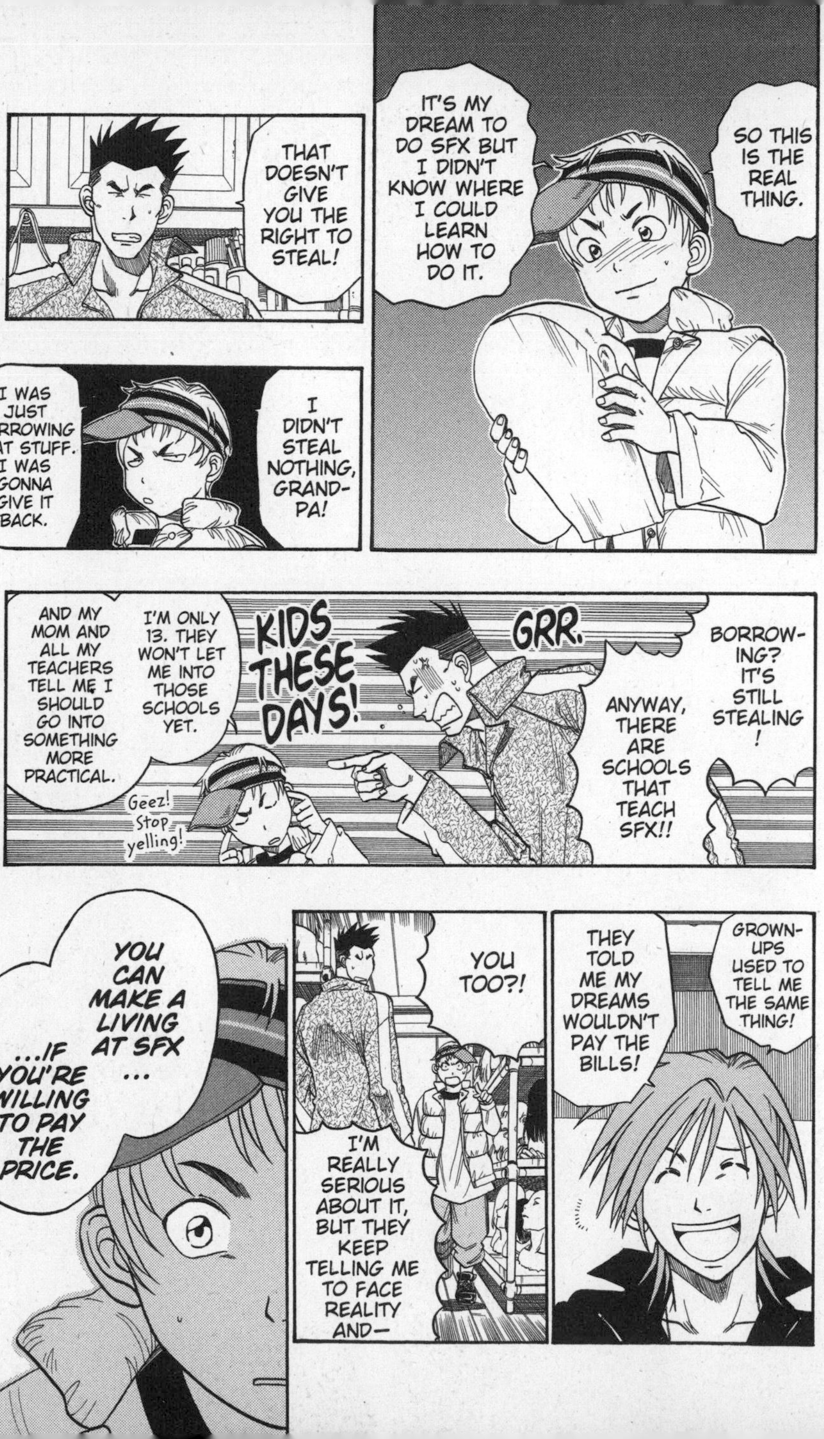
SO THIS IS THE REAL THING.
IT'S MY DREAM TO DO SFX BUT I DIDN'T KNOW WHERE I COULD LEARN HOW TO DO IT.
THAT DOESN'T GIVE YOU THE RIGHT TO STEAL!
I DIDN'T STEAL NOTHING, GRAND-PA!
I WAS JUST BORROWING THAT STUFF. I WAS GONNA GIVE IT BACK.
BORROW-ING? IT'S STILL STEALING!
GRR.
ANYWAY, THERE ARE SCHOOLS THAT TEACH SFX!!
KIDS THESE DAYS!
I'M ONLY 13. THEY WON'T LET ME INTO THOSE SCHOOLS YET.
AND MY MOM AND ALL MY TEACHERS TELL ME I SHOULD GO INTO SOMETHING MORE PRACTICAL.
Geez! Stop yelling!
GROWN-UPS USED TO TELL ME THE SAME THING!
THEY TOLD ME MY DREAMS WOULDN'T PAY THE BILLS!
YOU TOO?!
I'M REALLY SERIOUS ABOUT IT, BUT THEY KEEP TELLING ME TO FACE REALITY AND—
YOU CAN MAKE A LIVING AT SFX...
...IF YOU'RE WILLING TO PAY THE PRICE.

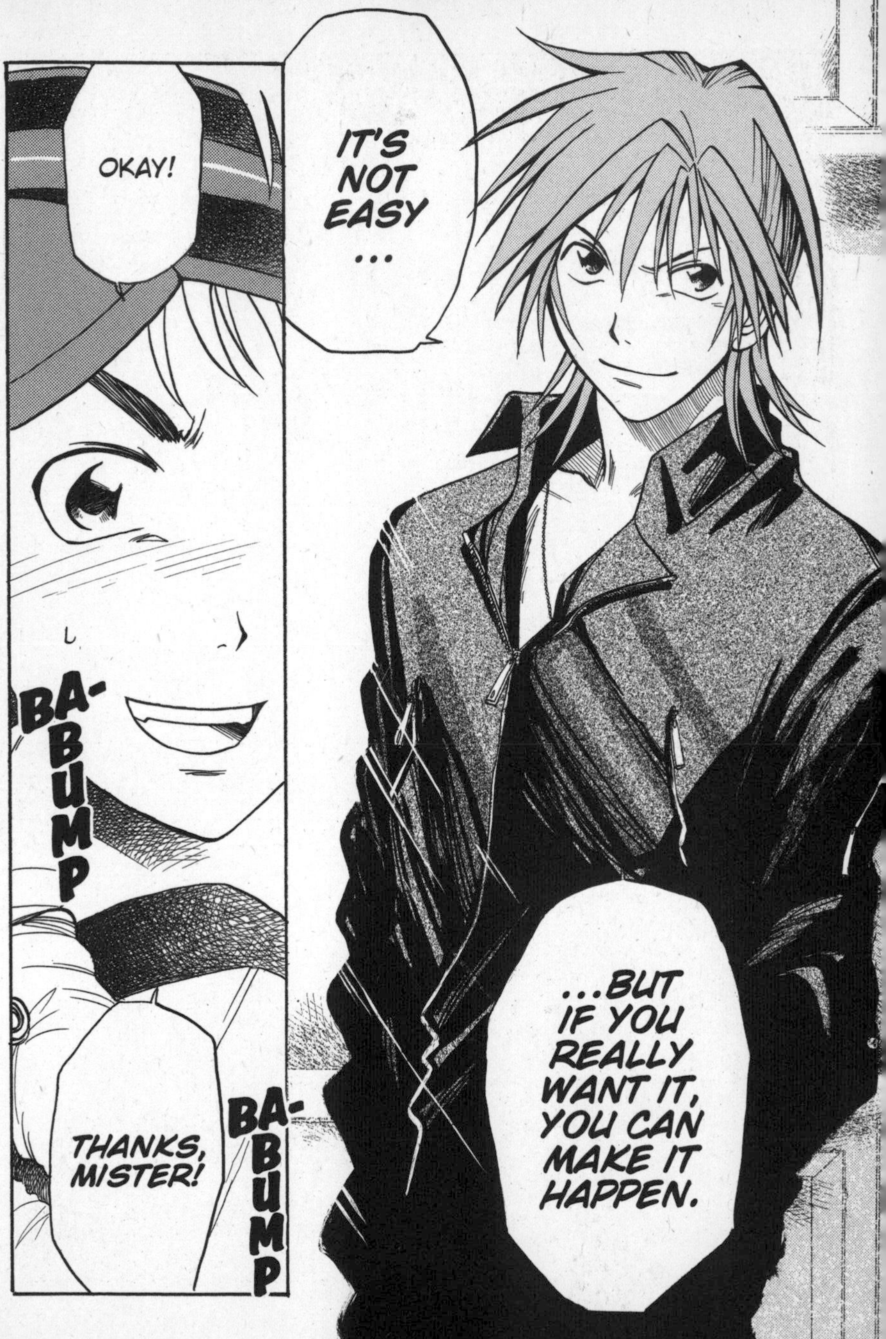
IT'S NOT EASY...
...BUT IF YOU REALLY WANT IT, YOU CAN MAKE IT HAPPEN.
OKAY!
BA-BUMP
BA-BUMP
THANKS, MISTER!

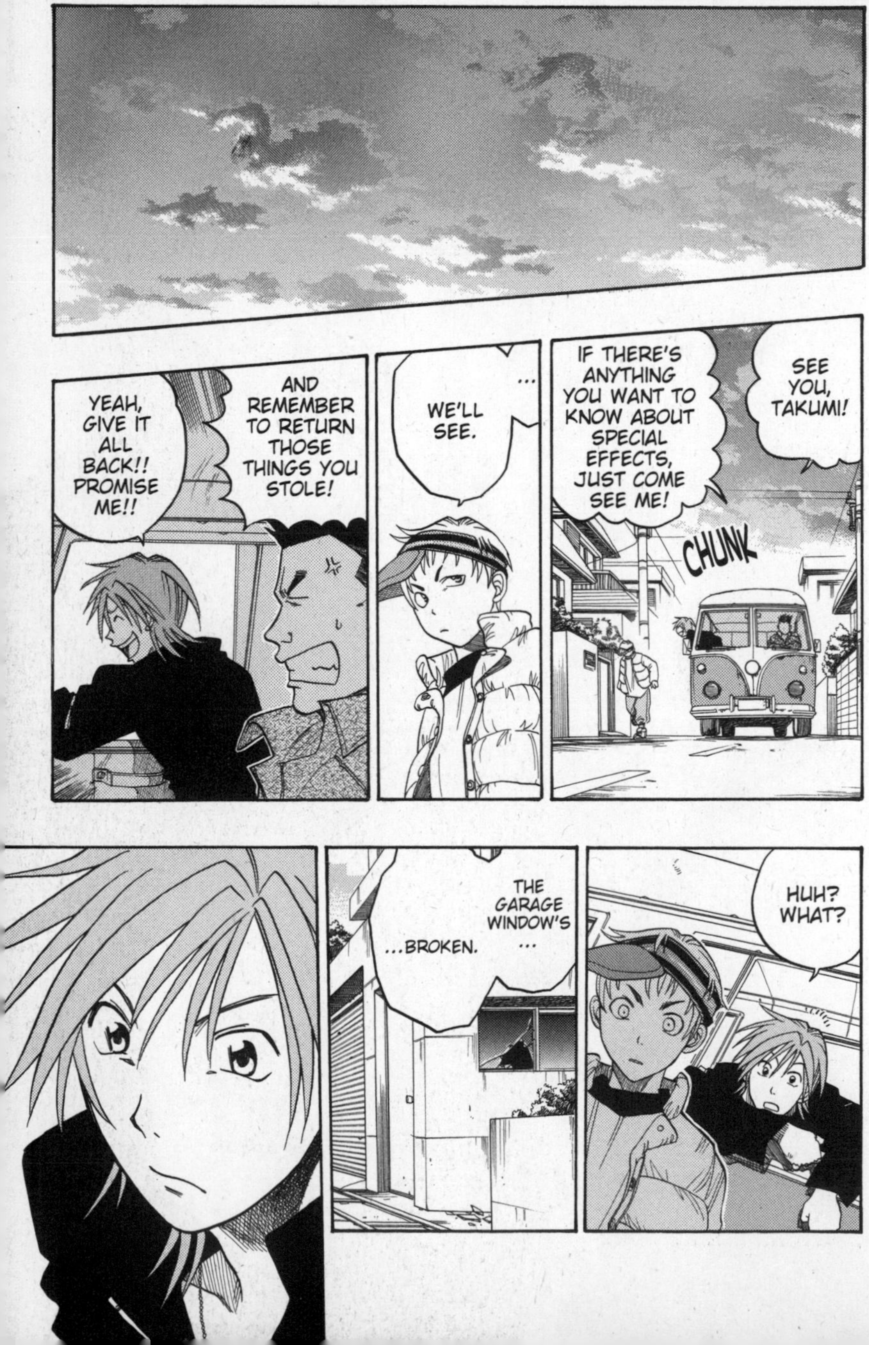
SEE YOU, TAKUMI!
IF THERE'S ANYTHING YOU WANT TO KNOW ABOUT SPECIAL EFFECTS, JUST COME SEE ME!
CHUNK
...
WE'LL SEE.
AND REMEMBER TO RETURN THOSE THINGS YOU STOLE!
YEAH, GIVE IT ALL BACK!! PROMISE ME!!
HUH? WHAT?
THE GARAGE WINDOW'S ...
...BROKEN.

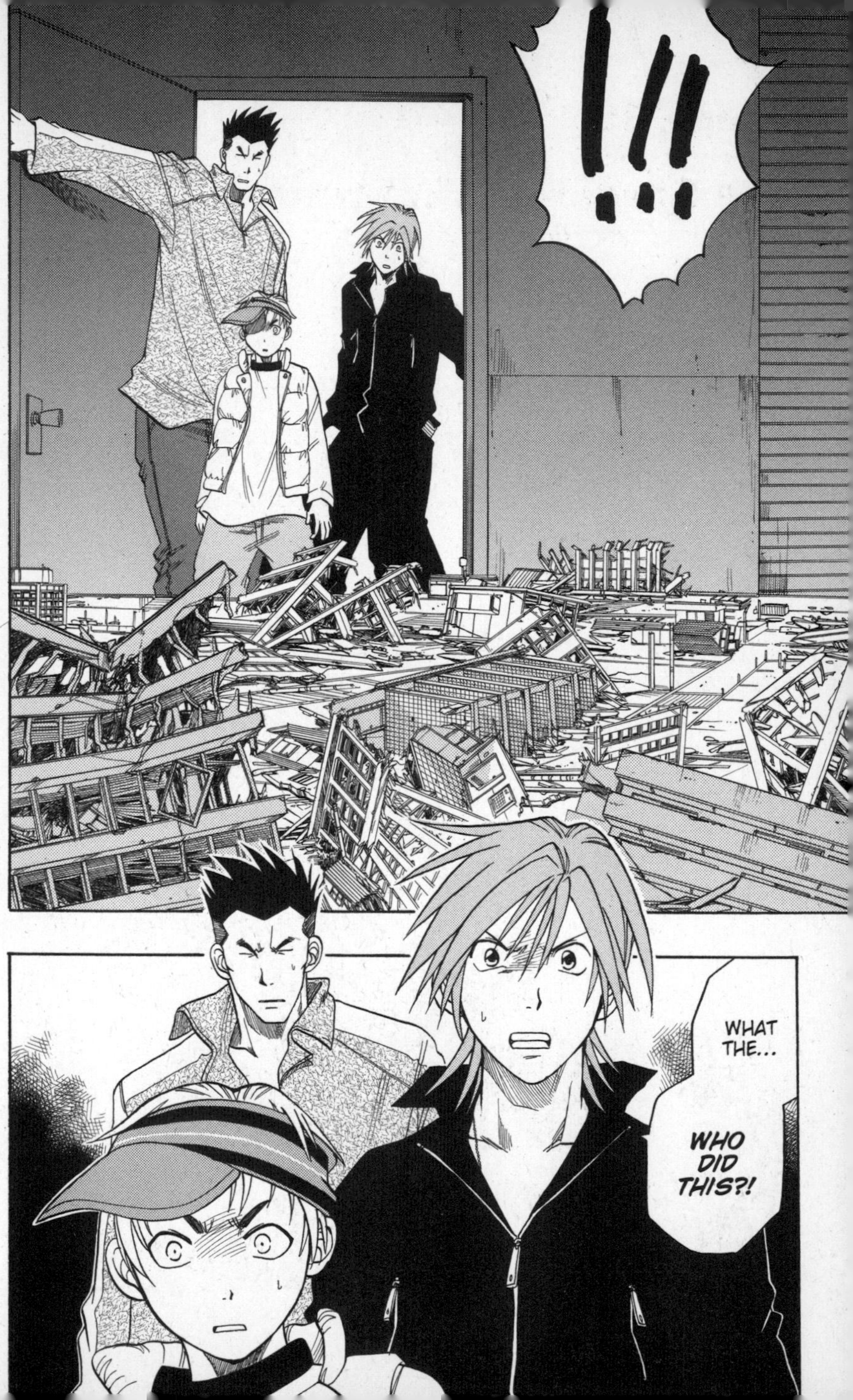
!!!
WHAT THE...
WHO DID THIS?!

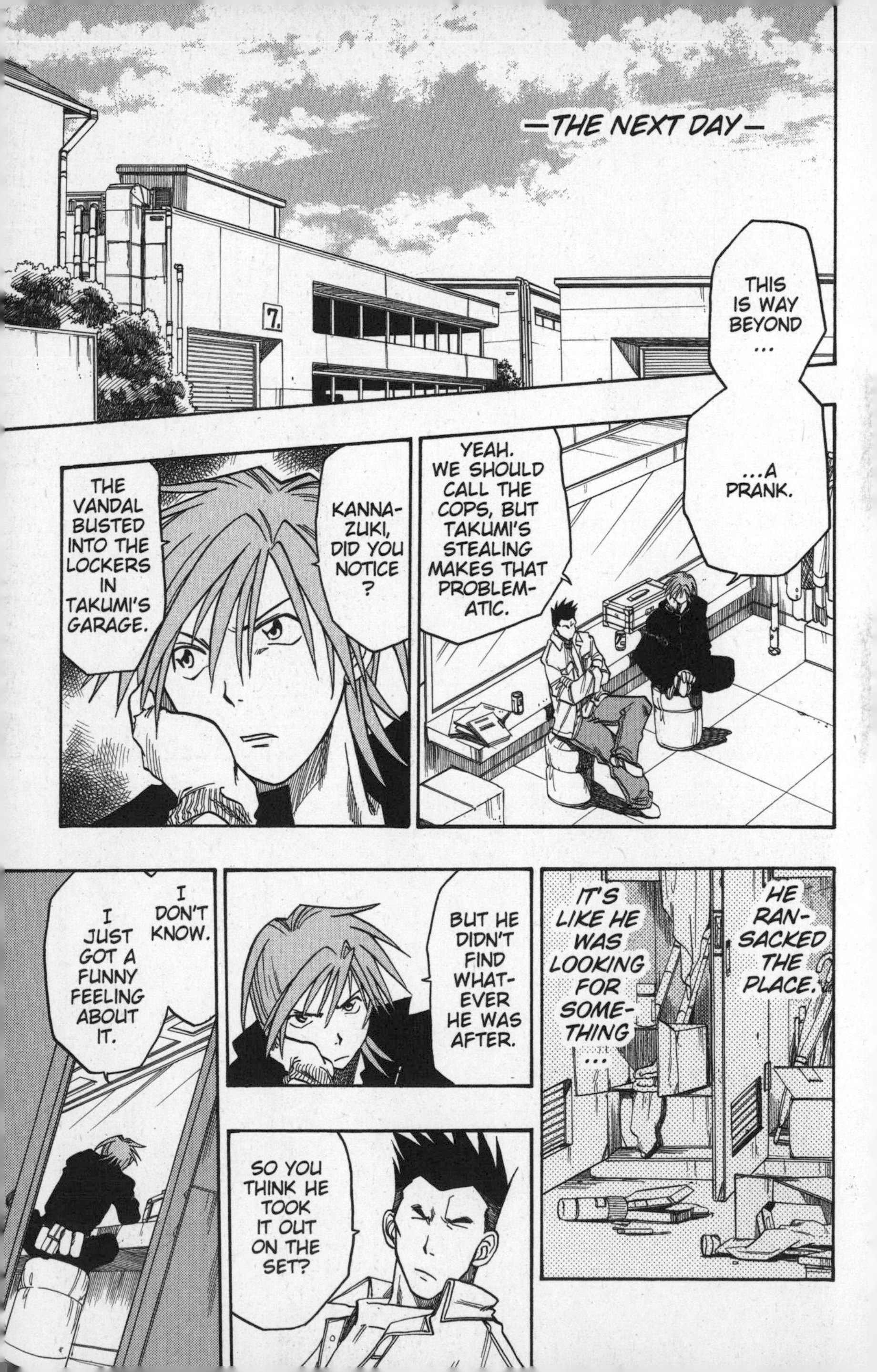
—THE NEXT DAY—
THIS IS WAY BEYOND ... ...A PRANK.
YEAH. WE SHOULD CALL THE COPS, BUT TAKUMI'S STEALING MAKES THAT PROBLEMATIC.
KANNAZUKI, DID YOU NOTICE?
THE VANDAL BUSTED INTO THE LOCKERS IN TAKUMI'S GARAGE.
HE RANSACKED THE PLACE.
IT'S LIKE HE WAS LOOKING FOR SOMETHING...
BUT HE DIDN'T FIND WHATEVER HE WAS AFTER.
SO YOU THINK HE TOOK IT OUT ON THE SET?
I DON'T KNOW.
I JUST GOT A FUNNY FEELING ABOUT IT.

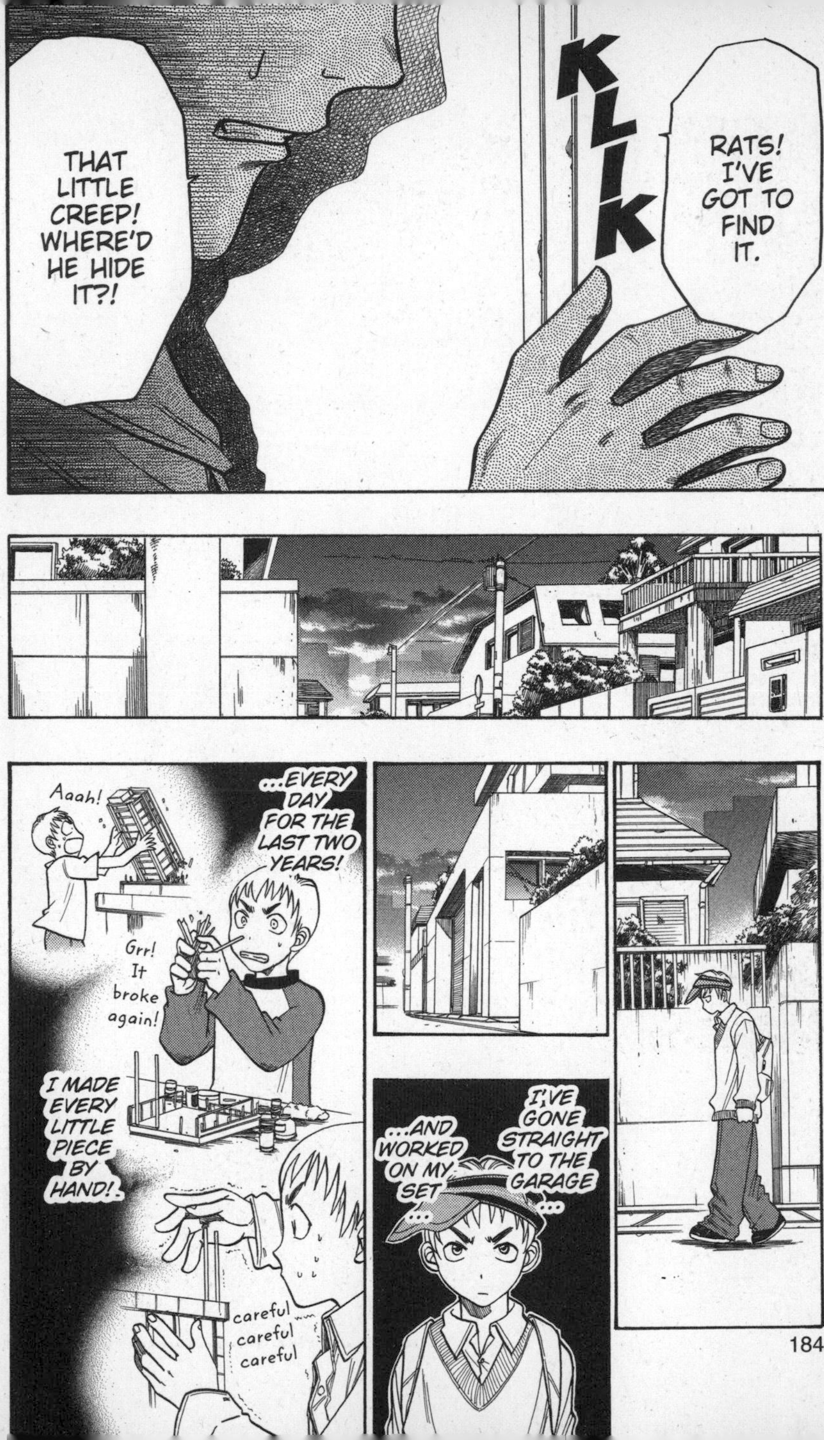
KLIK
RATS! I'VE GOT TO FIND IT.
THAT LITTLE CREEP! WHERE'D HE HIDE IT?!
I'VE GONE STRAIGHT TO THE GARAGE...
...AND WORKED ON MY SET...
...EVERY DAY FOR THE LAST TWO YEARS!
Aaah!
Grr! It broke again!
I MADE EVERY LITTLE PIECE BY HAND!
careful
careful
careful

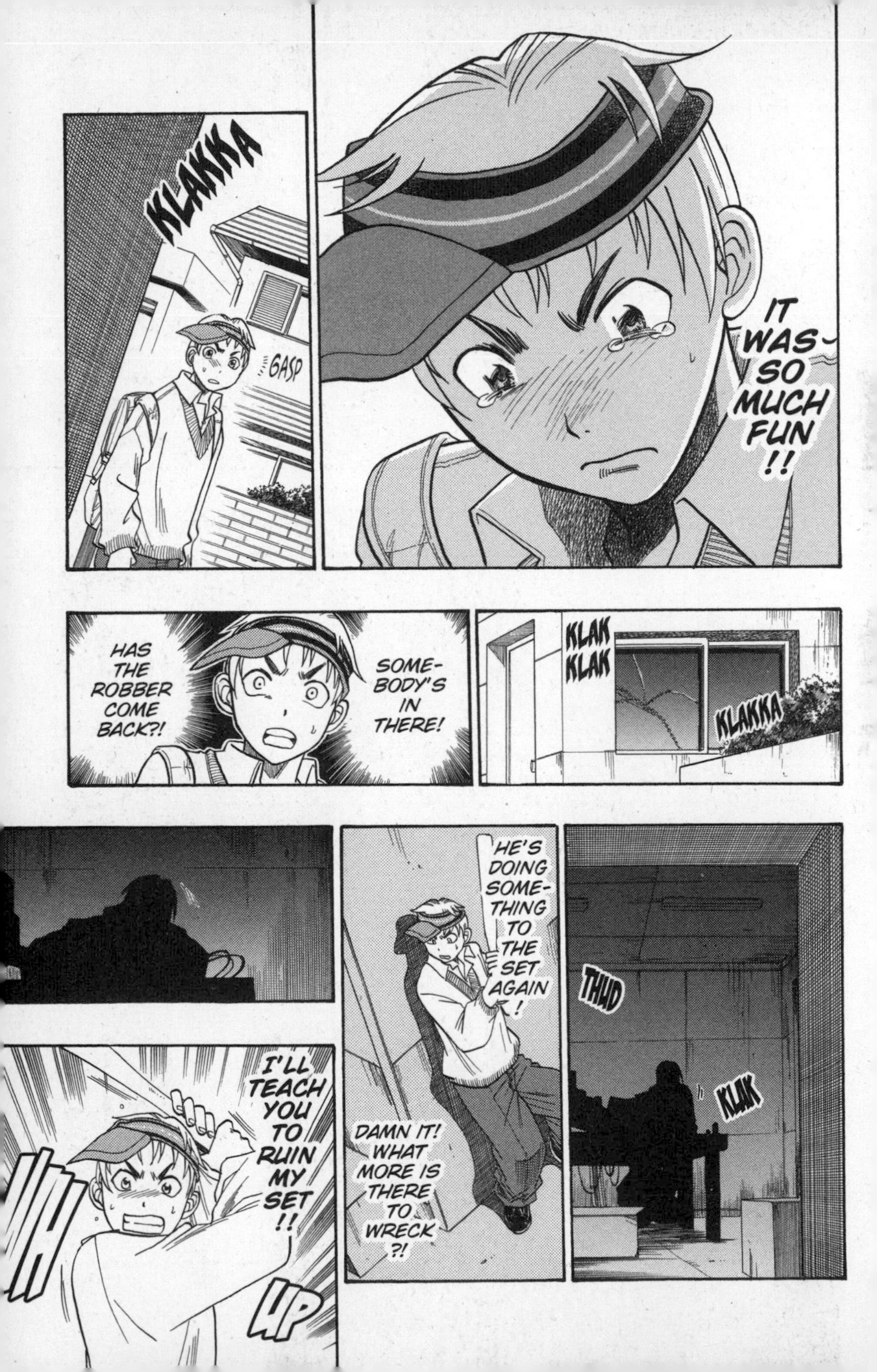
IT WAS-SO MUCH FUN!!
KLAKKA
GASP
KLAK KLAK
KLAKKA
SOME-BODY'S IN THERE!
HAS THE ROBBER COME BACK?!
THUD
KLAK
HE'S DOING SOME-THING TO THE SET AGAIN!
DAMN IT! WHAT MORE IS THERE TO WRECK?!
I'LL TEACH YOU TO RUIN MY SET!!
HUP

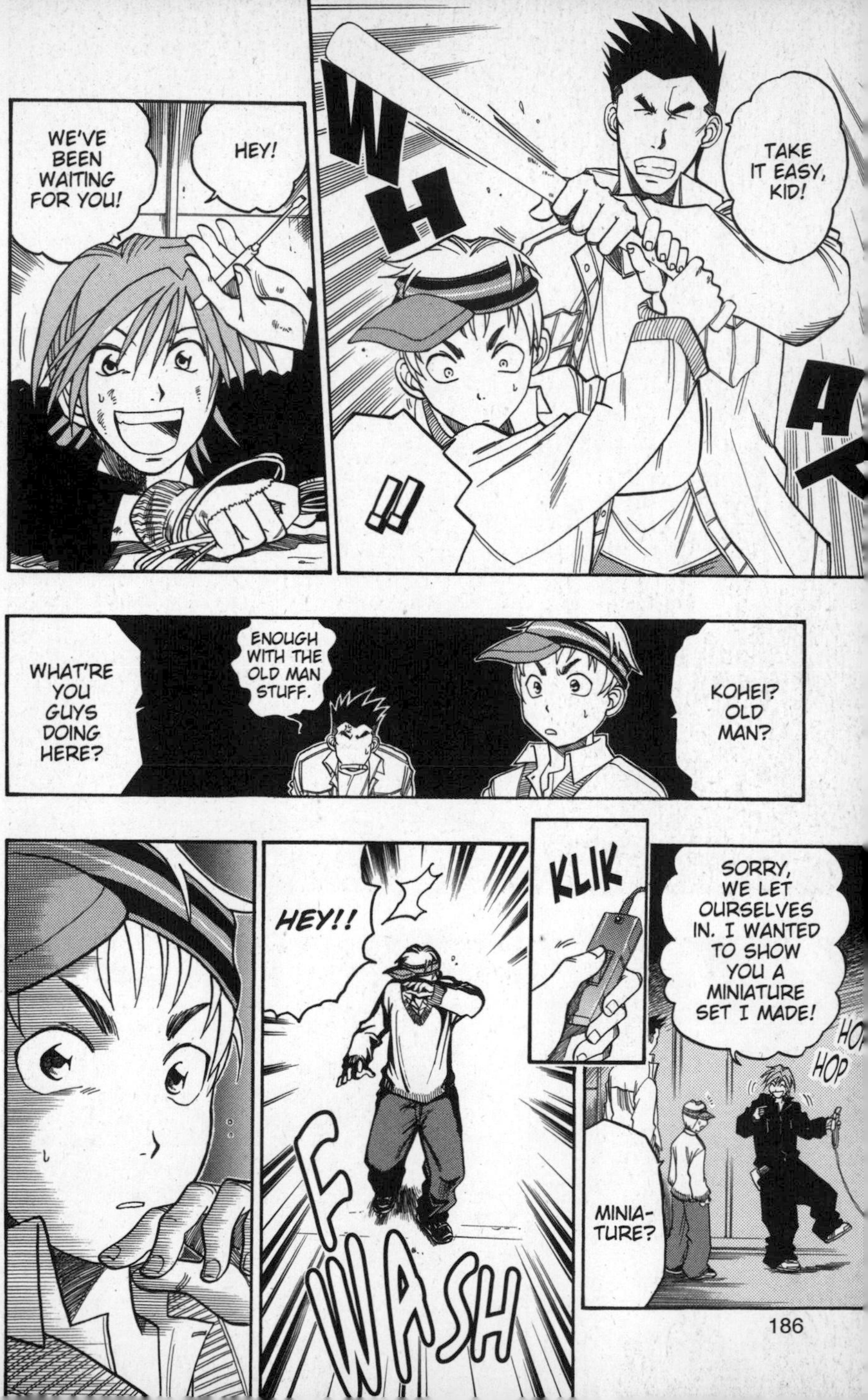

TAKE IT EASY, KID!
WH
A
!!
HEY!
WE'VE BEEN WAITING FOR YOU!
KOHEI? OLD MAN?
ENOUGH WITH THE OLD MAN STUFF.
WHAT'RE YOU GUYS DOING HERE?
SORRY, WE LET OURSELVES IN. I WANTED TO SHOW YOU A MINIATURE SET I MADE!
HOP
HOP
MINIA-TURE?
KLIK
HEY!!
FWASH

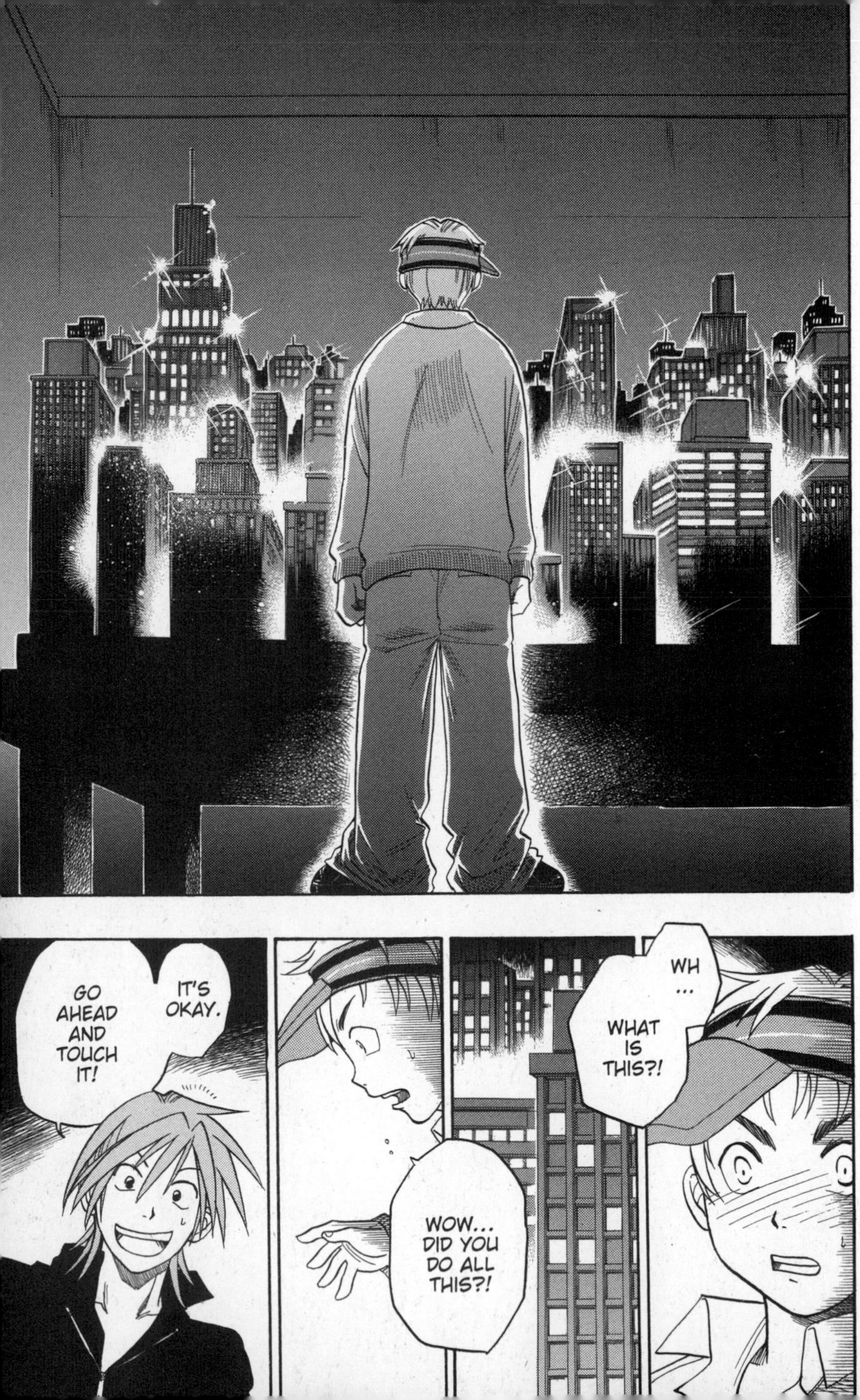
WH... WHAT IS THIS?!
WOW... DID YOU DO ALL THIS?!
IT'S OKAY.
GO AHEAD AND TOUCH IT!

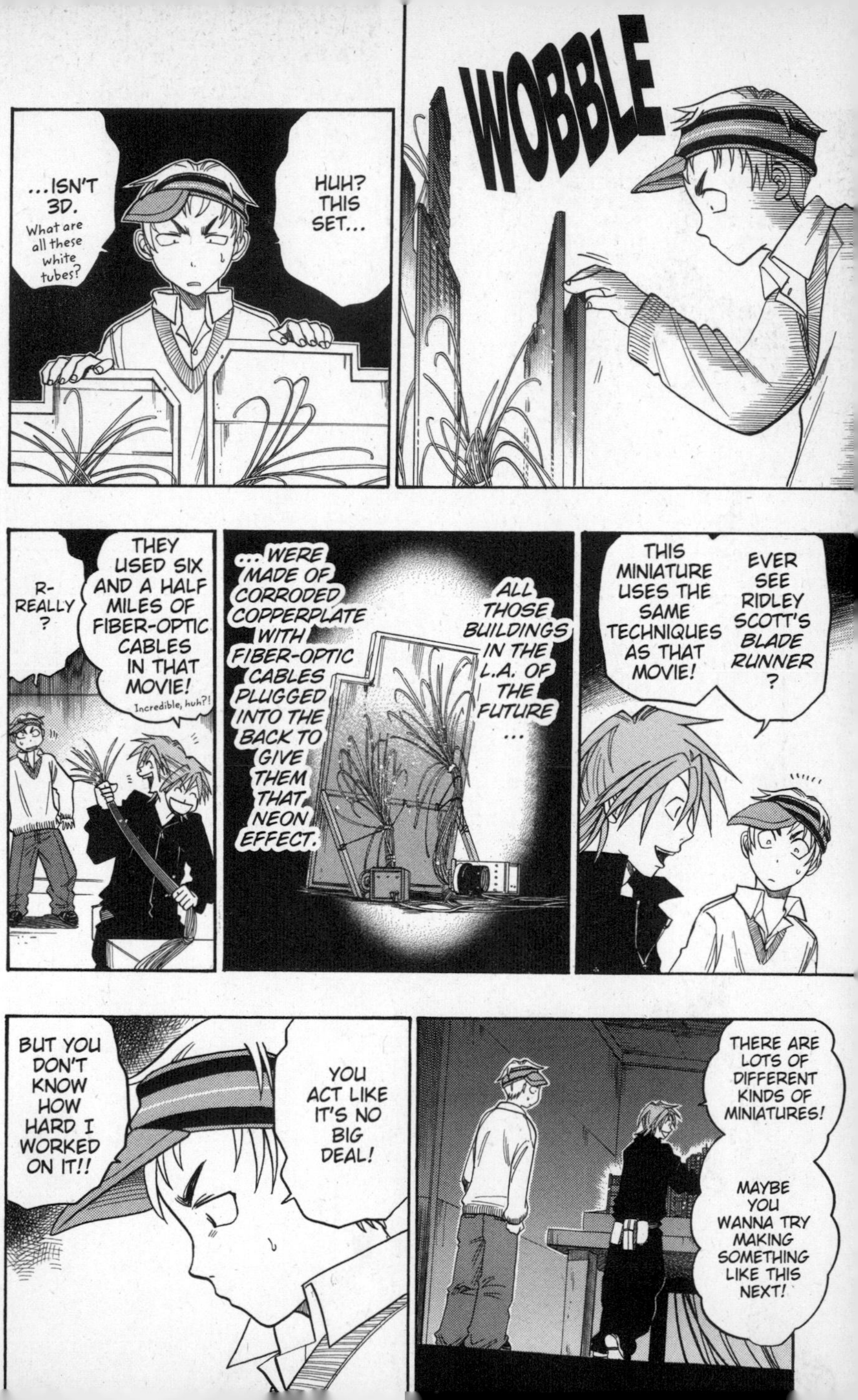
WOBBLE
HUH? THIS SET...
...ISN'T 3D.
What are all these white tubes?
EVER SEE RIDLEY SCOTT'S BLADE RUNNER?
THIS MINIATURE USES THE SAME TECHNIQUES AS THAT MOVIE!
ALL THOSE BUILDINGS IN THE L.A. OF THE FUTURE...
...WERE MADE OF CORRODED COPPERPLATE WITH FIBER-OPTIC CABLES PLUGGED INTO THE BACK TO GIVE THEM THAT NEON EFFECT.
THEY USED SIX AND A HALF MILES OF FIBER-OPTIC CABLES IN THAT MOVIE!
Incredible, huh?!
R-REALLY?
THERE ARE LOTS OF DIFFERENT KINDS OF MINIATURES!
MAYBE YOU WANNA TRY MAKING SOMETHING LIKE THIS NEXT!
YOU ACT LIKE IT'S NO BIG DEAL!
BUT YOU DON'T KNOW HOW HARD I WORKED ON IT!!

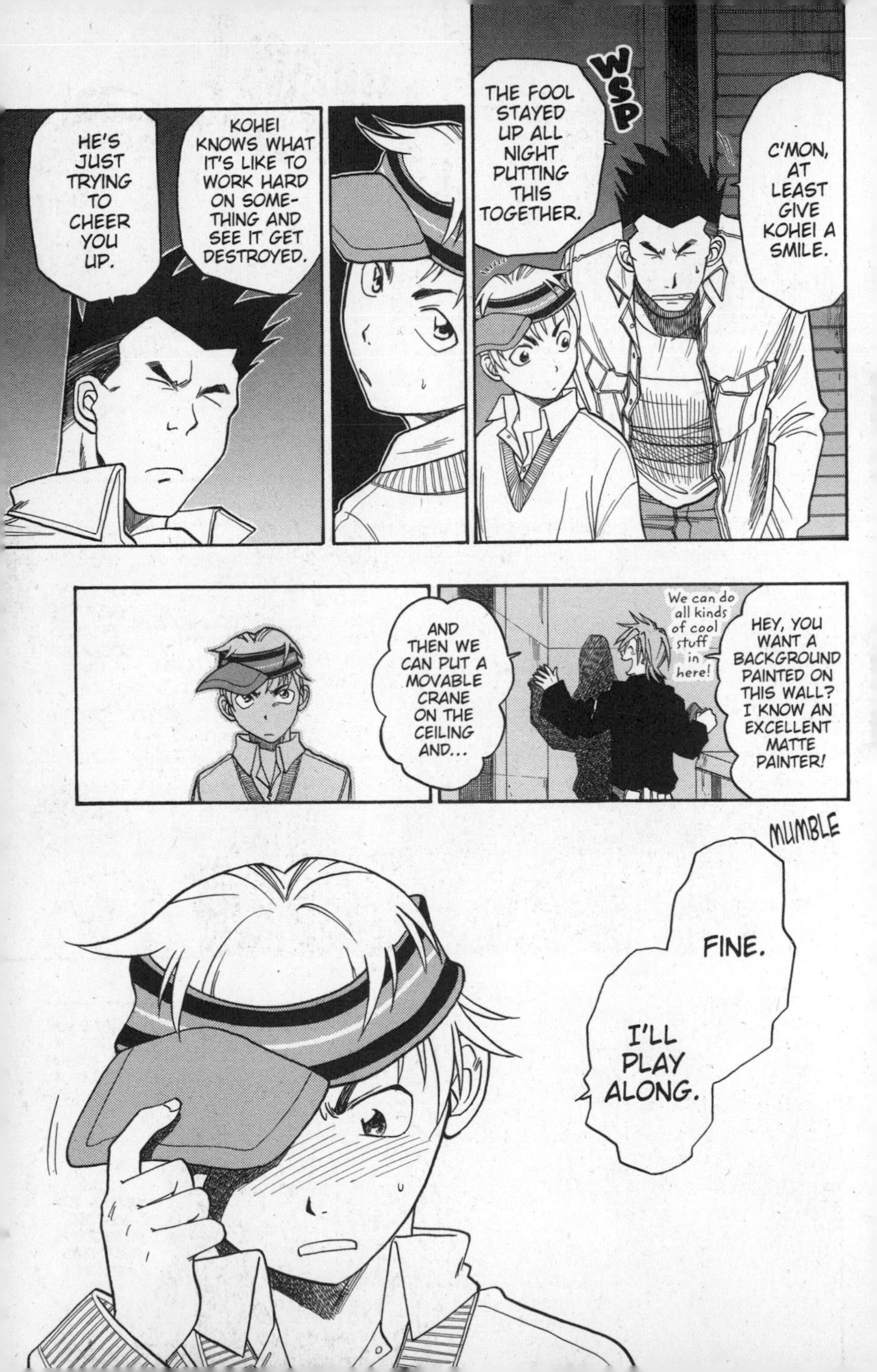
C'MON, AT LEAST GIVE KOHEI A SMILE.
WSP
THE FOOL STAYED UP ALL NIGHT PUTTING THIS TOGETHER.
KOHEI KNOWS WHAT IT'S LIKE TO WORK HARD ON SOME-THING AND SEE IT GET DESTROYED.
HE'S JUST TRYING TO CHEER YOU UP.
HEY, YOU WANT A BACKGROUND PAINTED ON THIS WALL? I KNOW AN EXCELLENT MATTE PAINTER!
We can do all kinds of cool stuff in here!
AND THEN WE CAN PUT A MOVABLE CRANE ON THE CEILING AND...
MUMBLE
FINE.
I'LL PLAY ALONG.

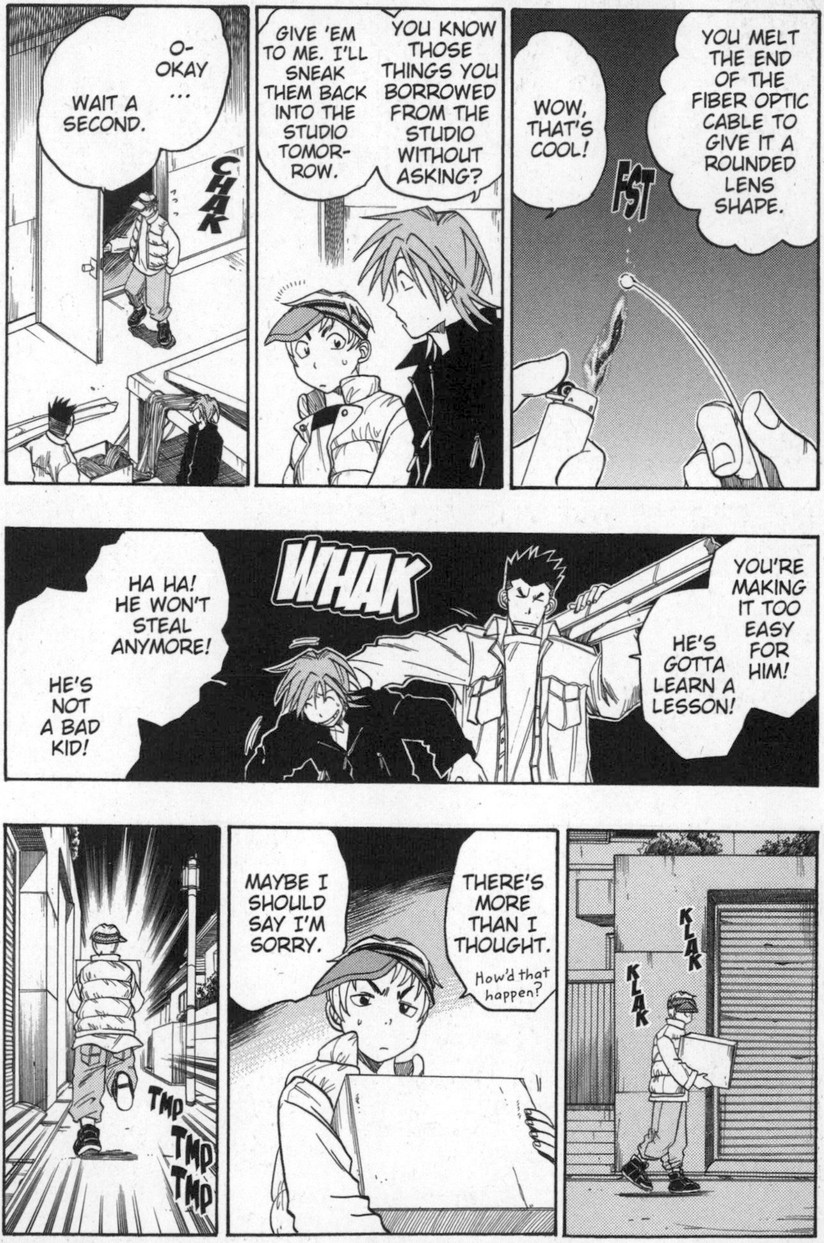
YOU MELT THE END OF THE FIBER OPTIC CABLE TO GIVE IT A ROUNDED LENS SHAPE.
WOW, THAT'S COOL!
FST
YOU KNOW THOSE THINGS YOU BORROWED FROM THE STUDIO WITHOUT ASKING?
GIVE 'EM TO ME. I'LL SNEAK THEM BACK INTO THE STUDIO TOMORROW.
O-OKAY ...
WAIT A SECOND.
CHAK
YOU'RE MAKING IT TOO EASY FOR HIM!
HE'S GOTTA LEARN A LESSON!
WHAK
HA HA! HE WON'T STEAL ANYMORE!
HE'S NOT A BAD KID!
KLAK
KLAK
THERE'S MORE THAN I THOUGHT.
How'd that happen?
MAYBE I SHOULD SAY I'M SORRY.
TMP
TMP
TMP
TMP

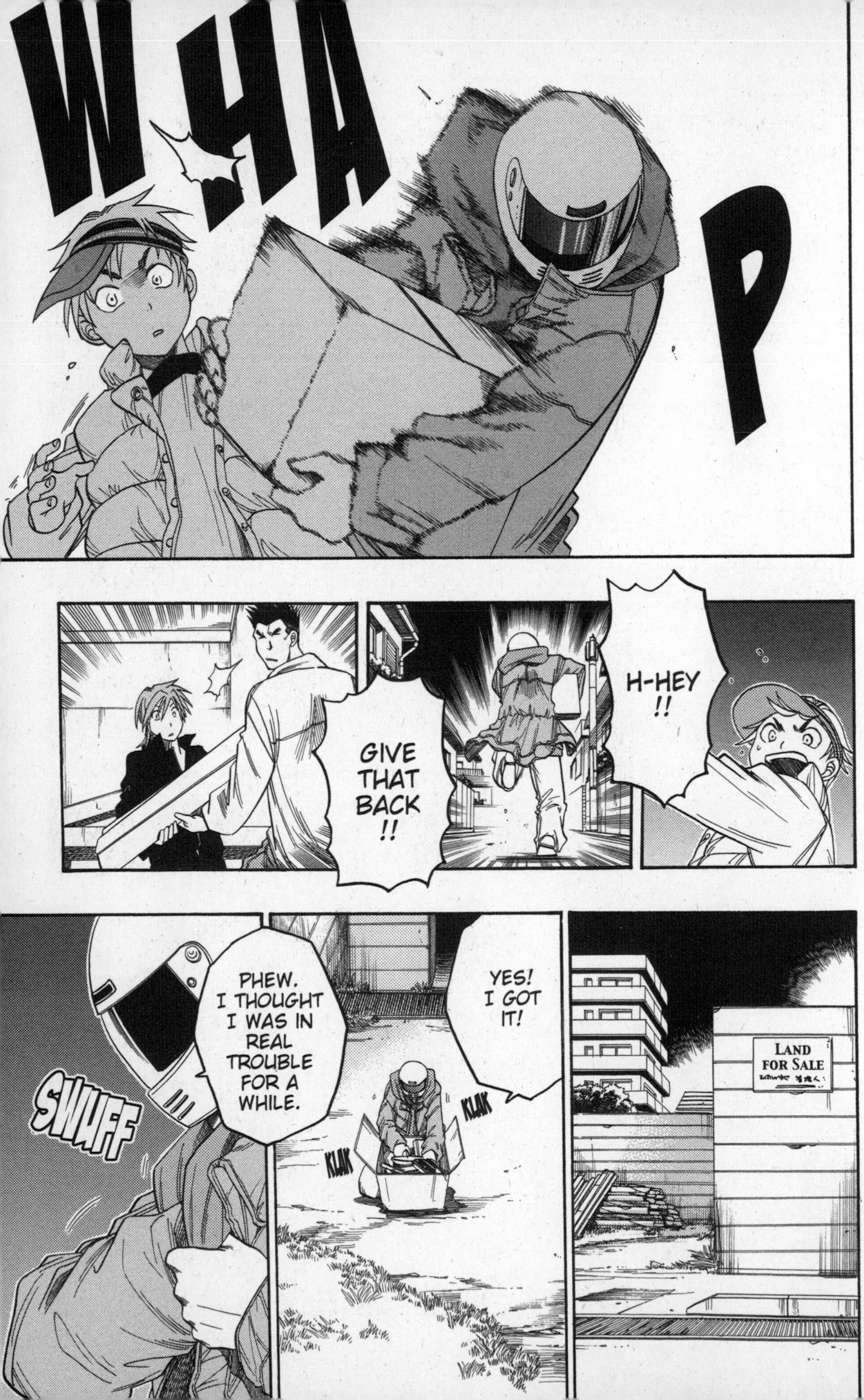
WHYAP
H-HEY !!
GIVE THAT BACK !!
LAND FOR SALE
YES! I GOT IT!
KLAK
KLAK
PHEW. I THOUGHT I WAS IN REAL TROUBLE FOR A WHILE.
SWUFF

AH...

DASH

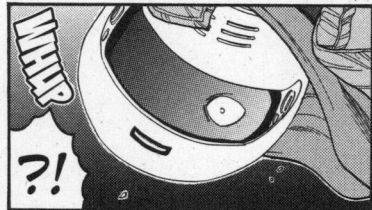

WHIP

?!

WHAT DID YOU JUST PUT IN YOUR POCKET?!

HEY!!

!!

THWA

SWIP

UGH!!

HUH?!

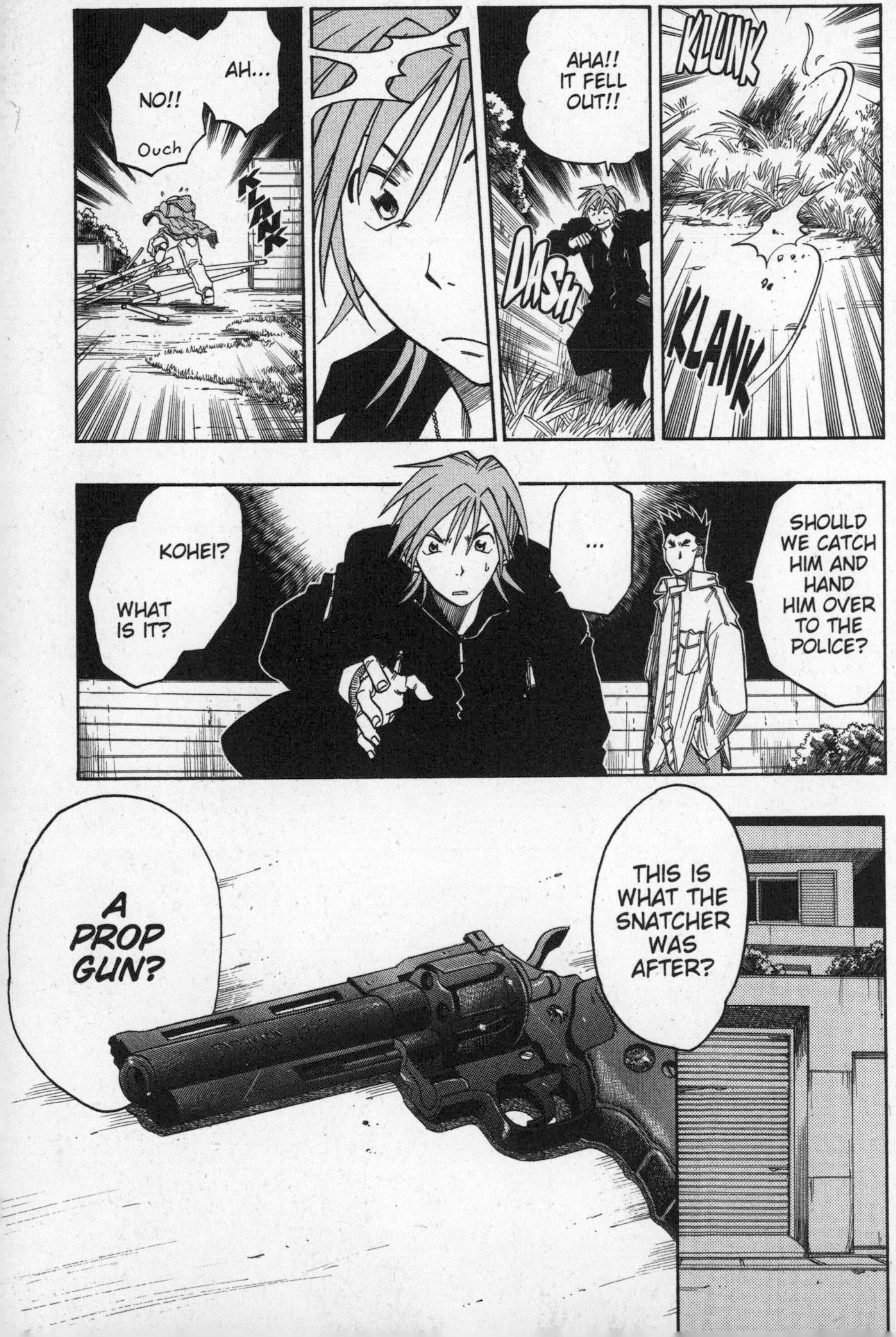
KLUNK
KLANK
AHA!! IT FELL OUT!!
DASH
AH...
NO!!
Ouch
KLANK
SHOULD WE CATCH HIM AND HAND HIM OVER TO THE POLICE?
...
KOHEI?
WHAT IS IT?
THIS IS WHAT THE SNATCHER WAS AFTER?
A PROP GUN?

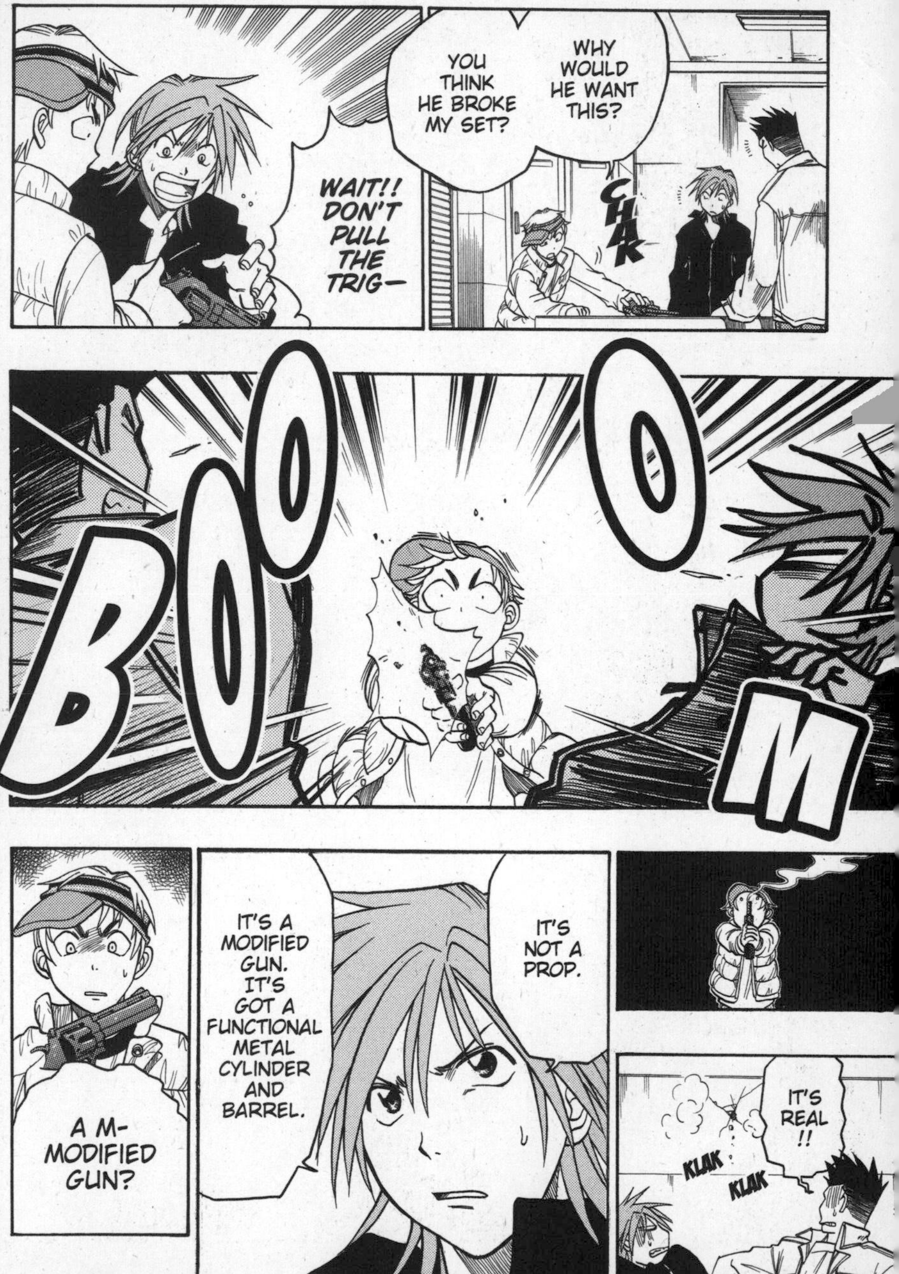
WHY WOULD HE WANT THIS?
YOU THINK HE BROKE MY SET?
CHAK
WAIT!! DON'T PULL THE TRIG—
BOOOOM
IT'S REAL!!
KLAK
KLAK
IT'S NOT A PROP.
IT'S A MODIFIED GUN. IT'S GOT A FUNCTIONAL METAL CYLINDER AND BARREL.
A M-MODIFIED GUN?

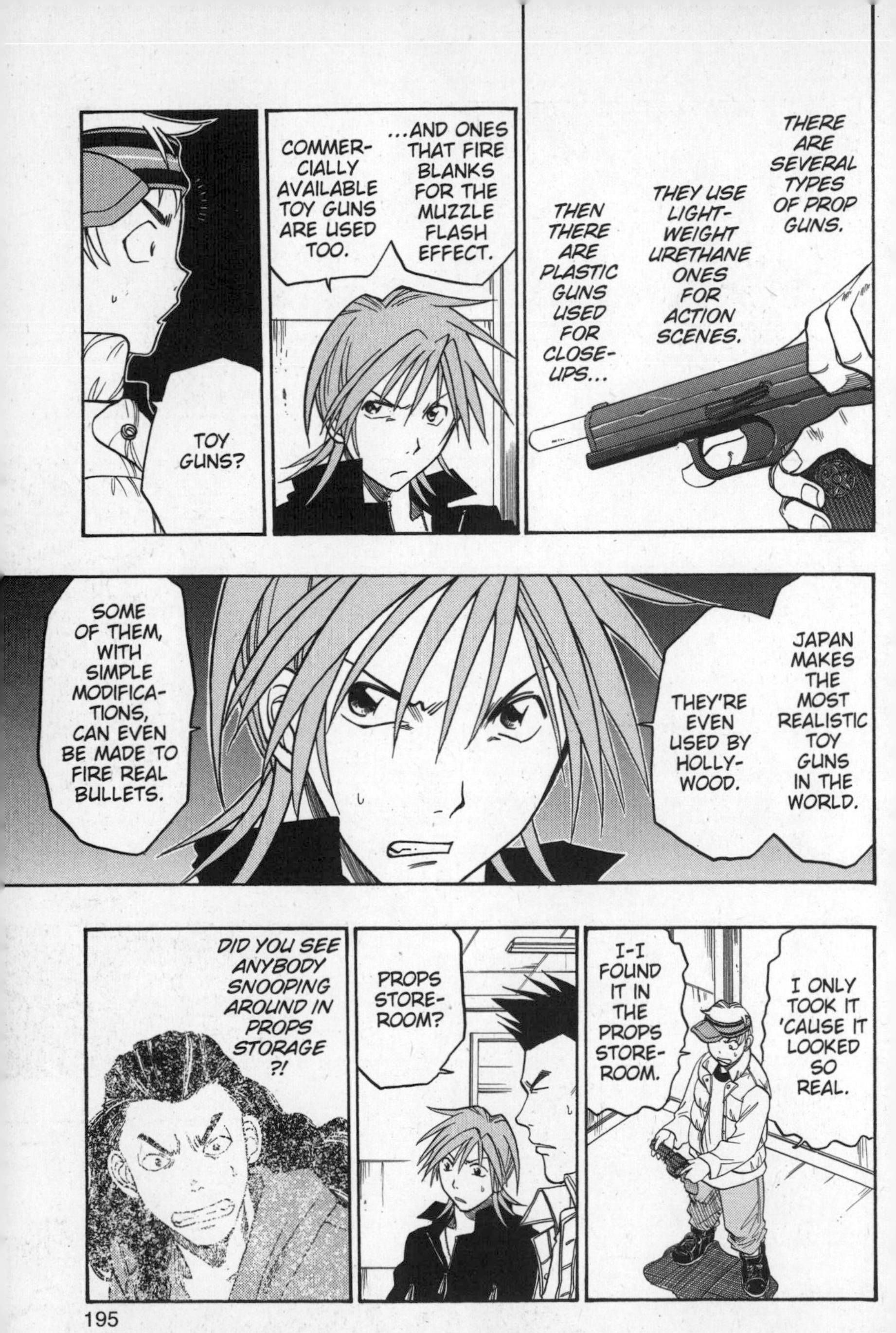
THERE ARE SEVERAL TYPES OF PROP GUNS.
THEY USE LIGHT-WEIGHT URETHANE ONES FOR ACTION SCENES.
THEN THERE ARE PLASTIC GUNS USED FOR CLOSE-UPS...
...AND ONES THAT FIRE BLANKS FOR THE MUZZLE FLASH EFFECT.
COMMER-CIALLY AVAILABLE TOY GUNS ARE USED TOO.
TOY GUNS?
JAPAN MAKES THE MOST REALISTIC TOY GUNS IN THE WORLD.
THEY'RE EVEN USED BY HOLLY-WOOD.
SOME OF THEM, WITH SIMPLE MODIFICA-TIONS, CAN EVEN BE MADE TO FIRE REAL BULLETS.
I ONLY TOOK IT 'CAUSE IT LOOKED SO REAL.
I-I FOUND IT IN THE PROPS STORE-ROOM.
PROPS STORE-ROOM?
DID YOU SEE ANYBODY SNOOPING AROUND IN PROPS STORAGE ?!

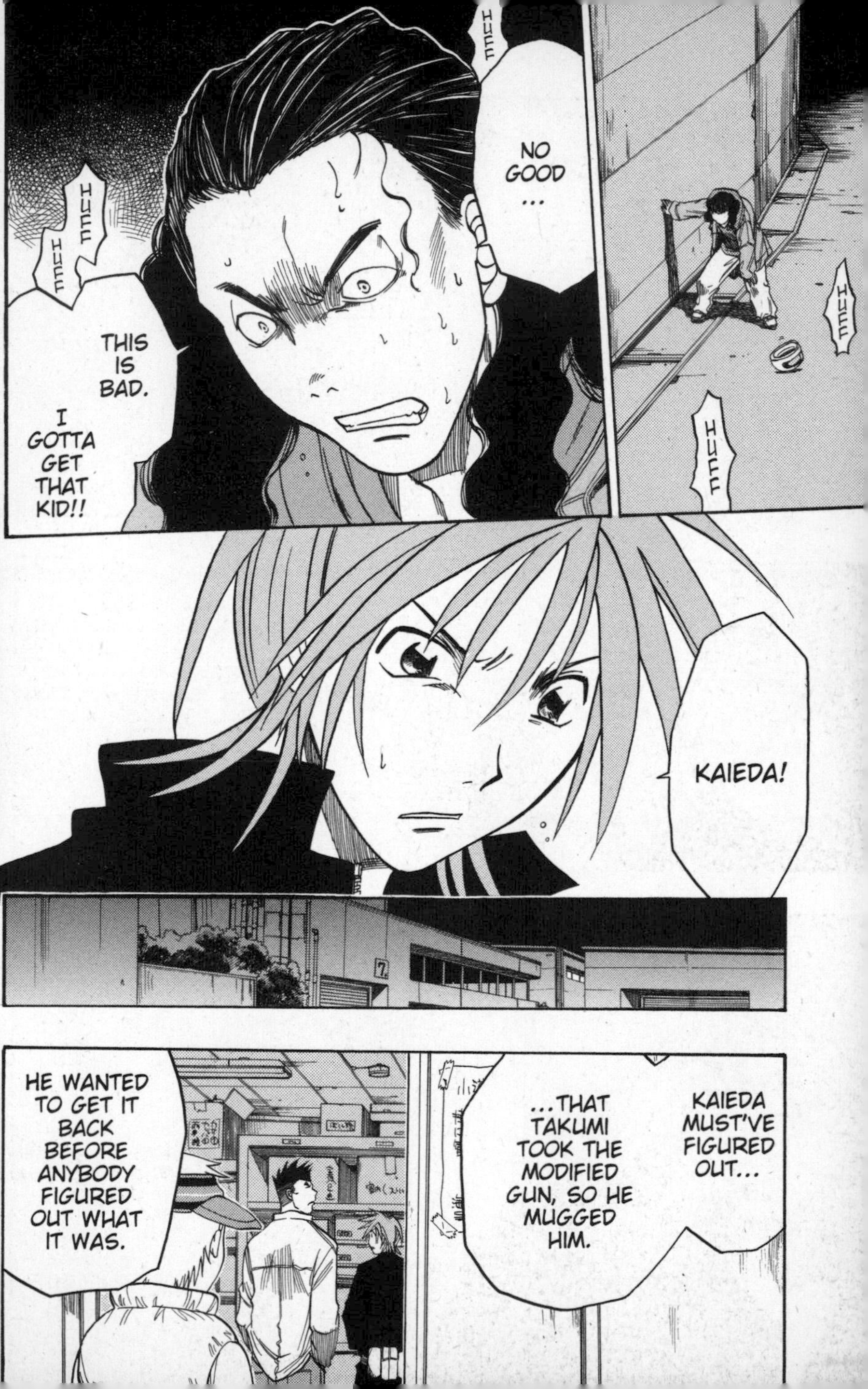
HUFF
HUFF
HUFF
NO GOOD ...
HUFF HUFF
THIS IS BAD.
I GOTTA GET THAT KID!!
KAIEDA!
KAIEDA MUST'VE FIGURED OUT...
...THAT TAKUMI TOOK THE MODIFIED GUN, SO HE MUGGED HIM.
HE WANTED TO GET IT BACK BEFORE ANYBODY FIGURED OUT WHAT IT WAS.

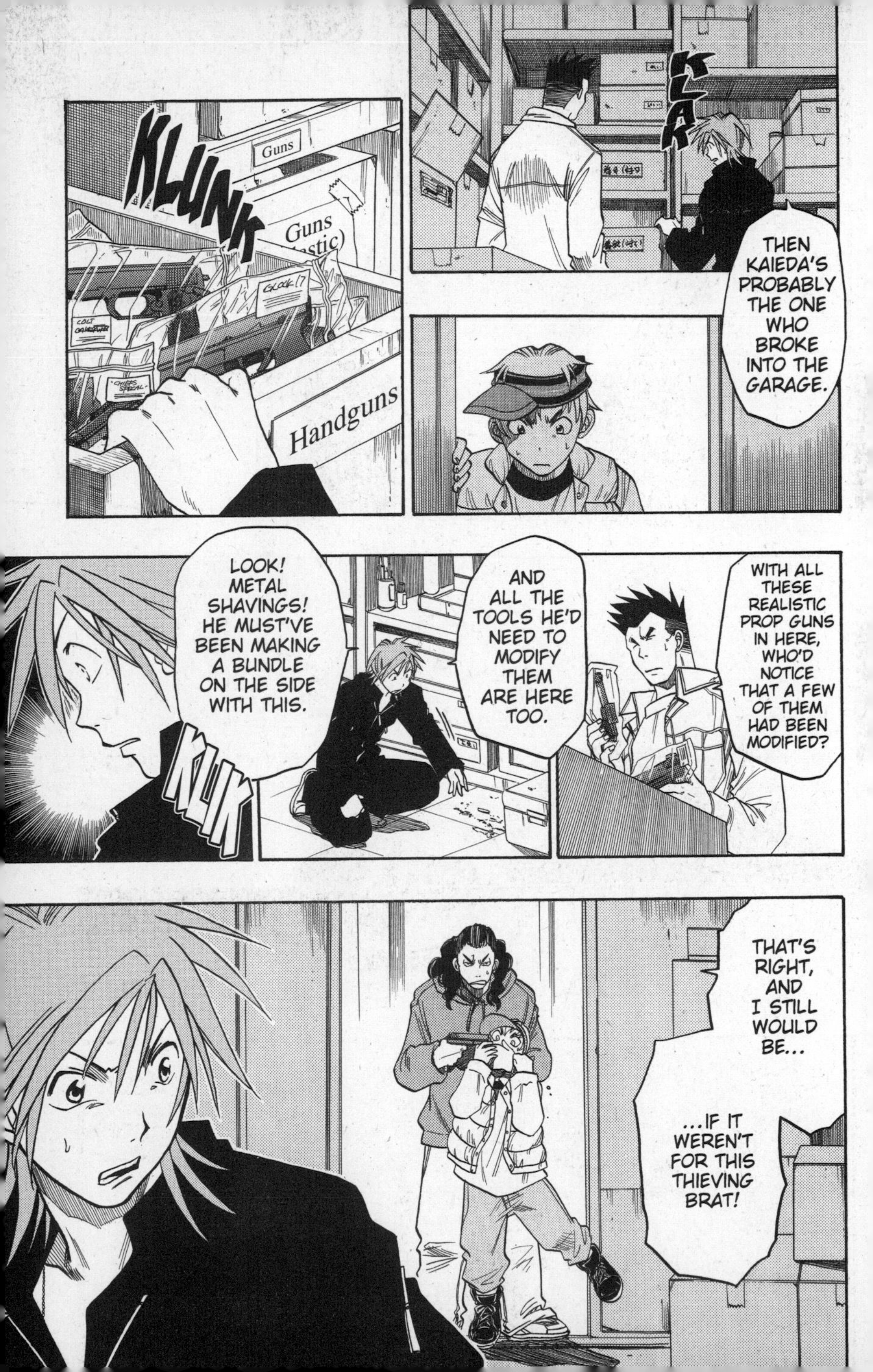
KLA
THEN KAIEDA'S PROBABLY THE ONE WHO BROKE INTO THE GARAGE.
KLUNK
Guns
Guns
astic)
GLOCK 17
Handguns
WITH ALL THESE REALISTIC PROP GUNS IN HERE, WHO'D NOTICE THAT A FEW OF THEM HAD BEEN MODIFIED?
AND ALL THE TOOLS HE'D NEED TO MODIFY THEM ARE HERE TOO.
LOOK! METAL SHAVINGS! HE MUST'VE BEEN MAKING A BUNDLE ON THE SIDE WITH THIS.
KLIK
THAT'S RIGHT, AND I STILL WOULD BE...
...IF IT WEREN'T FOR THIS THIEVING BRAT!

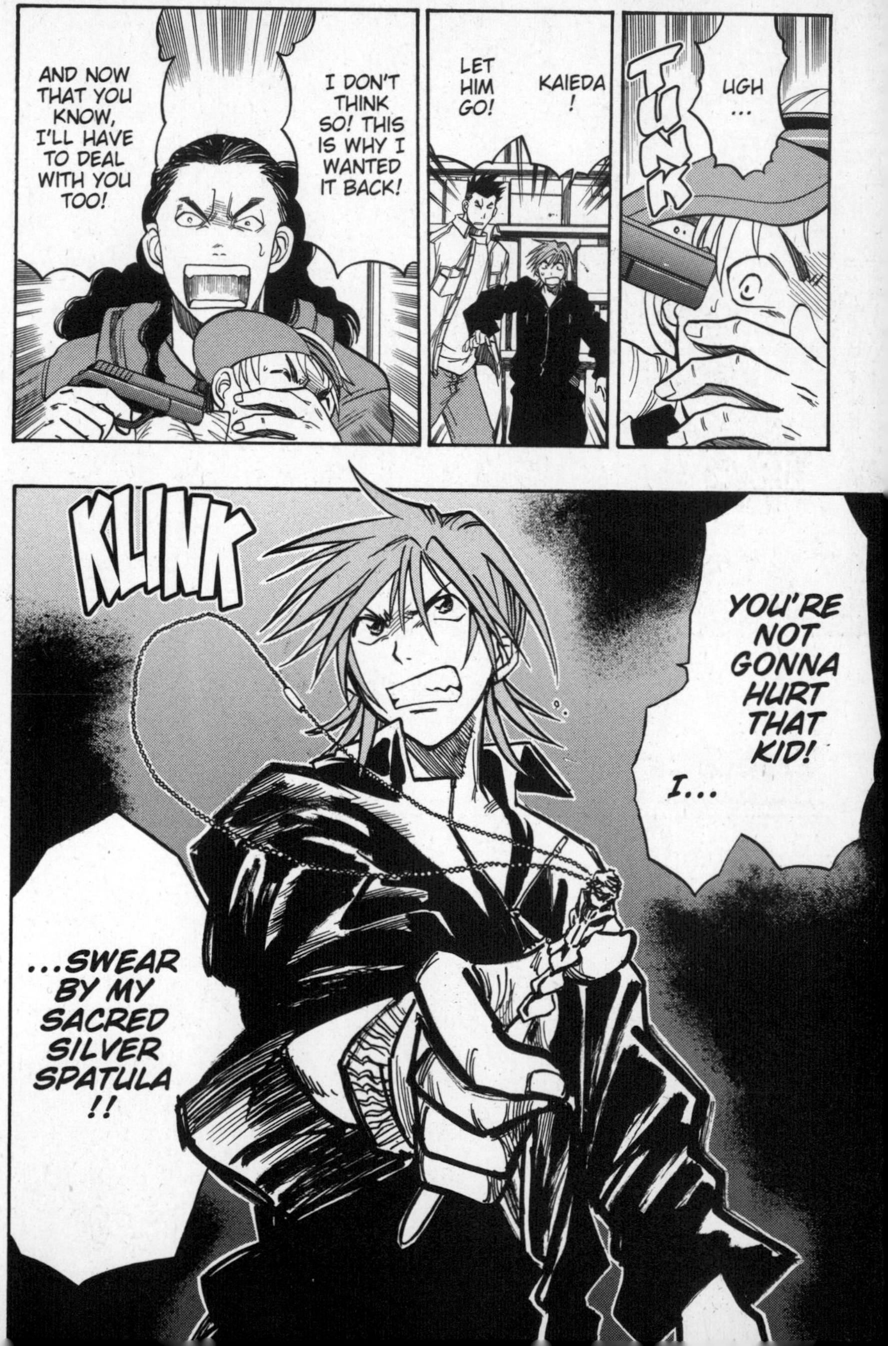
UGH ...
TUNK
KAIEDA!
LET HIM GO!
I DON'T THINK SO! THIS IS WHY I WANTED IT BACK!
AND NOW THAT YOU KNOW, I'LL HAVE TO DEAL WITH YOU TOO!
KLINK
YOU'RE NOT GONNA HURT THAT KID!
I...
...SWEAR BY MY SACRED SILVER SPATULA!!

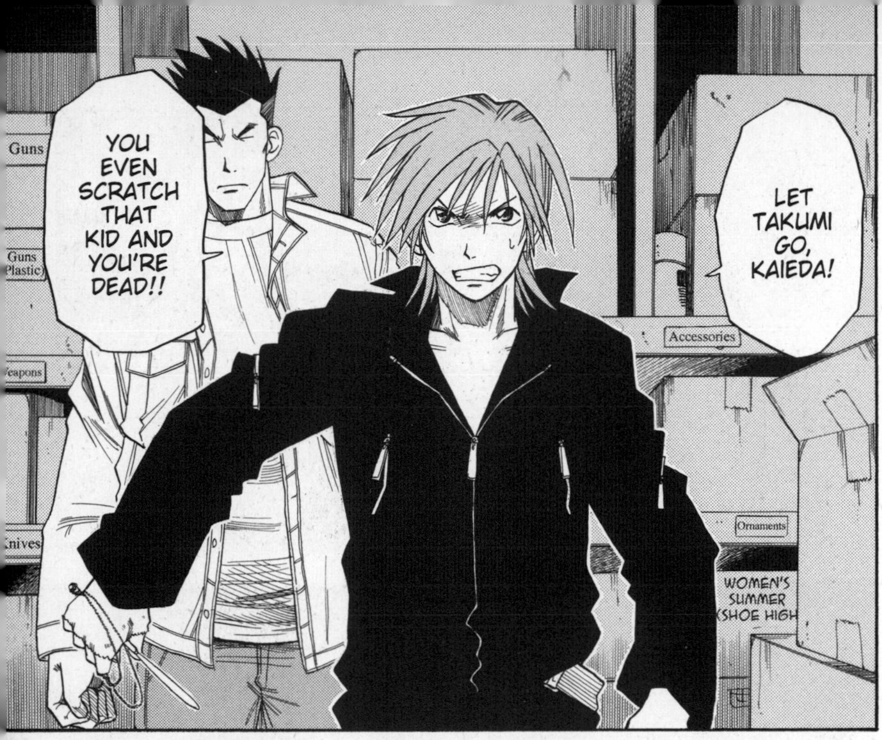
LET TAKUMI GO, KAIEDA!
YOU EVEN SCRATCH THAT KID AND YOU'RE DEAD!!
Guns
Guns Plastic
Accessories
Ornaments
WOMEN'S SUMMER SHOE HIGH

Scene 36:

The Sorcerer's Apprentice (Part 3)

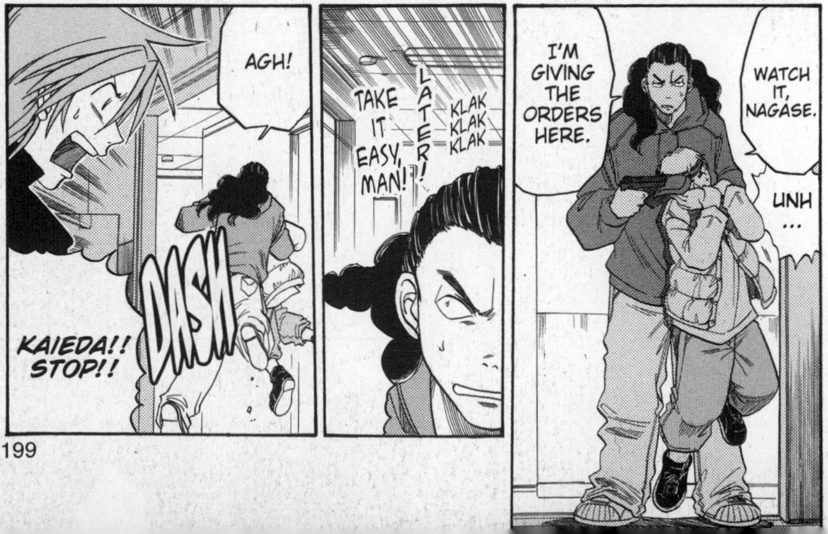
WATCH IT, NAGASE.
UNH ...
I'M GIVING THE ORDERS HERE.
LATER!
KLAK KLAK KLAK
TAKE IT EASY, MAN!
AGH!
DASH
KAIEDA!! STOP!!

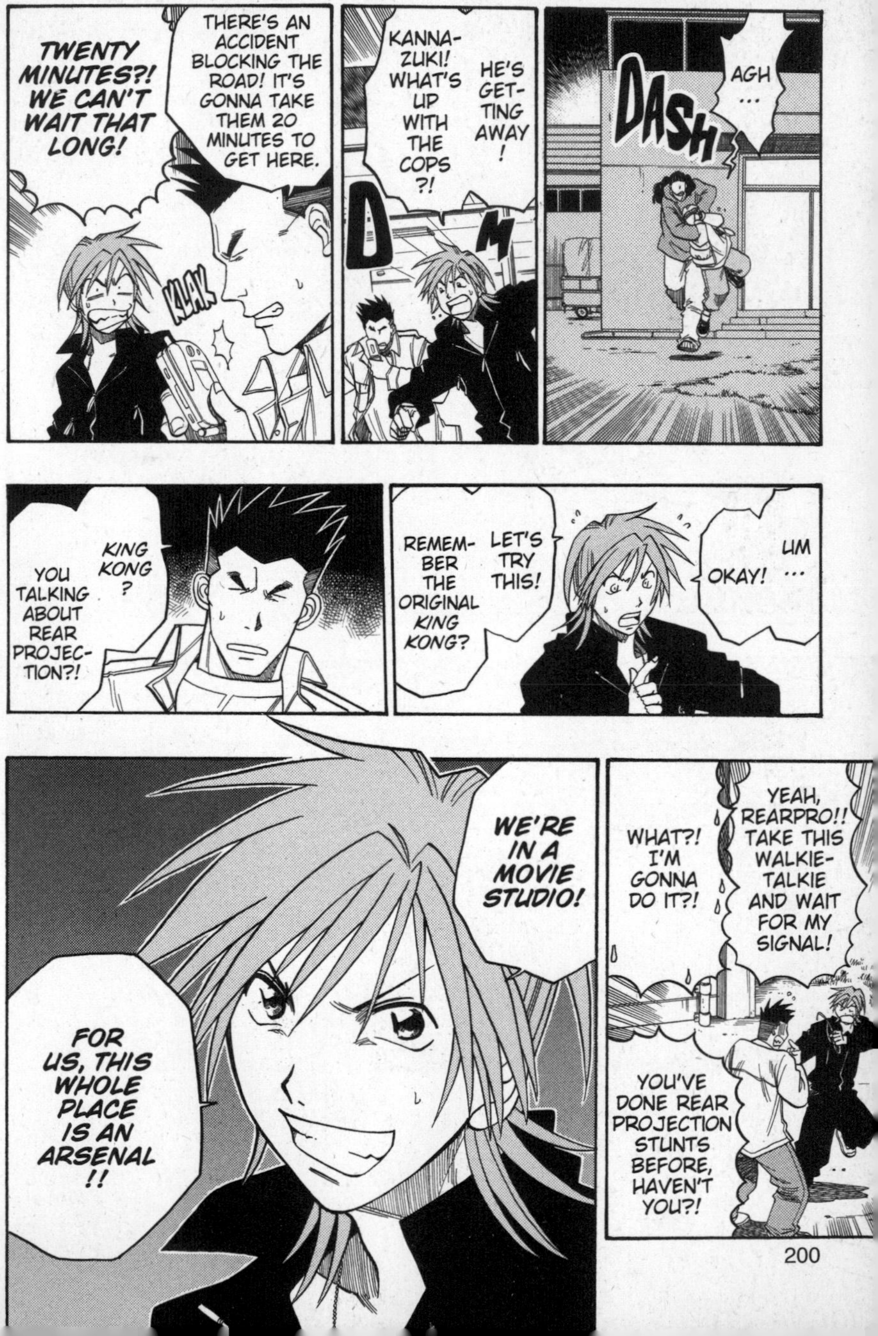
AGH ...
DASH
HE'S GETTING AWAY!
KANNAZUKI! WHAT'S UP WITH THE COPS?!
D M
THERE'S AN ACCIDENT BLOCKING THE ROAD! IT'S GONNA TAKE THEM 20 MINUTES TO GET HERE.
TWENTY MINUTES?! WE CAN'T WAIT THAT LONG!
KLAK
UM ...
OKAY!
LET'S TRY THIS!
REMEMBER THE ORIGINAL KING KONG?
KING KONG?
YOU TALKING ABOUT REAR PROJECTION?!
YEAH, REARPRO!! TAKE THIS WALKIE-TALKIE AND WAIT FOR MY SIGNAL!
WHAT?! I'M GONNA DO IT?!
YOU'VE DONE REAR PROJECTION STUNTS BEFORE, HAVEN'T YOU?!
WE'RE IN A MOVIE STUDIO!
FOR US, THIS WHOLE PLACE IS AN ARSENAL!!

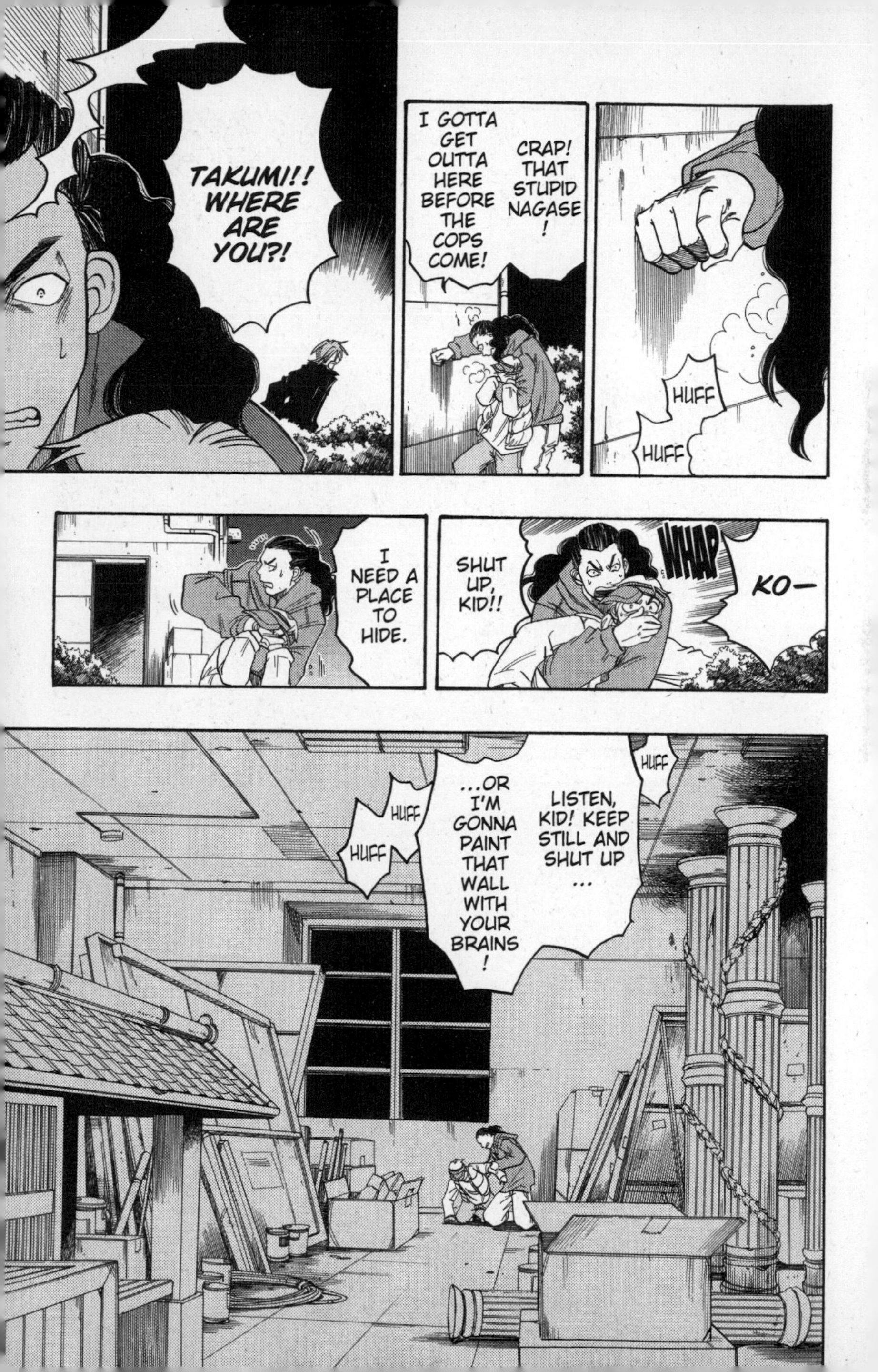
HUFF
HUFF
CRAP! THAT STUPID NAGASE!
I GOTTA GET OUTTA HERE BEFORE THE COPS COME!
TAKUMI!! WHERE ARE YOU?!
KO—
WHAP
SHUT UP, KID!!
I NEED A PLACE TO HIDE.
HUFF
LISTEN, KID! KEEP STILL AND SHUT UP...
...OR I'M GONNA PAINT THAT WALL WITH YOUR BRAINS!
HUFF
HUFF

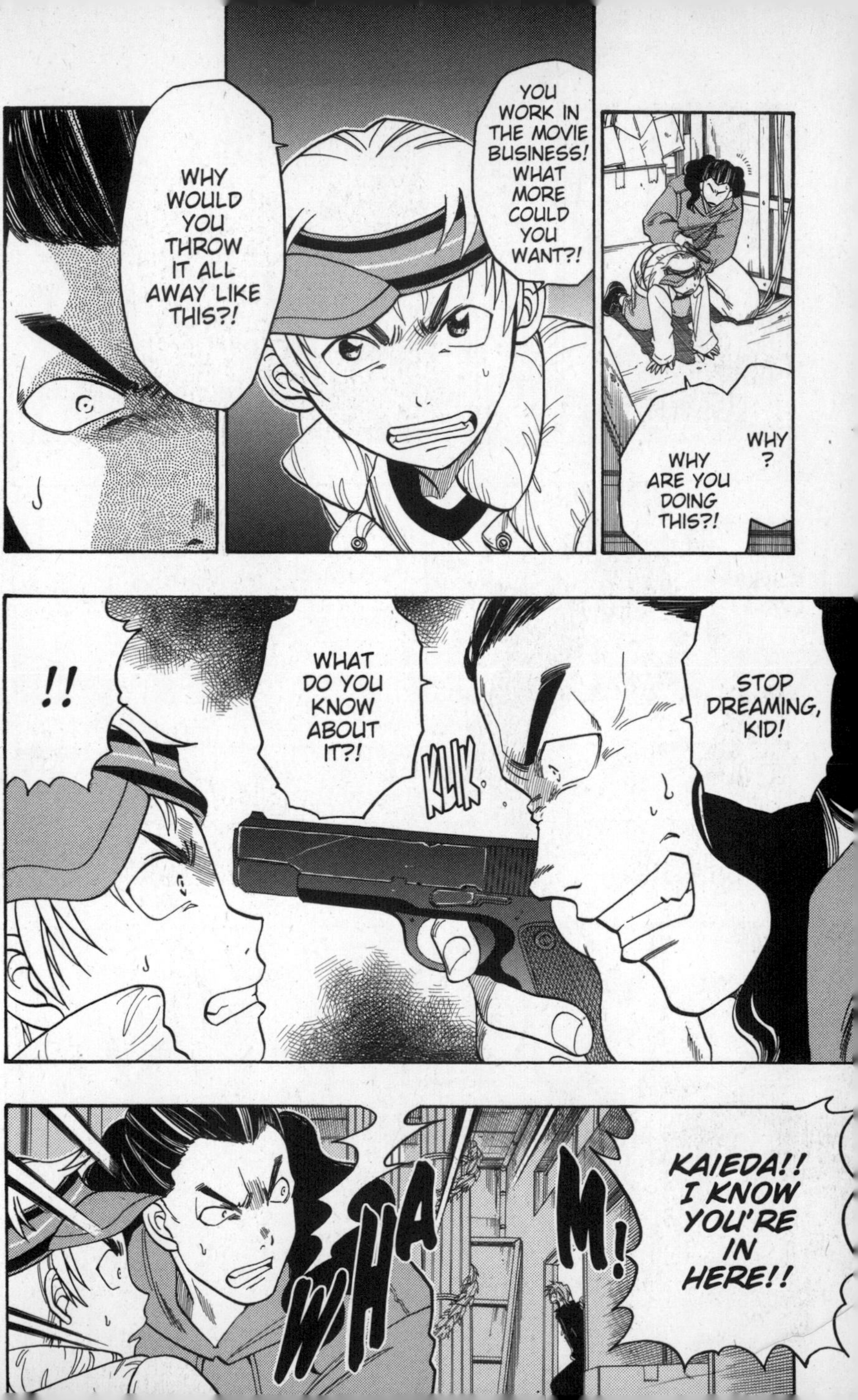
WHY? WHY ARE YOU DOING THIS?!
YOU WORK IN THE MOVIE BUSINESS! WHAT MORE COULD YOU WANT?!
WHY WOULD YOU THROW IT ALL AWAY LIKE THIS?!
STOP DREAMING, KID!
WHAT DO YOU KNOW ABOUT IT?!
KLIK
!!
KAIEDA!! I KNOW YOU'RE IN HERE!!
WHAM!

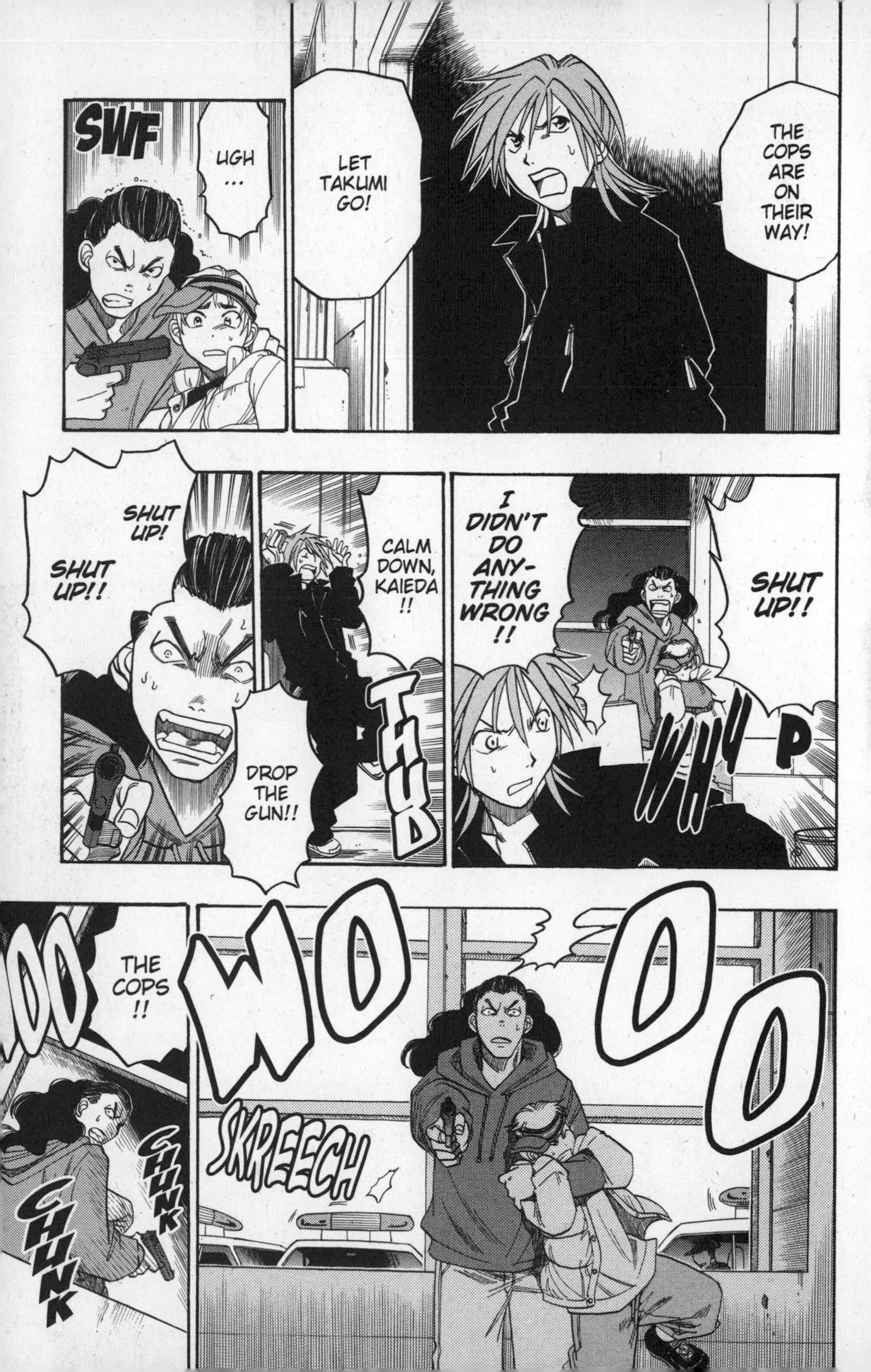
THE COPS ARE ON THEIR WAY!
LET TAKUMI GO!
SWF
UGH ...
SHUT UP!!
I DIDN'T DO ANY-THING WRONG!!
WHUP
CALM DOWN, KAIEDA!!
DROP THE GUN!!
THUD
SHUT UP!
SHUT UP!!
WOOOOO
SKREECH
THE COPS!!
CHUNK
CHUNK

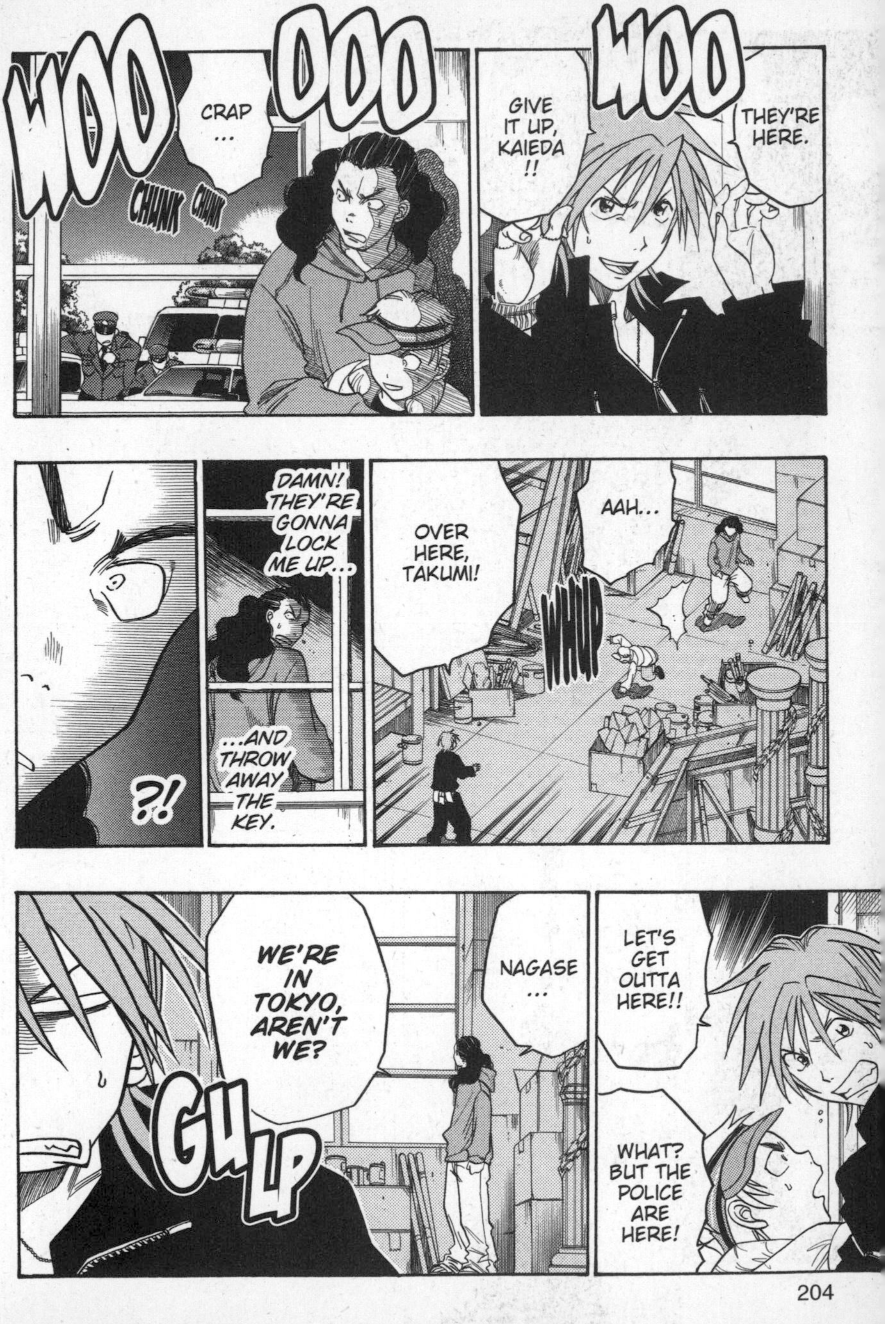
WOO OOO WOO
THEY'RE HERE.
GIVE IT UP, KAIEDA!!
CRAP...
CHUNK
CHUNK
AAH...
OVER HERE, TAKUMI!
WHUP
DAMN! THEY'RE GONNA LOCK ME UP...
...AND THROW AWAY THE KEY.
?!
LET'S GET OUTTA HERE!!
WHAT? BUT THE POLICE ARE HERE!
NAGASE...
WE'RE IN TOKYO, AREN'T WE?
GULP

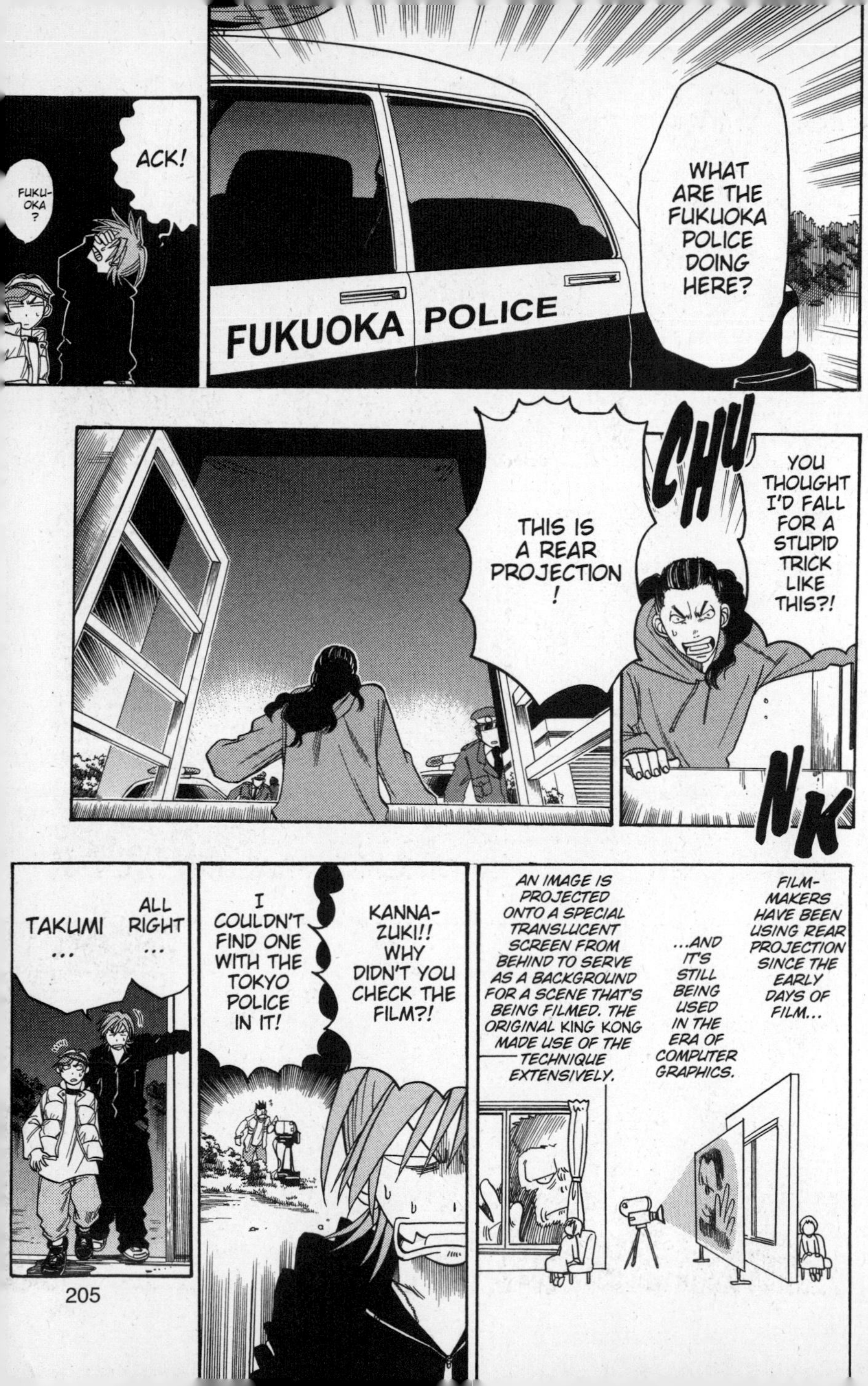
WHAT ARE THE FUKUOKA POLICE DOING HERE?
FUKUOKA POLICE
ACK!
FUKU-OKA?
YOU THOUGHT I'D FALL FOR A STUPID TRICK LIKE THIS?!
CHUNK
THIS IS A REAR PROJECTION!
FILM-MAKERS HAVE BEEN USING REAR PROJECTION SINCE THE EARLY DAYS OF FILM...
...AND IT'S STILL BEING USED IN THE ERA OF COMPUTER GRAPHICS.
AN IMAGE IS PROJECTED ONTO A SPECIAL TRANSLUCENT SCREEN FROM BEHIND TO SERVE AS A BACKGROUND FOR A SCENE THAT'S BEING FILMED. THE ORIGINAL KING KONG MADE USE OF THE TECHNIQUE EXTENSIVELY.
KANNA-ZUKI!! WHY DIDN'T YOU CHECK THE FILM?!
I COULDN'T FIND ONE WITH THE TOKYO POLICE IN IT!
ALL RIGHT...
TAKUMI...

LET'S GET OUTTA HERE!

THIS IS THE LAST TIME YOU MAKE A FOOL OUT OF ME!!

KLIK

OKAY!

RUN!!

TMP TMP TMP

2		OPEN SET MANAGER/YAMAMOTO	
2/1	CS Wolf of Edo	6:00 PM	
/2	"	#8	2:00 PM

IS EVERYTHING ALL RIGHT?

NAGASE?

Who's the kid?

TMP

TMP TMP

HEY!! WHERE ARE WE GOING?!

SORRY!! COMING THROUGH!!

HEY!! WHAT'RE YOU DOING?!

TMP

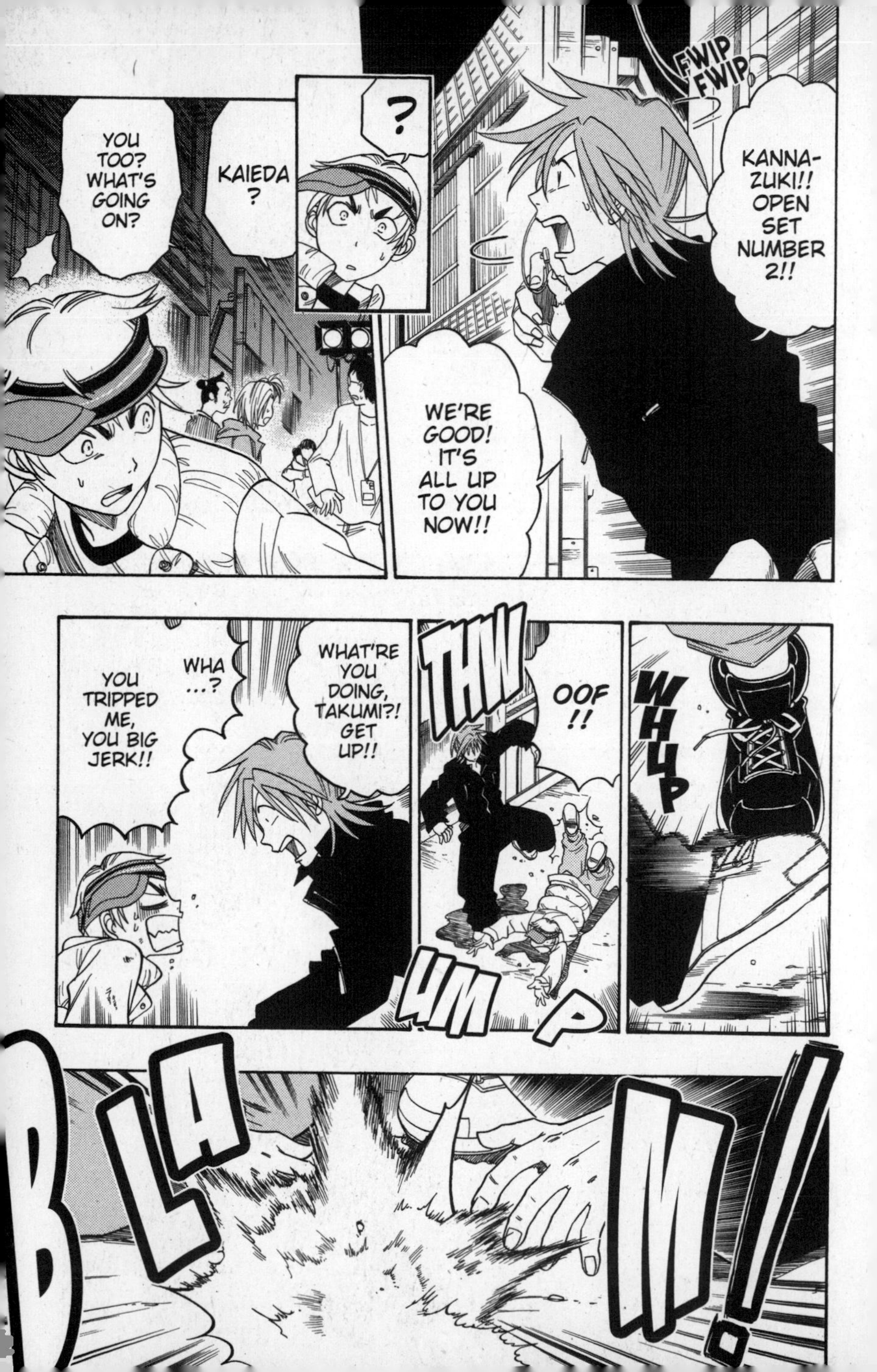
FWIP FWIP
KANNA-ZUKI!! OPEN SET NUMBER 2!!
WE'RE GOOD! IT'S ALL UP TO YOU NOW!!
?
KAIEDA?
YOU TOO? WHAT'S GOING ON?
WHUP
THWUMP
OOF!!
WHAT'RE YOU DOING, TAKUMI?! GET UP!!
WHA...?
YOU TRIPPED ME, YOU BIG JERK!!
BLAM!!

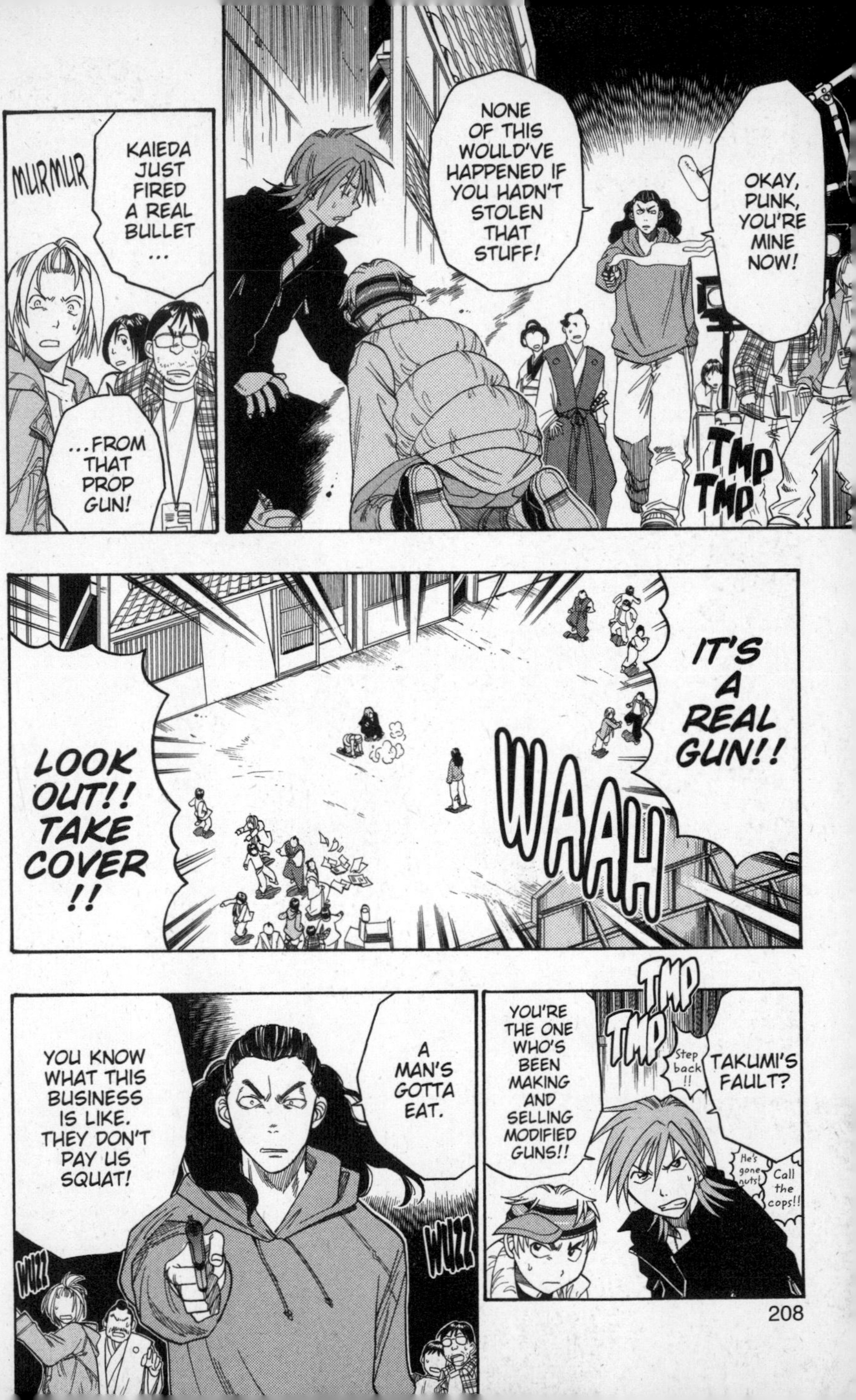
OKAY, PUNK, YOU'RE MINE NOW!
TMP TMP
NONE OF THIS WOULD'VE HAPPENED IF YOU HADN'T STOLEN THAT STUFF!
KAIEDA JUST FIRED A REAL BULLET ...
MURMUR
...FROM THAT PROP GUN!
IT'S A REAL GUN!!
WAAH
LOOK OUT!! TAKE COVER!!
TMP TMP
TAKUMI'S FAULT?
Step back!!
YOU'RE THE ONE WHO'S BEEN MAKING AND SELLING MODIFIED GUNS!!
Call the cops!!
He's gone nuts!
A MAN'S GOTTA EAT.
YOU KNOW WHAT THIS BUSINESS IS LIKE. THEY DON'T PAY US SQUAT!
WUZZ
WUZZ

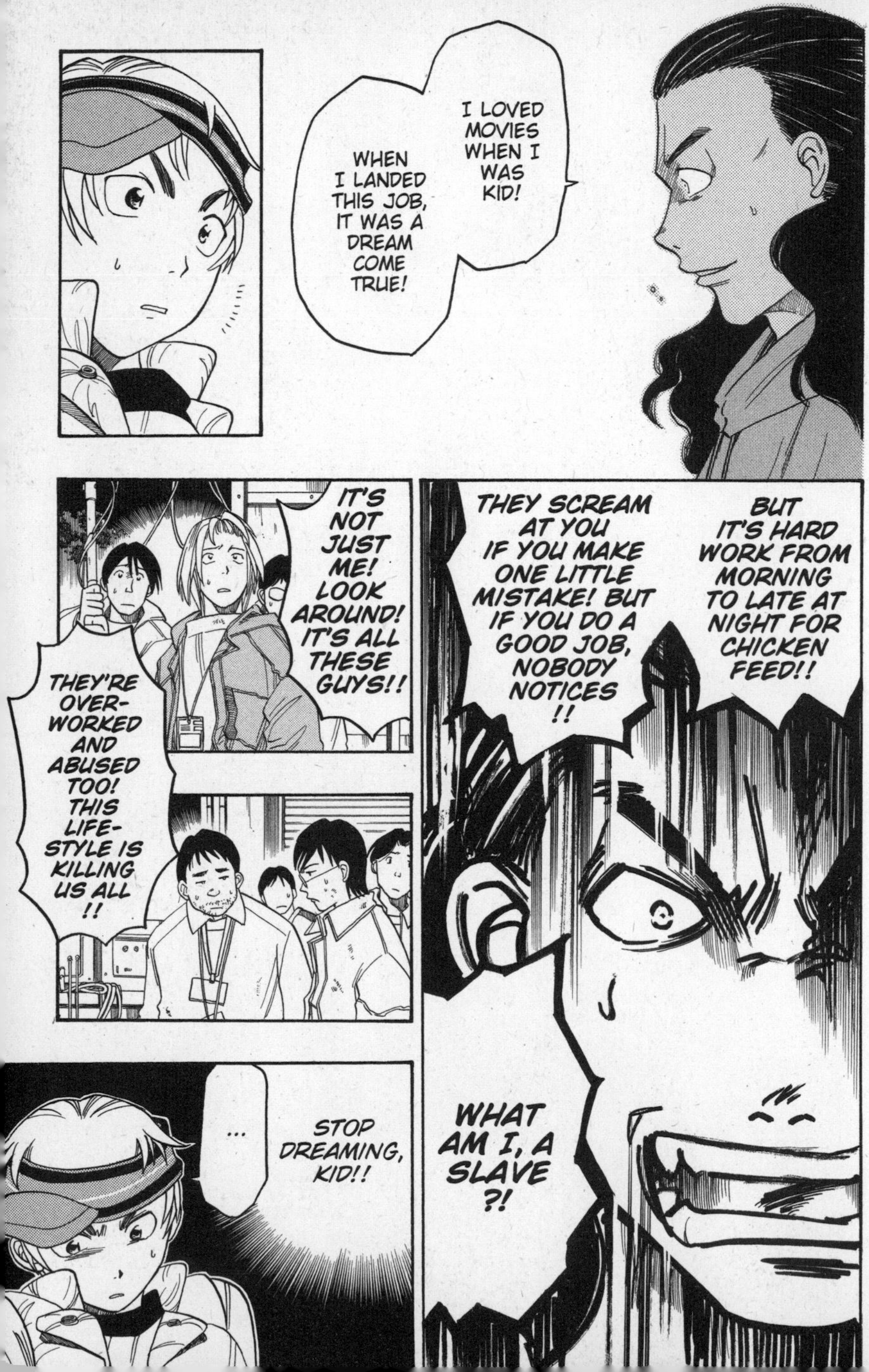
I LOVED MOVIES WHEN I WAS KID!
WHEN I LANDED THIS JOB, IT WAS A DREAM COME TRUE!
BUT IT'S HARD WORK FROM MORNING TO LATE AT NIGHT FOR CHICKEN FEED!!
THEY SCREAM AT YOU IF YOU MAKE ONE LITTLE MISTAKE! BUT IF YOU DO A GOOD JOB, NOBODY NOTICES!!
WHAT AM I, A SLAVE?!
IT'S NOT JUST ME! LOOK AROUND! IT'S ALL THESE GUYS!!
THEY'RE OVER-WORKED AND ABUSED TOO! THIS LIFE-STYLE IS KILLING US ALL!!
STOP DREAMING, KID!!
...

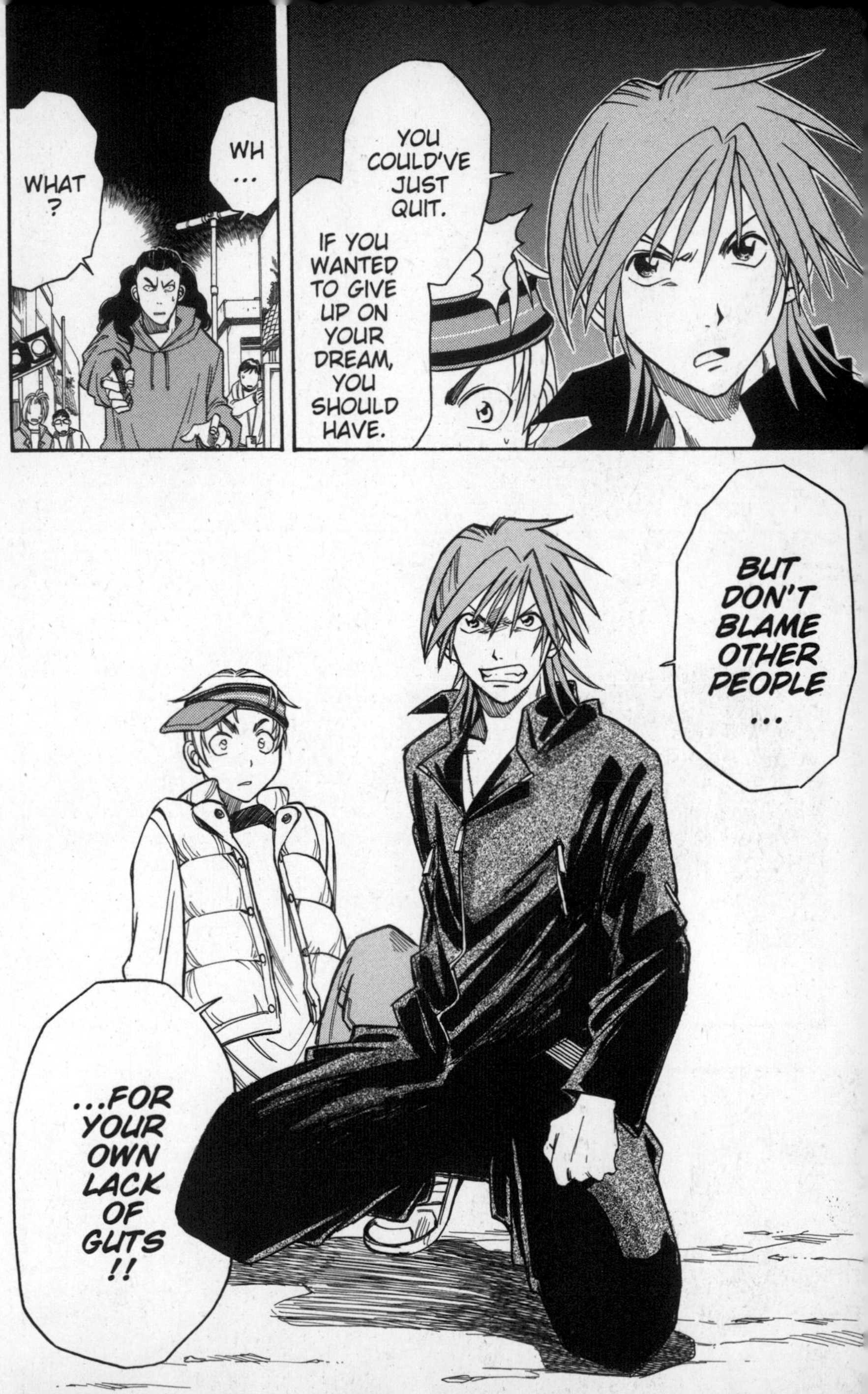
YOU COULD'VE JUST QUIT.
IF YOU WANTED TO GIVE UP ON YOUR DREAM, YOU SHOULD HAVE.
WH ...
WHAT ?
BUT DON'T BLAME OTHER PEOPLE ...
...FOR YOUR OWN LACK OF GUTS !!

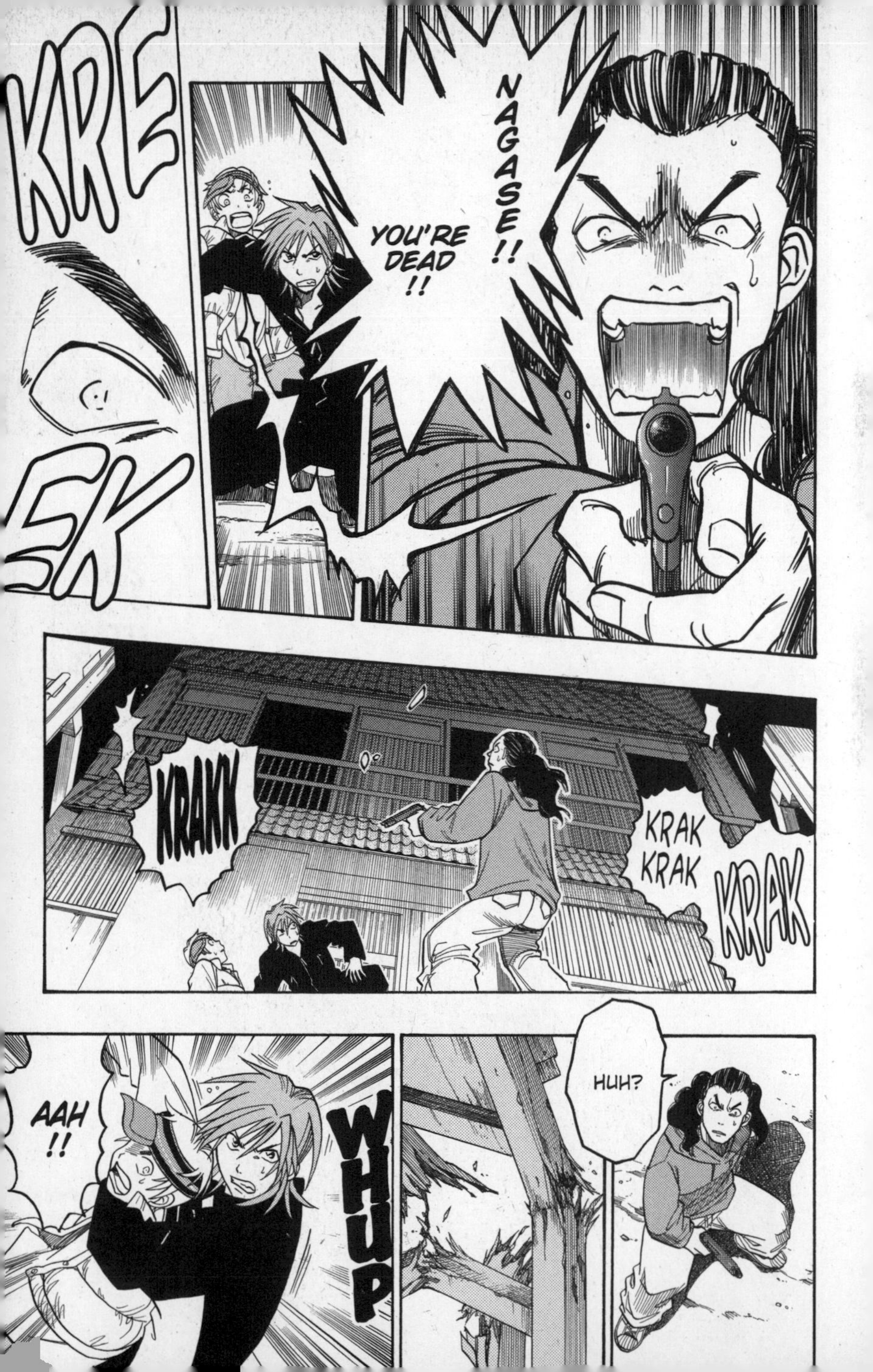
NAGASE!!
YOU'RE DEAD!!
KRESK
KRAK
KRAK KRAK
KRAKK
HUH?
WHUP
AAH!!

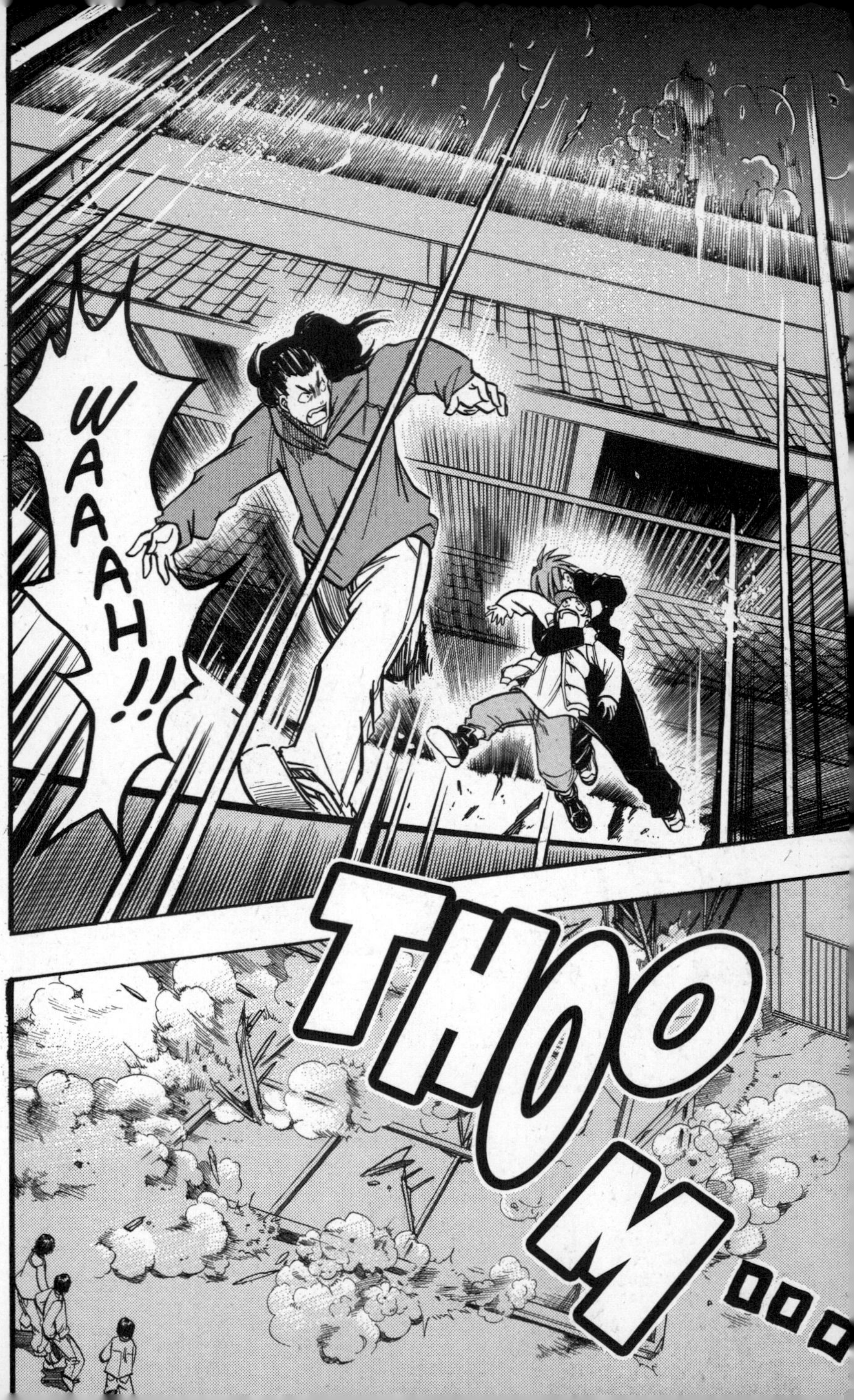
WAAAH!!!
THOOM...

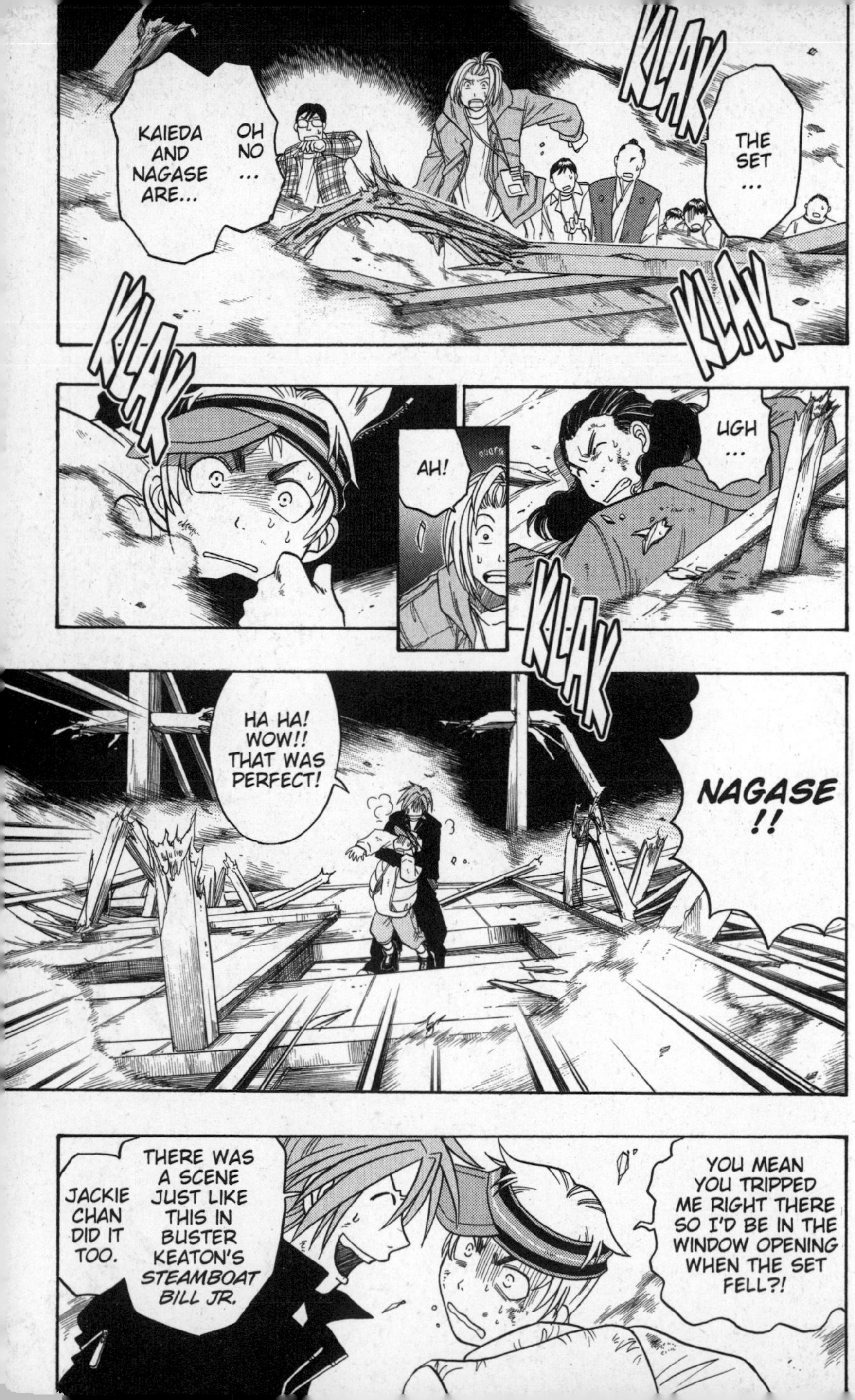
KLAK
THE SET ...
OH NO ...
KAIEDA AND NAGASE ARE...
KLAK
KLAK
UGH ...
KLAK
AH!
NAGASE !!
HA HA! WOW!! THAT WAS PERFECT!
YOU MEAN YOU TRIPPED ME RIGHT THERE SO I'D BE IN THE WINDOW OPENING WHEN THE SET FELL?!
THERE WAS A SCENE JUST LIKE THIS IN BUSTER KEATON'S *STEAMBOAT BILL JR.*
JACKIE CHAN DID IT TOO.

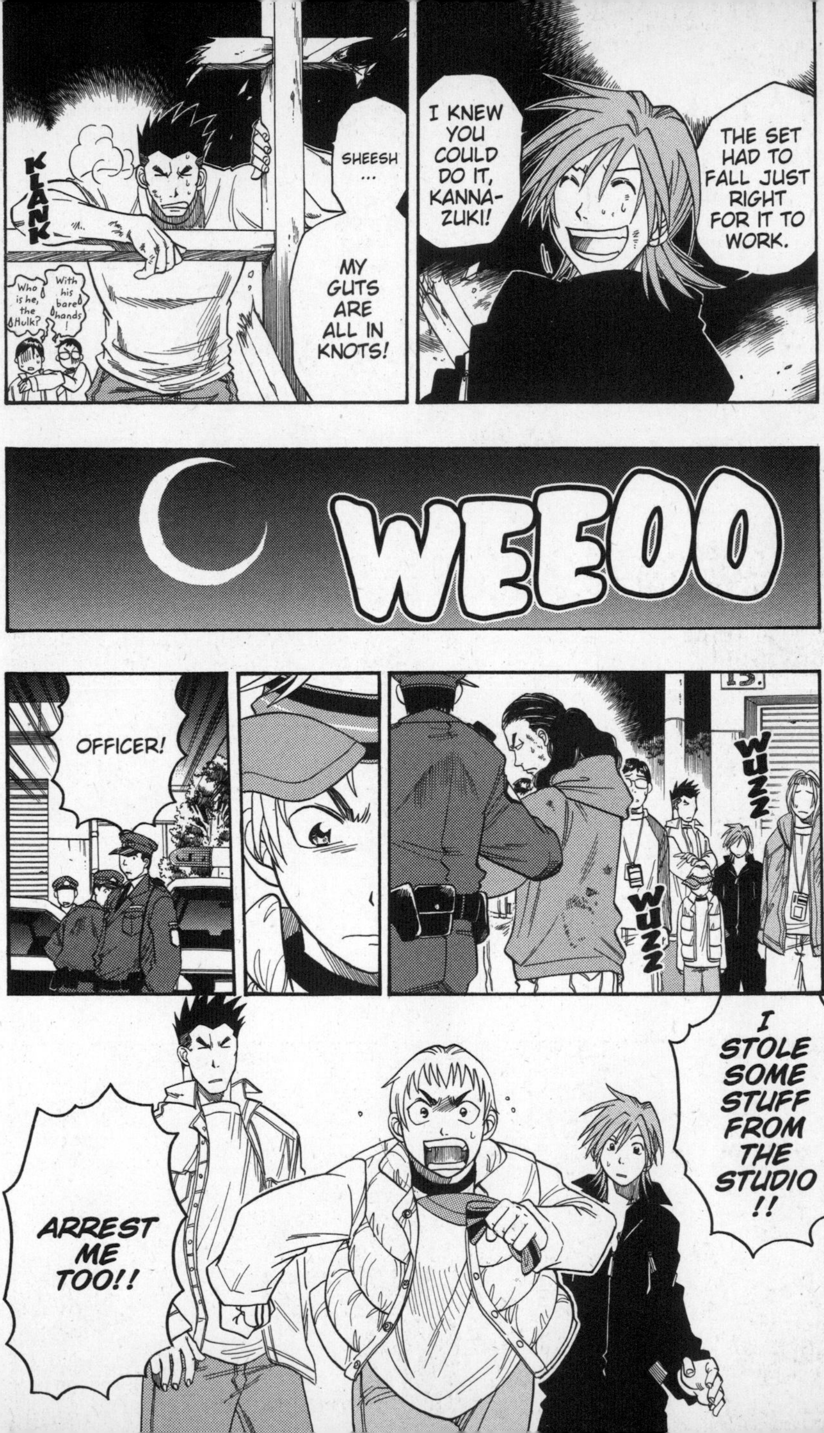
THE SET HAD TO FALL JUST RIGHT FOR IT TO WORK.
I KNEW YOU COULD DO IT, KANNAZUKI!
SHEESH ...
MY GUTS ARE ALL IN KNOTS!
KLANK
With his bare hands!
Who is he, the Hulk?
WEEOO
WUZZ
WUZZ
OFFICER!
I STOLE SOME STUFF FROM THE STUDIO!!
ARREST ME TOO!!

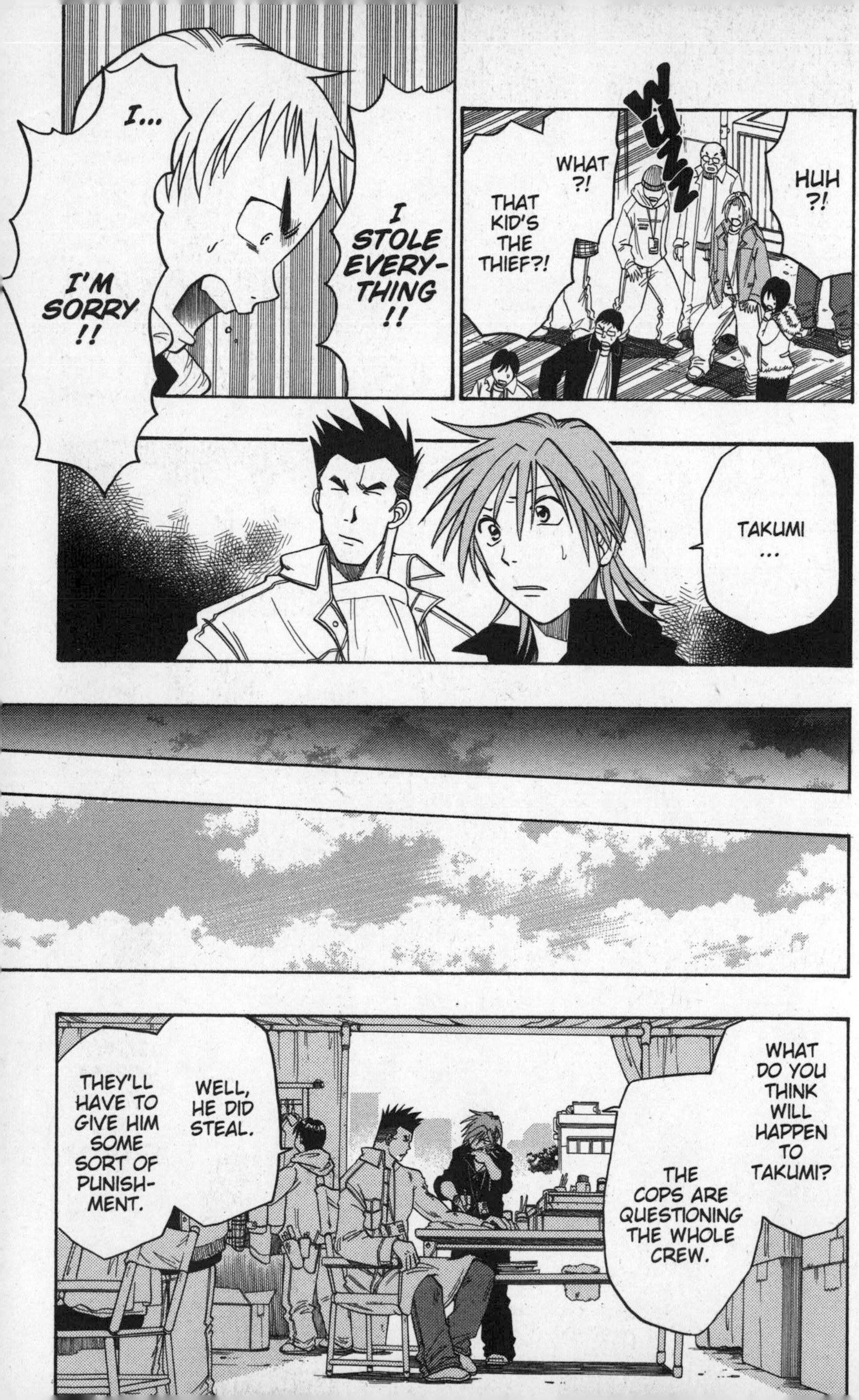
HUH?!
WUZZZ
WHAT?!
THAT KID'S THE THIEF?!
I...
I STOLE EVERY-THING!!
I'M SORRY!!
TAKUMI...
WHAT DO YOU THINK WILL HAPPEN TO TAKUMI?
THE COPS ARE QUESTIONING THE WHOLE CREW.
WELL, HE DID STEAL.
THEY'LL HAVE TO GIVE HIM SOME SORT OF PUNISH-MENT.

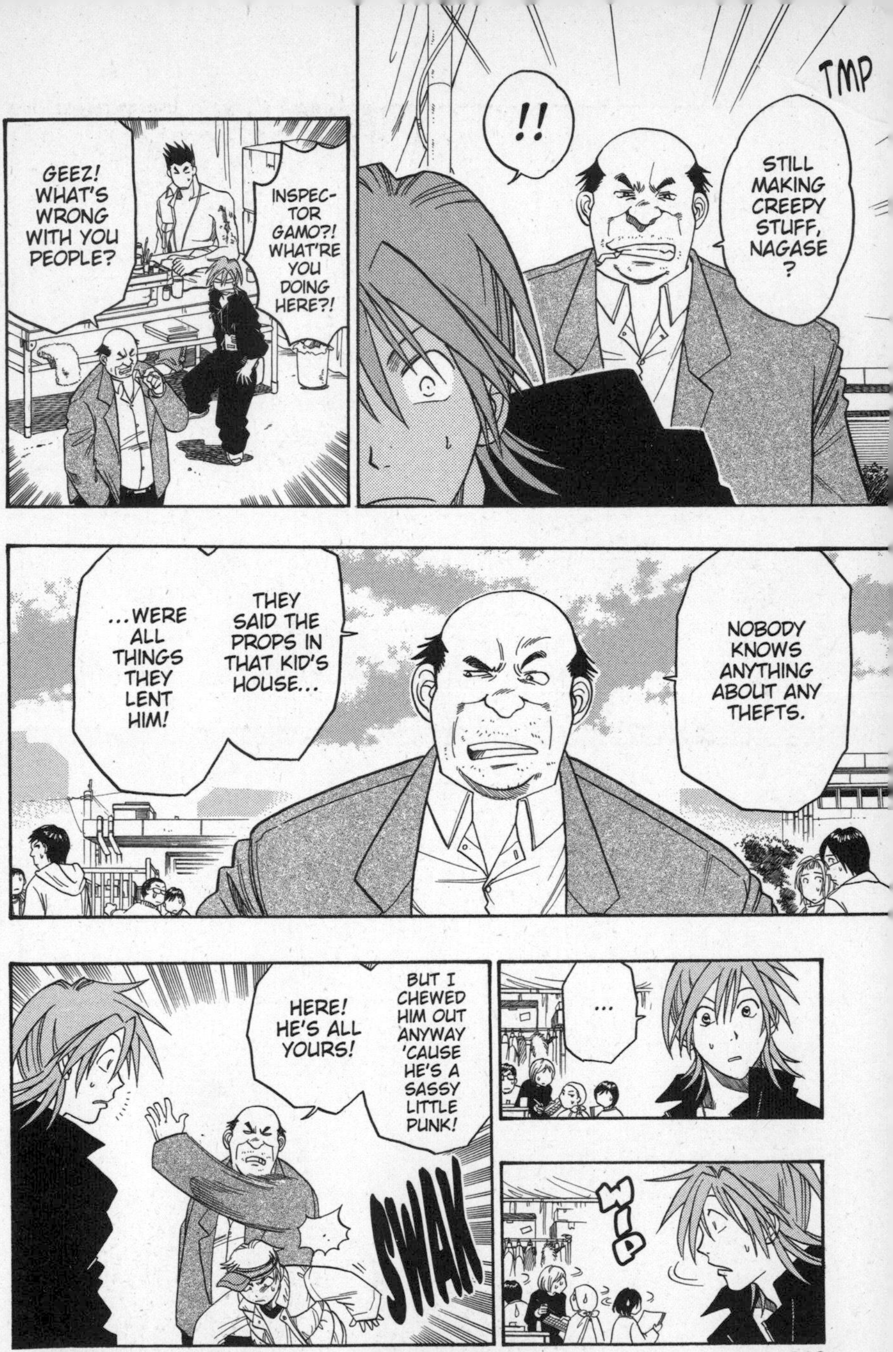
TMP
STILL MAKING CREEPY STUFF, NAGASE?
!!
INSPECTOR GAMO?! WHAT'RE YOU DOING HERE?!
GEEZ! WHAT'S WRONG WITH YOU PEOPLE?
NOBODY KNOWS ANYTHING ABOUT ANY THEFTS.
THEY SAID THE PROPS IN THAT KID'S HOUSE...
...WERE ALL THINGS THEY LENT HIM!
...
WIP
BUT I CHEWED HIM OUT ANYWAY 'CAUSE HE'S A SASSY LITTLE PUNK!
HERE! HE'S ALL YOURS!
SWAK

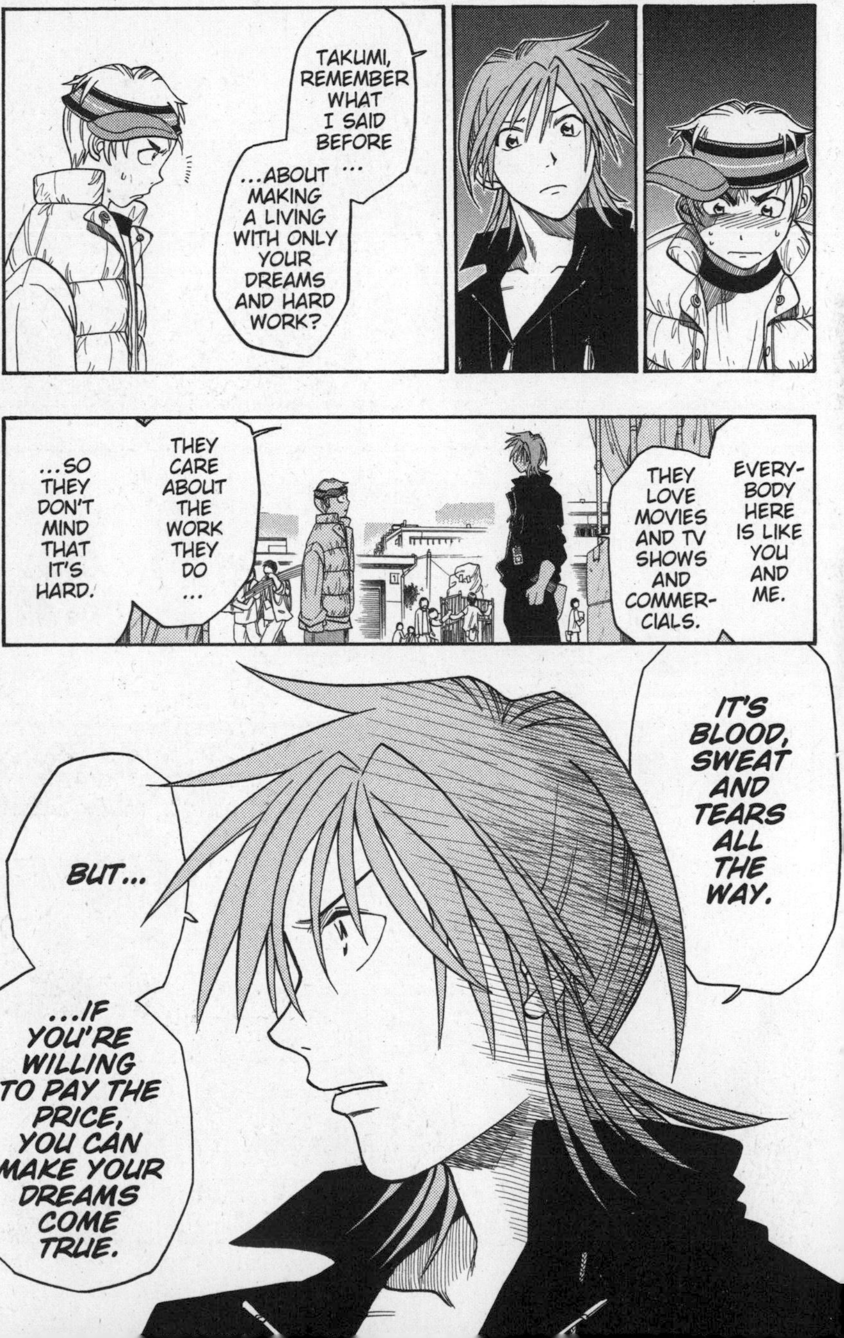
TAKUMI, REMEMBER WHAT I SAID BEFORE ...
...ABOUT MAKING A LIVING WITH ONLY YOUR DREAMS AND HARD WORK?
EVERY-BODY HERE IS LIKE YOU AND ME.
THEY LOVE MOVIES AND TV SHOWS AND COMMER-CIALS.
THEY CARE ABOUT THE WORK THEY DO ...
...SO THEY DON'T MIND THAT IT'S HARD.
IT'S BLOOD, SWEAT AND TEARS ALL THE WAY.
BUT...
...IF YOU'RE WILLING TO PAY THE PRICE, YOU CAN MAKE YOUR DREAMS COME TRUE.

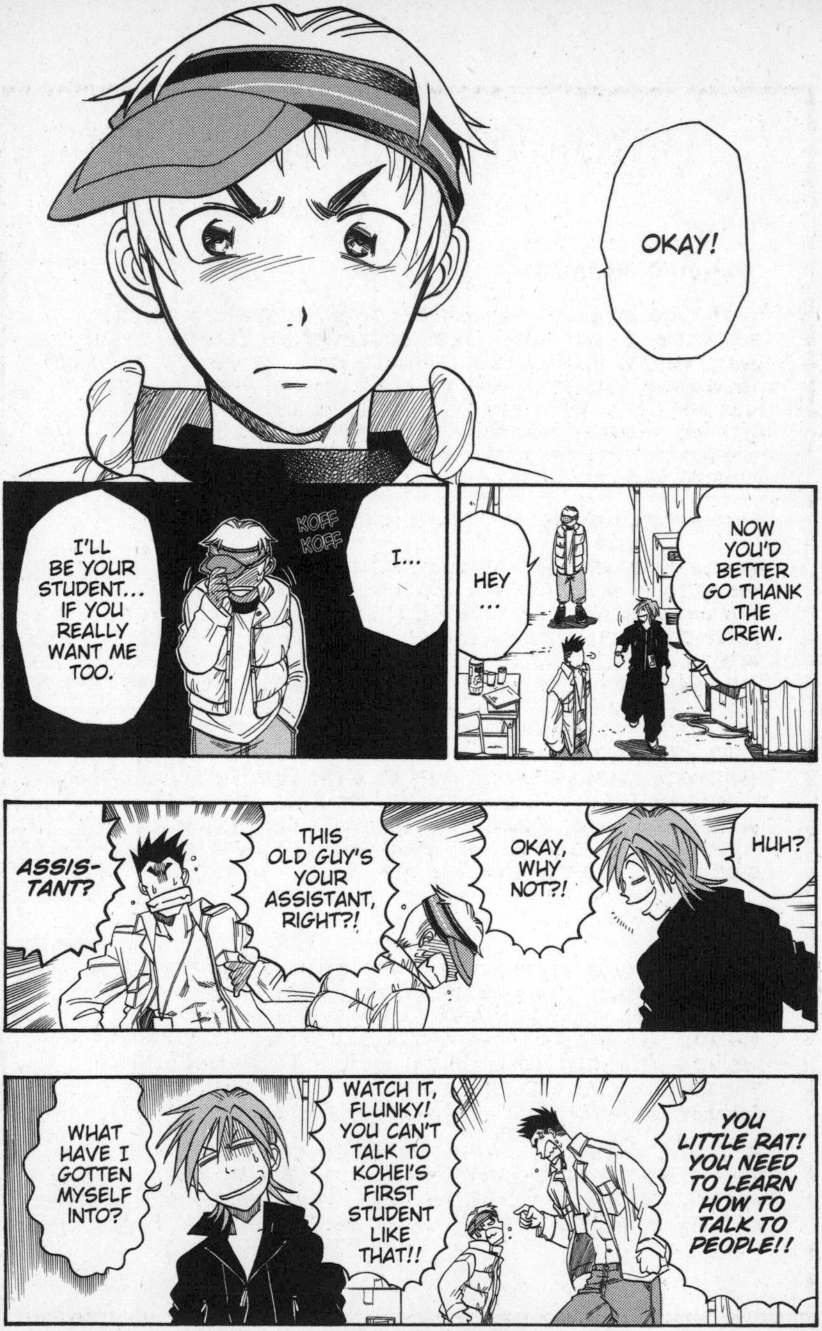
OKAY!
NOW YOU'D BETTER GO THANK THE CREW.
HEY...
I...
KOFF KOFF
I'LL BE YOUR STUDENT... IF YOU REALLY WANT ME TOO.
HUH?
OKAY, WHY NOT?!
THIS OLD GUY'S YOUR ASSISTANT, RIGHT?!
ASSIS-TANT?
YOU LITTLE RAT! YOU NEED TO LEARN HOW TO TALK TO PEOPLE!!
WATCH IT, FLUNKY! YOU CAN'T TALK TO KOHEI'S FIRST STUDENT LIKE THAT!!
WHAT HAVE I GOTTEN MYSELF INTO?

TO BE CONTINUED!

THE MAKING OF GIMMICK!
Episode 4 — By Youzaburou Kanari

"RUNAWAY ACTRESS"

THIS WAS OUR VERY FIRST STORY. AT FIRST I INTENDED TO WRITE SOMETHING LIKE *ROMAN HOLIDAY*. A BEAUTIFUL GIRL WHO'S IN TROUBLE SNEAKS OUT OF HER HOTEL AND WANDERS THE STREETS OF TOKYO AND THEN SOMEHOW KOHEI GETS INVOLVED WITH HER—SOMETHING LIKE THAT. BUT AS I WAS REWRITING IT, IT KEPT TURNING INTO A DIFFERENT STORY. AYAKA WAS A CHARACTER I REALLY LIKED. I HOPE SHE'LL SHOW UP AGAIN SOMEDAY.

"MONSTER HOUSE OF TERROR"

BOMB THREATS AND REVENGE AT AN AMUSEMENT PARK... MY IDEA WAS—WHAT IF I COULD INVOLVE KOHEI IN A STORY SIMILAR TO AN OLD MOVIE CALLED *ROLLERCOASTER*. THE VERY END FEATURES KOHEI COVERING UP A PHONY SCAR WITH AN APPLIANCE AND THEN TEARING IT OFF, SOMETHING I BORROWED FROM *THE GODFATHER*. I REMEMBER BEING SURPRISED WHEN I LATER LEARNED THAT THE SAME TECHNIQUE WAS USED IN MEL GIBSON'S *THE PASSION OF THE CHRIST* (2004) IN THE SCENE WHERE CHRIST IS WHIPPED. (ALTHOUGH IN *THE PASSION*, THE MAKEUP FOR THE WOUNDS WAS CONCEALED USING COMPUTER GRAPHICS.) THE VILLAIN KIYOSHI ITO IS ENORMOUSLY POPULAR WITH SOME OF THE FANS. HE'LL EVENTUALLY BECOME KOHEI'S RIVAL. OOPS, THAT'S A SECRET.

"WHILE NUDE"

THE TITLE WAS INSPIRED BY THE MOVIE *STRIPTEASE* WITH DEMI MOORE. IT WAS OUR FIRST ONE-SHOT STORY AND I REMEMBER HAVING A REALLY HARD TIME KEEPING IT SHORT. APPARENTLY THE MEDICAL COMMUNITY HAS BEGUN TO USE MAKEUP TECHNIQUES BORROWED FROM FILMMAKING TO HIDE SCARS AND GIVE PATIENTS A RENEWED SENSE OF ATTRACTIVENESS.

SPECIAL EFFECTS MAKEUP IS USED ON STAGE AND IN FILMS, BUT THERE'S NO REASON IT COULDN'T BE USED IN OTHER FIELDS. MIHO ACTS TOUGH, BUT SHE'S REALLY KIND AND FEMININE. DON'T YOU THINK SHE'S HOT?

CONTINUED IN VOLUME 5

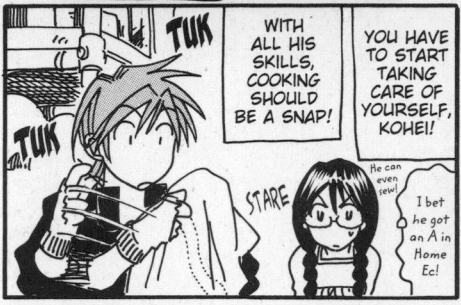

DO NOT KNEAD

Continued from vol. 3

YOU HAVE TO START TAKING CARE OF YOURSELF, KOHEI!
WITH ALL HIS SKILLS, COOKING SHOULD BE A SNAP!
TUK
TUK
I bet he got an A in Home Ec!
He can even sew!
STARE
Yes!
If he had all the ingredients and the right recipe...
...I think Kohei could become a really good cook!
You're meddling with forces you don't under-stand.
He might even enjoy it!
Mom's Extra-Wholesome Meatloaf
Ground Beef & Pork
Meat-loaf's ready!
Ground meat's like clay, huh? You can make anything out of it!
BURNED BODY
God help us...You were right.
The juices are oozing out like... Blegh!

HOW ABOUT STARTING WITH BOILED EGGS?

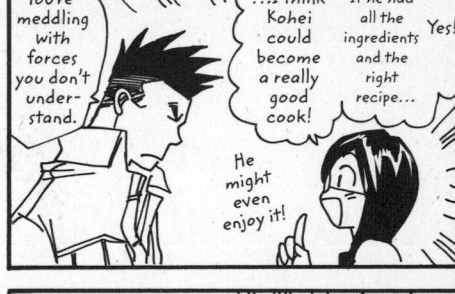

Kohei, there's something sticking out of the wrist.
I made veins out of spaghetti. Ketchup?

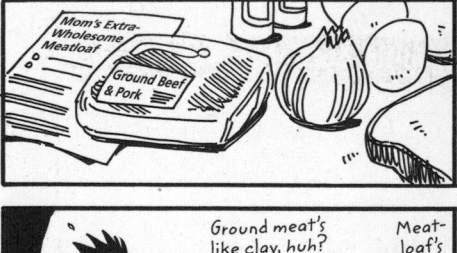

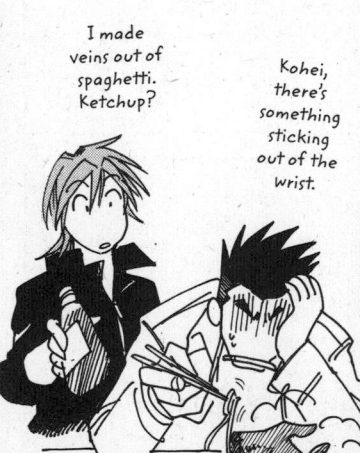

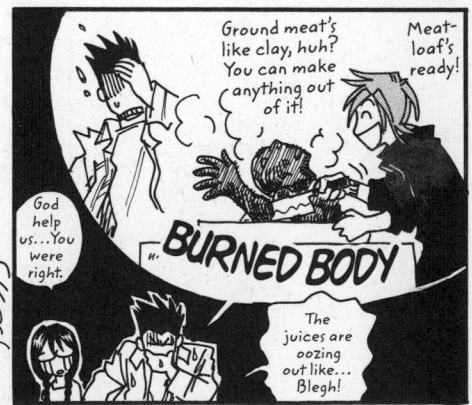

EXTRA

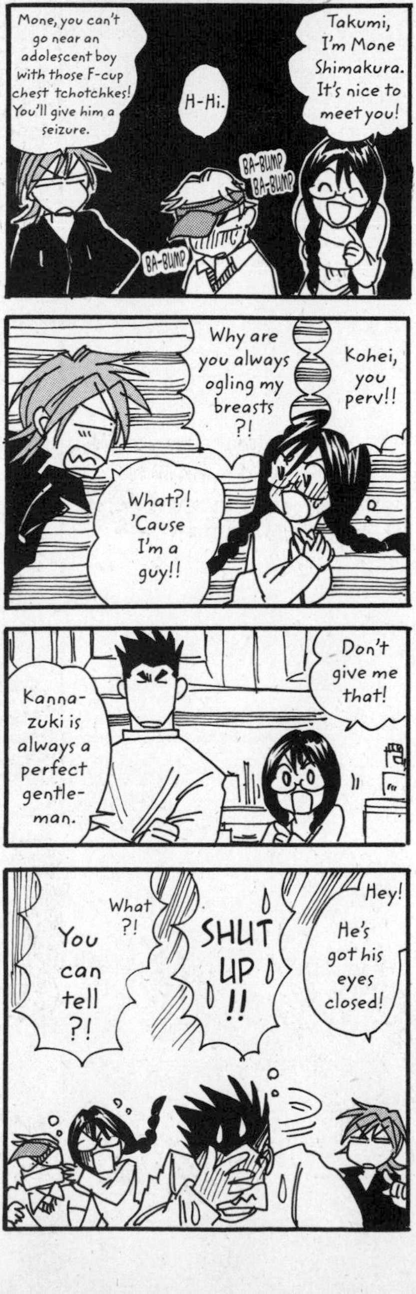
Takumi, I'm Mone Shimakura. It's nice to meet you!
H-Hi.
Mone, you can't go near an adolescent boy with those F-cup chest tchotchkes! You'll give him a seizure.
BA-BUMP BA-BUMP
BA-BUMP
Kohei, you perv!!
Why are you always ogling my breasts ?!
What?! 'Cause I'm a guy!!
Don't give me that!
Kanna-zuki is always a perfect gentle-man.
Hey! He's got his eyes closed!
SHUT UP !!
What ?!
You can tell ?!

COUNT ON YOUR FINGERS

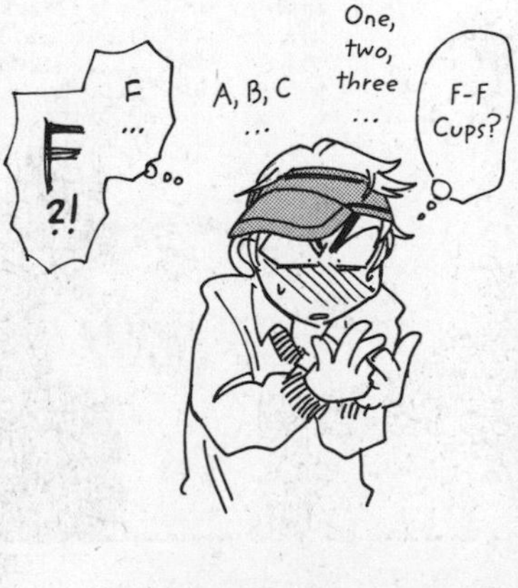
F-F Cups?
One, two, three ...
A, B, C ...
F ...
F ?!

I'M A SILVER SPATULA

Foreign movies are nice, but I like Japanese movies too. *Sabishinbou* and *Love Letter* are two of the best!

    —Kanari

I manage to get by with the help of a lot of people. It's *Gimmick!*'s one-year anniversary. Thank you.

    —Yabuguchi